D1247176

Psychiatric Malpractice: Cases and Comments for Clinicians

Psychiatric Malpractice: Cases and Comments for Clinicians

By

Robert I. Simon, M.D.
Clinical Professor of Psychiatry
Director, Program in Psychiatry and Law
Georgetown University School of Medicine
Washington, D.C.

Robert L. Sadoff, M.D.
Clinical Professor of Psychiatry
Director, Center for Studies in Social-Legal Psychiatry
University of Pennsylvania School of Medicine
Philadelphia, Pennsylvania

American Psychiatric Press, Inc.

Washington, DC
London, England

Note: The authors have worked to ensure that all information in this book concerning drug dosages, schedules, and routes of administration is accurate as of the time of publication and consistent with standards set by the U.S. Food and Drug Administration and the general medical community. As medical research and practice advance, however, therapeutic standards may change. For this reason and because human and mechanical errors sometimes occur, we recommend that readers follow the advice of a physician who is directly involved in their care or the care of a member of their family.

Copyright © 1992 American Psychiatric Press, Inc.
ALL RIGHTS RESERVED
Manufactured in the United States of America on acid-free paper.
94 93 92 91 4 3 2 1
First Edition

American Psychiatric Press, Inc.
1400 K Street, N.W., Washington, DC 20005

Library of Congress Cataloging-in-Publication Data
Simon, Robert I., 1934-
  Psychiatric malpractice : cases and comments for clinicians / Robert I. Simon, Robert L. Sadoff.
        p.   cm.
  Includes bibliographical references and index.
  ISBN 0-88048-107-2
  1. Psychiatrists—Malpractice—United States. 2. Actions and defenses—United States.   I. Simon, Robert I.   II. Title.
  [DNLM: 1. Malpractice—United States—legislation. 2. Psychiatry—United State—legislation.   WM 33 AA1 S24p]
  KF2910.P753S23   1991
  346.7303'—dc20
  [347.30633]
  DNLM/DLC
  for Library of Congress   91-4540
                                                                              CIP

British Library Cataloguing in Publication Data
A CIP record is available from the British Library.

Dedication

This book is dedicated to our teachers who instructed us in the art and science of our profession; to our patients who taught us through experience; and to our colleagues who may benefit from all we have learned from our patients and our teachers.

Contents

Acknowledgments

The authors wish to express their deep appreciation to the following individuals for their careful review of the manuscript and their very helpful suggestions in preparation of this work. We are grateful to Steven B. Bisbing, Psy.D., J.D., for his extensive editorial assistance. We are indebted to Professor Michael L. Perlin, New York Law School, for his careful review of the manuscript and his suggestions for legal accuracy. Finally, we want to thank Lynn Mourey, Esq., for her review of the references and legal citations for completeness and accuracy.

We also want to thank Susan Breglio for her dedication in typing and preparing the final manuscript. Also, to Ruth Borock, our appreciation for her typing and preparation of early versions of the text.

Foreword

New Directions in the Legal Regulation of the Mental Health Professions

Michael L. Perlin, J.D.

Over a decade ago, Third Circuit Court of Appeals Judge Ruggierio Aldisert, concurring in the court's judgment in *Romeo v. Youngberg* (1) (the case that eventually set the minimum standards of treatment for institutionalized mentally disabled persons) (2), wrote these pessimistic (perhaps fatalistic) words of consolation to mental health practitioners and to those considering entering the mental health professions:

> It has been almost 20 years since I faced a client across a law office desk. But were I to be placed in that position today, my advice would probably go something like this: if you are contemplating a position as an attendant in a mental hospital, seek another job: there is simply too much unpredictability in the law governing your conduct. If you are a physician, make certain that the state's malpractice insurance policy includes a clause protecting you from the new "constitutional torts" manufactured today by the Third Circuit Court of Appeals [3]. . . . If you are a governor or state legislator, cut back and retrench institutional programs for the mentally retarded, because the potential for lawsuits has now increased geometrically, with corresponding demands on the tax base to support the costs. If you are a parent with a retarded child, I simply feel sorry for you . . . [4]

The author is professor of law at New York Law School, 57 Worth St., New York, NY 10013. He was formerly director of the Division of Mental Health Advocacy in the New Jersey Department of the Public Advocate.

I thought at the time that Judge Aldisert had overreacted, and I still adhere to that view (5). The judge's alarmist rhetoric, however, strikes a nerve familiar to many psychiatrists and other mental health professionals, with his suggestion that legal regulation of their practice is inappropriate, oppressive, antitherapeutic, or somehow out of sync with legal regulation of other professions (6). His tone reifies Jonas Rappeport's marvelous neologism that mental health professionals are being unduly "belegaled" (7).

Is Judge Aldisert correct? Has the law somehow improperly encroached on the autonomy of psychiatrists, and, in doing so, has it threatened the quality of treatment made available to consumers of mental health services? When we consider the way that vivid, anecdotal evidence can cognitively so overwhelm reams of objective, "rational" data (8), we can understand how myths in this most tension-laden area can overtake reality. We now know, for instance, that, notwithstanding the general perception of a "litigation explosion" (a perception that is deeply flawed on many levels) (9), the reality is that the incidence of civil malpractice suits against mental health professionals remains substantially lower than rates for other medical specialties, a variance reflected in the comparatively "miniscule" insurance rate increases for mental health professionals (as opposed to those for providers in other areas of health care) (10). And yet, we also know, empirically as well as intuitively, that the legal regulation of mental health practice has expanded—in depth, in breadth, and in intensity—in ways not imagined a generation ago.

As of 1975, the number of reported cases involving psychiatric malpractice was so small as to be numerically insignificant (11). Of that small universe, most cases dealt with misapplications of organic interventions (such as the administration of electroconvulsive therapy without a proper accompanying muscle relaxant) (12), and many of the remainder dealt with fact patterns that were universally seen as so outrageous (13) that the underlying behavior was simply "beyond the pale" of acceptability. In short, it did not appear that legal developments would have a significant impact on most practitioners.

As the song goes, that was then and this is now. Consider the range of developments that we have seen in the past 15 years and think about their impact on the mental health professions:

- ❖ The increasing receptiveness of the tort law to suits alleging emotional injuries (14)
- ❖ The willingness of courts—both state and federal—to consider cases involving institutional conditions and, in some cases, to hold state-employed mental health professionals liable for the provision of inadequate care (15)
- ❖ The articulation in *Youngberg v. Romeo* (16) of a "substantial professional

judgment" standard to govern future federal court institutional litigation, and the implications of this standard for medical malpractice litigation (17)

- ❖ The application of the sovereign and qualified immunity doctrines to litigation involving alleged medical malpractice by state-employed mental health professionals (18)
- ❖ The shift in institutional litigation from federal courts to state courts (as a result of the increased hostility of the Burger and Rehnquist Supreme Courts to civil rights and public interest litigation, and the renascence of interest in state constitutional law), resulting in increased sensitivity on the part of many state court judges and litigators to the underlying substantive mental health issues (19)
- ❖ The emerging data base of information about drug side effects (especially tardive dyskinesia) and the emergence of the first generation of malpractice cases focusing on questions of inappropriate medication (20)
- ❖ The paradoxical shift in patients' rights litigation as a result of which patients are now joining with state mental health agencies and departments to force drug companies to make available alternative medications such as clozapine (21)
- ❖ The articulation of the *Tarasoff* doctrine (22), and its state-by-state recalibration, resulting in a staggering array of decisions turning on such issues as the identifiability of the victim, the professional training of the therapist, the type of protection that must be offered, and the length of time that the duty applies (23)
- ❖ The consideration of the power imbalances that are frequently present in forensic and therapeutic relationships, and the potential application of malpractice regulation principles to forensic matters (24)
- ❖ The potential conflict between "open door" policies (or other offshoots of the "least restrictive alternative" principle) and the imposition of liability based on premature release of dangerous patients (25)
- ❖ The growing awareness of the problems inherent in sexual contact between therapist and patient and the increased willingness of abused patients to "come forward" with their grievances (26)

What are practitioners to make of all of this, and how (if at all) must they change their behavior? Will all of this lead to increased passive-aggressive behavior on the part of mental health professionals ("litigaphobia," in Stanley Brodsky's apt term [27])? Is legal intervention in medical decision making inherently risky for all parties (a phenomenon characterized as "critogenesis" by Thomas Gutheil and his colleagues [28])? Should the focus shift to the legal systems, and must lawyers now employ a methodology (called "therapeutic jurisprudence" by David Wexler) through which they confront the therapeutic (or antitherapeutic) content of judicial decisions, statutes, and court rules (29)? Is the final irony here that, after years of arguing that mental health professionals cannot predict future dangerousness, courts are now—in effect—demanding that mental health professionals predict future *judicial* behavior, to ensure that clinical decisions do not run afoul of constitutional and common law proscriptions (30)? Do Judge Aldisert's words now come into clearer focus?

If it appears that all of these concerns are a cause for despair (or at the least, genuine confusion), then the publication of this volume is especially fitting and timely. For now—finally—there is a treatise that comprehensively, clearly, lucidly, and intelligently discusses all of the underlying policy issues, clinical considerations, and legal principles; what's more, it does so in a way that speaks meaningfully to the full range of mental health professionals, whether they come to this book totally unfamiliar with the underlying legal priniciples or with a significant degree of legal sophistication. As a bonus, the authors offer crystal-clear, practical, hands-on advice and suggestions to guide practitioner behavior so as to help avoid many of the more troubling potential minefields ahead.

The two authors are naturals to have collaborated on this volume. Bob Simon is a thoughtful scholar, a respected practitioner, and one of the leading theoretical thinkers in the area with which this book is concerned. Bob Sadoff is a gifted forensic psychiatrist, a superb teacher, and a skilled writer; he also has the rare ability to be able to take a mountain of data and distill it to its basic essence. Individually, each author is tops at what he does. Together, their synergy sets a new standard for clarity, coherence, and wisdom. It also does so in the context of a volume that can be read and appreciated by the most courtroom-seasoned practitioners as well as those who have never before given any serious thought to the underlying issues.

Psychiatric Malpractice: Cases and Comments for Clinicians works on every possible level. It provides a clear introduction to the often baffling procedural intricacies of the legal system, a comprehensive overview of malpractice law, and a primer on the practical problems faced by practitioners who are subject to malpractice litigation. It continues by offering in-depth analyses of all of the most important substantive subject matter areas with which practitioners must deal (i.e., somatic therapies, suicide, sexual exploitation, intentional torts, violent behavior, and premature release).

In each and every instance, the authors clarify the clinical issues, the controlling legal principles, and the type of behavior that will best ensure that practitioners *not* find themselves as defendants in long and painful court suits. Many of the chapters conclude with behavioral checklists and recommendations of "standard clinical practice" (that all too often are anything *but* standard) that in and of themselves make the book so valuable.

As a lawyer, professor, and consultant, I recognize the depth of feelings that the underlying issues raise in many mental health professionals who have been involved—either as parties, fact witnesses, or expert witnesses—in malpractice litigation. To an important extent, Drs. Simon and Sadoff defuse some of the tensions that permeate this area through their level-headed, even-tempered, sober, and thoughtful analyses of the issues; their assessment of the prevailing legal standards; and their recommendations for prophylactic behavior. The book is balanced, temperate, and intelligent, and is a major contribution to the literature. We all owe a debt of thanks to the authors.

References

1. 644 F2d 147 (Cir 3d 1981), vacated Youngberg v Romeo, 457 U.S. 307 (1982)
2. See Youngberg v Romeo, 457 U.S. 307 (1982)
3. The Supreme Court eventually reworked the standard of care specifically to limit damages liability in cases involving institutional mental health practitioners who had acted in good faith. See Youngberg v Romeo, 457 U.S. 323 (1982).
4. Romeo v Youngberg, 644 F2d 185 (Aldisert J, concurring)
5. See Perlin ML: Mental Disability Law: Civil and Criminal, Vol 1. Charlottesville, VA, Michie, 1989, pp 1–28
6. See Perlin ML: Institutionalization and the law, in Psychiatric Services in Institutional Settings. Chicago, IL, American Hospital Association, 1978, pp 75–84 (75, 76)
7. Rappeport J: Belegaled: mental health and the law in the United States. Can J Psychiatry 32:719, 1987
8. See Perlin ML: Psychodynamics and the insanity defense: "ordinary common sense" and heuristic reasoning. Nebraska Law Review 67:3–70, 1990 (3, 12–22); Saks MJ, Kidd RF: Human information processing and adjudication: trial by heuristics. Law and Society Review 15:123–160, 1980–1981
9. See Perlin ML: Power imbalances in therapeutic and forensic relationships. Behavioral Sciences and the Law 9:111–128, 1991
10. See Bonnie R: Professional liability and the quality of mental health care. Law, Medicine, and Health Care 16:229–240, 1988; see generally Herzog PF: The reform of medical liability: tort law or insurance. American Journal of Comparative Law 38:99–114, 1990
11. Trent CL, Muhl WP: Professional liability insurance and the American psychiatrist. Am J Psychiatry 132:1312–314, 1975; see p 1312. [As of 1975, psychiatrists faced one medical malpractice action for every 50 to 100 years of practice.]
12. See Bellamy WA: Psychiatric malpractice, in American Handbook of Psychiatry, 2nd Edition, Vol 5. Edited by Freedman DX, Dyrud JE (Arieta S,

editor in chief). New York, Basic Books, 1975, pp 899–923; see pp 899, 903

13. See, e.g., Roy v Hartogs 81 Misc 2d 350, 366 NYS2d 297 (Civ Ct 1975), modified, 85 Misc 2d 891, 381 NYS2d 587 (Sup Ct 1976); Zipkin v Freeman, 436 SW2d 753 (Mo 1968); Landau v Werner, 105 Sol J 1008 (CA 1961) [all involving sexual abuse]

14. See Ingber S: Rethinking intangible injuries: a focus on remedy. California Law Review 73:772–856, 1985

15. See, e.g., Zinermon v Burch, 110 S Ct 975 (1990)

16. 457 U.S. 307 (1982)

17. See generally Perlin ML: Mental Disability Law: Civil and Criminal, Vols 1–3. Charlottesville, VA, Michie, 1989

18. Ibid, Vol 3, § 12.41, pp 115–121

19. See Perlin ML: State constitutions and statutes as sources of rights for the mentally disabled. Loyola of Los Angeles Law Review 20:1249–1327, 1987

20. See Perlin ML: Mental Disability Law: Civil and Criminal, Vol 3. Charlottesville, VA, Michie 1989, § 12.11, pp 37–39

21. See Margulies P: A case study of the cognitive psychology of law reform: mental health advocates' ambivalence about new schizophrenia medication. Paper presented at the annual meeting of the Association of American Law Schools' Section on Law and Mental Disability, Washington, DC, January 1991

22. Tarasoff v Regents of the University of California, 17 Cal 3d 425, 131 Cal Rptr 14, 551 P2d 334 (1976)

23. See Perlin ML: Mental Disability Law: Civil and Criminal, Vol 3. Charlottesville, VA, Michie, 1989, §§ 13.05–13.21, pp 134–184

24. See Perlin ML: Power imbalances in therapeutic and forensic relationships. Behavioral Sciences and Law 9:111–128, 1991

25. See Perlin ML: Mental Disability Law: Civil and Criminal, Vol 3. Charlottesville, VA, Michie, 1989, § 13.23, pp 184–191

26. See Perlin ML: Power imbalances in therapeutic and forensic relationships. Behavioral Sciences and the Law 9:11–128, 1991

27. Brodsky S: Fear of litigation in mental health professionals. Criminal Justice and Behavior 15:492–500, 1988 (492, 497)

28. See Gutheil TG, Burstzajn H, Kaplan A, et al: Participation in competency assessment and treatment decisions: the role of the psychiatrist-at-torney team. Mental and Physical Disability Law Reporter 11:446, 449, 1987

29. See Wexler D (ed): Therapeutic Jurisprudence: The Law as a Therapeutic Agent. Durham, NC, Carolina Academic Press, 1990

30. Perlin ML: Reading the Supreme Court's tea leaves: predicting judicial behavior in civil and criminal right to refuse treatment cases. American Journal of Forensic Psychiatry (in press)

Preface

Malpractice cases in psychiatry have burgeoned over the past two decades and have been of great concern to practicing psychiatrists as well as to society. Patients have become more litigious in all specialties of medicine. Plaintiffs' lawyers have become increasingly creative in finding reasons to blame physicians and psychiatrists for unexpected outcomes or unforeseen events that affect patients and other individuals.

Most psychiatrists have always been concerned about the welfare of their patients and have adhered to the age-old dictum *primum non nocere*—first, do no harm. The practice of psychiatry has traditionally occurred both in hospitals and in private offices. Since the rise of community mental health centers in the 1960s, many patients have been treated in outpatient clinics, halfway houses, and community mental health centers. Laws affecting the mentally ill and restricting involuntary commitment procedures have changed the practice of psychiatry. Formally, patients would be committed to hospitals if they were mentally ill and in need of hospitalization. However, recent laws have declared that patients have a right to be at liberty, unless their mental health renders them a clear and present danger to self or others. Thus, the transition from treating a patient who is mentally ill and in need of hospital treatment to the belief that involuntary hospitalization is akin to incarceration has increased the likelihood that civil suits will be brought against psychiatrists.

The concept of "dangerousness" has entered the picture and has placed the psychiatrist in a position of responsibility for the safety of the community and the protection of citizens from dangers posed by mentally ill patients. Psychiatrists have acknowledged that they cannot accurately predict "dangerousness" except perhaps in certain clinical situations when violence appears imminent. Nevertheless, the courts have insisted that psychiatrists have a duty to control the violent behavior of their patients and may be sued if the patient becomes violent and others are injured.

In another area, psychiatrists have been sued increasingly for allegedly "mishandling the transference" and sexually exploiting their patients. Recently, there have been a great number of lawsuits against psychiatrists alleging sexual misconduct with patients. Some of the allegations have proven to be true, and others have proven false. How do psychiatrists handle such accusations, especially when these accusations may be untrue? All professional associations have declared such behavior unethical, immoral, unprofessional, egregious, and condemnable.

How do psychiatrists handle potentially suicidal patients who may or may not need hospitalization? Under what circumstances can psychiatrists take calculated risks with patients who prove to be suicidal or self-destructive? These issues, and the larger area of misdiagnosis and improper treatment, form the major concerns for psychiatrists who are charged with malpractice.

A psychiatric malpractice lawsuit may be frivolous or it may be based on negligence on the part of the psychiatrist that led to tragedy or serious damage to the patient or to others. The usual statute of limitations in which to bring the lawsuit is about 2 or 3 years in most jurisdictions. Therefore, by the time the psychiatrist realizes that he or she is being sued, the physician has usually put the patient in question out of mind and has gone on to other patients and other professional matters.

Most psychiatrists have very little contact with the law or with legal agencies. They are not familiar with the procedures of malpractice suits. Many psychiatrists have never contemplated being sued, because they practice conscientious medicine and care about their patients. Most react with disbelief when they are sued. Other psychiatrists, practicing in a high-risk population (e.g., chronic schizophrenic patients, patients with borderline personality disorder, and acting-out adolescents) expect that a number of cases will result in lawsuits. They practice what they consider to be good medicine, but they may need to take some risks with patients in order to achieve good results. Often, these are the cases that other psychiatrists have referred following unsuccessful treatment, and the safest course is the one that will maintain the patient with the least harm.

Psychiatrists take risks when they discharge patients into the community or treat patients using the "least-restrictive alternative." Psychiatrists have been fooled by patients who wish to get out of the hospital by claiming they are well. These patients act nonviolently in order to convince the doctor that they are well enough to be discharged. These same patients, however, may not be able to tolerate the stress of community living and may regress, requiring further hospitalization.

Psychiatric patients may be unpredictable, depending on the severity of their mental illness. They may act impulsively or react to hallucinations or the delusional belief that the patient is the victim of a broad conspiracy. Most patients can handle these problems in the restricted environment of a closed ward of a psychiatric hospital but have greater difficulty in the openness of the community setting.

Newer medications that significantly affect psychoses also may cause side effects that need to be monitored. Sometimes, the treating psychiatrist is faced with the dilemma of whether to continue the medication that leads to harmful side effects or to discontinue the medication and allow the patient to regress or deteriorate and again become psychotic. These are difficult choices, and the judgment is left to the treating physician. The doctor must make decisions based on risk-benefit assessments. Is the benefit to the patient greater than the risk involved in the treatment selected? Judgment calls are not deviations from the standard of care if acceptable guidelines are followed. Professional judgment can be the basis for a legal defense when a psychiatrist misdiagnoses a patient or treats the patient improperly if reasonably sound clinical practices were followed. We are all subject to errors in judgment, but sometimes those errors can be costly to our patients or to innocent bystanders.

Psychiatry requires a regulatory system to remind us when we have deviated from the standard of care, and when that deviation has led to damage to our patients. That regulatory system is the judicial system. The system is adversarial, where accusations are made and need to be proven. Psychiatrists have to defend themselves and their decisions, utilizing defense lawyers who are well trained in understanding the practical and theoretical considerations involved in psychiatric malpractice litigation.

Plaintiffs' attorneys will tend to put forward the statements of the family accusing the psychiatrist of wrongdoing, statements that may be distorted by emotion, by time, and by lack of understanding of complex psychiatric issues. Defense attorneys will present arguments to help the psychiatrist—arguments that may be based on the psychiatrist's records and recollections and that may also be distorted by time, by emotion, or by a similar lack of understanding. Attorneys are good at arguing and polarizing issues, sometimes to the extreme. Somewhere in between the polarized arguments lies the truth. It is for the judge or the jury to decide on the merits of the arguments and the validity of the defense.

This book is designed to provide the reader with an overview of psychiatric malpractice issues from the legal perspective as well as from the practitioner's viewpoint. The book is not designed as a comprehensive textbook on psychiatric malpractice. There are many books of that type to which the reader is referred. Neither is this exclusively a casebook on psychiatric malpractice, many of which also appear in the literature. Rather, this is an integrated approach to psychiatry and the law by two forensic psychiatrists sharing their experiences in this very difficult and complicated field.

Our goal is to help fellow practitioners to confront the anxieties and uncertainties concerning psychiatric malpractice through knowledge of the interaction between psychiatry and the law. We hope to communicate to our colleagues the changes in the professional environment that have led to the rise in psychiatric malpractice lawsuits and to guide the practitioner in prevention of malpractice allegations. Finally, we hope to demonstrate how to handle a very difficult situation if, in fact, a lawsuit is brought. Cases are utilized to develop guidelines for appropriate psychiatric practice. Preventing malpractice lawsuits also means better care of the patient, which is clearly our first goal. If the patient is treated according to the current clinical guidelines and laws affecting our practice, then prevention of malpractice lawsuits obviously will follow.

Robert I. Simon, M.D.
Robert L. Sadoff, M.D.

Chapter 1

Legal Regulations —————————————

The medical specialty of psychiatry is relatively young, constantly changing, and innovative. By comparison with many of the other medical specialties, it lacks firm definition with regard to diagnostic and treatment procedures. Currently, there are more than 450 schools of psychotherapy in existence (1), and this number appears to be increasing steadily. How can the public be protected against harmful or even useless treatments? Who will separate the competent therapist from the incompetent?

The legal regulation of psychiatric practice is also increasing. Certain psychiatric treatments, such as the use of neuroleptics in the treatment of institutionalized patients, have come under expanding regulatory control, particularly concerning informed consent requirements (2). The three major regulatory institutions governing these and a myriad of other critical issues in psychiatric practice are *judicial* (civil, criminal, and administrative), *legislative* (federal, state, and local), and *professional* (licensing boards and psychiatric and other mental health organizations) (3).

These regulatory institutions provide protection for the public through, among other things, the establishment of quality care standards, the control of supply distribution, and the enactment of cost containment measures of mental health care. For example, of great concern, both inside and outside the profession, is the evaluation of the competence of practitioners. State and local regulations typically define minimal competency requirements for the delivery of mental health services. Regulatory agencies working in concert with professional organizations oversee the effectiveness of professional performance and define, through ethical codes and other recognized "standards of conduct," practitioners' duties to patients. Also, professional standard review committees sponsored by state associations serve as arbitrators for complaints received about practitioners. Third-party payers also have become guardians of the quality of mental health care. The federal government, through the major health plans—including Medicare, Medicaid, Federal Employees Health Benefits Plan, and the Civilian Health and Medical Program of the Uniformed Services (CHAMPUS)—exerts a major influence on the quality of care rendered through utilization review and quality assurance efforts (4).

Consumers of mental health services can become easily bewildered by the plethora of psychological and organic therapies available. Most patients are unaware, and often are not told, of the risks and benefits of a proposed psychiatric treatment, available alternative treatments, diagnosis, and prognosis with and without treatment. Yet the law implicitly, if not explicitly, requires that patients be informed of these matters, with certain exceptions, from the first day of therapy (5). Therefore, regulations are needed to protect an often unknowing and naive public. As a result, a number of states have enacted statutes that enunciate the requirements for informed consent that must be provided by practitioners (6).

The judicial regulation of the psychiatric profession, either by statute or by certification (restricting the use of titles), serves, among other things, to establish requirements regarding education, experience, and evidence of good character in order to practice a particular profession. Practitioners failing to meet these criteria and assuming a professional title or conducting an unlicensed practice are subject to civil and possibly criminal penalties as established by statute (7).

As examples of statutory regulation, a number of states have defined by statute the psychiatrist's duty to warn endangered third parties (8), codified confidentiality requirements in psychiatric practice (9), and required reporting of sexual misconduct with attendant legal penalties (10). A primary purpose of regulatory policies, therefore, is to promote the healthy growth of the professions.

Psychiatrists cannot practice effectively while in ignorance of the regulations that are increasingly imposed upon their specialty. Psychiatrists need not become attorneys in order to practice their profession. However, a working knowledge of the law frequently permits integration of both legal and clinical issues for the full benefit of the patient and for the protection and piece of mind of the practitioner.

Legal System

Bases of the Law

The four principal bases of law in the United States are constitutional, administrative, statutory, and the common law. Statutes enacted by each state (statutory law), the written decision of courts (case law), and the rules and regulations of governmental agencies (administrative law) make up the main body of regulations that psychiatrists encounter daily in their practices. For example, quite often state legislatures will enact statutes address-ing primary issues in medical care delivery in relatively general terms or concepts. The function of actually defining the "specifics" of an issue or concept (e.g., standard of care) will typically be left to the courts to de-velop through case opinions (7).

Constitution

The United States Constitution, with its 26 amendments, is the supreme law of the land. *Constitutional law* deals with the nature, formation, amend-ment, operation, and interpretation of the United States Constitution. The interpretation of the Constitution in addressing the *specific* issues that are of concern here was not contemplated by the founding fathers. Instead, the Constitution was written in a flexible manner so that resolution of specific controversies was left to the judiciary (principally the United States Su-preme Court) to make. Constitutional questions abound in psychiatry. For instance, under the first amendment right to freedom of speech, it has been argued by civil libertarians that when the psychiatrist, as the state's agent, administers psychotropic medications, the state interferes with the genera-tion and communication of ideas (11). Most importantly, the Fourteenth Amendment's due-process clause applies to all decision making that is re-lated to the admission of individuals concerning their retention in and their release from public psychiatric hospitals (12).

Statutes

Statutory law is established by individual state legislatures that declare, command, or prohibit something in writing. Locally, municipal bodies pass ordinance statutes. According to each state, numerous statutes can govern various aspects of the practice of psychiatry. Informed consent, licensure, confidentiality, and duty-to-warn statutes are just a few examples of aspects of psychiatric practice that might be regulated by state law. Statutes may also govern specialized areas of law such as worker's compensation, Medi-care, and vocational rehabilitation programs. In essence, statutes enunciate general propositions that courts apply and, often times, interpret in specific circumstances. Generally, the courts help define a statute that is ambiguous through the rendering of court opinions. However, when interpretations of legislative language are made by the courts, they are usually narrow, incre-mental, and applicable only to certain fact situations.

Statutory authority supplements common law or court opinions, or may even supercede such authority. For example, when the state of Cali-fornia enacted a duty-to-warn statute (13), it *superceded* the earlier legal conclusions enunciated in the *Tarasoff* case (14). The California duty-to-warn statute superceded the legal conclusions in the *Tarasoff* decision to the extent that it imposes a duty to warn only when "the patient has communicated to the psychotherapist a serious threat of physical violence against a reasonably identifiable victim or victims" (15). The statute limits the duty imposed by the *Tarasoff* court by requiring the psychotherapist to take reasonable precautions only after the patient communicates a serious threat. The statute eliminates the burden on a psychotherapist to reasonably determine that a threat exists.

As noted earlier, all states have the legislative authority to regulate and control the professional conduct and activity of any profession that is recognized by law. Professions are specifically defined and regulated by the courts and by statutes enacted by individual state legislatures. Another example of the legislative regulation of psychiatric practice is the statutes enacted by some states that specify billing practices. For instance, in the District of Columbia, a psychiatrist is not to turn over a patient's account to a collection agency or lawyer until the patient receives "written notification that the fee is due and (the patient) has failed to arrange for payment . . . within a reasonable time after such notification" (16). If recourse to a collection agency or lawyer is taken, the act further states that disclosure should include only "administrative information," which is defined as the patient's name, age, sex, address, identifying number, dates and character of the session (individual or group), and fee.

The Federal Tort Claims Act (FTCA) (17) permits the government to be sued under certain limited circumstances. The government is liable in most instances for the failure of a government employee to carry out his or her duties with reasonable care and caution. For example, in *Andrews v. United States* (18) a physician's assistant induced a patient to engage in sexual intercourse with him. The patient alleged that during counseling sessions with the physician's assistant, sexual advances were made, and that he convinced her that the best course of treatment was to have sexual intercourse. As a consequence of the therapist's abusive treatment, the patient suffered severe depression and confusion about her self-worth. She also blamed the therapist's conduct for the dissolution of her marriage. The trial court awarded the patient $70,000 in damages and her husband $30,000 for his claim of severe depression.

On appeal, the United States Court of Appeals for the Fourth Circuit found that the employer's (i.e., the United States government's) liability could not be grounded in the sexual seduction itself, because liability under the FTCA is determined as if the United States were a private citizen subject to the laws of the applicable jurisdiction (e.g., South Carolina in this case). Therefore, under South Carolina law, an employer, while liable for an employee's conduct "in the scope of his employment," can only be so liable if the employee is actually engaged in his employer's business at the time of the malfeasance. Pursuant to this law, the appellate court held that the sexual exploitation perpetrated by the physician's assistant was in furtherance of his own self-interest, and not his employer's business. However, the court did find the United States government liable to the patient and her husband for the negligence of the supervising physician for failing to intercede once information about the assistant's impropriety (which was at an early stage of the exploitation) had been received. Consequently, the court upheld the trial court's award of damages.

Administrative Regulations

Government at all three levels (i.e., local, state, federal) has administrative agencies that make rules, regulations, and resolutions. The *administrative findings* from these agencies have the force of law when each agency's rulings are backed by specific statutes or ordinances. For example, former programs supported by the then Department of Health, Education and Welfare "involving the use of restraints or aversive stimuli were permitted with mentally handicapped persons, if informed consent by a parent or guardian was provided" (19). Administrative licensure boards and state medical boards usually operate under specific statutes regulating professions and occupations. The disciplining of errant mental health professionals often occurs under these administrative procedures (20). Other areas of practice covered by administrative regulations, among others, include defining a profession, professional practice, and due-process procedures.

Case or Judge-Made Law

Contemporary *case law* in the United States is fundamentally based on the common, or written, law of England as it existed when the English colonists settled in America (21). Case law, or judge-made law, embodies principles and rules that are dictated by natural reason and man's sense of justice, and are voluntarily adopted by society in order to be governed in social relations. Unlike the more rigid statutory law, case law is a flexible body of principles designed to accommodate the myriad disputes encountered in daily life. In the United States, both the law of contracts and the law of torts are based on the common law, although the majority of states have codified much of the law of contracts through adaptation of the Uniform Commercial Code (22). Psychiatric malpractice cases fall primarily within the law of torts (civil law). *A tort is any private or civil wrong by act or omission but not including breach of contract.*

A *precedent* is a court decision on a question of law that serves as authority for adjudicating similar questions in future cases. The principle that has been established becomes a binding precedent in future cases with similar fact patterns in the original court (jurisdiction) and other courts of equal or lower rank within the same jurisdiction. This legal principle is known as *stare decisis* (23). It is important to note that a case only has "precedential value" in the jurisdiction (state or federal district or circuit) in which it was decided. As a consequence, courts outside the affected jurisdiction are not bound by the earlier ruling. The only exception to this is rulings by the United States Supreme Court, which have national precedential authority and are, therefore, binding on all other courts. Although not bound by decisions made by courts outside of their jurisdiction, courts look to such opinions for guidance and may in fact rely on them as persuasive authority.

Precedent developed from the accumulated decisions of the courts produces a conservative evolution in the law. Therefore, before bringing a suit against someone (e.g., a psychiatrist), plaintiffs' attorneys typically research previous cases involving similar situations and advise their clients on the status of the law relating to their (potential) case. For example, in suicide cases, courts have generally held that the assessment and control of the patient's suicide risk and behavior rather than the prediction of suicide are the determinative factors in evaluating the standard of care (24). Therefore, a suit based primarily on the issue of prediction is unlikely to prevail because it would contravene precedent set by prior decisions adjudicating similar fact patterns.

Objectives of the Law

The law functions essentially to achieve four goals: 1) to prevent and settle disputes; 2) to distribute resources within society; 3) to establish relations between society and government; and 4) to enforce standards of social conduct (25).

Disputes

Civil suits are a means for settling disputes between individuals. For example, a psychiatric malpractice suit concerning the suicide death of a mental patient will generally involve conflicting assertions of the type of care that the patient received. The plaintiff (the person bringing the suit), after consultation with an attorney, may decide that expert testimony for his or her position is strong, in which case he or she may decide to go forward with a trial. On the other hand, the defendant (the person being sued) and his or her attorney may decide that the facts of the case clearly indicate liability, and therefore they may favor a quick settlement. If both sides cannot agree to settle, the case will go before an impartial trier of fact such as a judge or a jury. The party suffering an adverse verdict may appeal to a higher court based on many factors, including alleged procedural errors during the trial. In some states, a civil claim will not necessarily proceed to court if it *cannot* be settled. Instead, it must first be heard by an arbitration panel. Although arbitration appears typically to be easier, quicker, and less costly than trial litigation, empirical scholars have begun to question whether the value of arbitration always outweighs countervailing factors (e.g., a public hearing, right to jury trial, careful judicial consideration of ambiguous issues).

Distribution

The best example of the law's *second* goal—to distribute resources—is taxation. Money is taken by the government from citizens and corporations and spent according to the perceived needs of society. An example of distribution efforts in psychiatry is the right to treatment litigation. Here, the law attempts to provide minimal health care to disadvantaged sectors of the population (26).

Mediating Society and Government

The *third* function of the law involves establishing relations between society and government through the United States Constitution. The Constitution generally states the principles and establishes a foundation of law by which our government is created and from which it derives authority and power. The purpose of a constitutional government is to obtain for its citizens certain basic rights and remedies and to define the limits of government activities.

The Constitution mandates that no governmental office, body, or agency may deprive a citizen of his or her life, liberty, and property without observing elemental principles of fairness (i.e., due process of law). Only when a *government* body takes action against an individual are due-process guarantees applicable. When persons in their individual capacities act against others, due process is not violated, although other rights may be. However, when an individual or entity is acting at the direction of the state or is involved in activities that may otherwise be considered state action, then that individual or entity will be held to the same due-process standards as is a governmental body.

The Constitution identifies two kinds of due process: procedural and substantive. The former involves the methods the government uses to deal with its citizens; the latter involves the content of the laws passed by the government. Civil commitment illustrates the laws' relations between society and government. In psychiatry, civil commitment contains both procedural and substantive due-process issues. For example, in 1972, the court in *Lessard v. Schmidt* (27) promulgated a narrow, substantive standard of dangerousness in civil commitments to safeguard civil liberty. In addition, stringent procedural rights for involuntary hospitalization were made similar to those in criminal proceedings such as notice of hearing and the opportunity to be heard, the privilege against self-incrimination, right to counsel, and the exclusion of hearsay evidence. The court rulings in *Lessard* were later incorporated in a new civil commitment statute in Wisconsin (28).

Enforcement

The law enforces acceptable standards of social conduct, the fourth objective, for the psychiatric profession as well as for society at large. For instance, a number of states have enacted statutes establishing criminal penalties for the sexual exploitation of patients by health care providers (29).

The Legal Process

The legal process is adversarial. In both civil and criminal cases, each side tries to persuade the judge or jury that it is right. The aim of the adversarial procedure is not necessarily truth, but justice. That is, each party to a dispute will have his or her day in court in order to present his or her position before an impartial and fair-minded finder of fact.

Rules of procedure and evidence govern the nature and extent to which the judge and jury hear the relevant facts to a dispute. The function of the judge during the trial is to act as a referee or authority concerning all questions of law. The jury's task is to decide questions of fact. Jury trials usually are not permitted in cases of minor offenses with penalties less than $100. Twelve jurors sit on felony cases, while misdemeanors and civil cases may have a fewer number of jurors (30).

Civil Litigation

The following outline proceeds from the initial summons through the post-trial motions in a typical civil lawsuit (e.g., malpractice case against a psychiatrist) (31):

1. **Complaint.** A summons containing the complaint is prepared and served upon the defendant (psychiatrist). The complaint sets forth the general allegations that support the cause of action (i.e., those facts that, if alleged and proven in a law suit, would enable the plaintiff to attain a judgment).
2. **Answer.** A written response by the defendant to the specific allegations is made to the plaintiff's complaint. The answer may also assert affirmative defenses that if proven will serve to bar, in part or totally, the plaintiff's claims.
3. **Discovery.** The formal investigation of the other side's allegations, including the following:
   a. Written interrogatories

    b. Oral depositions
    c. Production of documents
    d. Physical and mental examinations
    e. Request for the admission of facts

4. **Motions.** A *motion* is a formal application to the court for a rule or other order. For example, motions will typically be made to the court for various kinds of relief, including clarification of the complaint. A motion to dismiss the complaint may be made by the defendant if the claim is not recognized by law or if it does not allege facts that are sufficient to demonstrate a violation of law (e.g., "prima facie case").

5. **Pretrial conference.** A pretrial conference is attended by the judge, attorneys, and, in some instances, the claimant. Settlement is discussed as well as methods of expediting and simplifying the trial.

6. **Trial.** The following is a rough outline of the major stages of a malpractice trial:

    a. Selection of jury ("voir dire")
    b. Opening statements
    c. Testimony of witnesses and the introduction of other evidence
    d. Various motions by the defense, if necessary. Motions by the defense may be made at this time. For example, a motion for a "directed verdict" is a request by the defense for the judge to instruct the jury of a particular decision that they are to render (e.g., a decision for the defense).
    e. Rebuttal evidence by plaintiff
    f. Renewal of motion for directed verdict
    g. Closing arguments
    h. Jury instructions
    i. Jury decision
    j. Post-trial motions (e.g., appeal)

Arbitration

An alternative to the litigation process is to resolve disputes through arbitration. A number of states have authorized some form of arbitration of medical malpractice cases, while other states are considering it. Arbitration is a contractual proceeding in which the parties to a dispute either mandatorily or voluntarily choose a third party to arbitrate or decide a dispute. The purpose of arbitration is to obtain an inexpensive and speedy disposition. Most jurisdictions permit specific differences to be submitted to arbitration but vary on the binding nature of the process. A number of states require initial submission of a malpractice claim for arbitration before court proceedings are instituted.

In recent years, arbitration has been gaining favor among physicians. However, psychiatrists must carefully consider the pros and cons of voluntary arbitration in malpractice cases (32). To process allegations of malpractice, states utilize a variety of quasi-judicial mechanisms such as pretrial sentencing panels, mediation, and arbitration. From the psychiatrist's perspective arbitration (voluntary or mandatory) holds a number of advantages. First, complex cases can be more readily explained in an arbitration format without undue constraint by evidentiary rulings. Second, unwanted publicity can often be avoided. In some jurisdictions, the records of the arbitration proceeding may be sealed. Finally, the available remedies are greater and extend beyond monetary awards. Often, the type of remedy can be negotiated (i.e., letter of apology, establishment of an annuity, etc.). The disadvantages include the possibility of a greater number of frivolous malpractice allegations and the preclusion of such affirmative defenses as contributory negligence, assumption of the risk, and expiration of the statute of limitations.

Court System

State Courts

Every state, to a certain degree, is a source or body of law unto itself. State courts are established by state constitutions and state legislatures. The state judicial system consists essentially of three trial levels: inferior (trial), intermediate (appeals), and courts of final authority (supreme). In some states, however, varying nomenclature may cause confusion. The trial court in New York is the *Supreme Court* and the highest court is the *Court of Appeals*. The *Tarasoff* (14) case wound its way through the lower courts in California before reaching the California Supreme Court. The highest court of California subsequently reversed the lower court's rejection of a duty to warn endangered parties. In *Tarasoff II* (33), the California Supreme Court reviewed the case again because of extenuating circumstances and defined an even broader "duty to protect."

Federal Courts

The federal court system has three levels: 1) district court, 2) circuit courts of appeal, and 3) United States Supreme Court. District courts represent the trial level of the federal system. Every state is served by at least one district court. Most psychiatric malpractice suits are brought in state courts. If the suit involves a federal statute, federal constitutional issues, or "diversity" of citizenship, it is brought in the federal court.

    A federal court has "diversity" jurisdiction when a resident of one state sues a resident of another state *and* more than $50,000 in damages are alleged. For jurisdiction purposes, a resident includes an individual or a state agency or other state entity.

The United States Supreme Court is the highest court of the land, and, as such, it hears appeals of important cases from federal circuit courts of appeals and from state supreme courts. Of the thousands of cases heard in the United States annually, only a small fraction make it to the Supreme Court. In these cases, the Supreme Court discretionarily accepts cases for review (known as granting *cert,* or *certiorari*) that in the court's view represent significant questions of law ripe for some degree of resolution. For the past two decades, a regular stream of cases involving issues of interest to mental health practitioners has come before the Supreme Court. For example, in *Youngberg v. Romeo* (34), the United States Supreme Court held that civilly committed mentally retarded patients possess certain constitutional rights that include the right to be free from unnecessary bodily restraints, to have safe conditions in which to live, and to receive some degree of training and treatment.

Unfortunately, significant issues considered by the United States Supreme Court are frequently not completely resolved and, instead, are merely redirected to a lower court for disposition. An example of how a case can work its way up the federal system and back is *Mills v. Rogers* (formerly *Rogers v. Okin*) (35), a Massachusetts case involving the right to refuse treatment. It originally was brought as a class action suit by the psychiatric patients at Boston State Hospital raising various constitutional violations and tort claims. The case was heard at the federal district court level and then was appealed to the United States Court of Appeals for the First Circuit. Later, the United States Supreme Court granted the petition for certiorari (36). However, in June of 1982, the Court (36) vacated the First Circuit judgment and remanded the case for further review in light of an intervening Massachusetts Supreme Judicial Court decision (37). In its latest incarnation, *Rogers v. Commission of the Department of Mental Health* (38), the Massachusetts Supreme Judicial Court ruled that mental patients, even when involuntarily committed, have an important right to arrive at their own treatment decisions. On remand, the First Circuit in *Rogers* held that the Massachusetts law regarding forcible antipsychotic medication of involuntarily committed mental patients provided procedures adequate to protect patients' due-process rights (39).

Appeals from district court opinions are heard by one of the 13 circuit courts of appeal, depending upon the location of the district court. For example, the civil suit against John Hinckley's psychiatrist was initially heard by the district court covering Colorado. (This case was heard as a diversity suit, because the plaintiff was from Washington, D.C. and the defendant from Colorado, and more than the then-current jurisdictional limitation was alleged.) The plaintiff lost and subsequently appealed to the

United States Court of Appeals for the Tenth Circuit, which later affirmed the lower court decision (40).

Administrative Action (Judicial)

When psychiatrists or other licensed practitioners breach professional ethics or practice in a manner reflecting immoral, deceitful, criminal, or fraudulent intent, state administrative agencies (e.g., state boards of occupational licenses) are usually empowered to investigate and impose appropriate disciplinary action (41). The most common sanctions include suspension or revocation of the practitioner's license to practice and/or the imposition of fines. For instance, in *Rudner v. Board of Regents of the New York State Department of Education* (42), the practitioner's license was revoked for sexual misconduct, breach of confidentiality, and verbal abuse of the patient.

A professional cannot be disciplined unless there are findings of fact, complete with certain due-process protection. Professional or disciplinary hearings are quasi-judicial in nature and are generally unencumbered by the formal trappings of a judge and jury. These proceedings are typically conducted before the full board of the administrative regulatory agency. The accused practitioner is typically permitted assistance by legal counsel as well as by other due-process protections (43). Because these proceedings are administrative (without penal consequences), the Sixth Amendment right to counsel is not considered a constitutional or basic right. Formal rules of evidence fundamental to legal trials are usually disregarded or greatly minimized at this type of proceeding, allowing some out-of-court testimony (hearsay) that is relevant to the issues at hand to be introduced and weighed by the board (7). Despite the absence of full judicial due process, the pursuit of truth and fundamental fairness govern these administrative hearings as in formal trials.

Despite these mechanisms for disciplining errant practitioners, licensing boards tend to be reluctant to impose strict, effective sanctions. Often, the underlying licensing sanctions or the statutes themselves lack the necessary authority to permit the investigation of offending professionals once these individuals are outside the state jurisdiction. Limited personnel resources for investigating complaints, difficulty in securing witnesses to testify, the reluctance of physicians to pass judgments against their peers, and controversy regarding what is the most effective way of addressing unethical practice all contribute to this problem.

Professional disciplinary proceedings against psychiatrists, while not uncommon, are far from being uniformly implemented from state to state or successful at reducing unethical practices. The reluctance or inability of licensing boards to impose truly effective sanctions against unethical practitioners is well illustrated by the officially unreported case *Walker v. Parzen* (44).

In *Walker,* an award of 4.6 million dollars was granted by a San Diego superior court jury after the patient testified and the defendant psychiatrist admitted that she had been physically, sexually, and psychologically abused by him. She ultimately agreed to a settlement of 2.5 million dollars in return for not pursuing further litigation. The complaint alleged that the psychiatrist had repeated sexual intercourse with her and advised her to commit suicide after giving her drugs with which to do so. In addition to the civil trial, licensure disciplinary hearings were held. The California Board of Medical Quality Assurance considered the same facts as were presented in the lawsuit, but concluded that Dr. Parzen should lose his license for only 1 year and be placed on probation for 10 years. Upon his return to practice, the California Board prohibited him from "treating female patients, working alone, or prescribing drugs that have the potential for abuse during the probationary period" (45). Given the seriousness of the charges against the psychiatrist, the California Board of Quality Assurance could have decided to permanently revoke the psychiatrist's medical license or some similar degree of punishment, but did not do so.

Professional Standard Review Committees

In addition to statutory and judicial regulation, psychiatric practice is strongly influenced by professional organizations. These regulatory bodies, though less formal, can exert substantial influence. The standards and policies of professional organizations are used to control professional entry, define training standards, and promulgate procedures and requirements for certification and licensing (46). In addition, all the major mental health disciplines in the United States have established codes of professional conduct (46). Professional standard review committees sponsored by state professional associations serve as arbitrators for complaints received against mental health practitioners. Action is initiated when a complaint is received. Formal and informal hearings are then conducted. Professional standard review committee findings are advisory and adopt no defined standards of competence but instead render opinions of what typically constitutes "usual and customary practice" (4).

Professional Ethics and Standards

Although the various mental health professions have not always been successful in exercising control over their members, these organizations have made considerable professional input into state regulations administered through licensing boards (46). Similarly, judicial opinions concerning mental health, such as standard-of-care issues, reflect practices largely defined by the profession (47).

Violation of ethical codes carries no direct legal consequences. Furthermore, ethical codes differ from governmental regulations in that the latter apply to every person holding a license, whereas ethical codes only apply to members in good standing of a particular organization (7).

Ethical codes primarily address the practitioner's responsibility not only to the patient but to the general public and to the physician. The venerable Hippocratic oath of the medical profession dates back at least 2,600 years. As a rule, an ethical code does not deal with the establishment of professional standards of care but instead promulgates general guidelines of conduct. For the general practitioner or specialist, standards of care are judicially determined. Nevertheless, courts of law and legislatures are substantially influenced by the codes of conduct of professional organizations (46). A profession's ethical code provides the foundation for enacting regulatory laws to judicial and legislative bodies. All of the major mental health disciplines in the United States have a code of professional conduct (46).

The American Psychiatric Association (APA), through its district branches, maintains ethical standards of behavior for its members according to "The Principles of Medical Ethics, With Annotations Especially Applicable to Psychiatry." Furthermore, alleged ethical violations are processed through the APA's "Procedures for Handling Complaints of Unethical Conduct."

The following example illustrates the kind of ethical violation investigated and commented upon by the APA. The APA's Ethics Committee reported to the membership that a member psychiatrist was charged with engaging in sexual activities with his patient (48). There was never any dispute that the sexual activity had taken place. However, the therapist argued that the sexual relationship did not begin until several weeks after the therapy was terminated. The district branch of the APA, with jurisdiction over the psychiatrist by virtue of his active membership, decided that the precise timing of the commencement of the sexual relationship was irrelevant. Even if the sexual relationship started after termination of therapy, the psychiatrist's sexual involvement constituted an exploitation of the "knowledge, power, and unique position that the psychiatrist held in the patient's life." The committee concluded that sexual involvement between a psychiatrist and a patient, even after the end of treatment, always raises concern about transference and countertransference. The termination of the formal doctor-patient relationship does not end the ethical concern.

National Practitioner Data Bank

On September 1, 1990, the United States government created the National Practitioner Data Bank containing the records of malpractice suits and disciplinary actions against physicians, dentists, and other health care professionals (49). The Data Bank was established by Congress through the Health Care Quality Improvement Act of 1986 by passage of Public Law 99-660, Title IV (50). The purpose of such a bank is to centralize the reporting of disciplinary actions by state licensing boards, hospital boards, and state medical societies against physicians so that interested parties (e.g., state licensing agencies, hospital review boards) can assess whether an applicant has ever had disciplinary or civil suits successfully brought against him or her, including all settled cases.

Hospitals, HMOs, professional societies, and state medical boards, as well as other health care organizations, are required to report any disciplinary actions against providers lasting longer than 30 days. Disciplinary actions include limitation, suspension, or revocation of privileges or membership in a professional society. Insurers who make malpractice payments on behalf of providers, including settlements, are required to participate. Immunity from liability is granted for health care entities and providers making peer review reports in good faith (51). Hospitals must query the Data Bank for information about physicians who make application for hospital privileges. Every 2 years, the Data Bank also must be queried about physicians who hold current staff privileges or who have lost immunity for professional peer review activities.

An additional, and quite valuable, consequence of such a resource is that errant professionals are prevented from changing hospitals or leaving the state in order to avoid detection of this information. Undoubtedly, the Data Bank will be very useful in rooting out incompetent professionals. Nevertheless, the mere fact of an adverse judgment against the doctor in a malpractice suit, by itself, likely proves nothing. It does not necessarily mean that the physician is incompetent or, even, that the physician committed malpractice. The accurate reporting of such a judgment or prior disciplinary action, however, will provide an inquiring agency the opportunity to investigate the relevancy and significance of the prior judgment. The Data Bank is creating considerable controversy. Legal commentators fear that the National Practitioner Data Bank will discourage settlement of legal claims, discourage hospital peer review, encourage litigation against hospitals over privileges, and encourage lower standards of medical practice by requiring the reporting of denial of requests for the upgrading of privileges (52).

Any disciplinary actions or malpractice payments made by physicians must be reported to the Data Bank. Failure to report is subject to civil monetary penalties of up to $10,000 for each unreported incident (53).

The public will not have access to the Data Bank. Plaintiffs' attorneys can have access to the Data Bank only if they can prove that the hospital failed to query the Data Bank regarding the physician in question. The information so obtained can be used only to sue the hospital for negligent credentialing (54). Physicians can request information from the Data Bank about their own file without paying the $2 standard fee per name.

Finding the Law: Legal Research

The psychiatrist who wishes to consult a particular legal opinion must be able to decipher case citations and then locate the appropriate book, called a *reporter,* that contains the case.

The general legal style for case citations is as follows:

Brady v. Hopper	751	F2d	329	(10th Cir. 1984)
Case name	*Volume*	*Reporter*	*Page*	*Jurisdiction Date*

Psychiatrists who need information and guidance on the legal regulation of their practices should consult attorneys knowledgeable in the mental health field. Obtaining legal references that may identify the sources of information directly, while possible for a psychiatrist to do, can be an arduous, confusing task. The different kinds of law books, reporters, digests, legal periodicals, and publications of federal, state, and municipal statutory codes have been identified by Statsky (55).

It can be stated with absolute certainty that the vast majority of psychiatrists have not seen the inside of a law library. Only an occasional forensic psychiatrist or, more likely, psychiatrists with law degrees know how to use a law library. This section on legal research is included for the intrepid psychiatrist who, for whatever reason, would like to use a law library. To the authors' knowledge, this kind of information has never been presented to the psychiatrist in either the general psychiatric or the forensic psychiatric literature.

Case decisions, statutes, administrative regulations, law review articles, and other legal documents and publications are not the easiest sources of information to track down, even when one has a correct citation. It therefore should not come as a surprise that conducting legal research, even if it is simply to check the accuracy of a reference, can be a bewildering and frustrating experience.

It is beyond the nature and scope of this book to provide a crash course in legal research. What will be addressed is a very rudimentary introduction to doing preliminary research in the areas of topical searching and specific case or statute citing.

Topical Search

Books of law. A *topical search* simply refers to a general review of the relevant legal literature regarding a particular subject or topic area. These types of reviews are valuable, in fact essential, for psychiatrists writing about or researching contemporary medicolegal issues. Legal research can personally be conducted in two ways. The fastest and most efficient means is with the use of a computer that has access to one of the main legal data bases such as WESTLAW (56) or LEXIS (57). However, this is an impractical solution for the novice legal researcher because of the equipment and subscriber service requirements, as well as the likely unfamiliarity with its on-line use. The second, and most common form, of legal research is the old fashioned way: "in the stacks" investigation.

One benefit associated with legal research is the fact that lawyers and other contributors to the law like to write and do *a lot* of it. As a result, there are a vast number of guides, encyclopedias, digests, summaries, etc., that condense, summarize, and generally facilitate finding legal information. A first step, therefore, in conducting a search of a particular legal topic such as the "standard of care for psychiatry" is to decide whether one is interested in the actual law from a specific jurisdiction (or nationally) or simply legal commentary on the subject. Legal research materials can essentially be classified into two groups: *books of law* and *books of search* (58). Books of law, as the name implies, are those materials that contain the actual laws and regulations such as statutes, constitutions, treaties, regulations, charters, ordinances, rules of court, opinions, and decisions. Therefore, to find the actual law in a given jurisdiction (e.g., state or federal district) requires researching the body of law containing that type of information (e.g., "statutory codes") for a given state or the federal judiciary.

Finding the right "body of law" to review is essential to any investigation because it can mean the difference between success or hours of wasted time and frustration. The guidance of the law librarian should be sought to help identify the volume of books desired, what books index or digest this area of law ("search books"), and where these materials are located in the library. It will be helpful (and likely engender positive relations with the librarian) if one has a clear idea of the topic issue (e.g., standard of care), jurisdiction requirements (e.g., the laws of state X), and time frame (e.g., most current). Because *nearly every* "book of law" has a set of indexes and sometimes digests ("books of search"), it is generally helpful to begin with them. This is true, of course, unless one is searching for a specific citation (e.g., case opinion cite or statutory code cite).

Unfortunately, there is generally no uniformity on how a particular topic will be phrased in the index or under what general heading or subheading the subject may be found. Therefore, before immediately proceeding to the state or federal "law" books, it is generally helpful to develop a variety of terms, topical phrases, or "key words" that might contain the subject being researched. For example, "standard of care in psychiatry" may be found in the section covering medicine, health care, malpractice, medical professions, public health, mental health, and so on. Again, the assistance of the law librarian can be invaluable for suggestions and guidance if initial attempts are not fruitful. Also, topics that are particularized or fairly specific such as "standard of care in *psychiatry*" will likely be subsumed under more general code provisions covering broad or global headings such as *physicians & surgeons* or simply *health care providers.*

Once the topic headings have been narrowed down to a workable number, one should refer to the volumes that index the "book of law" containing the desired information. For instance, a search of the "law" for the District of Columbia regarding the standard of care for psychiatrists might begin by looking in the book designated as the "index" for the D.C. Code. Any terms that refer to, or are possibly related to, "standard of care" would then be noted according to the book volume and section number given in the index. A review of this information will likely yield the desired information. If not, it is possible that the right key words were not searched or that "standard of care" is under another heading. Another possibility is that there is *no* statutory provision covering the issue being researched. If this is the situation, then the issue is likely governed by case law, which will require a second investigation of a separate set of books (e.g., a national reporter system such as a regional reporter like Atlantic 2d, or A2d). Fortunately these books have their own set of "books of search" that should be of assistance in tracking down the key word.

The last possibility, albeit a small one, is that the key word or issue is covered by a newly enacted statute. Because of this possibility, legal researchers should *always* check for updates to the statutory codes that are either slipped in the back cover of a volume (known as "pocket parts") or in separate paperback volumes along side the regular code books.

Legal periodical literature.   Reviewing the legal commentary or literature is a far simpler and less tedious process. Frequently, in the various statutory code books and their updates, there will be a "comments" section at the end of the statute. This section will generally contain the legislative history of the statute and, occasionally, citations to law review and other articles that deal generally or directly with the statute or statutory subject. Referring to the statutes in this manner is typically an inefficient process unless the researcher is looking for legal commentary that is *specific* to a particular code provision or statute. The more efficient and productive means of searching the legal periodical literature is to peruse one of the three main periodical indexes: Index for Legal Periodicals (ILP), Current

Law Index (CLI), and the Legal Resource Index (LRI). The ILP and CLI are in book form, whereas the LRI is on microfilm. Between these three sources, literally hundreds of medical, forensic, and legal periodicals are indexed. The only problem a researcher may encounter is that the library may not have the periodical that contains the article. In this case, a somewhat time-consuming interlibrary loan may be required or a visit to a second law library may be necessary.

Specific citation searching. Articles and commentary about malpractice or some other forensic psychiatric topic will contain numerous references to case opinions, statutes, and, on occasion, administrative regulations. Often, unfortunately, a case will be referenced or even cited in the text, but sufficient information about it will be lacking. Psychiatrists desiring more "first hand" knowledge about a case or statute may want to obtain a copy of the law for their reading and records. Unless the case is an unpublished trial opinion, which will be cited with a docket number, court, state, and date of opinion (e.g., *Golden v. Levy*, #CV-84-3686 PAR [USDC C.D. Cal. Nov. 23, 1984]), practically any published opinion can easily be obtained at a law library—provided it *has* been published. The following example of a case citation is all of the information a researcher should need in locating a published opinion:

Brady v. Hopper	751	F2d	329	(10th Cir. 1984)
Case name	*Volume*	*Reporter*	*Page*	*Jurisdiction Date*

In this example, the *Brady* opinion is published in Volume 751 of the *Federal Reporter, Second Series*. Opinions from the federal trial level or federal district courts (contained in the *Federal Supplements*, or F. Supp.), federal appellate level (contained in the *Federal Reporter*), or United States Supreme Court (the official edition is contained in *U.S. Reports*, and the unofficial are found in the *U.S. Supreme Court Reporter* [S. Ct.] or *U.S. Supreme Court Reporter, Lawyers Edition* [S. Ct. L.Ed.]) are all typically shelved in the same area of the library and easy to find.

State opinions are not always so easy to find. This is because of the lack of uniformity of books in which trial, appellate, and state supreme court opinions will be found. Many states do not regularly publish trial-level opinions, although these can sometimes be found in legal periodicals such as the *ATLA Law Reporter, Medical Malpractice: Verdicts, Settlements and Experts,* or the *Mental and Physical Disability Law Reporter,* to name a few.

The large majority of states, instead, only publish appellate opinions. These opinions can typically be found in one of the seven regional reporters (i.e., Atlantic, North Eastern, North Western, Pacific, Southern, South Eastern, and South Western). The "official" reporting of a state opinion may be found in a state reporter, if a state still publishes its opinions. A number of states have abandoned publishing state reporters and instead rely on independent law reporting companies such as West Publishing to report them in their reporter system. Like a federal case opinion, a citation to a state opinion will provide the researcher with all of the data needed to locate it. For example:

| *Peterson v. State,* | 100 Wn 2d 421, | 671 P2d 230 | (1983) |
| | (official reporter) | (unofficial, "regional" reporter) | |

In this example, the official opinion of *Peterson* can be found in Volume 100 of the *Washington Reports, Second Series* and the unofficial edition, in Volume 671 of the *Pacific Reporter, Second Series.* The distinction between official and unofficial opinions is more formal than substantive. The official version is the printing approved by the state, whereas the unofficial opinion, exactly the same in text content, is published by someone other than the state.

There are dozens of complex situations that can confront the legal researcher, such as trying to find a case that is only partially cited, locating a recently enacted statute that has not been officially codified, or determining the status of a case as to whether it is still valid "authority" (e.g., reversed, affirmed in part, superceded, etc.). The possible methods used to address these and other situations could consume a whole book.

For the reader interested in knowing more about legal research and legal periodical searches, two books are recommended. For an excellent pictorial and printed overview of the most common law books—their uses, applications, and practical research guidelines—the reader should refer to Statsky's *Legal Research, Writing and Analysis* (1982) (58). For a current synopsis of the books containing codified and uncodified state and federal law, as well as the format for proper legal citations, the current edition of *A Uniform System of Citation* by The Harvard Law Review Association should be consulted.

References

1. Simon RI: Clinical Psychiatry and the Law, 2nd Edition. Washington, DC, American Psychiatric Press, 1992
2. Simon RI: Concise Guide to Psychiatry and Law for Clinicians. Washington, DC, American Psychiatric Press, 1992
3. Simon RI: Clinical Psychiatry and the Law, 2nd Edition. Washington, DC, American Psychiatric Press, 1992
4. Clairborn WL: The problem of professional incompetence. Professional Psychology 13:153–158, 1982

5. Simon RI: Clinical Psychiatry and the Law, 2nd Edition. Washington, DC, American Psychiatric Press, 1992
6. Brakal SJ, Parry J, Weiner BA: The Mentally Disabled and the Law. Chicago, IL, ABA Foundation, 1985, pp 447–461
7. Smith JT: The regulation of psychiatric practice, in Medical Malpractice: Psychiatric Care. Colorado Springs, CO, Shepard's/McGraw-Hill, 1986, pp 570–588
8. See, e.g., Cal Civ Code § 43.92 (West Supp 1989)
9. See, e.g., DC Code Ann § 6-2003 (1981); DC Code Ann 43.92 (1985)
10. See, e.g., Minn Stat Ann § 372.148A.01-06 (West 1986)
11. Simon RI: Clinical Psychiatry and the Law, 2nd Edition. Washington, DC, American Psychiatric Press, 1992
12. O'Connor v Donaldson, 422 US 563 (1975); Jackson v Indiana, 406 US 715 (1972)
13. Cal Civ Code § 43.92 (West 1989)
14. Tarasoff v Regents of the University of California, 17 Cal 3d 425, 131 Cal Rptr 14, 551 P2d 334 (1976)
15. Cal Civ Code § 43.92(a) (1991)
16. DC Code Ann § 6-2024 (Supp 1981)
17. 28 USC § 2680 (1990)
18. 732 F2d 366 (4th Cir 1984)
19. Standards for Intermediate Care Facilities: HEW Rules and Regulations. 45 CFR 249 (1976)
20. Smith JT: The regulation of psychiatric practice, in Medical Malpractice: Psychiatric Care. Colorado Springs, CO, Shepard's/McGraw-Hill, 1986, pp 570–602; see p 575
21. People v Rehman, 253 Cal 2d 119, 61 Cal Rptr 65, 85 (1967)
22. UCC § 1-102 et seq
23. Hertz v Woodman, 218 US 205 (1910)
24. Simon RI: Concise Guide to Psychiatry and Law for Clinicians. Washington, DC, American Psychiatric Press, 1992
25. 325 F Supp 781 (MD Ala 1971)
26. Wyatt v Stickney, 325 F Supp 781, 334 F Supp 1341 (MD Ala 1971), 344 F Supp 373 (MD Ala 1972), affirmed sub nom, Wyatt v Alderholt 503 F2d 1305 (5th Cir 1974)
27. 349 F Supp 1078 (ED Wis 1972), vacated and remanded on other grounds, 414 US 473 (1974), redecided, 379 F Supp 1376 (ED Wis 1974), vacated and remanded on other grounds, 421 US 957 (1975), redecided, 413 F Supp 1318 (ED Wis 1976)
28. Wis Stat Ann § 51.20 et seq (1990)
29. Colo Rev Stat § 18-3-405.5; Maine Revised Statutes, Title 17-A § 253(2)(I) (Supp 1989); Minn Stat Ann § 609.344 (West 1989); Minn Stat Ann §§ 609.344(g),(v),(h–j) (West Supp 1985); Minn Stat § 609.341 et seq (Supp 1989); Cal Bus & Prof Code § 729 (Supp 1989); ND Cent Code § 12.1-20-06.1(1) (Michie Supp 1989); Wis Stat Ann § 940.22(2) (West 1989); 1990 Fla Sess Laws Serv 490.0112 § 1(1) (tentative assignment) (West 1990); Mich Comp Laws Ann §§ 750.520b(1)(d)(i), 750.90 (West Supp 1984–1985); NH Rev Stat Ann § 632-A:2 Part VIII (Supp 1986); Wyo Stat § 6-2-303 (1988)

30. Hibdon v United States 204 F2d 834 (6th Cir 1953)
31. Beis EB: Mental Health and the Law. Rockville, MD, Aspen, 1984, p 17–20
32. Simon RI: Clinical Psychiatry and the Law, 2nd Edition. Washington, DC, American Psychiatric Press, 1992
33. Tarasoff v Regents of the University of California, 17 Cal 3d 425, 131 Cal Rptr 14, 551 P2d 334 (1976)
34. 457 US 307 (1982)
35. Rogers v Okin, 478 F Supp 1342 (D Mass 1979), affirmed in part, reversed in part, 634 F2d 650 (1st Cir 1980), vacated and remanded sub nom Mills v Rogers, 457 US 291 (1982), remanded, 738 F2d 1 (1st Cir 1984)
36. Mills v Rogers, 457 US 291 (1982)
37. In re Guardianship of Richard Roe III, 383 Mass 415, 421 NE2d 40 (1981)
38. 390 Mass 489, 495, 458 NE 2d 308, 314 (1983)
39. Rogers v Okin, 738 F2d 1 (1st Cir 1984)
40. Brady v Hopper, 751 F2d 329 (10th Cir 1984)
41. Missouri ex rel Hurwitz v North, 271 US 40 (1926)
42. 105 AD2d 555, 481 NYS2d 502 (1984)
43. DC Code Ann § 2-3305.19-20 (Cum Supp 1987)
44. Walker v Parzen (Cal San Diego Super Ct, July 7, 1982), cited in 24 American Trial Lawyers Association Reporter 295 (1984)
45. Walker E, Young PD: A Killing Cure. New York, Henry Holt, 1986
46. Van Hoose W, Kottler J: Professional and legal regulation, in Ethical and Legal Issues in Counseling and Psychotherapy. San Francisco, CA, Jossey-Bass, 1982, pp 69–93
47. Simon RI: Clinical Psychiatry and the Law, 2nd Edition. Washington, DC, American Psychiatric Press, 1992
48. Recent ethics cases. Psychiatric News, Vol 17, April 16, 1982, pp 8–9
49. Johnson ID: Reports to the National Practitioner Data Bank. JAMA 265:407, 411, 1991
50. Walzer RS: Impaired physicians: an overview and update of legal issues. J Leg Med 11:131–198, 1990
51. 42 USC § 11101 (Supp V 1987)
52. Grad JD: Will national data bank encourage litigation? Virginia Medical (Richmond VA) 117:343–344, 1990
53. Federal data bank on disciplinary action opens. Clinical Psychiatry News 18(10):3, 20, 1990
54. Attorney limited in access to and use of information from malpractice data bank. Clinical Psychiatry News 18(8):12, 1990
55. Statsky WP: Legal Research, Writing, and Analysis, 2nd Edition. St Paul, MN, West Publishing, 1982, pp 12–14
56. WESTLAW is a trademark of the West Publishing Co, 50 W Kellogg Blvd, PO Box 3526, St Paul, MN 55102.
57. LEXIS is a trademark of Mead Data Central, 200 Park Avenue, New York, NY 10166.
58. Statsky WP: Legal Research, Writing, and Analysis, 2nd Edition. St Paul, MN, West Publishing, 1982, p 49

Chapter 2

Malpractice Law: An Introduction —————

Statistics: Overview

The incidence of lawsuits involving psychiatrists and other mental health professionals has shown a relatively steady rise over the past 20 years (1). This expansion is likely due to a number of factors, including, but not limited to, judicial activism as reflected by the court's acceptance of new and expanded areas of liability; consumerism on the part of patients who seem to be demonstrating a greater willingness to hold therapists accountable for their actions; a perceived "litigiousness" of society; and the creative expansion of the range of legal theories proffered by the plaintiff's bar upon which relief may be granted in such cases.

Statistically, however, psychiatrists still lag far behind nearly all other areas of medicine in terms of lawsuits filed against them and the average payment for claims (2). Putting these two seemingly divergent indices together, it would appear fair to conclude that the chances of psychiatrists being sued remain fairly small. Nevertheless, in addition to professional duty, the prospect of litigation increasingly behooves psychiatrists to conduct their practices in a professional and ethically sound manner. Failure to do so can only create an atmosphere that invites a lawsuit. Notwithstanding the "merit" of an allegation of negligence, the mere experience of being sued can be reason enough to want to avoid such an action (3).

Psychiatric Lawsuits: Historical Overview

Historically, legal actions alleging malpractice against psychiatrists, psychoanalysts, or anyone else providing mental health services were practically unprecedented (4, 5). This status of "minuscule incidence" remained relatively unchanged until the middle to late 1970s when publication of lawsuits against psychiatrists and psychologists began to be chronicled and publicly aired (6, 7, 8). Even then, the overall number of lawsuits, especially ones that were successful, remained relatively small.

Fishalow, in her article "The Tort Liability of the Psychiatrist" (9), notes eight reasons for this low incidence:

1. Psychiatrists usually treat relatively few patients, therefore their statistical potential for allegations of malfeasance are [*sic*] numerically more limited.
2. Psychodiagnostics is a young, fledgling science. As such, it is imprecise and more subject to reasonable disagreement than the more physical sciences.
3. In light of the variety and large number of recognized and "accepted" psychiatric treatment practices, it can be quite difficult determining a "standard of care" with which to evaluate a psychiatrist's acts and omissions.
4. The stigma associated with mental illness and having emotional problems has created for some patients a type of unspoken barrier to coming forward and disclosing confidential details in court. This factor is more a remnant of the past, than a present concern.
5. Transference feelings developed in treatment coupled with the mental perception that a therapist or psychiatrist was only there to help and would do "no harm" clouded the desire and motivation of some patients to initiate a lawsuit.
6. By virtue of their therapy skills, psychiatrists were capable of identifying and mollifying negative feelings before they developed into retaliatory actions.

Table 2-1.   Actions by therapist that may create a doctor-patient relationship

Giving advice

Making psychological interpretations

Writing a prescription

Supervising treatment by a nonmedical therapist

Holding lengthy phone conversation with a prospective patient

Treating an unseen patient by mail

Giving a patient an appointment

Telling a walk-in patient that he or she will be seen

Providing sample medications

Acting as a substitute therapist

Providing treatment during an evaluation

Providing psychiatric opinions to neighbors and friends

---

7. Notwithstanding the organic therapies (essentially ECT [electroconvulsive therapy] and medication), it is factually difficult for a patient to establish proof of damages when the injury is only psychic.
8. Proving causation was another stumbling block for the potential plaintiff when the alleged malfeasance is due to psychotherapy practice since the cause of most disorders is neither precise nor clearly established. As a result, distinguishing between an "alleged injury" from the natural course of the psychopathology and a doctor's act can be difficult.

Another factor, clearly distinguishable from today's "litigious mood," was the appearance that plaintiff's attorneys, in the past, were not eager to pursue malpractice claims against psychiatrists. This was likely due to the lack of precedent with which to guide counsel (and the courts). In addition, the reluctance of psychiatric experts to testify against colleagues also was an important factor. This latter barrier, commonly referred to as the "conspiracy of silence," is clearly not an issue today. Legal publications such as *Trial* or the *National Law Journal* contain numerous advertisements offering a wide variety of experts' services.

Litigation Frequency Research

The so-called "litigation crisis" in the early 1970s and then in the recent 1980s focused public attention on the continued, dramatic rise of malpractice and other civil lawsuits in general. Despite a considerable amount of media, legislative, and judicial attention, information regarding the cause(s) of this apparent upswing in litigation, and whether there was ever a "crisis" in the first place, is a source of considerable learned debate (10). Similarly, actual statistically significant data, projections, and "hard facts" from reliable sources concerning the incidence, frequency, and financial consequence of lawsuits against psychiatrists and other mental health professionals are equally questionable.

In fact, a close look at 11 published "studies" and at "research findings" covering nearly 30 years reveals little in the way of statistically valid or significant data. While it is apparent that the number of lawsuits involving psychiatrists has increased over time, any other conclusion from these data would be speculative. As Smith points out in the supplement to *Medical Malpractice: Psychiatric Care*, the reasons for this lack of confidence are numerous:

> The majority of this information is simply generalizations from the closed insurance files of a single insurance carrier or extremely limited sample pools. As a result, the total sample size is small. Moreover, the figures and supporting data published with these and other studies are poorly organized, lack operational definitions, and consistently fail to control for numerous contam-

inating and other variables that will skew the results. For instance, multiple law suits against a single doctor, settled cases that are unrecorded, suits that are filed but later dismissed are all not accounted for. (11)

In light of this information, any reference to these studies should be done with caution. Their value would appear to be for illustration and gross generalization purposes only. Certainly, any reliance on them to make finite cause-and-effect conclusions is risky. An unfortunate consequence to this dearth of "hard data" is that it forces individuals, groups, organizations, and agencies studying this issue to speculate when developing prevention policies and professional education. Given the lack of alternative sources of information for more accurate data, this speculation is likely to result in underestimating the seriousness of psychiatric malpractice. The newly created National Practitioner Data Bank (see Chapter 1) should be able to finally provide definitive malpractice data.

Future Trends

Notwithstanding the lack of statistically valid and reliable data regarding the incidence and scope of psychiatric malpractice claims, it is difficult to ignore the consistency of comparative data that are available. For example, data from the American Medical Association published in the December 14, 1987, issue of *U.S. News & World Report* indicated that for every 100 malpractice suits, claims against psychiatrists *before 1981* amounted to 0.6 (out of 100). This figure then increased to 2.4 out of 100 in 1985 (12). These figures, of course, must be placed in their proper perspective. From this set of data, it is obvious that the number of lawsuits against psychiatrists remains relatively low compared with the number of lawsuits in all other medical specialties. (In one "study," only the specialty of pathology had an incidence of lawsuits lower than that of psychiatry [13].)

Moreover, common sense would also suggest that a steady growth in the numbers of psychiatrists being sued can be expected. Many of the barriers that were thought, at one time, to diminish the likelihood of a lawsuit are no longer viable. For example, patient "stigma," the "omnipresent" perception of the doctor, and the reluctance of many members of the plaintiffs' bar to pursue psychic injury claims are all remnants of the past. In addition, the simple fact that psychiatry has grown in number and stature, has gradually made it a more appealing target of patients seeking redress for perceived wrongdoing by their therapists.

From a strictly numerical or statistical perspective, no one at this time can reasonably project what percentage of psychiatrists will be sued or what these suits will mean in terms of added malpractice premiums. However, it is safe to conclude that unless there is a radical change in the American system of civil law (e.g., to a strict liability system [14]), lawsuits against all professionals, including psychiatrists, will continue to increase. Even with this in mind, the lawsuits against mental health professionals will likely continue to increase gradually rather than sharply. Psychiatric malpractice suits, even with occasional new theories of causes of action, such as the "duty to warn and/or protect" (15), will continue to be limited to a small scope of causes. Moreover, suits alleging psychic harm remain difficult to prove and, as in any civil action, are expensive to litigate.

The Fundamental Elements of a Malpractice Claim

Psychiatric malpractice comes under the general heading of medical negligence. It consists of acts or omissions by physicians (psychiatrists) acting in their professional capacity that cause or aggravate an injury to the patient. The injury to the patient must be the direct result of a failure by the psychiatrist to exercise that *reasonable* degree of care, knowledge, and skill *ordinarily* possessed and exercised in similar situations by other psychiatrists (16). A plaintiff must establish four elements (often referred to as the "4D's") (17) by a preponderance of the evidence (51 out 100 chance) in order to prevail in a malpractice action. The plaintiff must establish the following:

1. That a psychiatrist-patient relationship existed, creating a *duty of care.*
2. That the psychiatrist *deviated* from (breached) the duty of care by an act or omission not in accord with professional standards.
3. That the patient was *damaged* (harmed).
4. That the harm to the patient was *directly* (proximally) caused by the psychiatrist's breach of duty.

This basic knowledge of medical negligence law is essential for practitioners so that unrealistic fears and fantasies about psychiatric malpractice can be dispelled. The words "reasonable" and "ordinary" permeate discussions of established standards in professional liability actions. Both terms refer to the standard of *average,* not perfect, medical or psychiatric care. Mental health professionals, in order not to practice too defensively, need to know the legal realities governing their professional lives. Denial is no less maladaptive for practitioners than it is for patients.

It is also important to realize certain maxims or rules accepted in the law. For example, if the psychiatrist provides substandard treatment but the patient is not harmed, there is no actionable malpractice. Even if the patient alleges injury from the provision of substandard care, liability will not be incurred unless the damage or harm is proximally caused by the deviation in care. Furthermore, there can be no malpractice liability unless a doctor-patient relationship is formed.

Also, a therapist is not held to be a warrantor of correct diagnosis and treatment unless, of course, an actual "guarantee" is made. Mistakes can be made without necessarily incurring liability as long as reasonable care was provided. Thus, for example, a risk-benefit analysis regarding treatment interventions can be critically important in averting liability. The psychiatrist who records in the patient's chart the clinical and factual factors that underlie a treatment decision is in a far better position to demonstrate that "reasonable care" was used than someone who has no such documentation. Clinical judgments that later prove to be wrong will likely not be considered negligent if reasonable care was used and the reasoning documented. The law, as a general rule, does not punish a mere error in judgment (18).

Elements of a Lawsuit

Legal basis of the psychiatrist-patient relationship.   No professional duty of care is owed a patient unless a doctor-patient relationship exists. Once that relationship is created, the duty of care required of the psychiatrist is concomitantly created and recognized by law, regardless of any agreement between a doctor and patient (19). For example, a psychiatrist cannot contract with a patient to "disclaim" liability should something happen to the patient because of substandard psychiatric care (20).

The legal basis of the psychiatrist-patient relationship is founded on contract and "undertaking" theory (19) (see Table 2-1). When a psychiatrist *agrees* (e.g., verbally) to provide services in exchange for a promise to pay a fee, a contract is created with corresponding duties and rights (21).

Circumstances arise in professional practice that do not always fit into the traditional contract model. For example, an unconscious patient may be treated without his or her knowledge or consent, or a patient may be treated free of charge, yet the standard of care owed is no different than if an explicit agreement between doctor and patient was reached (22).

The second theory on which psychiatrist-patient relations are based holds that a psychiatrist who *undertakes* to treat a patient creates a professional relationship with a duty of care regardless of any overt or expressed act by the patient (e.g., payment of a fee). Even when the patient is treated without charge, the psychiatrist remains liable for any negligence in the course of diagnosis and treatment (22). Although the psychiatrist-patient relationship is most often based on contract theory, the contract is not a guarantee of specific results but rather a promise to provide an acceptable standard of care. A claim based on an express contract theory, however, may be successful if the plaintiff proves that the physician expressly guaranteed a result (23).

Bianco (24) advises that a physician who wishes to avoid undertaking treatment of a particular person "must politely, emphatically, and clearly inform the individual that he [or she] is not undertaking to treat and, where advice is given, the advice should be no more than a recommendation to find other medical assistance while at the same time avoiding any detailed query concerning the person's past medical history or present illness." However, psychiatrists who perform evaluations of acutely mentally ill patients may not be able to remain aloof from the patient in crisis. Some immediate dispositional or treatment intervention that might create a psychiatrist-patient relationship may be necessary. Professional and ethical concern for the patient is required when a patient experiences a psychiatric emergency. Referring the patient to an immediately available mental health provider or even accompanying the patient to an emergency room may be necessary. However, the patient should be informed (both verbally and in writing) that no further services beyond the referral will be provided (25).

It may appear that a trivial or minor act of defendant-physicians may sometimes serve as the predicate for malpractice liability (26). For example, in *O'Neill v. Montefiore Hospital* (27), the decedent arrived at a hospital emergency room and had a telephone conversation with a doctor from his hospital insurance plan program about his condition. He was instructed to go home and come back when the doctor on duty was scheduled to arrive at the hospital. The Appellate Division found that the question of whether the doctor's or nurse's refusal of treatment constituted negligence was a question for the jury. It determined that such action may be sufficient to create a physician-patient relationship and that the decision should be left to the jury.

In another case, *Shane v. Mouw* (28), a telephone conversation between a physician and his patient involving an offer to prescribe medication was considered to be a continuation of the treatment relationship for purposes of determining the accrual date of a medical malpractice claim. However, in *Clayton v. Von Hamm* (29), a doctor treated a patient-plaintiff for one condition and then listened to the patient's symptoms over the telephone for something different. The court held that no relationship was established by the (second) "telephone treatment." Occasionally, a new patient who calls for an appointment will want to engage the therapist in a lengthy discussion. This should be tactfully discouraged. Clearly, the telephone should be avoided in making diagnoses or initiating treatment. In *Giallanza v. Sands* (30), a physician allowed his name to be used as a favor so that a patient could be admitted to a hospital for emergency treatment by the staff. Although the physician never saw the patient, the court held that a triable issue of fact existed as to whether a doctor-patient relationship had been created.

In *Rainer v. Grossman* (31), it was alleged by the plaintiff that the opinion of a medical school professor expressed during a teaching conference that surgery was recommended for the plaintiff made the professor liable for malpractice. The court declined to find liability, stating

> [P]resumably every professor or instructor in a professional school hopes, expects or foresees that his students will absorb and apply in their own careers at least some of the information he imparts. Does he thereby assume a duty of care and potential liability to those persons who may ultimately become clients or patients of those students? We think not.

The traditional view in tort law regarding the creation of the doctor-patient relationship limits the therapist's duty of care only to persons with whom a therapist-patient relationship has been established. However, a body of case law has developed during the past 15 years in which, under certain circumscribed situations, a therapist may be held liable to an endangered nonpatient third party (32, 33, 34, 35). Another "nonpatient duty" may theoretically arise when family members are involved in the therapy of a "basic patient." It is conceivable that they may be able to assert a relationship with the therapist or claim an expanded duty owed to them based on the idea that they are foreseeable victims of any negligence committed during the sessions with the primary patient (15). This issue is quite separate from the therapist-patient relationship established with all members in formal family or group therapy. In these circumstances, should any doubt exist for the therapist regarding to whom the duty is owed, it should be made absolutely clear to the (supportive) family members that no therapist-patient relationship exists with them. The therapist must take care in focusing treatment solely on the primary patient. If it is believed that the family members themselves require individual treatment, it is prudent to refer them to another therapist.

Many times, therapists are asked by friends, neighbors, or colleagues for advice about their problems. Therapists should make clear that in listening or giving advice, they are doing so only as friends and that no professional advice is intended. Moreover, the practice of providing psychoactive drugs to nonpatients (e.g., friends, colleagues) may create a doctor-patient relationship and a risk of malpractice if the new patient suffers an adverse reaction.

Radio and television shows and newspaper and magazine columns, as well as lectures to large groups, often invite therapists' views and opinions. Unless wanting to possibly risk (theoretically) creating a duty of care, therapists who engage in informational and educational activities directed toward the general public must make clear that they are speaking about general principles only and are not specifically advising individuals in the audience. The American Psychiatric Association (APA) offers guidelines for psychiatrists who make radio and television appearances (36).

Third-party requests for treatment also may create a duty of care. When parents request a therapist to treat their child, the therapist who accepts generally owes a duty of care to the child but also may have a degree of responsibility to the guardian parent as well. In addition, when a therapist who is employed by a company treats an employee and negligently causes injury, any ensuing lawsuit will likely be directed at the employer and not the employee-therapist. Even though both the therapist and the company will likely be sued, if liability is upheld, the company will pay under the doctrine of *respondeat superior*. In some situations, worker's compensation laws may provide an additional remedy (37). A plaintiff claiming under worker's compensation is limited to this remedy and may not pursue a claim under another approach.

The evaluation of a person for "nontherapeutic purposes" (e.g., examination for insurance application, worker's compensation assessment, prospective employees) can create a confusing picture in determining to whom a duty is owed. These situations can produce two classes of injuries that will determine whether the examining psychiatrist can be held liable to the examinee. The first class of injuries is *physical*. Generally, if a physician's negligent acts *actively* injure a nontherapeutic examinee, the physician would be liable regardless of who paid for the evaluation. For example, a physician who negligently fractures an employee knee cap while conducting a reflex test during a physical evaluation would be held liable. The issue is muddied, however, when there is a negligent *omission* (e.g., failure to diagnose a disease or notify the examinee of a potentially dangerous condition). The traditional position has been, "No doctor-patient relationship, no duty of care" (38). However, the courts have not been uniform in accepting this position (39).

The second class of injuries is *economic,* although not arising out of a physical harm. The classic example occurs when the examiner negligently and inaccurately reports finding a disease that results in the denial of employment or promotion. Again, the courts are divided regarding whether a physician hired by anyone other than the applicant or examinee might be liable to the examinee undergoing nontherapeutic evaluations in which examiner negligence causes noninjury economic loss (40, 41). Given this lack of judicial uniformity, King (42) advises that it would be prudent for examiners to consider the following in these situations: 1) explaining the nontherapeutic nature of the examination to the applicant, 2) obtaining authorization from the examinee to report the results to the individual who ordered the evaluation, and 3) making it clear that the evaluation process is not intended to take the place of treatment by the examinee's personal physician. If a condition or problem is diagnosed during the examination that should be attended to medically or psychiatrically, consent should be obtained from the examinee to send these findings to a designated primary physician, and the examinee should be encouraged to contact his or her private doctor (43).

It is important to note, however, that if some therapeutic benefit is deemed to accrue to the examinee through even a modicum of advice or treatment, then a doctor-patient relationship may be construed to have been created. Also, therapists who examine litigants at the request of the court are generally immune from liability (44). For example, absolute privilege was applied to a psychiatrist's letter to a mother's attorney concerning the father's fitness for custody of the children (45). In another case, a court-appointed psychiatrist was absolutely immune from liability for findings relating to the mental condition of a criminal defendant (46).

Similarly, psychiatrists who participate in commitment proceedings have been held to be immune from malpractice suits by a number of courts (46). A large number of states have immunity provisions in their commitment statutes for good faith actions. The reasoning is that, like judges, psychiatrists should be in the position of making decisions surrounding commitment without fear of legal liability (47). Psychiatrists acting in good faith and in compliance with state commitment statutes are considered to be functioning in a quasi-judicial role for the state and therefore are afforded immunity from liability (48). However, it is incumbent upon the certifying psychiatrist to act in good faith and pursuant to the requirements of the state commitment statute in order to receive immunity. A failure to do this can result in liability for the negligently committed patient (49). It is important to note, however, that when a psychiatrist-patient relationship exists, courts in some jurisdictions may be less willing to cloak the commitment process with immunity for the psychiatrist. This is largely because the (treating) psychiatrist has more knowledge and responsibility for the patient whom he or she is treating than does the psychiatrist examining the patient solely for the purpose of civil commitment (50).

The question of *terminating* the doctor-patient relationship can sometimes be a sticky issue. As a rule, once a doctor-patient relationship is created, the psychiatrist cannot unilaterally terminate the relationship without reasonable notice (25). If appropriate notice is given, the psychiatrist usually must be available for emergencies for a reasonable period of time. Moreover, it behooves the terminating therapist to provide, in writing, names of other therapists or mental health organizations in the area. Also, it is advisable not to terminate volatile or vulnerable patients (e.g., suicidal) until they have achieved a level of psychological stability.

Another rule or maxim in medical jurisprudence as well as in the ethical code for psychiatry (51) is the fact that a physician or psychiatrist has the right to choose what patients he or she wishes to treat barring any contractual agreement to do otherwise (e.g., emergency room doctors, involuntary civil commitment evaluation). To cope with the uncertainty that sometimes arises concerning whether to accept a patient for treatment, some therapists, when seeing a patient for the first time, seek to avoid initiating treatment until an adequate evaluation has been conducted. Accordingly, to avoid initially establishing a doctor-patient relationship, it is advisable for the psychiatrist to make it clear to the prospective patient that the initial meeting(s) is for assessment purposes only and that no treatment will be provided.

This may be a very difficult task and not always possible in actual clinical practice. For instance, the therapist usually does not know how ill the new patient will be when seen for the first time. Some patients are floridly psychotic or may present symptoms that suggest they are a danger to themselves or others. The therapist, therefore, may be compelled to intervene and forego the evaluation period. In this situation, what if the therapist does not want to accept the patient for treatment? Therapists in these circumstances may feel helpless and trapped when confronted with a patient in a crisis that requires immediate attention. Therapists who do not want to undertake the care of these patients should attempt to find immediate competent treatment for them. In some instances, this may require accompanying the patient to a hospital or emergency room. The possibility exists that the therapist who remains indifferent to the patient's immediate crisis can be sued for negligent evaluation or failure to treat if the patient is subsequently harmed. Legal issues aside, professional concern for the patient in a crisis dictates that the patient be directed to immediate help.

The defensive psychiatrist may find litigation concerns to be an additional incentive to see a prospective patient for a period of evaluation. Psychiatrists have become increasingly vulnerable to suits by patients seen for a short period of time, many for only 30 days (52). A new patient may have unrealistic expectations, unrecognized discontents, and litigious tendencies creating a high liability potential. It also has been estimated that 8 out of every 10 persons who commit suicide pay a visit to a physician within 6 months of their decision (53). Thus, the need to assess the potential for violence should not be overlooked.

Psychiatric supervision. Psychiatrists can under certain circumstances become legally responsible for the negligence committed by persons for whom they are providing supervision. In *Andrews v United States* (54), the court found the United States government liable under the Federal Tort Claims Act because of the negligent supervision of a physician's assistant who sexually exploited a therapy patient. Under the doctrine of *respondeat superior,* or vicarious liability, supervisors may become liable for the acts and omissions of anyone over whom they exert some control (such as the psychotherapist in training) who is directly treating a patient. The doctrine of vicarious liability or its Latin equivalent, *respondeat superior* (meaning "let the master answer"), originated from the master-servant relationship (55). The one with the right of control (e.g., supervisor, employer) can be held liable to the successful plaintiff under certain circumstances. Under this doctrine, vicarious liability may be imposed under certain circum-scribed situations. First, the "master," or, for example, the supervising or employing psychiatrist, must have a measure of *control* over subordinates (56, 57). Second, liability will only extend to tortious acts of subordinates that are committed within the *scope of their employment* or relationship (58, 59). When a subordinate deviates too far from the "scope" or "nature" of employment or supervisory duties and becomes engaged in some act for oneself, not connected with the employer-supervisor's business—histori-cally referred to as "frolic and detour" (60)—the liability of the employer will no longer exist (61).

Even in the absence of an employer-employee relationship, persons serving in the capacity of "master" may be liable for negligence of the subordinates they control under the "borrowed servant" doctrine (62). For example, the treating psychiatrist in a hospital will generally be supported by other physicians (e.g., residents, interns), psychiatric nurses, techni-cians, and so forth. Many of these individuals will be hospital employees or self-employed, but rarely formal employees of the treating psychiatrist. The imposition of vicarious liability in these situations, pursuant to the "borrowed servant" rule, requires proof that the subordinate assisting the psychiatrist was negligent, that the psychiatrist possessed the requisite de-gree of control, and that the subordinate was acting within the scope of his or her roles as assistant (63).

A common vicarious liability situation occurs when psychiatrists are collaborating with nonmedical professionals or psychotherapists. A distinc-tion should be made, however, between *supervising* and *consulting with* medical and nonmedical psychotherapists. With regard to the *supervisory relationship,* the APA's "Guidelines for Psychiatrists in Consultative, Super-visory, or Collaborative Relationships With Nonmedical Therapists" (64) states the following:

> In a supervisory relationship the psychiatrist retains direct responsibility for patient care and gives professional direction and active guidance to the therapist. In this relationship the nonmedical therapist may be the employee of an organized health-care setting or of the psychiatrist. The psychiatrist is clinically responsible for the initial workup, diagnosis, and prescription of a treatment plan, as well as for assuring that adequate and timely attention is paid to the patient's physical status and that such infor-mation is integrated into the overall evaluation, diagnosis, and planning.

The psychiatrist remains ethically and medically responsible for the patient's care as long as the treatment continues under his or her supervision. The patient should be fully informed of the existence and nature of, and any changes in, the supervisory relationship.

The guidelines do not specify the frequency of supervision. Thus psychiatrists, when supervising the nonmedical therapist, are responsible for the patient as if the patient were their own. From a legal standpoint, this guideline is consistent with the tenor of the law pursuant to principles underlying the theory of *respondeat superior.*

Consultation relationships generally present a different situation legally than do supervisory ones. Ethically, the APA guidelines advise that a psychiatrist "does not assume responsibility for the patient's care. The psychiatrist evaluates the information provided by the therapist and offers a medical opinion which the therapist may or may not accept" (64).

The law concerning consultative relationships is sparse and provides little guidance. If a psychiatrist confines his or her consultation to the narrow scope defined by the APA guidelines, then the likelihood of liability would seem to be small and probably limited to negligent advice or opinion based upon the facts provided by the therapist. Liability will also likely be limited if it can be demonstrated that the harm to the patient was due to the independent judgment of the therapist, because he or she is free to disregard the consulting psychiatrist's opinion. It is important to understand that a psychiatrist's liability will be limited only if he or she *actually* serves as a consultant. To simply call oneself a consultant, when actually one's role is more of a supervisor or employer, produces a different set of circumstances that likely broadens the potential for liability.

For psychiatrists supervising other psychiatrists, psychiatric residents, or interns, the rules regarding supervisory relationships are still governed by the requirement of control, even in "borrowed servant" situations. For example, if an intern or resident is treating the primary therapist's (psychiatrist's) patient, the intern may be considered a "borrowed servant," whereupon the psychiatrist will be vicariously responsible for any negligence that leads to harm. Interns and residents treating their own patients but supervised by a psychiatrist may themselves incur liability directly, while the psychiatrist may be vicariously liable in those cases in which supervising control has been established. In cases involving *consultation relationships,* the extension of liability to the consultant may depend on the disparity in training and experience. For instance, the closer the training gap, the less likely vicarious liability will be extended to the consultant. However, the beginning intern, as with the nonphysician provider, may be regarded as less free to disregard a psychiatrist's advice than another psychiatrist. In those situations, the consulting psychiatrist may not be successful in arguing that his or her opinions were "advisory" only (63).

The psychiatric team concept has gained considerable popularity in treating patients. The team may contain a psychiatrist, a psychologist, a social worker, and other mental health professionals, with a concomitant increase in the liability of individual members (65). Therapists, who have authority and control over the disposition of care for a patient, may be held liable for the negligent acts of team members (66), or similarly of partners, (67) even though they themselves were not negligent.

One final note: The laws concerning liability for the negligent acts of others are extremely varied, at times confusing, and not necessarily uniform from state to state. The variety of situations are numerous in which psychiatrists might find themselves owing a duty of care based on the acts of a third party. These occasions arise far more frequently than can be mentioned here. Therefore, whether a situation involves an employee, supervisee, partner, independent contractor, or consultation relationship, it is in the physician's best interest to understand the legal duties that may be produced from such a relationship (68, 69).

"No duty" rule.   The "no duty" rule states that a physician who is self-employed and not required by the policies of the organization or entity he or she may work for to accept patients (70) can refuse to accept any patient regardless of reason. King (19) feels that aside from common law precedent holding that no duty is owed by one individual to come to the aid of another, medical practice is essentially a private enterprise, consistent with individualism and independence, that is part of our nation's history. The courts have refused to abrogate the right of an individual to say "no" in a free society. In fact, some states have enacted "good Samaritan" laws to protect those who, while not required to, come to the aid of another (71).

Psychiatrists generally have no legal obligation to provide emergency medical care, just as a stranger has no moral obligation (of "common humanity") to go to the aid of another human who is in danger, even if the circumstances are potentially fatal (72). Nevertheless, the American Medical Association's *Current Opinions of the Judicial Council* (Section 8.11) (73) advises, "The physician should, however, respond to the best of his ability in cases of emergency where first aid treatment is essential."

If a psychiatrist does undertake to render assistance to the person "at the wayside," *good Samaritan* statutes, enacted by all states (71), protect against suit for damages arising out of any professional act or omission performed in "good faith" and not amounting to gross negligence. Good Samaritan laws cover the physician who is not licensed in the state where emergency care is rendered (74). However, once a psychiatrist decides to render aid, he or she has a duty to avoid any affirmative acts that make the person's situation worse, such as abandoning the person in need. Therefore, the "Samaritan psychiatrist" should exercise whatever reasonable means are available to continue the rescue effort, without jeopardizing his or her self. This reasonable care may involve waiting until competent medical assistance arrives, or accompanying the victim to the hospital and putting the victim into the hands of competent medical care. The good Samaritan, acting in good faith, does not bill the trauma victim for services, although billing is not prohibited by law (71).

Standard of Care

In a medical negligence lawsuit, the plaintiff bears the burden of establishing the four elements ("4D's") constituting actionable malpractice. The first significant hurdle is establishing what the standard of care was and that it was breached. This burden is generally accomplished through the use of expert witnesses (75). In the past, in judging the standard of care and whether there was a deviation, courts have applied the standards of practice from the defendant's geographic locality as its basis (known as the "locality rule") (76). However, most courts today judge psychiatrists by a national standard (77, 78). This trend is particularly true of the board-certified specialist (79).

A variety of "authorities," including medication package inserts, manufacturers' brochures, rules and regulations imposed by health care institutions, codes of ethics, and treatises and articles accepted as authoritative in their field, in addition to expert testimony, have been adopted in establishing the professional standard of care. The plaintiff may be relieved of the "burden of proof" if the facts allow for laypersons to conclude that there was a failure to conform to the applicable standard of care. This process refers to the *res ipsa loquitur* doctrine ("the thing that speaks for itself") and indicates that negligence may be inferred from the fact of an unexplained injury of a type that normally does not occur in the absence of negligence. To satisfy the standard, the following requirements must be met: 1) the injury would not have occurred in the absence of negligence; 2) the injury was caused by an instrumentality in the exclusive control of the defendant; and 3) the plaintiff did not contribute to his or her injury in any form (80). Technically speaking, the application of *res ipsa loquitur* applies to the issue of *fault,* (e.g., that substandard care has been provided) but does not establish the requirement of *causation*. If, however, there is a possible force *other than the alleged negligence* of more or equal likelihood of causing the injury in question, then *res ipsa loquitur* will not apply (81).

Psychiatric diagnosis and treatment is still an imprecise science despite the recent and continuing development of the *Diagnostic and Statistical Manual of Mental Disorders, Third Edition, Revised* (DSM-III-R) (82). Many feel that psychiatry is more art than science. For example, one psychiatrist's definition of deviation in care of patients may be another's cornerstone of patient management. Therapists commonly disagree concerning the indications and effectiveness of the myriad psychotherapeutic modalities currently utilized.

The standard of care in psychiatry is broadly based. Lazare (83) describes four separate conceptual models utilized in the treatment of patients in contemporary psychiatry: biological, behavioral, psychodynamic, and social. The biological and behavioral models are currently ascendant, while the psychodynamic and social models are declining (84). In between, the eclectic psychiatrist is under pressure from subspecialization in all four areas. Moreover, biological psychiatry seems to have ready credibility with the medical community, while behavioral principles and theories appeal to pragmatic physicians because of their relatively direct, uncomplicated approaches to treatment. Standard-of-care considerations for the behavioral approach appear to be the best defined and the easiest of the four to establish. Nonetheless, courts may be reluctant to find a psychiatrist negligent when following a method approved by at least a respectable minority of the profession (16).

The court usually derives the standards of the profession from expert testimony of psychiatrists and from sources that ordinary and prudent practitioners of the profession rely upon in conducting their practices (85). The law takes the position that it does not prefer one form of treatment over another and will typically measure therapists' care by the standard from their own school of treatment (86) if that school is supported by a respectable minority of fellow professionals (87).

The acceptance of experts from other professions in suits against psychiatrists rarely occurs (88, 89, 90). In some instances, however, the applicable standard may be defined by statute, or by the court imposing judicially determined standards, as in *Tarasoff v. Regents of the University of California* (91). In *Lundgren v. Eustermann* (92), a Minnesota court of appeals initially held that a licensed psychologist was competent to give expert testimony in a medical malpractice case challenging the chlorpromazine treatment a physician prescribed. This case was overturned by the Minnesota Supreme Court, which concluded that a licensed psychologist was not qualified to give an opinion in a medical malpractice action on the standard of care required of a medical doctor (93).

Expert testimony is not the only source of authority in terms of establishing the standard of care. Cases involving products, such as medication or medical equipment, will frequently rely on published industry standards (e.g., drug inserts [94] or manufacturers' brochures [95]). In addition, governmental and nongovernmental regulatory agencies also may specify standards of care. Informed consent statutes and other legislative mandates that set standards for peer review and record keeping are increasingly more common (96). Other sources, such as third-party payers, including private, state, and federal insurance programs, frequently are establishing standards for treatment. Long-term psychotherapy is being drastically limited as an "appropriate" treatment modality for a number of psychiatric diagnostic categories. Treatment manuals developed for the various types of psychotherapy provide standards for this very ambiguous area. Inevitably, it would appear that the standard of care will be influenced and shaped by third-party decision-makers.

Professionals, in general, or those individuals who undertake work requiring special skill, have a duty not only to exercise reasonable skill in what they do, but also to possess a standard minimum of special knowledge (97). Psychiatrists are no different (98, 99). Psychiatrists, like all physicians, have an ethical and professional duty to stay abreast of new developments. *The Principles of Medical Ethics, With Annotations Especially Applicable to Psychiatry* (100) states: "Psychiatrists are responsible for their own continuing education and should be mindful of the fact that theirs must be a lifetime of learning." Medical skill and knowledge are acquired by the psychiatrist through formal education, personal experience, and observation, and by continuing education in contemporary psychiatric advances (101). The law has imposed a duty on all physicians to keep current with changing concepts and new developments (102). This duty is much clearer for specialists than for general practitioners (103). Psychiatrists are held, with minor exceptions, to the standards and advances in diagnosis and treatment commonly utilized throughout the country (104). This is because formal psychiatric training and postgraduate specialty knowledge are generally disseminated uniformly throughout the United States and are reasonably consistent regardless of locality.

Knowledge concerning treatment efficacy and adverse effects of drug therapy is burgeoning. Psychiatrists who prescribe drug therapy also must apprise themselves of current developments in psychopharmacology. A failure to do so will likely shortchange the efficacy of patient treatment and increase the likelihood of a successful lawsuit if the patient is proximately harmed (104, 105, 106).

Stone (84) states that psychoanalysts and other psychodynamic therapists have been almost totally immune from malpractice suits because of virtually insurmountable technical and legal reasons. Patients dissatisfied with the lack of improvement after prolonged psychodynamic treatment may have found a way around these legal obstacles through the advancements of biological psychiatry. A suit for malpractice may be brought because biological treatments were indicated but not administered (107).

Nonmedical, unlicensed, and nontraditional therapists who hold themselves out to be specialists in the treatment of emotional and mental illness will generally be held to the same standard as other "more recognized" health care providers and mental health professionals (108). If diagnosis and treatment of medical disorders are undertaken, then medical standards may be utilized (19). Finally, specialists are held to a higher standard of care than nonspecialists, even in cases involving the same problem (97). Thus, for example, psychiatrists who do psychotherapy should not represent their work as psychoanalysis nor themselves as analysts if they are not so trained. For that matter, the use of the traditional couch in psychoanalysis should not be used for psychotherapy, nor should it be used by therapists who are not prepared to handle the transference complications that may develop. The couch is not just a formality.

Determination of Harm

No matter how clear the deviation from a reasonable standard of care, liability will not be assessed where there is no proximately caused *harm* to the patient. The courts typically rely on the testimony of expert witnesses to establish the presence or absence of an injury to the plaintiff. Until relatively recently, the courts generally have *not* been receptive to claims of emotional distress in the absence of some type of physical injury or impact (96, 109). However, the impact rule and other similarly dogmatic and unenlightened rules have increasingly fallen by the wayside as a result of the recognition of "psychic injury" as an independent and significant harm; advances in psychological theory, diagnosis, and methodology; and a general loosening of the American tort system. Today, courts have recognized not only psychic damages as a result of some direct stimulus or act but also recovery by bystanders who have neither a direct relationship with the tortfeasor (110) or who do not actually witness the distressing event but find out about it later (111). Other, even more far-reaching developments in the area of psychic damages include recovery for "preimpact terror" just before an airplane crash (112); fear of cancer (113); and even the apprehension of danger by plaintiffs who are not in any immediate danger of harm (114).

Proximate Cause

When a psychiatrist deviates from a standard of care in the diagnosis and treatment of a patient and the patient alleges damage, no malpractice can be assigned unless the damage is the *direct,* or *proximate,* result of that deviation from the standard of care (115).

The law divides causation into cause-in-fact and legal or proximate cause (116). Cause-in-fact is expressed by the "but for" rule which states that the harm would not have occurred *but for* the defendant's negligent conduct (104). For example, a patient may allege that *but for* the psychiatrist's lack of warning about serious side effects from taking a neuroleptic, the patient would not have taken the drug and not developed tardive dyskinesia. If, however, the injury would have occurred regardless of the psychiatrist's conduct, no causation exists. In another example, a borderline patient who became a paraplegic after impulsively attempting suicide between psychotherapy sessions from an unexpected rejection by a friend, but did not contact the psychiatrist, probably would not meet the "but for" test in assessing the psychiatrist's liability. The unexpected rejection and impulsive suicide became an independent variable that had nothing to do with the defendant's conduct and was the likely cause of the plaintiff's harm.

In cases in which there is more than one cause of injury, the "but for" test is sometimes substituted by the "substantial factor test" (117). This test requires the defendant's tortious conduct to have been a "substantial factor" in causing the plaintiff's injury. For instance, in cases in which more than one cause act together to bring about an injury of which any one alone would have been sufficient to cause the injury, the causation requirement may still be met if the defendant's conduct was a "substantial factor" in causing the injury (118). Many courts avoid this conundrum by considering as causes all the factors that were *substantial* factors in creating the damage or injury. Generally, an act or omission is considered to be a proximate cause of an injury if it was a substantial factor in bringing about the injury (i.e., if it had such an effect producing the injury that reasonable men would regard it as the direct cause of the injury) (119).

Where two or more individuals have been negligent but uncertainty exists about who caused the plaintiff's injury, the *alternative cause approach* may be utilized in some situations and jurisdictions (115). Here, the plaintiff must prove that harm has been caused by one of the individuals, although the plaintiff may be uncertain as to which one. The burden of proof then shifts to the defendants, who then must show that their negligence was not the actual cause. For example, two shotguns are negligently fired in the direction of the plaintiff who is hit by a pellet. The plaintiff cannot determine which shotgun fired the shot but can prove that it was one or the other. Under the alternative causes approach, each defendant who fired a gun will have to prove that the pellet did not come from his or her gun. If neither defendant is able to do so, both may be liable (115).

In addition to the cause-in-fact, the second type of causation theory most frequently utilized in malpractice suits is referred to as *proximate cause* (115). Proximate or legal cause exists when an uninterrupted chain of events occurs from the time of the defendant's negligent conduct to the time of the plaintiff's injury. However, intervening causes may occur after the time of the initial negligent act by the defendant that combine with the initial negligent act to cause injury to the plaintiff. The continuation of the subsequent negligence will not necessarily alleviate the initial defendant from liability. For example, a physician who is initially negligent in harming a patient may be liable for the aggravation of the patient's condition caused by the negligent acts of a subsequent treating physician (115).

A factor or event occurring after a defendant's negligence that becomes the *actual or direct cause* of a plaintiff's injury is said to be a "superceding intervening force" (115). The net effect of this force is that it will relieve the initial tortfeasor (defendant) of liability because it was not his or her negligence that was the actual or ultimate cause of the injury (115). As an example, suppose a physician carelessly leaves a prescription pad lying about the office. A new patient, prone to abusing medications, takes the form and forges the doctor's signature for a bottle of benzodiazepines. The patient becomes drowsy while driving and has an accident, injuring another person. The patient's act of driving while knowingly drowsy may be considered a superseding intervening force cutting off liability from the physician's original negligent conduct of leaving the prescription form out in the open (115).

In medical malpractice actions, proving the proximate cause link is generally the most difficult and complex issue. Causation of emotional and mental illness is imperfectly understood. It is sometimes very difficult to distinguish emotional harm allegedly caused by the psychiatrist's negligent act or omission from the natural course of the disorder or from other causes in the patient's life (e.g., preexisting personality factors). Expert psychiatric testimony almost always is necessary in establishing proximate cause (120). The expert is necessary to explain the nature and expected course of the patient's underlying emotional or mental condition and discuss the basis of his or her opinion that the alleged deviation from proper psychiatric practice altered an otherwise expected medical result (101). It is important to understand that expert testimony is simply a form of evidence to be weighed by the trier of fact. In other words, an expert may be used to establish the standard of care and the nature of the defendant's care in relation to that standard, but it is the *jury* who decides whether or not a breach has occurred (121).

Damages

Damages are divided into three classes: 1) compensatory, 2) nominal, and 3) punitive. *Compensatory* damages are based on the principle that the plaintiff should be restored as much as possible to his or her preinjury condition (i.e., to be made "whole"). Compensatory damages, therefore, would include recovery for pecuniary losses (e.g., past and future medical expenses and loss of earnings) as well as compensation for "pain and suffering" and "mental distress" (122). The cost of litigation, as well as attorney's fees, usually is borne by the litigants separately and is not part of the damages assessed. *Nominal* damages are awarded in cases in which an actual or technical wrong has been suffered that cannot be translated into dollar terms, such as when certain rights are violated (123). The fact-finder may make a symbolic award of one dollar (e.g., the relatively recent anti-trust suit by the United States Football League against the National Football League).

Punitive damages are awarded to punish the offender and serve as a public warning to others that certain actions or behaviors will not be tolerated (124). Punitive damages are awarded in those cases in which the defendant's conduct is reckless, malicious, willful (125), or wanton (126). It is clear that in order to be awarded punitive damages, something more egregious than the mere commission of negligence, even gross negligence, must have occurred (127). The amount awarded is at the discretion of the judge or jury if the circumstances warrant it. Some states do not permit awards for punitive damages (128). Punitive damages may be awarded in a civil-rights action when the psychiatrist acts with malice or reckless disregard of the patient's civil rights (129).

In actions involving a plaintiff who has died, the elements of damages may vary according to whether the action is a "survival action" or a "wrongful death action" (130). In survival actions, recovery is usually limited to losses incurred between the time of injury and the time of death. In other words, the law places the decedent's estate in the position in which it would have been had the deceased's life not been cut short (131). These losses typically involve conscious pain and suffering of the deceased as well as loss of earnings during that time. In wrongful death actions, recovery is restricted to the *pecuniary* or *financial* loss associated with the maintenance or assistance the deceased would have rendered to others (e.g., family members) had he or she lived (132). Compensable losses may include loss of support, prospective inheritance, services and society, and the companionship of the deceased (115).

Damages are assessed either by a jury or, in cases where there is no jury, by the trial judge. The judge or jury usually is afforded broad discretion in assessing the amount of damages awarded because many elements of damages do not readily lend themselves to a fixed formula. Determination of damages may be amended or set aside if the award can be shown to have been 1) inadequate or grossly excessive (133), 2) the result of a mistake of law or fact (134), 3) against the preponderance of the evidence (134\5), or 4) shocking to the court's conscience (136).

Theories of Liability

In addition to negligence suits, psychiatrists may be sued for the intentional and quasi-intentional torts such as assault and battery (137), false imprisonment (138), defamation (139), invasion of privacy (140), and the intentional infliction of emotional distress or outrage (141). Psychiatrists also may be held liable for a breach of contract (142). In those cases in which the plaintiff has difficulty establishing all elements of an action for malpractice, a claim for relief sometimes may be brought pursuant to contract theory (143) or based on the deprivation of state or federal civil rights (144).

Psychiatrists also may be liable for violations of constitutional rights (145). Public hospitals and their professional employees may be liable for violation of rights guaranteed patients by the United States Constitution, by a state constitution, or by federal civil rights statutes (146). Class action suits and individual suits affecting the lives of thousands of hospitalized mental patients have been successfully filed on behalf of patients during the past 10 years under the Civil Rights Act, alleging violation of the due-process clause of the Fourteenth Amendment in state admission standards and procedures (147), the right to protection and safety (148), the right to adequate treatment (149), and the right to refuse treatment (150). Fewer than a handful of these cases have involved damages; however, most have sought equitable relief, either *mandating* public officials to provide certain minimal constitutional rights or *enjoining* them from violating such rights.

The Civil Rights Act states:

> Every person who, under color of any statute, ordinance, regulation, custom, or usage, of any state or territory, subjects or causes to be subjected, any citizen of the United States or other person within its jurisdiction thereof to the deprivation of any rights, privileges, or immunities secured by the Constitution and laws, shall be liable to the party injured in an action at law, as suit in equity, or other proper proceeding for redress. (146)

Two essential elements must be established to maintain an action under Section 1983 of the Civil Rights Act. The patient must establish that the complaint of conduct is committed by an individual acting "under color" of state or territorial law, custom, or usage and that the conduct deprived the patient of rights, privileges, or immunities secured by the Constitution or United States laws—in other words, that the state was somehow involved in the deprivation of the plaintiff's federal rights. Under civil rights statutes, two kinds of rights are protected: substantive and procedural rights. The Fifth Amendment created due-process procedural rights in order to protect against deprivations of life, liberty, or property. This has been applied to the states through the Fourteenth Amendment. Constitutionally based tort actions against hospitals and their employees based directly on violation of the United States Constitution raise complex litigation issues. Civil rights claims also may be brought against state and county hospitals and their employees for violations of U.S. Code 1983, but these violations are narrowly defined. Mental health professionals working in federal and state institutions should determine whether their malpractice insurance covers 1983 actions.

Reisner (151) points out that hospitals have a level of control over a patient that provides ample opportunities for violation of that patient's civil rights. For example, the denial of the patient's right to vote in a federal election or the right of the patient to practice his or her religion would be cause for a civil rights action against the responsible person. In *Gerrard v. Blackman* (152), monitoring the patient's calls to an attorney by a psychiatrist was found to be the possible basis of a civil rights action, providing that the plaintiff sufficiently established the state action requirement. In *Jobson v. Frank R. Henne* (153), a patient was assigned 16-hours-a-day uncompensated work that was not part of a therapy program nor related to the patient's housekeeping needs. The court held that a cause of action existed based on a violation of the patient's Thirteenth Amendment right of freedom from involuntary servitude. However, there are limitations to these types of claims. For example, in *Jones v. Superintendent* (154), a patient who was a vegetarian for religious reasons was denied a special diet. The court, although realizing that the patient may have stated a cause of action, refused to award damages for civil rights violation because the plaintiff was unable to prove physical or other injury.

In those cases in which a mental health professional acts under color of law as a state executive official, he or she is generally entitled to qualified immunity similar to sovereign immunity (155). While the United States Supreme Court has rejected absolute immunity for executive officers from civil rights actions, balancing of individual rights against the needs of decision-makers to be free to exercise discretionary judgments has led to "good faith" immunity for many defendants (10, 156).

Therapists, like other citizens, may be sued for ordinary negligence if patients are injured around or within the therapists' office. For this reason, therapists should carry an insurance rider, or obtain a separate policy, that provides office-premises liability insurance. This type of insurance policy often covers only the key individual on the premises and may not provide coverage for suits of patients seen by colleagues renting or sharing office space.

Health Provider Organizations

Health maintenance organizations (HMOs), independent practice associations (IPAs), and preferred provider organizations (PPOs) may create additional ethical and legal dilemmas for psychiatrists. Such systems can interject burdensome costs and contractual pressures into treatment and dispositional decisions. Psychiatrists must not allow themselves to be put in the position of choosing between patients' need for quality care and the economic and administrative requirements of the health plan (157).

Before signing a contract, the psychiatrist must be aware of plan requirements that may interfere with the provision of good clinical care and the traditional doctor-patient relationship (157). Some plan agreements provide that medical records be made available to other providers in the plan. Thus, for patients using health provider organization plans who see a psychiatrist in his or her office, it may need to be explained that the same confidentiality that exists for other patients does not exist for them. Moreover, patients also may know other providers in the plan, and they may not want to have psychiatric information disseminated. Some contracts clearly state that the psychiatrist must provide information to administrators that may lead to loss of medical services to the patient. Patients who act out in self-destructive or violent ways or refuse to follow a treatment plan may be dropped from the plan. Sometimes plan contracts explicitly state that the physician will not make any communication or take any action that may adversely affect the confidence of patients in the plan. However, this does not supersede the psychiatrist's duty to comply with certain statutory requirements such as reporting child abuse or warning endangered third parties (158).

Psychiatrists must realize that their responsibilities to patients are not necessarily limited by the contractual services covered by an insurance plan or institutional policy manual. Should the plan limit services to the suicidal or dangerous patient, the psychiatrist's legal duty remains the same as if treating the patient independently (157). The psychiatrist must take whatever steps are necessary to adequately care for the patient. The majority of plans reserve the right to review all hospitalizations, refusing coverage even to the patient admitted as an emergency, if further treatment is not considered necessary. If the patient suffers harm as a result, the plaintiff's attorney can claim that in order to save money, the physician did not provide necessary care.

Courts will not accept the argument that a plan prevented the physician from providing accepted treatments or from referring the patient to appropriate specialists outside of the plan. For example, in *Wickline v. State* (159), the California Supreme Court let stand a landmark appellate court decision that placed responsibility for discharge decisions squarely on physicians. In this case, three doctors recommended that a thrombectomy patient remain hospitalized an additional 8 days, but acceded to a shorter hospitalization after Medi-Cal insurance reviewers approved only a 4-day extension. The patient subsequently developed complications requiring amputation of the affected limb. The patient sued the reviewers and won. However, the appellate court, in reviewing the $500,000 jury award, stated that it was the responsibility of the patients' physicians to protest utilization review decisions that violate their medical judgment. The court stated that the physician who complies without protest with limitations imposed by a third-party payer cannot avoid "ultimate responsibility" for patient care. The findings in *Wickline* are likely applicable to long-term psychiatric care. The treatment prerogatives of the psychiatrist may be limited by the conditions of an insurance plan, which can undermine the needs of some patients requiring long-term hospitalization. The temptation to cut corners in patient treatment, in this situation, can thus become a malpractice trap.

Some plans may also specify which hospital must be utilized or require that referrals be made to other providers in the plan. In this and similar situations, psychiatrists must not suspend their judgment in making competent dispositions and referrals; otherwise they may be held responsible for making a negligent choice. During periods when the psychiatrist is away, nonparticipating psychiatrists who provide replacement coverage must understand that they will have to accept the fees designated by the plan and abide by its review procedures (157).

Psychiatrists should also determine whether the contract contains a "hold harmless" and indemnification provision that will require repayment of the plan for any liability arising out of the psychiatrist's practice. Many malpractice policies will not cover any liability assumed under an oral or written agreement, such as a contract provision. Should the plan be sued because of care provided by the psychiatrist, the psychiatrist may be held personally liable for any resulting judgment while having no malpractice insurance to cover it. Obviously, the psychiatrist should consult an attorney before signing any contract with a health provider organization (157).

Peer Review Liability

During the past decade, many physicians have used federal antitrust laws to sue medical staff members involved in peer review. These doctors allege that they were denied staff privileges because the peer reviewers had anti-competitive motives. Antitrust suits are particularly dangerous because jury damage awards are automatically tripled. Most insurance policies owned by physicians will not cover the cost of the award (160).

Psychiatrists may be held legally liable for statements made during the course of participation in the work of professional committees (161). Psychiatrists who make comments in peer review meetings that are knowingly false or are a sham attempt to deny or impede the rights of a colleague may forfeit the legal privilege that surrounds such proceedings and be subject to a lawsuit for defamation or tortious interference with business relations (162). The frequency of such lawsuits is expected to rise (161). Most state statutes provide a substantial degree of confidentiality to the peer review process (163), although care must be taken not to abuse this privilege.

Currently, the great majority of states have laws making peer review reports privileged (164, 165, 166). A number of states have "qualified" peer review confidentiality. In these states, lawyers may have access to certain factual materials (167) but not generally to the opinions and conclusions of individual participants (168).

Problems arise when peer review committees are not monitored closely to rule out conflicts of interest among members that may lead to allegations of bias, conspiracy, and restraint of trade. In *Patrick v. Burget* (169), the United States Supreme Court unanimously ruled that a hospital peer review committee with the authority to grant hospital privileges is *not* immune from antitrust laws. The high court's ruling overturned a lower court decision that would have given hospitals absolute immunity to such hospital committees. This could have led to the systematic exclusion of nonmedical health care providers from hospitals pursuant to a doctrine called "state action." Writing for the majority, Justice Thurgood Marshall made the critical distinction that bodies such as peer review committees are afforded absolute immunity from antitrust laws under the state law doctrine "only when their anti-competitive acts were truly the product of state regulation" (108 S Ct 1658, 1662 [1988]). To meet that test (state law), 1) there must be a showing that the restraint of competition is clearly and affirmatively a part of state policy, and 2) the restraint of competition must be actively supervised by the state. It was this second prong that the Court closely scrutinized and determined that the state of Oregon did not meet. Concluding that the state failed to actively supervise the peer review process, the Supreme Court therefore upheld the original trial decision. In essence, this decision serves to provide some minimum standards for peer review by refusing to shield malevolent, bad-faith conduct from antitrust scrutiny. The net result is that hospital peer review committees cannot unreasonably or summarily exclude someone from applying and receiving hospital privileges.

Psychiatrists who are members of peer review committees on a hospital staff, medical society, or state licensing board (as well as medical staff credentialing, quality assurance, and disciplinary committees) should know the particular state statute that applies to their activities. State statutes differ as to which activities are covered and to the degree and extent they offer immunity. Some states cover only utilization review committees, whereas others offer immunity only to physician health care providers (170). Federal courts also have been divided on whether peer review records and proceedings clearly and unambiguously protected by state law should be revealed in a federal courtroom. Whether and when federal courts must follow state law is a thorny legal issue of civil procedure that scholars have followed through various twists and turns over the years (171). Greater access to peer review records can be expected in the future as courts place greater emphasis on public versus private interests. Without the protection of privilege, maligning a professional's qualifications may be "actionable per se," and the defamed person will not likely have to show monetary loss due to the libel or slander (172).

The key to comfortable participation on committees is to act reasonably and professionally. Professional committees are designed to further the vital interest of assuring quality care for patients. If statements made in this context are within the scope of this important interest, free from malice, and communicated in a proper manner, the conditional privilege will exist. Under the most scrupulous standards, recommending denial of hospital privileges, questioning a colleague's competence at staff meetings aimed at analyzing substandard patient care, or reporting an impaired colleague may not prevent a suit *from being filed*. However, good-faith actions consistent with the language of the applicable privilege statute will almost certainly prevent its success. For example, the Health Care Quality Improvement Act of 1986 (173) protects physicians and hospitals that conduct peer review from antitrust suits brought by physicians whom they discipline only when their procedures accord with the due-process standards dictated by the bill. The Act states that a peer review action is protected if taken "in the reasonable belief that [it] was in the furtherance of quality health care." Psychiatrists who serve on credentialing and peer review committees should check their professional liability insurance to see if they are covered against legal actions brought in the line of such committee work (174).

References

1. Smith JT: Medical Malpractice: Psychiatric Care, Supplement. Colorado Springs, CO, Shepard's/McGraw-Hill, 1988, pp 9–10
2. U.S. General Accounting Office: Medical Malpractice: Characteristics of Claims Closed in 1984: Report to Congressional Requesters. Washington, DC, U.S. General Accounting Office, 1985, Table 4.2
3. Charles SC, Kennedy E: Defendant. New York, Free Press, 1985
4. Sandusk JF, Watson FE: Professional liability claims in California. California Medicine 87:192–196, 1957
5. Bellamy WA: Malpractice risks confronting the psychiatrist: a nationwide fifteen-year study of appellate court cases, 1946 to 1961. Am J Psychiatry 118:769–780, 1962
6. Slawson PF: Psychiatric malpractice: a regional incidence study. Am J Psychiatry 126:1302–1305, 1970
7. Brownfain JJ: The APA professional liability insurance program. Am Psychol 26:648–652, 1971
8. Slawson PF: Psychiatric malpractice: the California experience. Am J Psychiatry 136:650–654, 1979

9. Fishalow SE: The tort liability of the psychiatrist. Bull Am Acad Psychiatry Law 3:191–230, 1975
10. Malpractice litigation news. Medical Malpractice: Verdicts, Settlements, and Experts 2:8–9, 1986
11. Smith JT: Medical Malpractice: Psychiatric Care, Supplement. Colorado Springs, CO, Shepard's/McGraw-Hill, 1988, p 4
12. AMA News, February 13, 1987, p 17
13. U. S. General Accounting Office: Medical Malpractice: Characteristics of Claims Closed in 1984: Report to Congressional Requesters. Washington, DC, U.S. General Accounting Office, 1985, Tables 14–15
14. Furrow BR: Malpractice in Psychotherapy. Lexington MA, Lexington Books, 1980, pp 81–93
15. Tarasoff v Regents of the University of California, 17 Cal 3d 425, 131 Cal Rptr 14, 551 P2d 334 (1976)
16. 70 Corpus Juris Secundum Physicians and Surgeons, § 41 (1951)
17. Restatement (Second) of Torts Section, § 282 (1965)
18. Simon RI: Psychiatric Interventions and Malpractice: A Primer for Liability Prevention. Springfield, IL, Charles C Thomas, 1982
19. King JH: The Law of Medical Malpractice, 2nd Edition. St Paul, MN, West Publishing, 1986, pp 15–20
20. Tunkl v Regents of the University of California, 60 Cal 2d 92, 383 P2d 441, 32 Cal Rptr 33 (1963)
21. Osborne v Frazier, 425 SW2d 768 (Tenn App 1968)
22. DuBois v Decker, 130 NY 325, 29 NE 313 (1891)
23. See, e.g., Salis v United States, 522 F Supp 989 (MD Pa 1981)
24. Bianco EA: The physician-patient relationship. Legal Aspects of Medical Practice 11:1, 1983
25. See, e.g., Bolles v Kinton, 83 Colo 147, 263 P 26 (1928)
26. What constitutes physician-patient relationship for malpractice purposes? 17 ALR4th 132–160 (1981)
27. 11 AD2d 132, 135–136; 202 NYS2d 436, 439–440 (1960)
28. 116 Mich App 737, 323 NW2d 537 (1982)
29. 177 Ga App 694, 340 SE2d 627 (1986)
30. 316 So 2d 77 (Fla App 1975) (per curiam)
31. 31 Cal App3d 539, 107 Cal Rptr 469 (1973)
32. Tarasoff v Regents of the University of California, 17 Cal 3d 425, 131 Cal Rptr 14, 551 P2d 334 (1976)
33. McIntosh v Milano, 168 NJ Super 466, 403 A2d 500 (1979)
34. Lipari v Sears, Roebuck & Co, 497 F Supp 185 (D Neb 1980) (construing Nebraska law)
35. Mavroudis v Superior Court, 102 Cal App 3d 594, 162 Cal Rptr 724 (1980)
36. Official actions: guidelines for psychiatrists working with the communication media. Am J Psychiatry 134:609–611, 1977
37. Halleck SL: Law in the Practice of Psychiatry. New York, Plenum, 1980
38. Lotspench v Chance Vought Aircraft, 369 SW2d 705 (Tex Civ App 1963)
39. Betesh v United States, 400 F Supp 238 (DDC 1974) (upholding a duty)
40. Davis v Tirrell, 110 Misc 2d 889, 443 NYS2d 136 (1981) (no duty)

41. Olson v Western Airlines, 191 Cal Rptr 502 (App 1983) (duty held)

42. King JH: The Law of Medical Malpractice, 2nd Edition. St Paul, MN, West Publishing, 1986, p 33

43. MacDonald v Clinger, 84 AD2d 482, 446 NYS2d 801 (4th Dept, 1982)

44. Doyle v Sclensky, 120 Ill App 3d 807 (1983)

45. Dolan v Von Zweck, 19 Mass App 1032, 477 NE2d 200 (1985)

46. Mullen v Kelley, 693 SW2d 837 (Mo Ct App 1985)

47. Enberg v Bonde, 331 NW2d 731 (Minn 1983)

48. Klein J, Onek J, MacBeth J: Seminar on Law in the Practice of Psychiatry. Washington, DC, Onek, Klein, and Farr, 1983

49. Lanier v Sallas, 777 F2d 321 (5th Cir 1985)

50. Davis v Tirrell, 110 Misc 2d 889, 443 NYS2d 136 (1981) [no duty]

51. American Psychiatric Association: The Principles of Medical Ethics, With Annotations Especially Applicable to Psychiatry, Section 6. Washington, DC, American Psychiatric Association, 1989, p 8

52. Paddock v Chacko, 522 So 2d 410 (Fla Ct App 1988)

53. Medicine devoting increasing attention to rising incidence of teenage suicides. AMA News, August 2, 1985, p 36

54. 732 F2d 366 (4th Cir 1984)

55. Williams RC: Vicarious liability: tort of the master or of the servant? L Q Rev 72:522, 1982

56. Restatement (Second) of Agency, § 220(1) (1958)

57. Baird v Stickler, 69 Ohio St 2d 652, 433 NE2d 593 (1982)

58. Restatement (Second) of Agency, § 228 (1958)

59. Barnes v Towlson, 405 A2d 137 (Del 1979)

60. Joel v Morrison, 6 CP 501, 172 Eng Rep 1338 (1834)

61. Ambrosia v Price, 495 F Supp 381 (D Neb 1980)

62. Restatement (Second) of Agency, § 227 (1958)

63. See, e.g., Moulton v Huckleberry, 150 OR 538, 46 P2d 589 (1935)

64. Guidelines for psychiatrists in consultative, supervisory, or collaborative relationships with nonmedical therapists. Am J Psychiatry 137:1489–1491, 1980; see p 1490

65. Cohen RJ, Mariano WE: Legal Guidebook in Mental Health. New York, Free Press, 1982, p 315

66. Baird v Stickler, 69 Ohio St 2d 652, 433 NE2d 593 (1982)

67. Keeton WP, Dobbs DB, Keeton RE, et al: Prosser and Keeton on Torts, 5th Edition. St Paul, MN, West Publishing, 1984, pp 516–521

68. Keeton WP, Dobbs DB, Keeton RE, et al: Prosser and Keeton on Torts, 5th Edition. St Paul, MN, West Publishing, 1984, pp 499–533

69. King JH: The Law of Medical Malpractice, 2nd Edition. St Paul, MN, West Publishing, 1986, pp 231–252

70. 2 Hospital & Law Manual, Admitting and Discharge §§ 1–2 (1980)

71. American Jurisprudence, Physicians and Surgeons § 306 [for a discussion of good Samaritan statutes]

72. Feldbrugge: Good and bad Samaritans: a comparative survey. American Journal of Comparative Law 14:630–656, 1967

73. American Medical Association: Current Opinions of the Judicial Council. Chicago, IL, American Medical Association, 1989
74. Md Cts & Jud Proc § 5-309 (1984)
75. Klein JI, MacBeth JE, Onek JN: Legal Issues in the Private Practice of Psychiatry. Washington, DC, American Psychiatric Press, 1984
76. Smothers v Hanks, 34 Iowa 286 (1872); annotated 18 ALR4th 603 (1982)
77. Slovenko R: Forensic psychiatry, in Comprehensive Textbook of Psychiatry IV, Vol 2. Edited by Kaplan HI, Sadock BJ. Baltimore, MD, Williams & Wilkins, 1985, pp 1960–1990
78. Medical specialties and the locality rule. Stanford Law Review 14:884–909, 1962
79. Aasheim v Humberger, 695 P2d 824 (Mont 1985)
80. Sullivan v Methodist Hospital of Dallas, 699 SW2d 265 (Tex App 1985)
81. Lasseigne v Dauterive, 433 So 2d 334 (La App 1983)
82. American Psychiatric Association: Diagnostic and Statistical Manual of Mental Disorders, 3rd Edition, Revised. Washington, DC, American Psychiatric Association, 1987
83. Lazare A: Hidden conceptual models in clinical psychiatry. N Engl J Med 288:345–351, 1973
84. Stone AA: The new paradox of psychiatric malpractice. N Engl J Med 311:1384–1387, 1984
85. Colten RJ: The professional liability of behavioral scientists: an overview. Behavioral Sciences and the Law 1:9–22, 1983
86. Roberts v Tardiff, 417 A2d 444 (Me 1980)
87. Brannan v Lankenau Hospital, 490 Pa 588, 417 A2d 196 (1980)
88. McDonnell v County of Nassau, 492 NYS2d 699 (Trial Term 1985)
89. Rudy v Meshorer, 146 Ariz 467, 706 P2d 1234 (1985)
90. Connelly v Kortz, 689 P2d 728 (Colo Ct App 1984)
91. 188 Cal Rptr 129, 529 P2d 553 (1974); reargued, 17 Cal 3d 425, 550 P2d 334 (1976)
92. 356 NW2d 762 (Minn Ct App 1984); revised, 370 NW 2d 877 (Minn 1985)
93. Ibid
94. Gowan v United States, 601 F Supp 1297 (D Or 1985)
95. Monk v Doctor's Hospital, 403 F2d 580 (DC Cir 1968) (per curiam)
96. Slovenko R: Malpractice in psychiatry and related fields. Journal of Psychiatry and Law 9:5–63, 1981
97. King v Murphy, 424 So 2d 547 (Miss 1982)
98. Cotton v Kambly, 101 Mich App 537, 300 NW2d 627 (1980)
99. Mazza v Huffaker, 61 NC App 170, 300 SE2d 833 (1983)
100. American Psychiatric Association: The Principles of Medical Ethics, With Annotations Especially Applicable to Psychiatry. Washington, DC, American Psychiatric Association, 1985, Section 5(1), p 7
101. Pegalis SE, Wachsman HF: American Law of Medical Malpractice. Rochester, NY, Lawyers Co-Operative Publishing, 1980, section 2:7
102. Holder AR: Failure to "keep up" as negligence. The Best of Law and Medicine 116:107, 1973
103. Weintraub A: Physician's duty to stay abreast of current medical developments. Medical Trial Technique Quarterly 31:329–341, 1985

104. Witherill v Weimer, 148 Ill App 3d 32, 499 NE2d 46 (1986)

105. Callan v Nordland, 144 Ill App 3d 196, 448 NE2d 651 (1983)

106. Doerr v Hurley Memorial Hospital, NM 82-674-39 (Mich August 1984)

107. Osheroff v Chestnut Lodge, 490 A2d 720, 722 (Md App 1985); see also Klerman GL: The psychiatric patient's right to effective treatment: implications of Osheroff v Chestnut Lodge. Am J Psychiatry 147:409–418, 1990; Stone AA: Law, science, and psychiatric malpractice: a response to Klerman's indictment of psychoanalytic psychiatry. Am J Psychiatry 147:419–427, 1990

108. Watts v Cumberland County Hospital System, Inc, 74 NC App 769, 330 SE2d 242 (1985)

109. Restatement (Second) of Torts, § 436A, comment b (1965); annotated, Right to recover for mental pain and anguish alone, 23 ALR 361 (1923)

110. Dillon v Legg, 69 Cal Rptr 72, 441 P2d 912 (1968)

111. City of Tucson v Wondergem, 466 P2d 383 (Ariz 1970)

112. Platt v McDonnell Douglas, 554 F Supp 360 (ED Mich 1983)

113. Ferrara v Galuchio, 5 NY2d 16, 152 NE2d 249 (1968)

114. Prince v Pittston, 63 Federal Rules Decisions 28 (SD WVa 1974)

115. Keeton WP, Dobbs DB, Keeton RE, et al: Prosser and Keeton on Torts, 5th Edition. St Paul, MN, West Publishing, 1984, pp 263–321

116. Kionka EJ: Torts: Injuries to Persons and Properties. St Paul, MN, West Publishing, 1977

117. Restatement (Second) of Torts § 431 (1965)

118. King JH: The Law of Medical Malpractice, 2nd Edition. St Paul, MN, West Publishing, 1986, pp 199–200

119. Prosser WL: Law of Torts, 4th Edition. St Paul, MN, West Publishing, 1971, § 41, p 244, and § 49, p 286; Restatement (Second) of Torts § 431 and comment at § 433 (1965)

120. Paul v Boschenstein, 105 AD2d 248, 482 NYS2d 870 (1984)

121. Baldwin v Williams, 104 Mich App 735, 306 NW2d 314 (1981)

122. Reisner R, Slobogin C: Law and the Mental Health System, 2nd Edition. St Paul, MN, West Publishing, 1990, p 197

123. Tatum v Morton, 386 F Supp 1308 (DDC 1974)

124. Simon RI: Clinical Psychiatry and the Law. Washington, DC, American Psychiatric Press, 1987, p 452

125. Blackman v Church of Scientology of California, No 78-403-J-CA (Fla November 26, 1980), cited in 24 American Trial Lawyers Association Reporter 222 (June 1981)

126. Scott v Donald, 165 US 58 (1896)

127. Milwaukee & St Paul Railroad Co v Arms, 91 US 489 (1875)

128. Reisner R: Law and the Mental Health System. St Paul, MN, West Publishing, 1985, pp 85–90

129. Reisner R, Slobogin C: Law and the Mental Health System, 2nd Edition. St Paul, MN, West Publishing, 1990, pp 153–164

130. Speiser WD: Introduction, in 1 Damages in Tort Actions, Section 1.30. New York, Matthew Bender, 1986

131. Semler v Psychiatric Institute of Washington, 575 F2d 922 (DC Cir 1978)

132. Runyon v District of Columbia, 463 F2d 1319 (DC Cir 1972)

133. Davis v Schuchat, 510 F2d 731 (DC Cir 1975)

134. 66 Corpus Juris Secundum New Trial § 207(g) (1950); 50 CJS Juries § 128(e) (1947)

135. Davis v Abbuhl, 461 A2d 473 (DC 1983)

136. Phillips v District of Columbia, 458 F2d 722 (DC Cir 1983)

137. Rains v Superior Court of Los Angeles, 150 Cal 3d 933, 198 Cal Rptr 249 (1984)

138. Plumadore v State, 427 NYS2d 90 (AD 1980)

139. Katz v Enzer, 504 NE2d 427 (Ohio Ct App 1985)

140. Prince v St Francis–St George Hospital Inc, 710 P2d 1250 (Kan 1985)

141. Restatement (Second) of Torts § 46 (1965); Anderson v Prease, 445 A2d 612 (DC 1982)

142. Davis v Monsanto Co., 627 F Supp 418 (SD W Va 1986)

143. Johnston v Rodis, 251 F2d 917 (DC Cir 1958)

144. Gordon v Sadasivan, 144 Mich App 113, 373 NW2d 258 (1985)

145. Houghton v South, 743 F2d 1438 (9th Cir 1984)

146. 42 USC § 1983 (1970)

147. In re Ballay, 482 F2d 648, 655 (DC Cir 1973)

148. Youngberg v Romeo, 457 US 307 (1982)

149. Wyatt v Stickney, 325 F Supp 781 (MD Ala 1971)

150. Jarvis v Levine, 418 NW2d 139 (Minn 1988)

151. Reisner R: Law and the Mental Health System. St Paul, MN, West Publishing, 1985, pp 127–128

152. 401 F Supp 1189 (ND Ill 1975)

153. 355 F2d 129 (2d Cir 1966)

154. 370 F Supp 488 (WD VA 1974)

155. Keeton WP, Dobbs DB, Keeton RE, et al: Prosser and Keeton on Torts, 5th Edition. St Paul, MN, West Publishing, 1984, pp 1032–1069

156. Canon v Thumudo, 430 Mich 326, 422 NW2d 688 (1988)

157. Contracts with PPO's and HMO's. American Psychiatric Association Legal Consultation Newsletter (Washington, DC), Winter 1985, pp 1–4

158. Cal Civ Code § 43.92 (West 1989)

159. 183 Cal 3d 1175, 228 Cal Rptr 661 (1986)

160. Brooten KE: How anti-trust laws affect your medical practice. Private Practice 21:7–9, 1989

161. Cassidy R: Can you really speak your mind in peer review? Medical Economics, January 23, 1984, pp 246–262

162. Doe v St Joseph's Hospital of Ft Wayne, 113 FRD 677 (D Ind 1987)

163. Feldman v Glucroft, 488 So 2d 574 (Fla App 1986)

164. Santa Rosa Medical Center v Spears, 709 SW2d 720 (Tex App 1986)

165. State ex rel St John's Mercy Medical Center v Hoester, 708 SW2d 786 (Mo App 1986)

166. Cofone v Westerly Hospital, 504 A2d 998 (RI 1986)

167. Gleason v St Elizabeth's Medical Center, 135 Ill App 3d 92, 481 NE2d 780 (1986)

168. Simon RI: Clinical Psychiatry and the Law, 2nd Edition. Washington, DC, American Psychiatric Press, 1992

169. 108 S Ct 1658 (1988)

170. Norman JC: So-called physician "whistle-blowers" protected. Legal Aspects of Medical Practice 11:3–4, 7, 1983
171. "Peer review confidentiality key issue in lawsuit." AMA News, October 25, 1985, pp 1, 7–8
172. Alsobrook HB: When you can—and can't—badmouth a colleague. Medical Economics, April 2, 1984, pp 72–85
173. 42 USC § 11101 (supp v 1987)
174. Simon RI: Clinical Psychiatry and the Law, 2nd Edition. Washington, DC, American Psychiatric Press, 1992

Chapter 3

Intentional Torts ──────

The majority of lawsuits against psychiatrists involve allegations of *negligence*, either nonfeasance (i.e., failing to do something that should have been done) or malfeasance (i.e., doing something in a way that was injurious to the patient). In either situation, the person (i.e., the defendant) does not intend to cause the result that occurred (i.e., injury to patient), but because of some dereliction in the duty to act *reasonably*, harm does occur.

On occasions, however, psychiatrists and other physicians are sued for harm or injuries caused by their deliberate or intentional acts. Conceptually, *intentional torts* are "wrongs perpetuated by one who intends to do that which the law has declared wrong as contrasted with *negligence* in which the tortfeasor fails to exercise that degree of care in doing what is otherwise permissible" (1). Similarly, *quasi-intentional torts* are wrongs that resemble intentional torts and from which intent can be inferred. For all practical purposes this distinction is more form than substance. As the name implies, an element common to all intentional torts is the defendant's intent. In other words, the defendant must have meant to commit the tort or wrong. Intent is usually defined as the desire to cause certain immediate consequences. Although intent is a state of mind and a *subjective* matter, the law applies an *objective* standard: persons are considered to have intended the consequences of their acts if they know or believe that the consequences are substantially certain to result, *whether or not they wish these results to come about*. For example:

> Patient X barges into an office in which Dr. Y is conducting group therapy, screaming obscenities. Patient X wants to offend and insult Dr. Y. He knows that other patients are present but has no desire to insult them and, in fact, would like to direct his anger only at Dr. Y. Nevertheless, because patient X knew that the other patients would hear his insults and obscenities and likely be offended, he is considered to have intended to "harm" (i.e., offend) them as well.

Doctors are always considered responsible for their actions undertaken in a professional capacity, especially those that can be reasonably foreseen to cause possible harm to a patient. Psychiatrists, in particular, must be cognizant of their relatively unique susceptibility to allegations of intentional harm. For instance, the confinement of a patient through the civil commitment process; the intentional touching required to medicate, restrain, or place a patient into seclusion; and the disclosure of confidential information to various parties involved in a patient's treatment are all necessary practices in certain clinical situations. In other situations, however, these practices can subject the psychiatrist to civil liability for one or more intentional torts.

The incidence of lawsuits for intentional and quasi-intentional torts or civil wrongs is quite low (2). Nevertheless, they represent an area of unacceptable clinical practice and potential litigation of which psychiatrists should be aware. In addition to the differences in *intent* that are represented by lawsuits alleging malpractice, as opposed to an intentional or quasi-intentional act, there are other distinctions that require comment. In some situations, proof of an intentional tort may not require expert evidence to establish the standard of care. As a result, the plaintiff may have an easier time in proving his or her case. Also, for many intentional torts (e.g., defamation), unlike negligence, an action can be brought for purely "dignitary" injuries, for example, injuries to reputation and good name. Finally, depending upon the language of a policy and the public policy of a state, coverage for some intentional torts *may expressly be denied* by a physician's malpractice insurance contract. Similarly, statutory immunity for federal, state, and local governmental officials is sometimes dropped and a lawsuit is allowed to go forward when the allegation involves an intentional act (3).

Intentional Torts

Assault and Battery

While commonly paired together as if they represented a single action, assault and battery are actually two separate wrongs. *Assault* is a threat, expressed or implied, to do bodily harm by someone whose ability to carry out the threat is such that the victim fears he or she is in imminent danger. There does not have to be physical contact for there to be an assault (4). *Battery,* on the other hand, is the harmful, wrongful, or offensive touching of another person's body without that other person's consent. The touching may be direct, such as one person striking another with his or her fist, or it can be indirect, as when one person throws and strikes another person with an object (5). Also, in contrast to assault, battery does not require that the patient be aware of the contact at the time of the touching (5).

Psychiatric application. Generally, when psychiatrists are sued for assault and battery, the allegations can basically be reduced to good faith errors emanating from the doctor's failure to obtain informed consent for a particular psychiatric procedure (e.g., administration of medication). In these situations, the courts generally regard these cases as ordinary negligence suits rather than intentional torts (6). However, a lawsuit is occasionally brought by a patient alleging some form of deliberate physical contact that is harmful or offensive to the patient and results in some form of injury. It is important to note that a psychiatrist's intentional act in a battery situation does not necessarily have to involve the intent to harm the patient. Instead, it is only *the intent to do the act* that results in offensive touching without consent that matters.

There are several relatively common situations in which an assault and battery might occur in a psychiatric practice. The first involves **the forcible administration of a physical intervention,** such as psychotropic medication or electroconvulsive therapy (ECT), without obtaining valid informed consent. The law is currently in a considerable state of flux regarding the rights of competent and incompetent patients to refuse psychotropic medication (7). Because the laws vary so much from state to state, psychiatrists are advised to be cautious in forcibly medicating patients who refuse treatment. Failure either to obtain the valid consent of a patient or to pursue forcible medication through legally approved channels could subject a psychiatrist to a lawsuit for assault and battery (8). Moreover, clinicians should not assume just because a patient is mentally ill or civilly committed that the patient does not retain the right to be informed of treatment decisions and the right to accept or reject them (9).

A second potential situation for an allegation of assault and battery exists when a psychiatrist engages in **atypical or unusual treatments that involve physical touching or contact with patients.** Patients, as well as the courts, are not likely to consider casual touching, such as hand shakes, occasional hugs, or pats across the back as "offensive and harmful." However, when physical contact rises to the level of being invasive, abusive, or injurious (mentally or physically), an action for assault and battery, intentional infliction of emotional distress, or malpractice becomes more likely. The few reported cases holding therapists liable for physical, nonsexual contact have all involved relatively outrageous contact. For instance, in the oft-cited case of *Hammer v. Rosen* (10), a psychiatrist admitted to physically beating his patients as a form of treatment, contending that it was an appropriate means of therapy for their problems. The court roundly rejected this argument, stating that "the very nature of the acts complained of bespeaks improper treatment and malpractice." In another celebrated case, a psychologist was held liable for poking, tickling, beating, and restraining a patient for more than 10 hours as part of his "rage-reduction therapy" (11).

In imposing liability in cases involving "physically oriented therapies," the courts have paid particular attention to the amount of recognition the treatment has in the mental health community and the degree to which it poses a risk of serious physical or emotional injury to the patient. For instance, in the case of *Woods v. United States* (12), the court held that a physician's unorthodox, but good faith use of "shock therapy" as a diagnostic device did not amount to an assault and battery.

A third scenario that might invoke a claim of assault and battery is when patients are **physically abused, mistreated, or punished by orderlies, staff, or other hospital personnel.** Mental institutions, especially in the past, have been frequently cited for patient abuses. In most situations, if an attendant beats or deliberately injures a patient, the hospital will be held liable for assault (13). This situation is of special concern to inpatient facilities that use seclusion rooms to manage violent and resistant patients. The American Psychiatric Association (APA) Task Force report *The Psychiatric Uses of Seclusion and Restraint* provides clear, practical standards for the appropriate, therapeutic use of seclusion and restraint procedures (14). As Simon notes, "Adherence to the [the APA Task Force] guidelines should protect patients from abuse and practitioners from legal liability" (15). It is when hospital staffs deviate from therapeutic purposes and instead use seclusion and restraint procedures for punishment, intimidation, or staff convenience that legal liability can arise.

A final situation in which a lawsuit for assault and battery might arise is when a therapist engages in some form of **sexual contact** with a patient. Sexual relations or activities with a patient is not only unethical and countertherapeutic (see Chapter 7) but also may constitute criminal assault (16), as well as battery and malpractice (17). There is no acceptable reason or excuse for a physician, psychiatrist, or other health care professional to ever engage in sexual activity with a patient. Moreover, courts have consistently recognized that because of the transference effect, patients are not capable of giving "consent" to this type of activity. In light of these facts, a doctor's sexual touching of the patient is automatically considered an unconsented, offensive touching or battery. Practically speaking, however, while sexual contact does technically amount to an assault and battery, the great majority of sexual exploitation lawsuits are brought under the laws of negligence as malpractice actions (18).

False Imprisonment

The concept of *false imprisonment* involves the notion that individuals have a basic right to be free from restrained and restricted movement (19). When legal authority is improperly, excessively, or invalidly exercised, resulting in a patient being confined, a cause of action for false imprisonment may follow.

The requirements for establishing a case of false imprisonment are essentially threefold (20):

1. The defendants must *commit* an act, or there must be a failure to act, that results in restraining, restricting, or confining the plaintiff (e.g., patient) to a limited area.
2. The defendant must possess the *intent* to restrain, restrict, or confine the plaintiff to a limited area.
3. The defendant's actions must *actually* have caused the plaintiff to be restrained, restricted, or confined.

Psychiatric application.　　There are basically two situations in which a psychiatrist might be sued for false imprisonment of a patient. The most common involves the civil commitment process. In a recent United States Supreme Court case, *Zinermon v. Burch* (21), a mentally ill patient who was unable to give informed consent was permitted to go forward with a civil rights action against state officials who committed him to a state hospital using voluntary commitment procedures. The Court held that Florida must have procedures to screen all voluntary patients for competency and exclude incompetent persons from the voluntary admission process. For the few states requiring competent consent to voluntary admission, screening procedures must be created to exclude incompetent patients. Although the Court did not directly address whether a voluntary patient must be competent to consent to admission, Appelbaum (22) opined that "Zinermon will refocus attention on the often-neglected process of voluntary admission."

Generally, if a doctor makes a good-faith misdiagnosis of a patient's condition and, based on that assessment, erroneously commits the patient, no suit will be upheld. This is because doctors are granted *qualified immunity* as officers of the court when they participate in "good faith" in a civil commitment proceeding. Immunity is *not* available if a psychiatrist involuntarily commits a patient out of malice (23), spite, or for reasons other than those contemplated by the state statute. For example, in *Marcus v. Liebman* (24), a psychiatrist was held liable for false imprisonment for threatening to civilly commit a voluntary patient as a means of keeping her confined in a state mental hospital. When a psychiatrist-patient relationship exists, however, courts in some jurisdictions may be less willing to cloak the commitment process with immunity. The psychiatrist has more knowledge and responsibility for the patient whom he or she is treating than does the psychiatrist examining the patient solely for the purpose and determination of civil commitment.

The second, and most common, situation in which psychiatrists have the greatest potential of being sued for false imprisonment is when they intentionally or with gross indifference fail to comply with the statutory requirements for civilly committing a patient. In order for a patient to successfully recover under these circumstances, the patient must demonstrate that the psychiatrist's diagnosis of mental illness and/or dangerousness was erroneous *and* that the doctor's efforts were not made in good faith (25). This is not an easy burden to meet, but it is not insurmountable. For instance, a physician or psychiatrist is legally held to know the statutory requirements regarding involuntary commitment before a certificate of commitment is signed.

Under no circumstances, not even in an apparent emergency, is it permissible for a psychiatrist to certify someone as meeting the requirements for commitment when he or she is without a good-faith basis for that determination. No court is likely to uphold a defendant's argument that circumstances required the physician to conduct something less than whatever examination was needed to ascertain a patient's fitness for involuntary hospitalization. The law is clear: a patient may only be committed on the basis of a good-faith determination that he or she meets all of the requirements for involuntary hospitalization (26). Failure to comply with this straightforward duty is sufficient grounds for a lawsuit for false imprisonment.

Several case examples illustrate this point. In *Gonzales v. State* (27), the plaintiff was found unconscious on some subway tracks and subsequently committed to a state psychiatric center for 3 days. The court upheld a recovery for $10,000 for false imprisonment, stating that his presence on the tracks was not adequate evidence of either a mental illness or dangerousness, as the state statute required. Moreover, the court noted that direct observation by a doctor of a serious mental illness was needed before the plaintiff could be legally detained. Similarly, in *Plumadore v. State* (28), a New York court affirmed a patient's suit for false imprisonment based on evidence that he had been illegally detained for a period of time after refusing to sign a voluntary admission form. The court highlighted the fact that at no time did the hospital ever conduct a psychiatric examination to determine his suitability for civil commitment.

Infliction of Emotional Distress

Emotional distress claims, on their own, against psychiatrists are quite uncommon. In most cases alleging mental distress, the claim involves physical injuries that produced the stress (e.g., obstetrics malpractice that results in the death of a newborn) (29). Liability in these cases is usually based on traditional negligence theories. The element of mental distress in such cases is generally compensable simply as a part of the damages recoverable for the underlying tort. In psychiatry, cases involving sexual exploitation are a good example. Some plaintiffs, in addition to a general claim of negligence or malpractice, will also allege numerous other lesser claims such as assault (30) and battery (31), negligent or intentional infliction of emotional distress (32), fraud, and other actions (33). There are, however, other situations in which the initial injury may be purely emotional in nature and not covered by another tort theory.

The tort of infliction of emotional distress has generally been divided into two categories. The first, the most egregious and least common, is reserved for instances indicative of *outrageous* conduct by which the defendant intentionally, willfully, or recklessly inflicts severe emotional distress on a victim (34). This conduct is frequently referred to as the tort of "outrage." The second category involves *negligently or intentionally inflicted emotional distress that falls short of being considered outrageous.* In addition to the difference in "degrees of severity" between the two classes of acts, most courts do not require that claims for outrage produce physical consequences, such as a miscarriage or heart attack, in order to sustain the action. However, the courts are split for the less serious form of inflicted emotional distress (35).

As noted earlier, psychiatric cases alleging the infliction of emotional distress (negligent, intentional, or outrageous) are quite rare. This is generally because emotional distress is considered as an element of the damages, rather than a basis for liability. Following the general trend in the law, some courts have entertained psychiatric claims involving the infliction of emotional distress (36), whereas others have not (37). Also, in some cases the claim of outrage or infliction of emotional distress is barred on immunity grounds (38).

The most likely scenario in which a claim for infliction of emotional distress is likely to occur in a psychiatric case is when allegations of sexual exploitation are involved. For instance, in *Marlene F. v. Affiliated Psychiatric Medical Clinic* (39), a mother was held to have stated a viable cause of action against a psychotherapist and psychiatric clinic for *negligent infliction of emotional distress* based on her allegations that the therapist had sexually molested her son. The court concluded that although the mother had not been present at the time of the molestations, nor was she the actual target of the exploitation, both were patients of the therapist and he either knew or should have known that his conduct toward the child would directly injure and cause severe emotional distress to the mother.

Occasionally, allegations of wrongful commitment will sustain a claim of infliction of emotional distress as well as other causes of action (40).

Defamation

The tort of *defamation* can be described as injuring someone's character or reputation by making false and malicious statements about him or her to other people. The law makes a distinction between defamation and mere criticism. The latter deals only with matters that legitimately invite public attention or call for public comment, whereas defamation usually involves a person's private life or domestic affairs. One may be subject to liability if the defamatory statements are communicated in writing (referred to as *libel*), or if spoken (referred to as *slander*).

There are five essential elements to establishing a cause of action for defamation (libel or slander) (41):

1. The defendant must communicate some form of defamatory language that adversely affects the reputation of another person. Language that impeaches another person's virtue, honesty, character, and the like is generally what occurs.
2. The defamatory language must identify or single out the injured party to a reasonable listener, viewer, or reader.
3. There must be publication of the defamatory language to a third party.
4. The plaintiff's reputation must be injured in some way.
5. If the plaintiff is a public figure or official, there is a fifth requirement that the defendant acted with malice. Legal malice usually is established if the person knew the matter was false, or failed to make even a minimal inquiry to find out if it was true or false, thereby acting in "reckless disregard of the truth."

In cases involving private individuals, which would be the situation in nearly all psychiatric situations, malice may be presumed. However, there are instances in which courts have required some showing that the defendant made little or no attempt to ascertain the truth, which would *imply* malice. There are other legal considerations, but the above represent the salient aspects of this type of action (42).

Psychiatric application.   The potential for an action involving defamation in a psychiatric setting is relatively high if a therapist deviates from the principles of professional ethics or notions of common courtesy and discretion. For instance, the psychiatrist who carelessly describes a patient as a "spouse abuser," "psychopath," or some other term in an insurance claim form or other document, when such a description is unnecessary or inappropriate, may be liable for defaming the patient (43). In one striking case, a Blue Cross plan committed libel per se when it falsely informed a doctor's patients that the doctor had been convicted of a crime (43).

The courts tend to cast a very critical eye on claims of defamation. Because we live in a society in which freedom of information and critical thought are cherished and closely protected by the First Amendment, what might be considered defamatory by a plaintiff may be dismissed by the court as simply in "bad taste," "critical," "obnoxious," or "unkind" (44). For example, a court ruled in *Dauw v. Kennedy & Kennedy, Inc.* (45) that a newspaper article referring to a psychologist and executive career counseling center as "schlock" was merely an opinion and therefore not actionable. However, when a defendant's comments more directly attack the character or reputation of a person, a suit for defamation may be upheld. Actionable slander per se thus occurred when, during a telephone conversation between a pediatrician and school officials concerning a psychologist who had conducted psychological testing at the school, the pediatrician stated that the psychologist was "incompetent," "unqualified," "ineffective," and had been dismissed from a hospital because of his incompetence. The court ruled that malice could be implied from what the pediatrician had said and that the intent and contents of the conversation were such that a jury could reject the defendant's claim that his conversation was privileged. An award of $100,000, which was upheld on appeal, was granted to the psychologist. In another case, a private mental health professional's civil rights were deemed to have been violated when the director of a mental health center disparaged his services and competence and discouraged the referral of patients to him (46).

Psychiatrists or other physicians who are sued for defamation may have a number of legally recognized defenses:

1. **The alleged defamatory language is true.** For example, in *Katz v. Enzer* (47), a social worker filed a defamation action against a psychiatrist for statements he made regarding the social worker's alleged improper practice of psychotherapy. An Ohio appeals court ruled that a lower court erred in refusing to admit testimony from qualified witnesses concerning the function of social workers in the field of psychotherapy. This was because such concerns were vital in assessing the truthfulness of the psychiatrist's statements and whether he was guilty of actual malice that would defeat his defense of qualified privilege.

2. **The plaintiff consented to the disclosure.** Consent to disclose what is normally considered confidential patient information can be expressed or implied. Common psychiatric examples are filing of insurance forms that contain patient diagnoses, presenting a patient's case at hospital rounds, or preparing psychiatric reports for third-parties such as insurance companies, employment agencies, worker's compensation boards, and the like. In the latter situation, consent is implied or presumed on the basis of the patient's participation in the evaluation. This is due to the understanding that for the patient to receive reimbursement (e.g., insurance), consideration for employment, or work injury benefits, the examining psychiatrist must communicate his or her clinical impressions to a third party. Where some psychiatrists go wrong, and basically violate the implied consent of the patient, is when their conclusions are loosely based, without any rea-

sonable foundation, or negligently arrived at. A psychiatrist risks an even greater likelihood of liability if he or she communicates statements or information about a patient that are knowingly false.

3. **The communication was proper because there was a legal obligation to disclose it.** In the case of *Davis v. Monsanto* (48), a company counselor concluded that an employee he was treating in therapy posed a risk of danger to himself and fellow employees because of his mental instability and daily access to dangerous chemicals. He advised the company of his conclusions, and the plaintiff was subsequently fired. The plaintiff sued the counselor for invasion of privacy and defamation, but the court ruled that the company had a legitimate interest in protecting itself and its employees that exceeded the personal reputation of the former employee.

4. **The disclosure was privileged and was required in order to implement an important social function or policy.** This defense is most common in situations in which a psychiatrist testifies in court or on behalf of the court. Disclosures, even extremely offensive ones, are generally protected by qualified immunity in order to facilitate the important social and public function that court proceedings represent. Testimony in any court proceeding, including civil commitment (49), criminal trials, personal injury cases, and domestic and custody cases (50), is generally protected. Investigatory proceedings such as hospital peer review meetings (51), psychiatric residency selections (52), and reports of child abuse to local agencies (53) will also generally be protected from a defamation action.

Invasion of Privacy

Often times claims alleging defamation will also contain a charge of *invasion of privacy*. This is because the two are closely linked to the issue of patient confidentiality. In a sense, the right to privacy involves the simple right "to be left alone." A mere intrusion on a person's private thoughts or personal space is typically not an actionable event. In order for a case to be made for invasion of privacy, four elements must be met (54):

1. There is an appropriation of the plaintiff's picture or name.
2. The plaintiff's private affairs or seclusion is intruded upon.
3. Certain facts about the plaintiff's private life are publicized that place the plaintiff in a false light.
4. There is a public disclosure of certain private details or facts about the plaintiff.

Unlike some of the torts mentioned, there need not be special damages or harm other than emotional distress. Also, liability may be for either intentional or negligent invasion, just as in defamation. The defenses to a claim for invasion of privacy include consent and privilege. However, good faith, truth, and lack of malice are *not* viable defenses.

Psychiatric application. The most common basis for an invasion of privacy claim against a psychiatrist is when unauthorized confidential information is disclosed to a third party not privileged to receive it. As a general rule, any discussion or disclosure of patient information, without proper consent, that permits the patient to be identified by name, description, or appearance may result in a successful action for invasion of privacy (55). This is true even of information that is published for scientific or professional purposes, as opposed to commercial purposes. Generally, though, the courts seem to be a bit more flexible in evaluating disclosures in professional journals than in commercial venues or the popular press (56). There is, however, definite distrust and dislike of breaches in confidentiality for whatever reason (57). Even if a patient consents to having his or her name, picture, or certain medical information disclosed in a professional journal, a cause of action may still be justified if the defendant exceeds the scope of the patient's consent (58). It is sound clinical and ethical practice for a psychiatrist to go beyond simply obtaining a patient's consent. The psychiatrist should also make every attempt to sufficiently alter those details that will safeguard the identity and integrity of the patient without sacrificing the scientific purpose of the publication.

Any time a psychiatrist intentionally or negligently breaches confidentiality, he or she has also likely invaded the patient's privacy. Unconsented verbal disclosures (59) can be just as damaging *and actionable* as those in writing. Written breaches of confidentiality that invade a patient's privacy usually can occur in the form of, for example, an unauthorized description of a patient in a psychiatric report or insurance form (60) or unconsented inclusion in a book for commercial distribution (61).

Other forms of invasion of privacy that are less common but probable include the following:

❖ Permitting nonessential persons to be present during treatment or patient sessions (62)
❖ Mailing repeated documents, notices, letters, and so forth to a patient's home who had terminated treatment, died (63), or had requested that this information not be sent in order to avoid disclosing to the family that he or she had been in treatment (64).

Misrepresentation and Fraud

Fraud is a comprehensive term describing any manner or way in which one person gains or attempts to gain an advantage over another person by false suggestion, concealment of the truth, dishonesty, or deception (65). It is often used interchangeably with the terms *misrepresentation* and *deceit*. Fraud may be classified as actual or constructive. "Actual" fraud consists of a deception practiced to induce a person or entity to part with property (e.g., money) or to surrender some legal right (e.g., individual freedom of movement) (65). "Constructive" fraud is a breach of duty that becomes legally fraudulent because of its tendency to deceive, violate confidence, or injure public interests (65). Constructive fraud is most commonly found when there has been a breach of a duty arising from a fiduciary relationship. There does not have to be an intent to deceive or a dishonest purpose for a constructive fraud to be found.

Psychiatric application. It is generally uncommon for a psychiatrist or other physician to be successfully sued for fraud, deceit, or intentional misrepresentation. However, there are several situations in which such an allegation might occur.

Situations requiring informed consent are always susceptible to claims of fraud, as well as other charges, if the psychiatrist knowingly or intentionally misrepresents the treatment, its risks, or its benefits (66). This is especially true if the misrepresentation is done in order to coerce patient compliance.

Psychiatrists who give some warranty of result on which the patient relies in accepting the treatment offered always run the risk of an action for breach of contract should the warranted result not occur. However, if a doctor gives a warranty or guarantee of result *knowing that no such guarantee is possible,* a lawsuit for fraudulent inducement may also be available. Because it is generally accepted that psychiatry is an inexact science and that no guarantees of "cure" presently exist, it does not make sense that a psychiatrist would ever guarantee treatment success.

Another treatment-related circumstance that could invite an allegation of fraud is when a patient is induced to try an unnecessary or therapeutically inappropriate procedure. Similarly, when a doctor minimizes or conceals a mistake, error, or injury that has been caused by his or her treatment, an action for fraud might occur. An excellent example is the case of *Rains v. Superior Court* (67). In *Rains,* several patients complained that their psychiatrist had misrepresented to them the therapeutic value of their "treatment" and that it required that they be subjected to physical violence. A trial court accepted the defendant's contention that he had not misrepresented his treatment and that all of the patients had consented to participate in it. On appeal, the appellate court reversed the lower court stating that the defendant had indeed misrepresented the nature and value of his unique treatment approach and that misrepresentation vitiated the plaintiffs' otherwise informed consent.

The final and *most likely* situation in which a psychiatrist might be sued for fraud is in the filing of false insurance claims and billings. Therapists who engage in deceptive or unlawful practices related to billing and reimbursement run the risk of several forms of punishment: civil suit (68), criminal prosecution (69), and licensure revocation (70). A variety of acts or conduct could result in a claim of fraud by individual patients, insurers, or the government:

❖ Billing a patient or payer for services not rendered
❖ Billing a patient or payer at a rate greater than what was agreed upon
❖ Billing a patient or payer for unnecessary services
❖ Waiver of copayments or deductibles
❖ Providing untruthful or misleading information about the nature of treatment provided, the identity of the provider of service, or the problem(s) being treated
❖ Billing for services of personnel not authorized to be reimbursed
❖ Billing more than one payer for the same service
❖ Paying or receiving kickbacks or referral fees, or engaging in fee splitting
❖ Billing for services known to be excluded from coverage

One issue associated with billing fraud that has captured significant attention and produced a considerable amount of litigation is the question of whether those investigating fraud are barred from reviewing patient records, in part or totally, because of patient privilege (43). In other words, when fraud investigators want to verify what services actually took place, by whom, and under what conditions, and therapy clients want their treatment communications kept confidential, whose rights take precedent?

Courts across the country have split on this issue. For example, in *Matter of Camperlengo v. Blum* (71), the New York Court of Appeals granted the state's Department of Social Services the right to look at patients' records to determine whether any Medicaid fraud had occurred. On the other hand, some courts have resisted, at least initially, any attempt by investigators to override the psychiatrist-patient privilege and obtain unbridled access to patient records (72). Other courts, in what appears to be the majority view, have recognized that patients still have to some degree a right to privacy. Accordingly, these courts have restricted the nature and extent of information the states can obtain from patient records in order to pursue reimbursement fraud claims (73). Typically, this information is limited to the patient's name, medical services provided, diagnoses, and service dates. Several courts have held that this type of information is sufficient in meeting both interests when balancing the privacy rights of patients with the state's right not to be defrauded (73).

Conclusions: Psychiatric Practice Considerations

By and large, psychiatrists are not commonly sued for allegations of intentional or quasi-intentional torts. However, the potential is certainly available, especially when patient contact is sloppy, unconventional, deceptive, or unethical.

There is no set of guidelines, precautions, or formulae that can ensure that a patient will not sue his or her therapist for one of the torts outlined in this chapter. As with any aspect of psychiatric practice, however, there are several sensible practices that can considerably reduce the risk. They include, but are not limited to, the following:

Prior to the initiation of any treatment, obtain appropriate informed consent. Even in situations in which authorization is implied or is assumed to be given, it is a sound clinical practice to solicit the patient as a treatment partner. This process can be facilitated by clearly explaining treatment procedures and their benefits and risks, and then by obtaining the patient's input.

Know the law or laws that affect your practice and practice within them (74). This does not mean that a psychiatrist must now become a lawyer. What it does mean (and as a part of the duty of care) is that professionals have a responsibility to practice within the limits of the law. For instance, efforts to civilly commit or forcibly medicate a patient can only be *legally* accomplished according to the law of the state in which the psychiatrist practices. Ignorance of these details will be no defense if sued for noncompliance.

Maintain accurate, up-to-date records. Careful record keeping will not only facilitate treatment, improve one's clinical skills and insights, and help one keep track of his or her practice, but also serve as a valuable resource if ever an allegation of wrongdoing is made.

Adhere to the principles of ethics. Such common restrictions and prohibitions as maintaining confidentiality and not engaging a patient for personal reasons are written for a purpose. *The Principles of Medical Ethics, With Annotations Especially Applicable to Psychiatry* is not only a compendium of ethical guidelines but a sound *malpractice prevention plan*. It is hard to imagine an allegation of malpractice or intentional tort that does not violate at least one, and likely many, ethical principles.

Establish an expertise and maintain a level of competence. Too often, professionals are sued because their actions go beyond the scope of their knowledge, training, or experience. As a result, they have exceeded their level of competence and expertise. Psychiatrists who experiment with a lot of unconventional treatment approaches, "freelance" into areas of practice in which they have little or no training, or attempt to be too much of a generalist by trying to treat every patient that comes to their office, are at a high risk to invite an intentional tort. Choosing an area of professional interest, staying abreast of the current literature, consulting peers with similar interests, becoming licensed or certified in that practice area, and participating in continuing education are all important ways of establishing and maintaining competency.

The following practices are also recommended:

❖ **Select patients that are appropriate for your practice** and enlist them as treatment partners.
❖ **Follow up** and in good faith reconcile errors in judgment or accidents in practice.
❖ **Regularly consult with peers** and seek professional support.

These few common-sense practical recommendations should aid the practitioner in preventing lawsuits by patients accusing the psychiatrist of intentional or quasi-intentional torts.

References

1. Black HC: Black's Law Dictionary, 6th Edition. St Paul, MN, West Publishing, 1990, p 1489
2. See, e.g., Bellamy WA: Malpractice risks confronting the psychiatrist: a nationwide fifteen-year study of the appellate court cases, 1946–1961. Am J Psychiatry 118:769–780, 1962; Slawson PF: Psychiatric malpractice: the California experience. Am J Psychiatry 136:650–654, 1979; Psychiatry claims closed 1980–1985. Psychiatric News, Vol 22, April 3, 1987, p 11; Hogan DB: The Regulation of Psychotherapists, Vol 3. Cambridge, MA, Ballinger, 1979, p 382
3. See, e.g., Hayes v New York, 80 Misc2d 498, 363 NYS2d 986 (Ct Cl 1975); Hipp v Hospital Authority, 104 Ga App 174, 131 SE2d 273 (1961). But also see Miele v United States, 800 F2d 50 (2d Cir 1986) [assault and battery by a mentally ill soldier considered "intentional act" and thus barred by the intentional tort exception to the Federal Tort Claims Act for lawsuits against the federal government]
4. Original rule established in I de S et ux v Wde S, 1348 Y.B. Lib Assis f 99, pl 60. For current discussion see Keeton WP, Dobbs DB, Keeton RE, et al: Prosser and Keeton on Torts, 5th Edition, St Paul, MN, West Publishing, 1984, pp 43–46
5. Original rule established in I de S et ux v Wde S, 1348 Y.B. Lib Assis f 99, pl 60. For current discussion see Keeton WP, Dobbs DB, Keeton RE, et al: Prosser and Keeton on Torts, 5th Edition, St Paul, MN, West Publishing, 1984, pp 39–42
6. See, e.g., Wilson v Scott, 412 SW2d 299 (Tex 1967); Mink v University of Chicago, 460 F Supp 713 (ND Ill 1978); Beck v Lowell, 361 So 2d 245 (La Ct App 1978)

7. See Rappaport D, Parry J (eds): The Right to Refuse Antipsychotic Medication. Washington, DC, American Bar Association, 1986, pp 7–31; Washington v Harper, 110 S Ct 1028 (1990)

8. See Winters v Miller, 446 F2d 656 (2d Cir 1971)

9. Winters v Miller, 446 F2d 658 (2d Cir 1971)

10. 181 NYS2d 805, 7 AD 216 (1959), modified, 7 NY2d 376, 198 NYS2d 65, 165 NE2d 756 (1960)

11. Abraham v Zaslow, No 245862 Super Ct (Cal June 30, 1972), affirmed Cal App (February 2, 1975)

12. 720 F2d 1451 (9th Cir 1983)

13. See, e.g., Davis v New York, 70 Misc 2d 112, 332 NYS2d 569 (Ct Cl 1972); Bellardi v Park Sanitorium Association, 214 Cal 472, 6 P2d 508 (1931); Wheeler v Glass, 473 F2d 983 (7th Cir 1973); Townsend v Memorial Medical Centers, 529 SW2d 264 (Tex 1975)

14. See American Psychiatric Association: Seclusion and Restraint: The Psychiatric Uses (Task Force Report No 22). Washington, DC, American Psychiatric Association, 1985; Gutheil TG, Tardiff K: Indications and contraindications for seclusion and restraint, in The Psychiatric Uses of Seclusion and Restraint. Edited by Tardiff K. Washington, DC, American Psychiatric Press, 1984, pp 11–17

15. Simon RI: Concise Guide to Psychiatry and Law for Clinicians. Washington, DC, American Psychiatric Press, 1992

16. See, e.g., Minnesota v Nevers, SJIS 21-31-1-000004 Douglas Cty Dist Ct (Minn filed July 30, 1987) [psychologist: extradited from Nev]; Peer v Municipal Court of South Bay Judicial District, 128 Cal App 3d 733, 180 Cal Rptr 137 (1982) [psychologist]; Annot 70 ALR2d 824 (1951) [intercourse accomplished under pretext of medical treatment as rape]

17. See, e.g., Osborne v Leonard, No 21788/77 NY Cty Sup Ct (NY November 5, 1982); Richard FH v Larry HD, 198 Cal 3d 591, 243 Cal Rptr 807 (1988) [psychiatrist]

18. Smith JT, Bisbing SB: Sexual Exploitation by Health Care Providers, 2nd Edition. Potomac, MD, Legal Medicine Press, 1987

19. Keeton WP, Dobbs DB, Keeton RE, et al: Prosser and Keeton on Torts, 5th Edition. St Paul, MN, West Publishing, 1984, p 47

20. Ibid, pp 47–53

21. 110 S Ct 975 (1990)

22. Appelbaum PS: Voluntary hospitalization and due process: the dilemma of Zinermon v Burch. Hosp Community Psychiatry 41:1059–1060, 1990

23. See, e.g., Stowers v Wolodzko, 386 Mich 119, 191 NW2d 355 (1971); Chudy v Chudy, 243 Ark 332, 420 SW2d 401 (1967); Lowen v Hilton, 351 P2d 881 (Colo 1961)

24. 59 Ill App 3d 337, 375 NE2d 486 (1978)

25. See, e.g., St Vincent's Medical Center v Oakley, 371 So 2d 590 (Fla Dist Ct 1979)

26. See, e.g., Boaz v Taylor, Tenn Ct App (Jan 27, 1986), cited in Mental and Physical Disability Law Reports 10:198, 1986

27. 121 Misc 2d 210, 467 NYS2d 538 (Ct Cl 1983)

28. 75 AD2d 691, 427 NYS2d 90 (1980)

29. See, e.g., Stiles v Sen, 544 NYS2d 259 (App Div 1989)

30. Roy v Hartogs, 81 Misc2d 350, 366 NYS2d 297 (Civ Ct 1975), affirmed 85 Misc 2d 891, 381 NYS2d 587 (App Term 1976) [psychiatrist]
31. See, e.g., Doe v Bodwin, 119 Mich App 264, 326 NW2d 473 (1982) [psychologist]
32. See, e.g., Rosenstein v Barnes, No NWC 78755 "B" Van Nuys Sup Ct (Cal March 14, 1984) [psychologist]
33. See, e.g., Mazza v Huffaker, 61 NC App 170, 300 SE2d 833 (1983) [psychiatrist sued for medical malpractice and criminal conversation]
34. Restatement (Second) of Torts § 46
35. Williams v Baker, 540 A2d 449 (DC Ct App 1988)
36. Rowe v Bennett, 514 A2d 802 (Me 1986)
37. Gihring v Butcher, 138 Ill App 3d 976, 487 NE2d 75 (1985)
38. Spencer v King County, 39 Wash App 201, 692 P2d 874 (1984)
39. 257 Cal Rptr 98, 48 Cal 3d 583, 770 P2d 278 (1989)
40. See, e.g., Long v Rothbaum, 68 Md App 569, 514 A2d 1223 (1986)
41. Keeton WP, Dobbs DB, Keeton RE, et al: Prosser and Keeton on Torts, 5th Edition. St Paul, MN, West Publishing, 1984, pp 771–813
42. Keeton WP, Dobbs DB, Keeton RE, et al: Prosser and Keeton on Torts, 5th Edition. St Paul, MN, West Publishing, 1984, pp 771–842; Smith JT: Medical Malpractice: Psychiatric Care. Colorado Springs, Shepard's/McGraw-Hill, 1987, pp 257–258
43. Simonds v Blue Cross–Blue Shield of Michigan, 629 F Supp 369 (D Mich 1986)
44. Liberty Lobby, Inc v Anderson, 746 F2d 1563 (DC Cir 1984), 471 U.S. 1134
45. 130 Ill App 3d 163, 474 NE2d 380 (1984)
46. Corbitt v Andersen, 778 F2d 1471 (10 Cir 1985)
47. 290 Ohio App 3d 118, 133, 504 NE2d 427 (1985)
48. 627 F Supp 418 (SD Va 1986)
49. See, e.g., Gross v Haight, 496 So 2d 1225 (La Ct App 1986)
50. See, e.g., Dolan v Von Zweck, 477 NE2d 200 (Mass App Ct 1985)
51. See, e.g., Sibley v Lutheran Hospital of Maryland, Inc, 709 F Supp 657 (D Md 1989)
52. See, e.g., Ross v University of Minnesota, 439 NW2d 28 (Minn App 1989)
53. See, e.g., Shurn v Monteleone, 769 SW2d 188 (Mo App 1989)
54. Restatement (Second) of Torts § 652A
55. Keeton WP, Dobbs DB, Keeton RE, et al: Prosser and Keeton on Torts, 5th Edition. St Paul, MN, West Publishing, 1984, pp 849–869
56. See, e.g., Commonwealth v Wiseman, 256 Mass 251, 249 NE2d 610 (1969)
57. See, e.g., Griffin v Medical Society, 11 NYS2d 109 (Sup Ct Spec Term 1939)
58. See, e.g., Feeney v Young, 191 AD 501, 181 NYS 481 (1920)
59. See, e.g., Bratt v IBM, 785 F2d 352 (1st Cir 1986); Cutter v Brownbridge, 183 Cal App 3d 836, 228 Cal Rptr 545 (1986)
60. See, e.g., Prince v St Francis–St George Hospital, Inc, 484 NE2d 265 (Ohio Ct App 1985)
61. See, e.g., Doe v Roe, 400 NYS2d 668 (Sup Ct 1977)
62. See, e.g., DeMay v Roberts, 46 Mich 160, 9 NW 146 (1881)
63. See, e.g., McCormick v Haley, 37 Ohio App 2d 73, 307 NE2d 34 (1973)

64. See, e.g., Prince v St Francis–St George Hospital, Inc, 484 NE2d 265 (Ohio Ct App 1985)

65. Keeton WP, Dobbs DB, Keeton RE, et al: Prosser and Keeton on Torts, 5th Edition, St Paul, MN, West Publishing, 1984, pp 725–736

66. See, e.g., Kabel v Brady, 519 So 2d 912 (Ala 1987)

67. 150 Cal App 3d 933, 198 Cal Rptr 249 (1984)

68. See, e.g., Metropolitan Life Insurance Co v Ditmore, 729 F2d 1 (1st Cir 1984)

69. See, e.g., United States v Monick, 753 F2d 1085 (9th Cir 1984)

70. See, e.g., Eisenberg v Myers, 148 Cal 3d 814, 196 Cal Rptr 270 (1983)

71. 56 NY2d 251, 436 NE2d 1299 (App Div 1982); McKirdy v Superior Court of the City and County of San Francisco, 188 Cal Rptr 14 (1982)

72. See, e.g., in re Grand Jury Subpoena Duces Tecum, dated December 14, 1984, 495 NYS2d 365 (AD 1 Dept 1985)

73. See, e.g., Reynaud v Superior Court, Santa Clara County, 138 Cal 3d 1, 187 Cal Rptr 660 (1982); Commonwealth v Kobrin, 395 Mass 1004, 479 NE2d 674 (1985); in re Supoena Served Upon Zuniga, 714 F2d 632 (6th Cir 1983)

74. Simon RI: Clinical Psychiatry and the Law, 2nd Edition. Washington, DC, American Psychiatric Press, 1992

Chapter 4

Breach of Confidentiality —————

onfidentiality refers to the right of a patient to have communications spoken or written in confidence not disclosed to outside parties without implied or expressed authorization. Privilege—or, more accurately, *testimonial privilege*—can be viewed as a derivation of the right of confidentiality. Testimonial privilege is a statutorily created rule of evidence that permits the patient as holder of the privilege the right to prevent the psychiatrist to whom confidential information was given from disclosing it in a judicial proceeding (1).

Foundations of Confidentiality

The basis for recognizing and safeguarding patient confidences is derived from four general sources. States have acknowledged this right of protection by including confidentiality provisions in either professional licensure laws or confidentiality and privilege statutes. A second source, and probably the most traditional, is the ethical codes of the various mental health professions. Third, while common law recognized an attorney-client privilege, developing case law also has carved out this source of protection for physicians and psychotherapists. Fourth, the right of confidentiality may be subsumed under the constitutional right of privacy.

Portions of this chapter were adapted from Simon RI: *Clinical Psychiatry and the Law,* 2nd Edition (Washington, DC, American Psychiatric Press, 1992), and Simon RI: *Concise Guide to Psychiatry and Law for Clinicians* (Washington, DC, American Psychiatric Press, 1992).

Breaching Confidentiality

Regardless of the basis of the right of confidentiality, once the doctor-patient relationship has been created, the professional assumes an automatic duty to safeguard a patient's disclosures. This duty is not absolute, and there are circumstances in which breaching confidentiality is both ethical and legal.

Patients waive confidentiality in a variety of situations. Medical records are regularly sent to potential employers or to insurance companies for benefits. A limited waiver of confidentiality ordinarily exists when a patient participates in group therapy. Legally, whether one group member can be compelled in court to disclose information shared by another group member during group therapy is still unsettled. Many state statutes mandate disclosure by the psychiatrist in one or more situations.

Patients' access to their own records is normally controlled by statutes. These statutory provisions are found under the heading of medical records or the much broader term, *privilege.*

Testimonial Privilege

The patient—not the psychiatrist—is the holder of the privilege that controls the release of confidential information. Because privilege applies only to the judicial setting, it is called testimonial privilege. Privilege statutes represent the most common recognition by the state of the importance of protecting information provided by a patient to a psychotherapist. This recognition moves away from the essential truth-finding purpose of the American system of justice by insulating certain information from disclosure in court. This protection is justified on the basis that the special need for privacy in the doctor-patient relationship outweighs the unbridled quest for an accurate outcome in court.

Privilege statutes usually are drafted in one of four ways, depending on the type of practitioner:

❖ (General) physician-patient
❖ Psychiatrist-patient
❖ Psychologist-patient
❖ Psychotherapist-patient

Cases have been successfully litigated in which the broader physician-patient category was applied to the psychotherapist when an applicable statute did not exist.

Exceptions to Testimonial Privilege

Privilege statutes also specify exceptions to testimonial privilege. While exceptions vary, the most common include

- Child abuse reporting
- Involuntary hospitalization
- Court-ordered evaluations
- Cases in which a patient's mental state is in question as a component of litigation

This last exception, known as the *patient-litigant exception,* commonly occurs in will contests, worker's compensation cases, child custody disputes, personal injury actions, and malpractice actions in which the therapist is sued by the patient.

Liability

An unauthorized or unwarranted breach of confidentiality can cause a patient considerable emotional harm. As a result, a psychiatrist can typically be held liable for such a breach based on at least four theories:

- Malpractice (breach of confidentiality)
- Breach of statutory duty
- Invasion of privacy
- Breach of (implied) contract

Valid Authorization to Release Information

A valid, informed authorization for the release of information protects a psychiatrist ethically and legally (2). State law and mental health confidentiality statutes generally specify the requirements for a valid authorization. Statutes may forbid release of certain information even when the patient consents, as with information supplied to third-party payers.

Consent should be obtained in written form. This creates a permanent record of the fact and the scope of the consent. Patients need to be able to make a considered judgment about the impact of their decision. Written forms do possess this advantage (3).

Blanket consents should be avoided (4). Instead, consent should be given for a specific release of information. The purpose and any limitation should be specified. The form should have a place to indicate whether a one-time or continuing consent is being given. Patients also should be informed on the document that they have the right to revoke consent at any time, as well as a right to inspect and copy any information authorized for release. *The Principles of Medical Ethics With Annotations Applicable to Psychiatry* (5) states: "The continuing duty of the psychiatrist to protect the patient includes fully apprising him/her of the connotations of waiving the privilege of privacy" (Section 4, Annotation 2). Psychiatrists should satisfy themselves that the patient understands the kind of information requested and the type of information in the record. Whenever possible, the patient should be allowed to see all information that will be released to others as well as the opportunity to be the final decision-maker on release. The information can be provided to the patient in an addressed envelope without a stamp. The intent is not to save money but to emphasize to patients their responsibility and consent in releasing such information. The walk to the mailbox has produced a change of heart in some patients in regard to releasing certain information. If the patient does not wish to know the content of the disclosure, the psychiatrist should assess if the request is competent and record the patient's wish in the medical record.

The American Psychiatric Association (APA) Task Force on Confidentiality (6) states that psychiatrists are most concerned about statutory requirements of disclosure and judicial compulsion. Apart from these requirements, there is no other legal requirement to provide information. By far, the most frequent occasions for release of information are by patients themselves when they authorize disclosure by the psychiatrist for insurance, employment benefits, welfare benefits, drivers licenses, or even charge accounts (7). Often, however, psychiatrists needlessly reveal the identity of patients in correspondence involving the peer review process, even though the latter is set up to maintain patient anonymity.

The situation is entirely different when an evaluation is being performed for a third party, as in court evaluations, preemployment interviews, or disability evaluations. Unless a treatment relationship has been established between the therapist and patient, a duty of confidentiality does not arise. For example, at the very beginning of the examination, the person being examined is told that the examination is at the request of a third party (8). Quite apart from legal constraints, the individual should be told at the outset that information obtained is not confidential and that the individual will not be given a report by the psychiatrist. The report will be sent directly to the interested third party. Consent is implied when the individual proceeds with the evaluation. *The Principles of Medical Ethics* (5) states: "Psychiatrists are often asked to examine individuals for security purposes, to determine suitability for various jobs, and to determine legal competence. The psychiatrist must fully describe the nature and purpose and lack of confidentiality of the examination to the examinee at the beginning of the examination" (Section 4, Annotation 6).

The psychiatrist's duty to confidentiality remains even when blanket consent forms are signed. As stated in the *The Principles of Medical Ethics* (5): "Ethically the psychiatrist may disclose only that information which is relevant to a given situation. He/she should avoid offering speculation as fact. Sensitive information such as an individual's sexual orientation or fantasy material is usually unnecessary" (Section 4, Annotation 5).

Defenses to a Legal Action for Unauthorized Disclosures

Psychiatrists have been sued for unauthorized release of information to patients' employers (9), to insurers (10), to defendants in personal injury cases (11), to spouses (12), and in writing books about patients (13). Psychiatrists have raised various defenses in these cases. When a valid consent is obtained, the psychiatrist is legally and ethically protected (5).

The consent, however, must be given competently, knowingly, and voluntarily. Because of the influence of the transference in psychiatric treatment, voluntariness of consent needs to be considered. In *Doe v. Roe* (13), the psychiatrist's allegation that consent was obtained for a book about the patient met with the following comment from the court: "This defense is without substance. Consent was sought while the plaintiff was in therapy. It was never obtained in writing. . . . I need not deal with the value of an oral waiver of confidentiality given by a patient to a psychiatrist during the course of treatment." Legal commentators (14) suggest that consent under these circumstances be obtained in writing. Also, consideration should be given to obtaining a consultation from a psychiatrist or attorney to discuss the confidentiality issue with the patient and to determine if consent is competent, knowing, and voluntary.

The defense of an overriding public interest may be used under certain circumstances. The public interest defense is carefully scrutinized for possible self-interest. In *Doe v. Roe* (13), the public interest defense (educational contribution to the medical profession) appeared self-serving. Careful risk-benefit analysis should be conducted when unauthorized disclosures are made in the service of public interest.

Allegations of unauthorized disclosure also may occur in the course of warning endangered third parties. The competing interests of confidentiality and warning are discussed in Chapter 8. If a therapist suspects that a patient is physically abusing a child, child abuse statutes require reporting of such a suspicion. Many statutes also provide for the reporting of psychological abuse. The actual consequences for the therapy make such reporting a highly problematic matter. Reporting of contagious disease, epilepsy, and gunshot wounds are just some of the other reporting requirements contained in many statutes.

The defense of the lack of a statute addressing the particular right of confidentiality was raised in *Alberts v. Devine* (15). The court held that the lack of statute was no bar to the recognition of a nonstatutory remedy. The court also noted that other courts had in fact established a similar duty of confidentiality.

Breaching confidentiality in the interest of protecting the patient may occur. While a psychiatrist does not have a legal duty to warn others of a patient's possible suicide attempt, good clinical practice may require such an action. *The Principles of Medical Ethics* (5) are very clear on confidentiality and protecting the patient or the community from danger: "Psychiatrists at times may find it necessary, in order to protect the patient or the community from imminent danger, to reveal confidential information disclosed by the patient" (Section 4, Annotation 8).

Courts rarely support the gratuitous invoking of "protecting the patient or community" in order to make unauthorized disclosures to spouses or family members. In *MacDonald v. Clinger* (16), the court stated: "Disclosure of confidential information by a psychiatrist to a spouse would be justified whenever there is a danger to the patient, the spouse; otherwise, information should not be disclosed without authorization." This is sound advice to follow.

Whenever psychiatrists who practice in jurisdictions having mental health confidentiality statutes abide by these statutes, or disclose confidential information as required by reporting statutes, a defense against legal claims of unauthorized disclosure is present. Psychiatrists also may be vulnerable to ethical complaints filed by patients with the APA district branch and the APA over unauthorized disclosures. Justified claims may result in reprimand, suspension, or expulsion from these organizations. In a number of states, licensing statutes contain confidentiality requirements that if breached may lead to suspension or revocation of the psychiatrist's license (14).

Common Breaches of Confidentiality

One of the most common but most indefensible ways in which confidentiality is breached is by "loose lips." Sargent (17) describes this syndrome and provides a very credible psychological interpretation for its continued prevalence among psychiatrists. Because secrets confer power on their guardians, the temptation exists to display that power. The psychiatrist's stock-in-trade is secrets. Lacking the technological skills of the surgeon and the wonder drugs of the internist, psychiatrists depend on their unique knowledge of the mind and the secrets entrusted to them to impress others.

When yearning for recognition, the temptation to reveal confidential patient information can be very great. Thus, at one time or another, many psychiatrists have been chagrined by an "inadvertent" disclosure of confidential information.

Weiss (18) compared patients' expectations with those of physicians concerning the likelihood that a breach of confidentiality might occur. Weiss questioned patients, medical students, house officers, and senior physicians about the chances of confidentiality lapses. Whereas patients mostly believed that confidentiality was not breached, a significant number of medical students and physicians at each level believed that lapses were common. Although psychiatrists generally are acutely sensitive to confidentiality issues, constant vigilance is required to prevent unauthorized release of confidential patient information.

The Confidentiality of Minors

The "law of adolescence" is evolving. Historically, the legal status of all minors from age 7 to 17 was considered the same. Currently, the rights of a 15- to 17-year-old are not the same as those of a 6-year-old. In addition, all states allow young people to consent to treatment for venereal disease. Most states permit young people to secure birth control devices without parental notification. States are beginning to lower the age of medical consent from 18 to 14 or 15 (19).

During the past 30 years, no lawsuits for civil damages or criminal charges have been brought against physicians who have beneficially treated a minor over 15 for any condition on the consent of the minor. Because of an alarming rise in venereal disease, alcohol and drug abuse, and teenage pregnancies, "enabling laws" have been passed by states providing minors with access to medical care without parental approval.

The general rule is that confidentiality follows the legal ability to consent to treatment. Mental health confidentiality statutes usually provide a definition of who is a young minor. If a child is under age 12, the APA suggests relying on parental consent (20). With young minors, the parents or guardians are the legal decision-makers. Thus, parents have a right to know about the course of treatment as well as the diagnosis and prognosis. Obviously, revealing confidential information must be done cautiously so that damage is not done to the treatment or to the child's relationship with caregivers.

States require the reporting of child abuse, and some states require reporting the suspicion of child abuse. The psychiatrist is fully protected by the reporting statute from suit for breach of confidentiality in these cases. Every statute has criminal penalties for not reporting. At least three states exempt the physician from reporting child abuse if the physician is attempting to deal with the child abuse by counseling (21).

When releasing medical records or testifying about treatment, one parent's consent is generally sufficient. If divorce or custody litigation is taking place, parents may disagree about waiver of confidentiality. The therapist should wait before releasing confidential information until the court has ruled on the validity of the waiver. In the absence of a court ruling, the therapist should consult state law requirements (14). In some jurisdictions, the state may require an attorney to represent the interest of the child regarding waiver of confidentiality. If a minor is too young to personally exercise the privilege, courts may appoint a guardian to act in the best interests of the child. Under such circumstances, the parents, neither alone nor together, may agree or refuse to waive the privilege on the child's behalf (22).

After a divorce is final, usually one parent is granted custody of any minor children. The custodial parent holds the health care decision-making power. Psychiatrists may be asked to perform an examination or evaluation of a minor child at the request of a noncustodial parent. Psychiatrists who perform such examinations expose themselves to legal action. While no court has found a psychiatrist liable for failure to obtain the custodial parent's consent prior to examination or evaluation, such decisions appear likely (23). Court decisions as well as statutory interpretations of the term "parent" have limited the use of that word to the parent who has been awarded custody under a divorce decree's term (24, 25). Before performing an evaluation or examination upon a minor child, the psychiatrist should obtain the consent of the parent with legal custody.

As minors are able to consent to treatment independently and legally, they are able to control disclosure of medical information. Usually from age 14 to 15, minors may be considered *emancipated minors* when not living at home or when they are self-supporting. Minors who have been judged by physicians to possess sufficient maturity to understand and consent to treatment have been considered mature minors. Consent of a parent is never required in a genuine emergency. Unemancipated minors can be treated in all states for venereal disease without consent or knowledge of parents for the protection of the community.

Relying on parental consent alone for these groups is insufficient. When disclosures are made to interested third parties, consent of both the patient and the parents may be advisable. In addition, the risk of treatment is an important consideration that enters into treatment interventions provided without parental consent and knowledge. In psychiatry, the use of psychoactive drugs increases the risk of treatment. Not only are adverse drug effects a possible side effect, but also important activities such as educational performance, sports activities, or newly learned driving skills may be harmed.

Thus, the risk of treatment and the maturity of the minor are crucial issues to be weighed in proceeding with or without parental consent.

Whether the minor patient has consent rights or not, every effort should be made to preserve confidentiality for the sake of the treatment. The conflicting interests of the minor's independent right to confidentiality with the parent's need to have information for making reasonable treatment and confidentiality decisions are always present. *The Principles of Medical Ethics* (5) is sensitive to these conflicting interests: "Careful judgment must be exercised by the psychiatrist in order to include, when appropriate, the parents or guardian in the treatment of a minor. At the same time the psychiatrist must assure the minor proper confidentiality" (Section 4, Annotation 7).

In psychiatric practice, the parents of minors undergoing treatment will often need to be involved at some level. The problems of minor children are often inextricably wound together with those of their parents. Ground rules for confidentiality must be set out from the beginning of treatment. For the most part, the therapist may choose to avoid disclosure as much as possible, perhaps encouraging the child and parents to improve communications with each other. The parents must live with the child from day to day, and often the parents feel the psychic pain of their child's emotional disturbance. Almost all parents have some useful knowledge of the child and of the family's psychological dynamics that are a source of essential information to the therapist.

Economic reality rather than legal theory may determine the right to confidential information. Therapists or hospitals will often be unwilling to treat a minor patient without the signature of a financially responsible person. When the parent receives an itemized bill or statement from a therapist or insurance provider, privacy can no longer be maintained. If parents do not consent to nonemergency treatment of a minor, the parent is not responsible for payment of care. Some state statutes make this explicit (19).

Responding to a Subpoena

When a psychiatrist is subpoenaed to testify about a patient, conflicting ethical and legal issues immediately arise. Physician-patient or psychotherapist-patient privilege statutes may allow patients to prevent a treating psychiatrist from disclosing information obtained during the course of treatment in court. In the case of *In re B* (26), the Pennsylvania Supreme Court ruled that a patient's constitutional right to privacy protects confidential communications in psychotherapy.

As an ethical matter, *The Principles of Medical Ethics* (5) states: "A psychiatrist may release confidential information only with the authorization of the patient or under proper legal compulsion" (Section 4, Annotation 2).

The psychiatrist also should explain to the patient the possible impact of testimony or disclosure of the psychiatric record upon his or her treatment or possibly on the outcome of the lawsuit. When presented with a subpoena, the psychiatrist should question the subpoena on behalf of the patient to protect the confidentiality of the information gathered during psychotherapy. The standard professional liability policy covers the costs of legal services when responding to a subpoena relating to a psychiatrist's practice (27).

A subpoena by itself is not "proper legal compulsion." The subpoena merely compels the psychiatrist to appear, not to testify (14). A subpoena may be issued by various governmental authorities and administrative agencies. Not all of these agencies have the power to issue subpoenas, but this does not necessarily prevent them from trying to compel testimony (28). Attorneys have an absolute right to obtain a subpoena without prior review by a judge by merely attesting to a belief that certain individuals have information that is relevant to the issue at court. There are two basic types of subpoenas: 1) *subpoena duces tecum,* which requires the physician to bring medical records; and 2) *subpoena ad testificandum,* which only requires the attendance of the physician, usually for testimony. Trying to avoid being served a subpoena is both unrealistic and unethical. Psychiatrists should not deny reality when it is essential that they know their own rights and the rights of patients in the legal matter at hand.

After receiving a subpoena, the psychiatrist must still regard all information obtained during the course of therapy as privileged from testimonial disclosure until reviewed and properly resolved by legal authority. The subpoena often will be accompanied by a signed consent form from the patient. The psychiatrist may testify and provide records if the consent complies with state law requirements and is an informed consent. The psychiatrist is ethically obligated to provide only information that is relevant to the issue at court. The pursuit of irrelevant information should be directly questioned by the testifying psychiatrist. An appeal to the judge by either the patient's attorney or the psychiatrist may be necessary. In a deposition, irrelevant, sensitive information should not be provided without a court order or specific consent by the patient (14).

When no consent form accompanies the subpoena, the psychiatrist should ascertain whether consent will be forthcoming. If the patient fails to consent, the patient's attorney or the psychiatrist may file a motion to quash the subpoena on the basis of protection under physician-patient privilege and the duty to maintain confidentiality. The court will rule on the motion, settling the question of whether or not the psychiatrist must testify or turn over records.

If there is no motion to quash, the psychiatrist must appear at the deposition or trial. When asked to testify, the physician-patient privilege should be raised, and the court should be requested to rule on this issue. If the court rules that the psychiatrist must testify, the psychiatrist must do so or risk a contempt-of-court citation. A similar procedure should be followed in depositions. If necessary, attorneys at the deposition will arrange for a court resolution of the issue (14).

Keeping Records

Clinically, keeping a record during the course of the patient's treatment serves a number of purposes. Review of the record between sessions helps summarize treatment sessions and permits a better understanding of the patient and the treatment process. If the patient interrupts or terminates treatment but later decides to resume therapy, the previous record will prove helpful in refreshing the therapist's memory. Accurate record keeping will also help resolve disputes over billing. Additionally, pressure for record keeping is increasing because of the need to maintain quality of care for accreditation, for financial reimbursement, and for legal purposes.

Some courts have concluded that what is not recorded was not done (29, 30). Generally, in the absence of corroborating records, assertions in court that certain actions were taken is a question for the fact-finders who must consider the issue of proof. When an adequate record exists, the possibility of proving that an action (e.g., treatment or procedure) was taken is significantly enhanced.

Usually, no useful purpose is served by noting the patient's fantasies, derogatory opinions toward others, or any other information not directly relevant to documenting treatment decisions. Records documenting intimate details may be necessary for supervision of student psychotherapists or analysts. These records should not be kept after their educational function is served. A consistent policy of destroying treatment process records should be considered. The destruction can be certified and the certificate kept permanently. State law may forbid destruction of records if the intent is to prevent disclosure at a judicial proceeding. If the psychiatrist discloses at a judicial hearing that treatment process records are routinely destroyed, the presence of a consistent policy will tend to negate questions about credibility.

Psychiatrists must also realize that the psychiatric record can become an iatrogenic factor in exacerbating a patient's condition, particularly if it contains damaging or frightening information. Many states allow patients access to their records. The physical record maintained by the psychiatrist is the property of the psychiatrist. The information contained in the record, however, belongs to the patient. The original record should never be relinquished to the patient. Only a copy of the record should be provided. The psychiatrist should be present whenever patients wish to inspect their records in order to answer questions, and to avoid harm to the patient who may react negatively to the information provided.

A number of states have enacted patient access statutes permitting patients to have access to medical records in the absence of litigation, after the payment of administrative costs such as photocopying charges (31). Some jurisdictions make a distinction between mental health records and other medical records. Access to records may also depend on who is making the request (i.e., patient, next of kin, or legal representative) and the reason for the access request. A minority of jurisdictions permit direct access by the patient's attorney, physician, or near relative but not by the patient. Many states provide an exception for the release of mental health treatment records on the grounds that the psychological welfare of the patient might be impaired by knowledge of the contents of the record.

In *Bartlett v. Danti* (32), the Rhode Island Supreme Court held that the provision of the State Confidentiality of Health Care Information Act, exempting confidential health care information from compulsory legal process, violated the Rhode Island Constitution. The act was amended, defining situations in which physicians may be compelled to testify or produce evidence regarding a patient's medical condition. Medical information was defined as privileged rather than confidential.

A few states have passed statutes expressly prohibiting the release of mental health records to anyone except under court order (33). Most state statutes protect institutional records independently of the therapist's obligation to maintain confidentiality (31). This is frequently the case in state hospitals for the mentally ill and retarded. However, some states treat state hospital records as nonprivileged public documents or privileged under government privilege statutes that are subject to waiver by the government without the patient's consent (34).

Psychiatrists sometimes keep two separate sets of records: one set for diagnosis, prognosis, and treatment decisions; the other for speculations of the psychiatrist and the fantasies and intimate details of the patient's life. Although Illinois and the District of Columbia permit dual records, such a distinction is not normally accepted by the courts (35). The work product privilege that protects attorneys' records has not been applied to medical practice. Concealing records is a violation of the law. Instead of using illegal means, the psychiatrist should exercise extreme caution when writing in the patient's record, entering only information that is pertinent to the diagnosis and treatment plan for the patient.

Records should be kept until the relevant statute of limitations has lapsed. Psychiatrists who retire should keep their records at least until the statute of limitations runs out. The statute of limitations may be tolled (i.e., suspended) when a person is under a legal disability at the time that the alleged injury arises. Legal disability is defined as the lack of legal capacity to perform an act. Thus, a minor or a mentally incompetent person is considered to be incapable of initiating a lawsuit in his or her own behalf. For minors not otherwise disabled, the statute of limitations begins to run at the age of majority as defined by state statutes.

Some statutes spell out the nature, content, and style of record keeping to be maintained, who may receive records, and under what conditions. Psychiatrists need to be aware of these provisions and conduct their record keeping accordingly.

Professional organizations do not provide specific guidelines on record keeping. State licensing and certification laws may contain record-keeping requirements. Violation of these legal requirements may lead to suspension or loss of the practitioner's license. The statute of limitations for ethical charges filed by professional organizations or licensing authorities may be longer than the time established for legal actions. No time limit for filing ethical charges may exist in some states.

Confidentiality After a Patient's Death

The duty to maintain confidentiality of patient records that existed in life follows the patient in death, unless a specific court decision or statute in a particular jurisdiction provides otherwise. The APA's *Opinions of the Ethics Committee on the Principles of Medical Ethics With Annotations Especially Applicable to Psychiatry* (36) presents the following question and answer asked by a psychiatrist on this very point:

Question: Can I give confidential information about a recently deceased mother to her grieving daughter?

Answer: No. Ethically, her confidences survive her death. Legally this is an unclear issue varying from one jurisdiction to another. Further, there is a risk of the information being used to seek an advantage in the contesting of a will or in competition with other surviving family members.

Many patients feel they have horrible secrets that they must hide at all costs. If the confidentiality of their therapy were to cease to exist after their death, many patients would be deterred from treatment. This is particularly true if death seems imminent, as in the patient considering suicide or patients with terminal illnesses.

Many occasions arise in which information is requested after a patient's death. As a general rule, written authorization should be obtained from the executor or administrator of the deceased patient's estate before releasing a copy of the medical records. If the estate has been settled and an executor or administrator no longer exists, a copy of the medical records should be released only to properly appointed legal representatives.

For a variety of reasons, psychiatrists often decide to disclose confidential information after the patient's death despite ethical and legal strictures to the contrary. Criminal investigations, will contests, and families seeking information about the patient as part of their grieving are not uncommon reasons for postmortem requests for information. When a patient commits suicide, family members may request a meeting with the treating psychiatrist to try to understand the suicide. This is a very stressful time for the family and the psychiatrist. The psychiatrist may feel defeated, guilty, and defensive. The family invariably feels guilt, anger, and blame. In an effort to exculpate himself or herself, too much information may be revealed by the psychiatrist. Releasing to the family additional painful details of the patient's life that are not relevant to the inquiry must be avoided. The immediate priority should be to console the family and assist them in their grief. The psychiatrist should not refuse to see the family unless litigation has been threatened or instituted by the family against the psychiatrist.

If the psychiatrist feels compelled to reveal confidential information after the patient's death, legal risks may be minimized by providing just enough information for the task at hand. Details of the patient's therapy are rarely, if ever, required. Relevancy is the guiding rule. Second, revealing information about third parties learned from the patient may be legally dangerous. The dead or their survivors cannot sue for defamation or the invasion of privacy because these are personal rights that die with the individual (37). Even if a person is defamed while alive, the cause of action under common law dies with the person. However, a legal cause of action may exist when words contained in a medical record independently reflect on and defame those living. Slovenko (37) states that "[o]ne who divulges an allegation by another may find himself liable although he did not indicate his own belief in the truth of the statement" (p. 126). Unless privilege exists to make disclosures, mental health professionals are responsible for statements made, even though the views are purported to be those of the patient.

Detailed comments about third persons are rarely, if ever, necessary for the purposes of record keeping (e.g., facilitating ongoing treatment, a record to be available in the future for other physicians, research, or legal purposes). Unless a state law provides otherwise, confidentiality must be preserved after the death of the patient just as it was in life.

Furthermore, the physician-patient privilege does not expire upon the patient's death. Privilege continues after death and may be claimed by the deceased patient's next of kin or legal representative. Privilege seeks to protect the patient from embarrassment, which could extend to family members after the patient dies (38). Psychiatrists must be careful not to make unauthorized extrajudicial or statutorily prohibited disclosure of patient records unless the disclosure is justified by overriding public interest.

A majority of states have enacted legislation subjecting physicians to loss of their license for the unauthorized release of medical records. In addition, such a release could constitute the basis for a lawsuit. A major controversy was raised concerning the postmortem disclosures by the treating psychiatrist of the famous American poet Anne Sexton. This controversy underscores many of the complex legal and ethical issues surrounding release of confidential information after a patient's death (39).

The American Psychiatric Association Guidelines on Confidentiality (40) are explicit concerning disclosure of information by a psychiatrist after the death of a patient:

> Psychiatrists should remember that their ethical and legal responsibilities regarding confidentiality continue after their patients' deaths. . . . In cases in which the release of information would be injurious to the deceased patient's interests or reputation, care must be exercised to limit the released data to that which is necessary for the purpose stated in the request for information. (p. 1523)

Conclusions

Confidentiality is an ethical issue in psychiatry unless it is improperly breached, at which time it becomes a legal matter, especially if the patient is damaged as a result of the negligent breach of confidentiality. However, there are appropriate instances when confidentiality is necessarily breached by legal mandate and approved by ethical guidelines, that is, when the welfare of the patient or the safety of the community is jeopardized by maintaining silence. For example, physicians will breach confidentiality in *Tarasoff*-like situations when the patient threatens suicide, or when child abuse is suspected.

By knowing the laws and rules of confidentiality and privilege that guide and regulate psychiatric practice, psychiatrists will be in a better position to act appropriately with their patients. The laws concerning confidentiality vary in different jurisdictions, so it behooves all practitioners to learn the specific laws in their particular state.

References

1. Simon RI: Concise Guide to Psychiatry and Law for Clinicians. Washington, DC, American Psychiatric Press, 1992 (in press)
2. Slovenko R: Accountability and abuse of confidentiality in the practice of psychiatry. Int J Law Psychiatry 2:431–454, 1979
3. Simon RI: Clinical Psychiatry and the Law, 2nd Edition. Washington, DC, American Psychiatric Press, 1992,

4. American Psychiatric Association Official Action: Model law on confidentiality of health and social service records. Am J Psychiatry 136:137, 1979

5. American Psychiatric Association: The Principles of Medical Ethics With Annotations Especially Applicable to Psychiatry. Washington, DC, American Psychiatric Association, 1989

6. American Psychiatric Association: Confidentiality: A Report of the Conference on Confidentiality of Health Records. Washington, DC, American Psychiatric Association, 1975

7. Slovenko R: Psychotherapy and confidentiality. Cleveland State Law Review 24:375, 1975

8. Reisner R, Slobogin C: Law and the Mental Health System, 2nd Edition. St Paul, MN, West Publishing, 1990, p 236

9. Hopewell v Adebimpe, 130 PHL J 107 (Pa Ct Com Pl 1981)

10. Hammonds v Aetna Casualty & Surety Co, 243 F Supp 793 (N D Ohio 1965)

11. Horne v Patton, 291 Ala 701, 287 So 2d 824 (1973)

12. MacDonald v Clinger, 84 AD2d 482, 446 NYS2d 801 (NY App Div 1982)

13. Doe v Roe, 93 Misc 2d 201, 400 NYS2d 668 (NY Sup Ct 1977)

14. Klein JI, Macbeth JE, Onek JN: Legal Issues in the Private Practice of Psychiatry. Washington, DC, American Psychiatric Press, 1984, p 33

15. Alberts v Devine, 395 Mass 59, 479 NE2d 113, cert denied, Carroll v Alberts, 474 U.S. 1013 (1985)

16. MacDonald v Clinger 84 AD2d 482, 446 NYS2d 801 (NY App Div 1982)

17. Sargent DA: Viewpoint: loose lips. Psychiatric News, October 18, 1985, pp 2, 16

18. Weiss BD: Confidentiality expectations of patients, physicians and medical students. JAMA 247:2695–2697, 1982

19. Holder AR: Minors' rights to consent to medical care. JAMA 257:3400–3402, 1987

20. Sloan JB, Hall B: Confidentiality of psychotherapeutic records. J Leg Med 5:435–467, 1984

21. Me Rev Stat Ann tit 22:4011(L) (1986); 62 Maryland Op Att'y Gen 157 (1977); or Rev Stat § 40.225, 40.295 (1986)

22. Nagle v Hooks, 296 Md 123, 460 A2d 49 (1983)

23. Kuder A: Legal Alert: Treatment and Consent. Washington Psychiatric Society Newsletter, Summer 1986, pp 8–9

24. Gary v Gary, 631 SW2d 781 (Tex Ct App 1982)

25. Texas Fam Code Ann § 14.08 (C) (I) (Vernon 1990)

26. In re B, 482 Pa 471, 394 A2d 419 (1978)

27. Slovenko R: Forensic psychiatry, in Comprehensive Textbook of Psychiatry IV. Edited by Kaplan HI, Sadock BJ. Baltimore, MD, Williams & Wilkins, 1985, p 1986

28. Marvit RC: You and the law: problem areas. Psychiatric News, April 2, 1982, p 12

29. Whitree v State, 56 Misc 2d 693, 290 NYS2d 486, 489–499 (1968)

30. Abille v United States, 482 F Supp 703, 708 (ND Cal 1980)

31. Brakel SJ, Parry J, Weiner BA: The Mentally Disabled and the Law. Chicago, IL, American Bar Foundation, 1985, pp 574–575

32. Bartlett v Danti, No 83-453-Appeal (RI Jan 14, 1986)
33. Bromberg J, Hirsh HL: Medical records and hospital reports. Medical Law 1:253–272, 1982
34. Reisner R: Law and the Mental Health System. St Paul, MN, West Publishing, 1985, p 244
35. Illinois Stat Ann 91-1/2, 802, § 2(4)(iii) (Smith-Hurd Supp 1985); DC Code § 6-2003
36. American Psychiatric Association: Opinions of the Ethics Committee on the Principles of Medical Ethics With Annotations Especially Applicable to Psychiatry. Washington, DC, American Psychiatric Association, 1989
37. Slovenko R: The hazards of writing or disclosing information in psychiatry. Behavioral Sciences and the Law 1:109–127, 1983
38. Thoren J: The physician-patient privilege. Medical Trial Technique Quarterly 29:61–78, 1982
39. Goldstein RL: Psychiatric poetic license? Post-mortem disclosures of confidential information in the Anne Sexton case. Psychiatric Annals (in press)
40. American Psychiatric Association Committee on Confidentiality: Guidelines on confidentiality. Am J Psychiatry 144:1522–1526, 1987

Chapter 5

Somatic Therapies ───────

Modern psychiatry primarily relies on two distinct treatment approaches: biological intervention and psychological intervention. Biological procedures are typically referred to as *somatic* or *organic* therapies because they act upon the biochemistry of the brain to produce a change in mood or behavior. This class of treatments involves two basic forms: psychopharmacotherapy (i.e., medication) and shock treatment (chemical and electrical).

Psychopharmacotherapy

Major Medication Classes

The primary form of somatic intervention used by psychiatrists is drug therapy. Under the broad heading of "psychopharmacology" are the *psychotropic drugs,* which are chemical agents that have an altering impact on the brain and its various functions. The impact that psychotropic medication has had on psychiatric medicine is immeasurable. For instance, the number of patients requiring institutionalization because of the lack of viable treatment alternatives has been greatly reduced over the past 25 years because of the discovery and refinement of various psychotropic drugs. While enormous social, political, and economic pressures have led to increased awareness of the abysmal conditions and circumstances frequently associated with the institutional care and treatment of psychiatrically ill patients, much credit must be given to the discovery and use of psychotropic medication. These drugs have proved effective, with many patients, in reducing the number and severity of acute psychotic episodes as well as maintaining stable thought and mood function over extended periods of time.

Notwithstanding the general benefits of medication in psychiatric practice, there are limitations. Foremost, psychotropic drugs may produce symptomatic improvement, but they **do not** completely alleviate or cure the disorder or illness (1). Also important is the recognition that not all patients respond favorably to a given medication, or even any medications. This may be true even when their symptoms are appropriate for the planned medication regimen. Finally, and possibly most distressing, is the fact that no medication is "risk free." All of the psychotropic medications have a wide range of side effects that are associated with acute and chronic use (2). These side effects are often, at a minimum, uncomfortable and irritating and can sometimes be permanently disabling (3) and even lethal (5).

The usefulness and effect of psychotropic medications can best be understood by the classification group they occupy. Each class of drugs tends to act upon a particular set of symptoms. A common division of the various psychotropic drugs is referred to as the *major tranquilizers* and the *minor tranquilizers*. The major tranquilizers are frequently referred to as *antipsychotic* or *neuroleptic* agents; their effects are both sedative and antipsychotic. Together with *antidepressants and antimanic drugs,* these three classes of medications comprise the primary group of psychotropics. This large group of drugs is "symptom specific"—that is, if taken by someone without the target mental illness (e.g., depression, psychosis), those individuals will not experience the therapeutic effect of the drug. For instance, a "normal" person taking an antipsychotic agent will experience no change in thought process, whereas a schizophrenic patient, for whose symptoms the drug is indicated, likely will.

A second general group of medications exists. These drugs include the *minor tranquilizers,* or *antianxiety agents, stimulants,* and *sedative-hypnotics.* Unlike the primary class of psychotropics, these medications are less symptom-specific and, therefore, produce their chemical effects regardless of the presence of a specific mental disorder. Because of this characteristic, they are prescribed to both mentally ill and nonmentally ill people and are much more commonly misused and abused than are the primary psychotropic agents.

Tardive Dyskinesia

The development of neuroleptic medications in the mid-1950s was heralded as a breakthrough in psychiatric medicine and a savior for thousands of chronically ill mental patients. However, in a relatively short period of time following the introduction of these medications as psychotropic agents, researchers and clinicians began to observe a variety of abnormal muscle movements in patients taking the medication (5). These abnormal movements were later referred to as *tardive dyskinesia* (sometimes abbreviated TD). Although identification of tardive dyskinesia was made early (6), widespread recognition and concern among clinicians took years to emerge. *Today, many medical and psychiatric researchers, clinicians, and*

*commentators consider tardive dyskinesia a major public health problem
(7). As a consequence, it is projected to be a significant source of future
malpractice litigation (8).*

Tardive dyskinesia is most commonly manifested by choreoathetoid
movements of the buccal, lingual, and facial muscles, but any muscle
group may be involved, and the dyskinesia may be myoclonic, dystonic,
tic-like, or ballistic (9). It is topographically indistinguishable from many
other neurological disorders of the basal ganglia, such as Parkinson's disease (10) and Huntington's chorea (11). The abnormal movements associated with tardive dyskinesia may range in severity from mild to severe and
occasionally can be life threatening (12).

Neuroleptic-produced dyskinesia may be transient and self-limiting or
persistent and irreversible (13). The diagnosis of tardive dyskinesia is
made on the basis of three indices: abnormal movements, the exclusion of
likely alternative causes of the dyskinesia (14), and a history of known
exposure to a precipitating medication (15). At the present time, there is
no definitive neurological sign or diagnostic test that will confirm the presence or absence of tardive dyskinesia. The diagnosis in individual cases is
sometimes unclear. Diagnosis is further complicated when dealing with
geriatric patients, because these patients are prone to developing *spontaneous oral-facial dyskinesia* (16). Moreover, schizophrenic and devel-
opmentally impaired patients, who frequently manifest abnormal
movements, stereotypies, posturing, and compulsive behaviors, also may
be difficult to assess (17).

The most effective treatment for tardive dyskinesia is gradual discontinuation of neuroleptic medication (18). In some patients, the symptoms of
tardive dyskinesia can be reversed if the precipitating medication is
stopped early enough. In others, symptoms persist or worsen despite discontinuation. The tapering and discontinuation of neuroleptics in order to
manage and treat signs of tardive dyskinesia create a medical dilemma for
the treating psychiatrist. If neuroleptics are discontinued or tapered below
therapeutic doses, patients may experience a relapse of their psychiatric
symptoms. For this reason, the decision to discontinue neuroleptic treatment must be made carefully and be individualized for each patient based
on such factors as past history of relapse and length and severity of the
tardive dyskinesia.

An alternative to complete discontinuation of neuroleptics is maintenance of the patient on the lowest effective therapeutic dose. While there
is currently no single satisfactory treatment for tardive dyskinesia, several
options are being researched with some individual success (19). At present,
the best advice in guarding against the development of tardive dyskinesia
is to think *prevention*. This would entail wise prescription practices, gradual tapering of neuroleptics, and careful monitoring for early symptoms of

tardive dyskinesia. If tardive dyskinesia is detected, various management strategies are recommended (20).

For clinicians with questions concerning tardive dyskinesia, several excellent texts are available (21). Also, the American Psychiatric Association (APA) Task Force report on tardive dyskinesia (22) continues to represent a respected summary of many of the primary issues and a source of sound, conservative guidelines for preventing and managing this condition. (The updated APA Task Force report on tardive dyskinesia will be available in early 1992.) Official guidelines, however, can never substitute for sound clinical judgment.

Electroconvulsive Therapy

Electroconvulsive therapy (ECT) is intended to alter the various emotional and mood states of a patient by creating a temporary grand mal seizure. There are three forms of shock treatment: electroconvulsive, insulin, and Metrazol. The latter two interventions are considered pharmacoconvulsive therapies and are not used today.

Electroconvulsive therapy is likely the most misunderstood and maligned treatment in psychiatry (23). Commentary in the popular press has depicted ECT as cruel, barbaric, and archaic. Nevertheless, a significant number of clinicians believe it to be one of the most humane and efficacious treatments for certain disorders that are available to psychiatrists (24).

In simple terms, the administration of ECT involves the induction of a grand mal seizure by means of a prescribed electrical pulse through the brain. Each treatment consists of the induction of a single seizure while the patient is under anesthesia. A course of ECT typically is comprised of several of these inductions. Given either bilaterally or unilaterally (25), once a patient appears to have achieved maximum therapeutic effect (i.e., when no further beneficial effect is determined), two to three additional administrations may be given in order to prevent early relapse.

Research and clinical trials have demonstrated that ECT can be useful with patients with endogenous depression, acute mania, and schizophrenia (26). The precise mechanism by which ECT exerts its therapeutic effect is presently not known, although numerous theories exist.

Numerous side effects have been reported with the use of ECT (27). The most common include memory loss, headaches, muscle aches, weight gain, amenorrhea, apnea, cardiac arrhythmia, systematic hypertension, and increased permeability of the blood-brain barrier.

Like any medical procedure, ECT has its risks that must be weighed with its anticipated benefits. However, with proper screening of patients and preparation these risks can be greatly reduced. For instance, the APA Task Force report, *The Practice of Electroconvulsive Therapy: Recommenda-*

tions for Treatment, Training, and Privileging," outlines a number of sound, conservative recommendations for the use of ECT (28). These recommendations address such topics as when ECT is indicated, informed consent implications and information, and administration considerations (pretreatment, treatment, and posttreatment). Official guidelines, however, cannot replace sound clinical judgment.

One final risk that a clinician should also consider is the risk of not using ECT when it is therapeutically indicated and all other appropriate interventions have been tried. It is the responsibility of the treating psychiatrist to see that every patient receive complete and accurate information about all viable treatment options, and not just the ones that the media has accepted.

Standard of Reasonable Care

The therapeutic use of somatic therapy, including ECT, is evaluated no differently than any other medical or psychiatric procedure with respect to its application and potential liability. The same general standard of ordinary and reasonable care will, therefore, govern the assessment of whether a psychiatrist's use or failure to use an organic intervention is actionable (29).

It is generally acknowledged within the psychiatric profession that there is no standard protocol for the administration of psychotropic medication or ECT. However, the existence of certain standards, procedures, and authoritative resources regularly accepted or used by a significant number of psychiatrists should alert clinicians to consider these resources as a reference and guide. The APA has published comprehensive guidelines in the form of Task Force reports concerning electroconvulsive therapy (28) and tardive dyskinesia (30). Both of these publications thoroughly review the professional literature available at the time of publication. As a result, a number of clinically sound administration, management, and follow-up procedures have been developed for using ECT and neuroleptic medication. It is important to note that "on their own," these or any other publications do not per se establish the standard of care by which a court might evaluate a psychiatrist's treatment. It could be argued, however, that they do represent a credible source of information that a reasonable psychiatrist should at least be familiar with and have considered (31).

There is some evidence that there is less autonomy and flexibility associated with the use of ECT. Normally, the "reasonable care" standard that is applied to psychiatric treatment is construed in a fairly broad manner because psychiatry is currently considered inexact. However, some psychiatric treatments such as ECT appear to be more rigidly regulated than others. For instance, the Joint Commission on Accreditation of Healthcare Organizations (JCAHO) considers ECT a special treatment procedure, requiring hospitals to have written, informed consent policies concerning its use (32). These standards, coupled with any specific regulations a facility might promulgate regarding ECT, could serve as the basis for liability if violated.

The "standard" for judging the use and administration of medication, on the other hand, appears to be consistent with the more flexible and general "reasonable care" requirement. Another information source that bears highlighting is the use of the *Physicians' Desk Reference* (PDR) to establish or dispute a psychiatrist's pharmacotherapy procedures. The PDR is a commercially distributed, privately published reference regarding medication products used in the United States. The Food and Drug Administration requires that drug manufacturers have their official package inserts reported in the PDR. Accordingly, in order to keep abreast of new medication treatments and provide patients with current and accurate medication information, psychiatrists should periodically consult publications like the PDR. **However, while numerous courts have cited the PDR as a credible source of medication-related information in the medical profession (33), it is not generally viewed as establishing *the* standard of care.** Instead, the PDR may be used as one piece of evidence to support what the standard of care in a particular situation might be (34). The PDR or any other reference cannot be used as a substitute for the clinician's judgment:

> Psychiatrists are themselves responsible for making informed decisions, taking into account their own clinical experience and the relevant literature. They also must be prepared to justify their decisions based on professional standards. Since the *PDR* is not an official medical practice text, patient care may be compromised if clinicians view the *PDR* as their primary source of professional guidance, rather than the professional literature and the usual community standards of practice. In essence, the *PDR* should be considered as *one* of several sources of information that a psychiatrist can rely upon for making medication decisions. (35)

In general, the exercise of reasonable care with either ECT or psychotropic medication should involve, *at a minimum,* some variation of the following considerations and measures:

Pretreatment

- ❖ Clinical history (e.g., medical, psychological)
- ❖ Physical examination
- ❖ Administration of necessary laboratory tests and review of past test results
- ❖ Disclosure of sufficient information to obtain informed consent, including information regarding the consequences of *not* being treated

❖ Thorough documentation of all decisions, informed consent information, patient responses, and any other relevant treatment data

Posttreatment

❖ Careful monitoring of the patient's response to treatment, including frequent patient interviews and appropriate laboratory testing
❖ Prompt adjustments in treatment, as needed
❖ Continual obtaining of informed consent when appreciably altering
treatment or initiating new treatment

Legal Liability

Informed Consent

The legal duty to exercise reasonable care in selecting and administering
somatic procedures and treatments **always** includes obtaining the competent patient's *informed consent* before proceeding with the treatment. Incompetent patients require the consent of substitute decision-makers. In
certain situations, circumscribed exceptions to informed consent requirements exist (36).

The term *informed consent* is a legal principle in medical jurisprudence
that requires that a physician disclose to a patient sufficient information
that will enable the patient to make an "informed" decision about a proposed treatment or procedure (37). The failure of a psychiatrist to adequately provide a patient with this information can subject him or her to
liability for any injury that is proximally caused by this omission. Liability
for a failure to obtain a patient's informed consent is based upon the mate-
rialization of certain inherent risks of the treatment about which the patient
should have been forewarned. **The fact that the contemplated procedure was the most appropriate or best treatment possible or was not
administered negligently is immaterial.**

The theory of informed consent as a cause of action is grounded in the
belief that *every person has a right to determine and control what is to be
done to his or her body.* This principle is clearly described in the much
celebrated case *Schloendorff v. New York Hospital:*

> Every human being of adult years and sound mind has a right to deter-
> mine what shall be done with his own body; and a surgeon who performs
> an operation without his patient's consent commits (a battery) for which
> he is liable in damages. (38)

In addition to safeguarding a patient's right to self-determination, other
functions served by informed consent (39) include the following:

1. The promotion of individual autonomy

2. The protection of the patient's status as a human being
3. The avoidance of fraud and duress
4. The encouragement of self-regulation by the physician
5. The fostering of rational decision making
6. The involvement of the public (e.g., patient) in medical matters

In order for a patient's consent to be considered informed, it must adequately address three essential elements: **information, competency, and voluntariness.** In general, the patient must be given *adequate information* in which to make a truly knowing decision, and that decision (consent) must be made *voluntarily* by a person who is *legally competent.* Each of these elements must be adequately met or any consent given will not be considered informed and legally valid (40).

Information.   By far, the information requirement is the most difficult for psychiatrists and other physicians to meet. The threshold question— How much (information) should a patient be provided and by what standard will that disclosure be judged?—has consumed the medical and legal community for years.

When the principle of informed consent was first conceived and applied in practice, courts generally regarded the standard of disclosure (e.g., the test by which the adequacy of a psychiatrist's disclosure was measured) much the same way it did the standard of care in malpractice cases. Typically, it was held that the extent of a physician's duty to disclose was judged by the standards of the profession (41). For example, a psychiatrist's disclosure of information regarding the efficacy of a particular medication or the risks of ECT would be measured by what was commonly disclosed by other psychiatrists in that community. Commonly referred to as the "majority rule" or "medical community standard," courts typically were willing to defer to the profession itself, because it was generally felt that the medical community was in the best position to judge what risks and information warranted disclosure (42).

This position was severely challenged in 1972 by the landmark case *Canterbury v. Spence* (43). The Court of Appeals for the District of Columbia soundly rejected the medical community standard and instead adopted a standard based on what a "reasonable" patient might consider "material" to the decision to consent or not. The Court's repudiation of the traditional standard was based on its lack of faith that a cognizable medical standard for disclosure existed, the subjectiveness of the medical standard, and the incompatibility of regulating the rights of patients based on the opinions of third parties (e.g., physicians). In an effort to redirect the right of self-determination away from the doctor and back to the patient, the court fashioned a standard of disclosure that focused on how material a piece of information was to a patient's consent:

Thus the test for determining whether a particular peril must be divulged is its materiality to the patient's decision: all risks potentially affecting the decision must be unmasked. And to safeguard the patient's interest in achieving his own determination on treatment, the law must itself set the standard for adequate disclosure. (44)

The court then went on to say:

From these considerations we derive the breadth of the disclosures of risks legally to be required. The scope of the standard is not subjective as to either the physician or the patient; it remains objective with due regard for the patient's informational needs and with suitable leeway for the physician's situation. In broad outline, we agree that: [a] risk is thus *material* when a reasonable person, in what the physician knows or should know to be the patient's position, would likely attach significance to the risk or cluster of risks in deciding whether or not to forego the proposed therapy. (45)

After the holding of *Canterbury,* now considered the majority view, physicians were concerned that this new standard required them to disclose to a patient every minute risk associated with a treatment in order to avoid being sued. Such fears are exaggerated and distort the intent of the law. A patient's consent will usually be considered informed if the patient or a bona fide representative is given an adequate description of the intervention. An adequate description details the risk, benefits, and prognosis both *with* and *without* the treatment or procedure. The patient must voluntarily consent to or refuse the proposed treatment. There are four exceptions to the requirement of informed consent from the patient: 1) incapacity of the patient, 2) emergencies, 3) therapeutic privilege, and 4) waiver (46). If the patient lacks sufficient mental capacity, consent must be given by a substitute decision-maker (47).

There is generally no set form, outline, or list of information to be disclosed for any given medical or psychiatric situation. As a rule, however, psychiatrists should fashion what they tell a patient about a procedure around five general areas:

1. *Diagnosis:* clear, understandable description of the condition or problem
2. *Treatment:* overview description of the nature and purpose of the proposed treatment or procedure
3. *Risks and benefits:* description of the most likely risks and benefits of the proposed treatment or procedure *and* of any potential risks that the patient has expressed or implied a concern about *or* might want to know about
4. *Alternate treatment:* description of the risks and benefits of viable alternative treatments to the one being proposed, *including the choice of doing nothing*

5. *Prognosis:* likely or projected outcome if the treatment is accepted *and* if it is not accepted

As mentioned in previous sections, psychiatrists who plan to use neuroleptic drug treatment or ECT are advised to at least consider the disclosure information outlined in the two APA Task Force reports (48). Moreover, with new developments in psychopharmacological research constantly being published, it is always within the psychiatrist's (and patient's) best interest to become familiar with this information and then appropriately communicate it to the patient.

Competency.   Only a *competent* person is legally recognized as being able to give informed consent. For psychiatrists, because of their work with patients who sometimes are of questionable competence because of mental illness, this can be a particularly important issue. The law presumes that a person is competent unless judicially determined to be incompetent or unless the person has been incapacitated by a medical condition or emergency. It is important for clinicians to bear in mind that the mere fact that a person is being treated for a mental illness (49) or institutionalized (50) *does not* automatically render him or her incompetent. Accordingly, a psychiatrist has a duty to make a reasonably complete and fair disclosure of the risks of treatment and to obtain, in most situations, a psychiatric patient's informed consent prior to the imposition of treatment (51).

From a legal perspective, the term competency is narrowly defined in terms of *cognitive* capacity. There are no established set criteria for determining a patient's competence. In fact, some authors have likened "the search for a single test of competency" as "a search for a holy grail" (52). Physicians and psychiatrists should, however, ensure that at a minimum the patient is capable of 1) understanding the particular treatment being offered (53), 2) making a discernable decision, one way or another, regarding the treatment that has been offered (54), and 3) communicating, verbally or nonverbally, that decision (55). The problem with this standard is that it obtains a simple consent from the patient rather than an informed consent because alternative treatment choices are not provided. A review of case law and scholarly literature reveals four standards for determining incompetency in decision making (56). In order of levels of mental capacity required, these standards include 1) communication of choice, 2) understanding of information provided, 3) appreciation of one's available options, and 4) rational decision making. Psychiatrists feel most comfortable with a rational decision-making standard in determining incompetency. Most courts, however, prefer the first two standards. A truly informed consent reflecting the patient's autonomy and personal needs and values occurs when rational decision making is applied to the risks and benefits of appropriate treatment options provided to the patient by the clinician.

Mental patients who have been determined to lack the requisite competency to make a treatment decision, except usually in cases of an emergency (57), will have an authorized representative or guardian appointed to make medical decisions on their behalf (58).

Voluntariness. The element of voluntariness requires that a patient's consent must be given freely and without the presence of any form of duress, coercion, or fraud. Courts, when evaluating this aspect of a patient's consent, will commonly look closely at all of the circumstances that surrounded the decision-making process. Factors such as the psychiatrist's choice of words in explaining the procedure, manner, environmental state, and the patient's mental state will all likely be examined. As an example, making a patient's participation in a favorite activity (e.g., going to the hospital snack shop) contingent upon providing consent to a treatment would be considered coercive (58).

Consent of Minors

Traditionally, minors have been considered by the law to be incompetent for most purposes, including the right to make treatment decisions (59). The mental health professional must obtain the consent of the parent or legal guardian. However, statutory and judicial exceptions exist to this rule. Mental health professionals should acquaint themselves with the law in their jurisdiction.

The "law of adolescence" is evolving. Historically, the legal status of all minors from age 7 to 17 was considered the same. Currently, the rights of a 15- to 17-year-old are not the same as those of a 6-year-old. These changes are reflected in the United States Supreme Court holding that state statutes providing for parental permission in abortion decisions of pregnant teenagers are unconstitutional. In addition, all states by statute allow young people to consent to treatment for venereal disease. Most states permit young people to secure birth control devices without parental notification. States are beginning to lower the age of medical consent from 18 to 14 or 15 (60). Because of an alarming rise in venereal disease, alcohol and drug abuse, and teenage pregnancies, "enabling laws" have been passed by states providing minors with access to medical care without parental approval (61).

Exception exists for emergencies and in most states is an extension of that provided for adults. A few states narrowly apply this exception if the delay in treatment would result in death or serious injury (62). Exception for the physician's judgment is made in some states, allowing treatment if the delay in obtaining parental consent would, in the physician's judgment, endanger the health of the minor (59). Exception also exists for the emancipated minor who is no longer under parental control. Marriage or military service always emancipates a minor. Age, residence, financial indepen-dence, property ownership, pregnancy, or parenthood also will be consid-ered by the court in determining the appropriate status. More than half the states, through emancipation statutes, give minors the right to make treat-ment decisions if certain criteria are met.

The mature minor exception allows treating a minor on his or her own consent in those cases in which the minor demonstrates capacity to appre-ciate the nature, extent, and consequences of medical treatment (63). Al-though every state has not adopted the mature minor exception, physicians have not been held liable for treating minors over 15 years old. Annas (64) states that "no court in recent history has found any health care provider liable for treating a minor over 15 years old without parental consent, where the minor has consented to his own care."

In the involuntary hospitalization of minors, the United States Supreme Court in *Parham v J.R.* (65) held that in addition to prescribed state law procedures, the federal due-process clause requires review of a parental decision to commit a minor child by an independent and neutral physician. However, the court rejected the claim that the due-process clause necessi-tates more rigorous procedural safeguards.

Electroconvulsive Therapy

Areas of Negligence

While a significant proportion of psychiatrists believe ECT is a viable treat-ment for certain mental disorders (66), it has been estimated that *no more* than 3% to 5% of all psychiatric inpatients in the United States receive it (67). As can be expected from these figures, the potential number of legal actions alleging negligence associated with ECT is likely to be low. Com-mentators who have reported on the incidence of ECT-related malpractice suits have corroborated this suspicion (69).

Despite this low potential, occasional lawsuits are filed, and a brief review of some of these cases is at least instructive. Medical malpractice can be defined as any act or failure to act by a physician (e.g., psychiatrist) that is not in accord with the degree of "skill and learning ordinarily pos-sessed and exercised, under similar circumstances, by the members of his profession in good standing" (69), and that is the direct or proximate cause of the patient's injuries.

Cases involving ECT-related injuries have represented a variety of cir-cumstances in which negligence has occurred. These cases can be catego-rized into three groups: pretreatment, treatment, and posttreatment.

Pretreatment.   Before the administration of any procedure, but espe-cially one with potentially serious risks involved, a psychiatrist has an ethical, professional, and legal responsibility to properly prepare his or her patient. This includes, but would not be limited to, 1) obtaining all necessary information about the patient and the proposed procedure (e.g., patient's records, lab reports, and the professional literature) in order to select the most appropriate treatment for the patient's problem; 2) having the patient properly evaluated; and 3) adequately explaining the nature and risks of the procedure and then obtaining the patient's informed consent.

Failure to adequately conduct one of these pretreatment procedures could endanger the welfare of the patient and may result in a lawsuit for negligence. The following outlines some of the grounds on which a lawsuit involving ECT might be based:

❖ Failure to provide adequate informed consent (70)
❖ Failure to adequately screen a patient in order to determine whether he or she is a suitable candidate for ECT
❖ Breach of a guarantee or warranty that ECT was "perfectly safe," despite the knowledge that various risks are associated with the procedure (71)

Treatment. It is well established in the law that a psychiatrist will not be held liable for a mere mistake in judgment, nor will he or she be held to a standard of 100% accuracy or perfect performance (72). Consequently, a bad result (e.g., a patient injury) does not automatically establish a claim for malpractice (73). Instead, a patient must prove, by a preponderance of the evidence, that the physician deviated from the standard of care and that deviation proximately caused the patient some injury or damage (73). The procedure for evaluating the care and treatment afforded a patient when ECT is used is no different. Cases involving ECT-related injuries in which the negligence has centered around the actual treatment process include the following:

❖ Failure to use a muscle relaxant to reduce the chance of a bone fracture (74)
❖ Negligent administration of the procedure (75)
❖ Failure to conduct an evaluation of patient, including the use of X-rays, before continuing treatment (76)

Posttreatment. It is not uncommon for patients being treating with ECT to experience side effects such as temporary confusion, disorientation, and memory loss following its administration (77). Because of this temporary debilitating effect, sound clinical practice requires that the psychiatrist provide reasonable posttreatment care and safeguards. Courts have held in several cases that the failure to properly attend to a patient for a period of time following the administration of ECT can result in action for malpractice (78). The following outlines some of the posttreatment circumstances in which negligence may occur:

❖ Failure to evaluate complaints of pain or discomfort following treatment
❖ Failure to evaluate a patient's condition before resuming ECT treatments (79)
❖ Failure to properly monitor a patient in order to prevent falls (80)
❖ Failure to properly supervise a patient who had been injured as a result of ECT (80)

As a source of civil liability, ECT-related lawsuits today are quite rare and not likely to represent a significant problem area for clinical psychiatrists. But, as Perlin correctly points out, "recent developments in right-to-refuse treatment law and statutory regulation of intrusive therapy are likely to insure that any future ECT litigation will still be considered carefully" (81).

Medication

Common Areas of Malfeasance and Nonfeasance

The potential for negligence by a psychiatrist would appear to be greatest in clinical situations involving psychotropic medication. This is in large part due to the frequency in which drugs are used in psychiatric practice and the variety of risks and side effects inherently associated with their use. While no reliable compilation of malpractice claims data exists, anecdotal information suggests that medication-related lawsuits do constitute a significant share of the litigation filed against psychiatrists. For example, insurance data collected by the Medical Protective Company revealed that medication-related injuries constituted 20% of the total claims against psychiatrists between 1980 and 1985 (82). Similar figures are reported by the APA's insurance committee (83) and other commentators studying the incidence of psychiatric malpractice claims (84).

A review of the relevant case law indicates that there are a variety of mistakes, omissions, and poor treatment practices that commonly result in a malpractice action against a psychiatrist or physician. The following summary, while not exhaustive, should provide a workable framework for identifying problem areas associated with medication treatment.

Failure to properly evaluate: negligent diagnosis.   Sound clinical practice requires that before any form of somatic treatment is initiated, the patient should be properly examined. The nature and extent of an examination is largely dictated by the type of treatment being contemplated. At the very minimum, a physical examination, if indicated, as well as a clinical history and mental status examination, should be conducted. This will not only provide useful information about the patient's complaints but also alert the physician to any physical or emotional limitations. Moreover, the duty to ensure that proper informed consent is obtained can also be fulfilled at this time. Many psychiatrists do not perform physical examinations upon their patients. Recent medical examinations performed by other physicians or referral of the patient for a medical evaluation ordinarily suffices.

Numerous lawsuits have resulted from a physician's or psychiatrist's failure to properly evaluate a patient before administering psychotropic medication (85). As a result of this negligence, if the patient's condition is misdiagnosed, he or she may remain untreated and subject to unnecessary and unconsented side effects and risks. In the case of *Chambers v. Ingram* (86), an inmate filed a lawsuit against a psychologist following the wrongful prescription of haloperidol. Pretending to be suicidal, in order to be protected against violence by several other inmates, the inmate was first seen by the defendant psychologist. The psychologist then referred the inmate to a consulting psychiatrist, who met briefly with him. Following this meeting, the psychiatrist prescribed doxepin and hydroxyzine. A few days later, the psychologist again contacted the consulting psychiatrist, indicating that the inmate-patient was experiencing a number of ill effects from the medication. The psychiatrist subsequently prescribed haloperidol. The inmate experienced a number of significant adverse effects from the haloperidol. He complained about the problems he was having, but nothing was done. A lawsuit, alleging a variety of acts of negligence, was filed against the psychologist for physical and emotional injuries. At trial, the psychiatrist testified that in prescribing the haloperidol he had relied on the information provided by the psychologist. The jury concluded that the psychologist, who was the inmate's primary health care provider, had breached the standard of care by 1) failing to conduct a thorough mental status examination during the initial interview, 2) failing to make a detailed report of the interview containing impressions and bases for diagnosis, 3) failing to report all information about the inmate's alleged suicidal tendencies to the psychiatrist, 4) failing to record all courses of treatment in his daily treatment notes, and 5) failing to recognize when the medication prescribed was not consistent with his recorded observations and then passing this information to the consulting psychiatrist.

In *Osheroff v. Chestnut Lodge* (87), long-term psychotherapy was prescribed for a patient suffering from a major depression. After approximately 7 months, the patient's psychiatric condition had considerably worsened. The plaintiff was transferred to another hospital, where antidepressant medication was started. Improvement occurred rapidly. An arbitration panel found for the plaintiff. Both sides, however, exercised their right to a trial. Before trial, the case was settled for an undisclosed amount. The treatment of a psychiatric disorder exclusively by psychotherapy when proven, effective biological treatments exist can bring a suit for negligent treatment if the patient's condition remains unimproved or worsens. An intense debate involving biologic versus psychodynamic treatment in psychiatry continues to rage (88, 89).

Failure to monitor or supervise: negligent treatment. Once psychotropic medication has been prescribed to a patient, it is the physician's duty to monitor or supervise the patient's physical and emotional responses. It is a common practice in psychiatric medicine to change a patient's medication several times in order to determine which medication provides the best therapeutic effectiveness. In order to make such a determination, as well as safeguard against a patient suffering from prolonged medication side effects, it is necessary that periodic monitoring take place. This monitoring may require the use of laboratory testing, repeated physical examinations, and direct interviewing of the patient and other reliable parties. A failure to properly supervise the use of psychotropic medication can unnecessarily subject patients to harmful side effects and delay changing to a more effective treatment. If a patient is harmed from this form of negligence, a malpractice action might result (90).

The case of *McManus v. St. Josephs Hospital Corporation* provides a good illustration (91). The plaintiff alleged that the hospital, through its residents and interns, negligently prescribed unsupervised doses of tranquilizers and antidepressants that led to the development of a drug dependency. The former patient argued that this dependency caused him to lose past and future wages, led to the breakup of his marriage, and caused him mental anguish and humiliation. A jury agreed with the plaintiff's arguments and awarded him $750,000. The defendant subsequently filed an appeal disputing not the claim of negligence, but the alleged excessiveness of the award.

Negligent prescription practices: negligent treatment. The selection of a medication, initial dosage, form of administration, and other related procedures are all decisions left to the sound discretion of the treating psychiatrist. The law recognizes that the doctor is in the best position to "know his or her patient" and to determine what course of treatment is best under the circumstances. Accordingly, the standard by which a psychiatrist's prescription practices will be evaluated is whether they are reasonable. In administering psychotropic medication, a psychiatrist need only conform his or her procedures and decision making to that which is *ordinarily* practiced by other psychiatrists under similar circumstances (92).

Looking at the case law that has involved allegations of negligent prescription procedures, there are several common practices highlighted that represent fairly serious deviations in acceptable treatment practice. These include the following:

- ❖ Exceeding recommended dosages and then failing to adjust the medication level to therapeutic levels (93)
- ❖ Negligent mixing of drugs, or "polypharmacy" (94)
- ❖ Prescribing medication for unapproved uses (95)
- ❖ Prescribing "unapproved" medications

Failure to disclose medication effects: informed consent. As stated earlier, any physician who prescribes medication has a duty to explain the purpose, action, and risks of the drug, within reason and as circumstances permit. This is especially true of psychiatrists, because their patients may have a diminished cognitive capacity because of mental illness, physical or psychological trauma, or organic impairment.

It is important to also keep in mind that every time a medication is changed and a new drug is introduced, informed consent must be obtained. A failure to properly inform a patient of the risks and consequences of ingesting a medication is ample grounds for a malpractice action if the patient is injured as a result (96). In the case of *Kirk v. Michael Reese Hospital and Medical Center* (97), an automobile passenger was severely injured in an accident with another driver, whose ability to drive was impaired because of fluphenazine and chlorpromazine that had been prescribed by the defendant. An Illinois court ruled that the passenger was entitled to maintain an action for his injuries against the hospital, the physicians who had medicated the driver, and the manufacturer of the drugs on the theory that each had negligently *failed to warn the driver of the drugs' adverse effects.* The vehicular accident, the court ruled, was sufficiently foreseeable for the defendants to have known that in the absence of adequate warning, an injury to the patient or members of society could have resulted.

Other areas of negligence involving medication that have resulted in legal action include failure to treat side effects once they have been recognized or should have been recognized (98); failure to monitor a patient's compliance with prescription limits (99); failure to prescribe medication or appropriate levels of medication when treatment needs called for it (100); failure to refer a patient for consultation or treatment by a specialist (101); and negligent withdrawal from a medication (102).

Tardive Dyskinesia Case Law

The introduction of neuroleptic drugs in the mid-1950s produced a tremendous advance in patient management and treatment. Shortly after the introduction of these drugs as therapeutic agents, however, researchers and clinicians observed unusual muscle movements, later referred to as *tardive dyskinesia,* in patients being treated with neuroleptic medication. In addition to the treatment and public health concerns that this condition represents, it has the *potential* for becoming one of the largest areas of liability to face psychiatrists.

Numerically, the number of psychiatric patients being treated with neuroleptics is quite high (103). It is estimated that at least 10% to 20% of patients (104), and as high as 50% of patients (in- and outpatients) (105), exposed to neuroleptic drugs for more than a year exhibit some degree of probable tardive dyskinesia. This estimate is projected to be even higher for elderly patients (106). Given these data, the potential for a flood of litigation due to tardive dyskinesia appears obvious. In fact, several commentators have made such predictions (107). Surprisingly, there have been relatively few lawsuits *reported* in the case law literature to date (108).

Several reasons for this dearth of reported lawsuits are suggested. First, chronically ill patients who develop tardive dyskinesia may be unaware that a possible legal recourse is available to them. Second, even if mentally ill patients are aware of the potential for recovery, they may be legally barred from seeking recovery on the grounds that the statute of limitations has run out (109). Third, it is not uncommon for a patient to have been treated by several different doctors in several different facilities. Determining who caused the tardive dyskinesia can be quite a problem. Fourth, lawsuits involving tardive dyskinesia are relatively difficult to prove, costly to litigate, and not currently enjoying wide appeal in the court system. As a result, plaintiffs' lawyers have not yet demonstrated a significant interest in pursuing these cases.

Cases that involve allegations of negligence which result in a patient developing tardive dyskinesia are based on the same legal elements as any other malpractice action. Moreover, the bases for negligence mirror those that had previously been identified with general medication cases. These areas include, but are not limited to, 1) failure to properly evaluate a patient, and 2) negligent diagnosis of a patient's condition.

For instance, in the case of *Hyde v. University of Michigan Board of Regents* (110), a woman was awarded one million dollars against a medical center for misdiagnosing her condition as Huntington's chorea instead of tardive dyskinesia. This verdict was later reversed on the basis of a subsequent case that expanded the state's sovereign immunity coverage (111).

Wrongful prescription of neuroleptic medication.   In *Dovido v. Vasquez* (112), a net award of $700,000 went to a 42-year-old plaintiff who suffered from tardive dyskinesia as a result of the defendant-psychiatrist's negligent prescription of extremely high doses of fluphenazine. However, unreported cases such as *Dovido v. Vasquez* have *very* limited precedential value.

The indiscriminate use of neuroleptics occurs when these drugs are prescribed for nonindicated disorders. The APA Task Force on Tardive

Dyskinesia (48) presents clear indications for the prescribing of neuroleptics. Nevertheless certain patients, particularly patients with borderline personality disorder, may respond favorably to neuroleptics even though clear indications for the use of neuroleptics in these patients may not exist (113). Sound clinical judgment that includes detailed knowledge of the patient should take precedence over official treatment guidelines. The psychiatrist, though, should be aware of official guidelines.

Failure to monitor medication side effects.   In *Clites v. State of Iowa* (114), the plaintiff was a mentally retarded man who had been institutionalized since age 11. He had been treated with major tranquilizers from ages 18 to 23. Tardive dyskinesia was diagnosed at age 23, and the plaintiff subsequently sued. The parents claimed that the defendants had negligently prescribed medication, had not informed them of the potential of developing tardive dyskinesia resulting from the medications the plaintiff was being given, and failed to monitor and subsequently treat resulting side effects. The jury returned a verdict for the plaintiff and awarded damages in the amount of $760,165. This award was affirmed on appeal.

The court ruled that the defendants were negligent because they deviated from the standards of the "industry." Specifically, they cited a variety of omissions in common psychiatric practice that reasonable psychiatrists would not have omitted. Among the "deviations" noted were the failure to conduct regular physical examinations and laboratory tests; the failure to intervene at the first sign of tardive dyskinesia; the inappropriate use of multiple medications at the same time; the use of drugs for convenience (e.g., "behavior management") rather than therapy; and the failure to obtain the parents' informed consent.

Other areas of negligence.   Other areas of negligence that have been identified in the tardive dyskinesia case law include 1) failure to obtain informed consent (115), and 2) failure to treat side effects once they are recognized or when they should have been recognized (116).

The defenses and preventive measures applicable to malpractice claims involving tardive dyskinesia are consistent with those used in any case alleging negligent drug treatment. In general, the application of sound clinical practice that is appropriately communicated to the patient and documented in the treatment chart will serve as an effective foil to any allegation of negligence should tardive dyskinesia appear to develop (117).

Conclusions: Projected Trends and Recommendations

Medication-related issues constitute the greatest potential of injury to patients. While the use of ECT does pose some risks, these are far more manageable than those related to psychotropic medication. Moreover, the number of patients annually receiving ECT as opposed to receiving some form of psychotropic medication is infinitesimal.

Interestingly, while tardive dyskinesia was first "officially" recognized around 1960, it is projected that prior to the landmark *Clites v. Iowa* decision in 1982 (118), there probably was little, if any, litigation related to tardive dyskinesia. A review of the few early studies investigating the incidence of malpractice actions against psychiatrists seems to support this conclusion because there was no mention of lawsuits involving injuries related to tardive dyskinesia (119).

Times have changed, however, and the potential for increased tardive dyskinesia litigation is present. The prevalence of tardive dyskinesia is estimated to range from 15% to 33% of chronically treated patients (120). When this figure is coupled with the estimate that no less than 3,000,000 people are currently taking neuroleptics and that over 900,000 new patients receive neuroleptics each year (121), the potential for new tardive dyskinesia cases each year is substantial. The vast majority of important tardive dyskinesia litigation has come in the context of equity rather than malpractice cases (e.g., injunction, mandatory relief such as in the case of *Rennie v Klein* [122]).

Since 1973, the Food and Drug Administration has required manufacturers of neuroleptics to include a warning about tardive dyskinesia in the package insert (123). Also in 1973, the American College of Neuropsychopharmacology issued guidelines for the management of tardive dyskinesia (124). In 1979, the APA published the results of its task force report concerning tardive dyskinesia (125). Despite all of these warnings and guidelines for prevention of this condition, no appreciable decline in the number of neuroleptic prescriptions each year has been reported (126).

Sound, conservative treatment practices remain the best means of preventing tardive dyskinesia. The APA Task Force report (125), although now dated in terms of current research, still remains a reliable source of preventive management information. (The updated APA Task Force report on tardive dyskinesia will be available in early 1992.) Obviously, providing neuroleptic drugs at the lowest dosages consistent with good clinical care is axiomatic (127).

Patients requiring high doses of neuroleptics for prolonged periods of time are at a substantially increased risk for tardive dyskinesia. Risk-benefit judgments favoring such drug regimens will go a long way in providing clinically sound treatment and diminishing the threat of successful lawsuits. Guttmacher (128) offers a number of reasonable, pragmatic, and sound approaches to pharmacological decision making:

❖ Document those signs and symptoms that are amenable to pharmacotherapy and are useful indicators of the patient's overall clinical state.

❖ Establish a meaningful set of differential diagnoses.

❖ Obtain a detailed drug history.

❖ Do not begin drug treatment before completing the first three steps. The only exception should be for frank emergencies, and these are decidedly rare.

❖ If the patient is taking clinically significant doses of medication that are not causing toxicity when first encountered, then continue the medication while you are performing your initial evaluation.

❖ Whenever possible, avoid changing more than one variable at a time.

❖ Within a group of drugs, you must prescribe on the basis of side effects; no convincing data exist to support differences in efficacy.

❖ Establishing a dose is done by titrating benefit versus toxicity.

❖ Psychotropics are used to treat symptoms, not diseases.

❖ Avoid medications that can obscure the collection of valuable data.

❖ Enlist your patients in a collegial fashion in fighting their illness.

❖ Compliance is one of the most difficult problems in psychopharmacology.

❖ Consider cost when prescribing.

❖ Avoid polypharmacy.

❖ Never use a fixed-combination drug.

❖ Dealing with an acute episode is different from prophylaxis.

❖ Do not try to learn all of the psychotropic agents.

❖ Maintain a healthy skepticism of new products and prescription trends.

❖ There are no rules.

This last suggestion underscores that no official guidelines or recommendations by medical authorities can ever take the place of the practitioner's sound clinical judgment combined with a detailed clinical knowledge of the patient.

These suggestions not only will facilitate sound clinical treatment but will serve as evidence of "reasonable" care, if the question of negligence ever arises. However, it cannot be overemphasized that the treating psychiatrist has the ultimate responsibility for deciding what the medical needs of the patient are and the best way to address them, given the surrounding circumstances. Reliance on set or fixed formulae of precautions and procedures may result in the provision of substandard care. Therefore, every treatment situation should be addressed on a case-by-case basis.

References

1. Guttmacher LB: Concise Guide to Somatic Therapies in Psychiatry. Washington, DC, American Psychiatric Press, 1988, p 3
2. Crammer J, Barraclough B, Heine B: The Use of Drugs in Psychiatry. London, Royal College of Psychiatrists, 1982, pp 123–210

3. Kane JM, Smith JM: Tardive dyskinesia: prevalence and risk factors, 1959–1979. Arch Gen Psychiatry 39:473–481, 1982

4. Levenson JL: Neuroleptic malignant syndrome. Am J Psychiatry 142:1137–1145, 1985

5. Uhrbrand L, Faurbye A: Reversible and irreversible dyskinesia after treatment with phenothiazines, chlorpromazine, reserpine, ECT treatment. Psychopharmacologia 1:408–418, 1960

6. Schonecker M: Ein eigentumliches Syndrom im oralen Bereich bei Magaphen Applikation [A peculiar syndrome in oral region as a result of the administration of Megaphen]. Nervenarzt 28:35, 1957

7. Crane GE: Clinical pharmacology in its 20th year. Science 181:124–128, 1973; American College of Neuropharmacology–Food and Drug Administration Task Force: Neurologic syndromes associated with antipsychotic drug use. N Engl J Med 289:20–23, 1973; Gardos G, Cole JO: Overview: public health issues in tardive dyskinesia. Am J Psychiatry 137:776–781, 1980

8. Baker B: Expect a flood of tardive dyskinesia malpractice suits. Clinical Psychiatry News 12(1):3, 35, 1984

9. Paulson GW: Tardive dyskinesia. Annu Rev Med 26:75–81, 1975

10. Cohen G: The pathobiology of Parkinson's disease: biochemical aspects of dopamine neuron senescence. J Neural Transm 19 (suppl):89–103, 1983

11. Wexler NS: Perceptual-motor, cognitive, and emotional characteristics of persons at risk for Huntington's disease, in Advances in Neurology, Vol 23. Edited by Chase TN, Wexler NS, Barbeau A. New York, Raven, 1979, pp 239–255

12. Baldessarini RJ, Tarsy D: Tardive dyskinesia, in Psychopharmacology: A Generation of Progress. Edited by Lipton MA, DiMascio A, Killam KF. New York, Raven, 1978, pp 993–1004

13. Faun WE, Smith RC, Davis JM, et al (eds): Tardive Dyskinesia: Research and Treatment. New York, Spectrum Publications, 1980

14. American Psychiatric Association: Tardive Dyskinesia (APA Task Force Report No 18). Washington, DC, APA, 1980, p 30 [see Table 7: Differential diagnoses to consider in evaluating tardive dyskinesia]

15. Gardos G, Cole JO, La Brie R: The assessment of tardive dyskinesia. Arch Gen Psychiatry 34:1206–1212, 1977; Granacher RP Jr: Differential diagnosis of tardive dyskinesia: an overview. Am J Psychiatry 138:1288–1297, 1981

16. Varga E, Sugerman AA, Varga V, et al: Prevalence of spontaneous oral dyskinesia in the elderly. Am J Psychiatry 139:329–331, 1982

17. Schooler NR, Kane JM: Research diagnoses for tardive dyskinesia. Arch Gen Psychiatry 39:486–487, 1982

18. Jeste D: Prevention, management and treatment of tardive dyskinesia. J Clin Psychiatry 46:14–18, 1985

19. Simpson GM, Pi EH, Sramek JJ: An update on tardive dyskinesia. Hosp Community Psychiatry 37:362–366, 1986

20. Simpson GM, Pi EH, Sramek JJ: An update on tardive dyskinesia. Hosp Community Psychiatry 37:362–366, 1986; American Psychiatric Association: Tardive Dyskinesia (APA Task Force Report No 18). Washington, DC, APA, 1980, p 169 [see Table 16: Suggested guidelines for the avoidance and management of tardive dyskinesia]

21. See, e.g., Jeste DV, Wyatt RJ: Understanding and Treating Tardive Dyskinesia. New York, Guilford, 1982; Fann WE, Smith RC, Davis JM, et al: Tardive Dyskinesia: Research and Treatment. New York, Spectrum Publications, 1980; Jeste DV, Wyatt RJ: Neuropsychiatric Movement Disorders. Washington, DC, American Psychiatric Press, 1984

22. American Psychiatric Association: Tardive Dyskinesia (APA Task Force Report No 18). Washington, DC, APA, 1980

23. Commentary—ECT: underused and misunderstood. Hosp Community Psychiatry 33:425, 1982

24. Janicak PG, Davis JM, Gibbons RD, et al: Efficacy of ECT: a meta-analysis. Am J Psychiatry 142:297–302, 1985

25. Sand-Stromgen L: Unilateral vs bilateral ECT. Acta Psychiatr Scand (Suppl) 240:1–65, 1973

26. Runck B: Consensus panel backs cautious use of ECT for severe disorders. Hosp Community Psychiatry 36:943–944, 1985

27. O'Connell RA: A review of the use of electroconvulsive therapy. Hosp Community Psychiatry 33:469–473, 1982

28. American Psychiatric Association: The Practice of Electroconvulsive Therapy: Recommendations for Treatment, Training, and Privileging (APA Task Force Report). Washington, DC, American Psychiatric Association, 1990

29. See, e.g., Annot, 94 ALR4th 317 [ECT-malpractice]; Annot, 42 ALR4th 586 [drug prescription–liability]

30. American Psychiatric Association: Tardive Dyskinesia (APA Task Force Report No 18). Washington, DC, APA, 1980

31. See, for example, Stone v Proctor, 259 NC 633, 131 SE2d 297 (1963)

32. Joint Commission on Accreditation of Healthcare Organizations: Consolidated Standards Manual. Chicago, IL, Joint Commission on Accreditation of Healthcare Organizations, 1988

33. See generally Witherell v Weimer, 148 Ill App 3d 32, 499 NE2d 46 (1986); Gowan v United States, 601 F Supp 1297 (D Or 1985)

34. Doerr v Hurley Medical Center, NM No 82-674-39 (Mich August 1984); Callan v Norland, 114 Ill App 3d 196, 448 NE2d 651 (1983)

35. Simon RI: Concise Guide to Psychiatry and Law for Clinicians. Washington, DC, American Psychiatric Press, 1992

36. Simon RI: Somatic therapies and the law, in American Psychiatric Press Review of Clinical Psychiatry and the Law, Vol 1. Edited by Simon RI. Washington, DC, American Psychiatric Press, 1990, pp 3–79

37. Black HC: Black's Law Dictionary, 6th Edition. St Paul, MN, West Publishing, 1990, p 779

38. Schloendorff v New York Hospital, 211 NY 125, 105 NE 92 (1914)

39. Capron AM: Informed consent in catastrophic disease control research and treatment. University of Pennsylvania Law Review 123:340, 364–376, 1974

40. See, for example, Canterbury v Spence, 464 F2d 772 (DC Civ 1972), cert denied, 409 US 1064 (1973)

41. See, e.g., Natanson v Kline, 186 Kan 393, 350 P2d 1107 (1960); Aiken v Clary, 396 SW2d 668 (Mo 1965). Note: Physician's duty to warn of possible adverse results of proposed treatment depends upon general practice followed by medical profession in the community. Harvard Law Review 75:1445, 1962

42. Fuller v Starnes, 268 Ark 476, 597 SW2d 88 (1980) [adopting the "majority view" that "emphasizes the interest in the medical profession to be relatively free from vexations and costly litigation and holds that what a patient should be told about future medical treatment is primarily a medical decision"]

43. 464 F2d 772 (DC Cir 1972), cert denied, 409 US 1064 (1972)

44. Ibid, pp 786–787

45. Ibid, p 787

46. Rozovsky FA: Consent to Treatment: A Practical Guide. Boston, MA, Little, Brown, 1984, pp 87–125

47. See, for example, Allen v Roark, 625 SW 2d 411 (Tex App 1981), modified, 633 SW2d 804 (1981)

48. American Psychiatric Association: Tardive Dyskinesia (APA Task Force Report No 18). Washington, DC, APA, 1979; American Psychiatric Association: The Practice of Electroconvulsive Therapy: Recommendations for Treatment, Training, and Privileging (APA Task Force Report). Washington, DC, American Psychiatric Association, 1990, pp 11–14, 64–71

49. See, e.g., Wilson v Lehmann, 379 SW2d 478 (Ky Ct App 1964)

50. See, e.g., Rennie v Klein, 462 FSupp 1131 (D NJ 1978), affirmed, 476 FSupp 1294 (D NJ 1979), affirmed in part, modified in part, and remanded, 653 F2d 836 (3d Cir 1980) (en banc), vacated and remanded, 458 US 1119 (1982)

51. See, e.g., Rivers v Katz, 504 NYS2d 74 (App Ct 1986) [psychopharmacotherapy]; Pickle v Curns, 106 Ill App 3d 734, 435 NE2d 877 (1982) [ECT]

52. Roth LH, Meisel A, Lidz CW: Tests of competency to consent to treatment. Am J Psychiatry 134:279–284, 1977; see pp 279, 283

53. Meisel A, Roth LH, Lidz CW: Toward a model of the legal doctrine of informed consent. Am J Psychiatry 134:285–289, 1977; see pp 285, 287

54. Perlin M: Mental Disability Law: Civil and Criminal, Vol 3. Charlottesville, VA, Michie, 1989, p 80

55. Meisel A, Roth LH, Lidz CW: Toward a model of the legal doctrine of informed consent. Am J Psychiatry 134:279–284, 1977 (see pp 285, 287), citing American Law Reports 139:1370, 1942. But see Lipscomb v Memorial Hospital, 733 F2d 332, 335–36 (4th Cir 1984)

56. Appelbaum PS, Lidz CW, Meisel A: Informed Consent: Legal Theory and Clinical Practice. New York, Oxford University Press, 1987, pp 84–87

57. See, e.g., Frasier v Department of Health and Human Resources, 500 So 2d 858, 864 (La Ct App 1986)

58. See, e.g., Aponte v United States, 582 F Supp 555, 566–569 (DPR 1984)

59. Klein J, Onek J, Macbeth J: Seminar on Law in the Practice of Psychiatry. Washington, DC, Onek, Klein, and Farr, 1984

60. Law of adolescence gradually maturing. AMA News, September 9, 1983, pp 7, 12

61. Simon RI: Clinical Psychiatry and the Law, 2nd Edition. Washington, DC, American Psychiatric Press, 1992

62. ND Cent Code 51417.1 (1981)

63. Younto v St Francis Hospital, 205 Kan 292, 469 P2d 330 (1970)

64. Annas GJ: The Rights of Hospital Patients. New York, Avon Books, 1975

65. 442 US 584 (1979)

66. O'Connell RA: A review of the use of electroconvulsive therapy. Hosp Community Psychiatry 33:469–473, 1982

67. Weiner RD: The psychiatric use of electrically induced seizures. Am J Psychiatry 136:1507–1517, 1979

68. See, for example, Perr IN: Liability and electroshock therapy. Journal of Forensic Sciences 25:508–513, 1980; Krouner LW: Shock therapy and psychiatric malpractice: the legal accommodation to a controversial treatment. Journal of Forensic Science 20:404–415, 1975

69. 70 Corpus Juris Secundum Physicians & Surgeons § 41 (1951)

70. Mitchell v Robinson, 334 SW2d 11 (Mo 1960). But see Lester v Aetna Casualty & Surety Co, 240 F2d 676 (5th Cir 1957); Stone v Proctor, 259 NC 633, 131 SE2d 297 (1963)

71. Johnston v Rodis, 251 F2d 917 (DC Cir 1957). But see Eisle v Moore, 143 F Supp 816 (D Pa 1956), denied, 158 NYS2d 761 (1957); Collins v Hand, 431 Pa 378, 246 A2d 398 (1968)

72. See, e.g., Smith JT: Medical Malpractice: Psychiatric Care. Colorado Springs, Shepard's/McGraw-Hill, 1986, p 68; Holton v Pfingst, 534 SW2d 786, 789 (Ky 1976)

73. Howe v Citizens Memorial Hospital of Victoria County, 426 SW2d 882, reversed sub nom, Constant v Howe, 436 SW2d 115 (Tex 1968)

74. McDonald v Moore, 323 So 2d 635 (Fla 1976); Pettis v State, 336 So 2d 521 (La 1976). But see Foxluger v New York, 23 Misc 2d 933, 203 NYS2d 985 (1960)

75. Quinley v Cocke, 183 Tenn App 428, 192 SW2d 992 (1946)

76. Stone v Proctor, 259 NC 633, 131 SE2d 297 (1963)

77. O'Connell RA: A review of the use of electroconvulsive therapy. Hosp Community Psychiatry 33:469, 472, 1982; American Psychiatric Association: The Practice of Electroconvulsive Therapy: Recommendations for Treatment, Training, and Privileging (APA Task Force Report). Washington, DC, American Psychiatric Association, 1990

78. Pettis v State Department of Hospitals, 336 So 2d 521 (La 1976)

79. Quick v Benedictine Sisters Hospital Association, 257 Minn 470, 102 NW2d 36 (1960); Brown v Moore, 143 F Supp 816 (D Pa 1956), affirmed, 247 F2d 711 (3d Cir 1957). But see O'Rourke v Halcyon Rest Home, 281 AD 838, 118 NYS2d 693, affirmed, 306 NY 692, 117 NE2d 639 (1953); Carrier v Regents of the University of California at Los Angeles, No WEC 88734, Los Angeles Cty Super Ct (Cal 1986)

80. Adams v Ricks, 91 Ga App 494, 86 SE2d 329 (1955)

81. Perlin ML: Mental Disability Law: Civil and Criminal, Vol 3. Charlottesville, VA, Michie, 1989, pp 47–48; see generally Winslade, et al: Medical, judicial, and statutory regulation of ECT in the United States. Am J Psychiatry 141:1347, 1984; Colorado ex rel M.K.M., 765 P2d 1075 (Colo Ct App 1988) [petition to compel patient to undergo ECT was properly denied in light of state's failure to establish by clear and convincing evidence that treatment was needed]; Price v Shepard, 239 NW2d 905 (Minn 1976); Lillian F. v Superior Court, 160 Cal App 3d 314, 206 Cal Rptr 603 (1984)

82. Psychiatry claims closed. Psychiatric News, Vol 22, April 3, 1987, p 11

83. Malpractice Digest, March/April 1979, p 2

84. Hogan DB: The Regulation of Psychotherapists, Vol 3. Cambridge, MA, Ballinger, 1979, p 382

85. See, for example, Blanchard v Levine, No D 014550 Fulton Cty Super Ct (GA 1985) [Negligent diagnosis and treatment using haloperidol by a physician resulting in an $80,000 settlement]; Shaughnessy v Spray, No A7905-02395 Multnomah Cty Cir Ct (Ore February 16, 1983) [negligent prescription of propoxyphene, failure to obtain adequate history (psychiatrist); $250,000 verdict]

86. 858 F2d 351 (7th Cir 1988)

87. 62 Md App 519, 409 A2d 720 (Md Ct App), cert denied, Chestnut Lodge v Osherhoff, 304 Md 163, 497 A2d 1163 (1985)

88. Klerman GL: The psychiatric patient's right to effective treatment: implications of Osheroff v Chestnut Lodge. Am J Psychiatry 147:409–418, 1990

89. Stone AA: Law, science, and psychiatric malpractice: a response to Klerman's indictment of psychoanalytic psychiatry. Am J Psychiatry 147:419–427, 1990

90. See, e.g., Chaires v St John's Episcopal Hospital, No 20808/75 NY Cty Sup Ct (NY February 21, 1984) [chlorpromazine—failure to supervise/restrain (psychiatric ward–general hospital); $950,000 settlement]; Clifford v United States, No 82-5002 USDC (SD 1985) [amitriptyline—overprescription/failure to monitor consumption (VA hospital); liability held]; Kilgore v County of Santa Clara, No 397-525 Santa Clara Cty Super Ct (Cal 1982) [fluphenazine—improper monitoring (psychiatrist); $230,000 settlement]

91. 167 Mich App 432, 423 NW2d 217 (1987)

92. Hubbard v Calvin, 83 Cal App 3d 529, 147 Cal Rptr 905 (1978)

93. See, e.g., No CU81-0950 USDC (SD NY 1986) [lithium—overprescription (VA hospital); $101,000 verdict]; Estate of Verenna v Commonwealth of Pennsylvania, No 82-C-4486 (Harrison Cty Ct Comm Pleas PA, June 1985) [psychotropic medication—excessive dose (state psychiatric hospital); $115,000 settlement]; Badger v Greenfield, No 79-2068 USDC, (CD Ill July 1, 1980) [chlorpromazine—overmedication (psychiatrist); $100,000 settlement]

94. See, e.g., French v Corbett, No 84-4063 (USDC NJ 1985) [Elavil—negligent mixing of medication (physician); $10,000 settlement]; Hand v Krakowski, 453 NYS2d 121 (AD 1982) [polypharmacy—negligent prescription (pharmacy); liability upheld]; Karasik v Bird, 98 AD2d 359, 470 NYS2d 605 (1984) [polypharmacy (antidepressants and other meds)—over prescription; negligent monitoring; failure to advise of risks (e.g., driving) (psychiatrist); $222,000 verdict]. But see Allen v Kaiser Foundation Hospital, 707 P2d 1289 (Or App 1985) [chlorpromazine—negligent polypharmacy (general hospital and psychiatrist) defense verdict]

95. See, for example, Shaughnessy v Spray, No A7905-02395 Multnomah Cty Cir Ct (Ore February 16, 1983) [propoxyphene—negligent prescription; failure to obtain adequate history (psychiatrist); $250,000 verdict]

96. Moran v Botsford General Hospital, No 81-225-533 Wayne Cty Cir Ct (MI October 1, 1984) [haloperidol—negligent prescription and monitoring (psychiatrist, other defendants); $437,500 settlement]; Wright v State, No 83-5035 Orleans Parish Civ Dist Ct (LA April 1986) [lithium—failure to monitor and failure to obtain informed consent (psychiatrist); $456,000 settlement]; Karasik v Bird, 98 AD2d 359, 470 NYS2d 605 (1984) [polypharmacy (antidepressants

and other medications)—overprescription; negligent monitoring; failure to advise of risks (e.g., driving) (psychiatrist); $222,000 verdict]; Kilgore v County of Santa Clara, No 397-525 Santa Clara Cty Super Ct (Cal 1982) [fluphenazine—improper monitoring (psychiatrist); $230,000 settlement]

97. 136 Ill App 3d 945, 483 NE2d 906 (1985); but see Schuster v Altenberg, 144 Wis 2d 223, 424 NW2d 159 (1988), rev'd, Schuster v Altenberg, 86-CV-1327 (Cir Ct Racine CTy 1990)

98. See, e.g., LaTour v St Luke's Hospital, No 147547 (St. Louis Cty Dist Ct MO September 22, 1983) [haloperidol—failure to restrain (psychiatrist and general hospital); $880,000 verdict]

99. See, e.g., Clifford v United States, No 82-5002 USDC (SD 1985) [amitriptyline—overprescription; failure to monitor consumption (VA hospital); liability held]

100. See, e.g., Daniels v McCurtain County, No 77-433-C Muskogee Cty Dist Ct (OK March 1980) [antidepressants—denial of medication (psychiatrist); $100,000 verdict]

101. See, e.g., Dolly v Skodnek, New York Sup Ct, Nassau Cty (NY 1986) [thioridazine—negligent monitoring; failure to refer (psychiatrist); $1,000,000 verdict]

102. See, e.g., Bloch v Alhambra Community Hospital, No C 385,300 Pasadena Super Ct (Cal 1986) [diazepam—negligent withdrawal from medication (psychiatric hospital) defense verdict]

103. Parry HJ, Balter MB, Mellinger GD, et al: National patterns of psychotherapeutic drug use. Arch Gen Psychiatry 28:769–783, 1973

104. Task Force on Late Neurological Effects of Antipsychotic Drugs: Tardive dyskinesia: summary of a task force report of the American Psychiatric Association. Am J Psychiatry 137:1163–1172, 1980; see pp 1163, 1165

105. Gardos G, Cole JO: Overview: public health issues in tardive dyskinesia. Am J Psychiatry 137:776–781, 1980

106. Klawans HL, Barr A: Prevalence of spontaneous lingual-facial-buccal dyskinesia in the elderly. Neurology 32:558–559, 1982; Kane JM, Weinhold P, Kinon B, et al: Prevalence of abnormal involuntary movements ("spontaneous dyskinesia") in the normal elderly. Psychopharmacology (Berlin) 77:105–108, 1982

107. Baker B: Expect a flood of tardive dyskinesia malpractice suits. Clinical Psychiatry News 12(1):3, 35 1984; Tardive dyskinesia malpractice suits may be rising. Clinical Psychiatry News 15(12):13, 1987; Wettstein RM, Appelbaum P: Legal liability for tardive dyskinesia. Hosp Community Psychiatry 35:992, 1984

108. Steven B Bisbing, personal communication, February 1990 [Comprehensive survey of the largest reporters of published and unpublished (e.g., settled, trial level) cases revealed less than 30 suits as of 12/89]

109. See, e.g., Lackey v Bressler, 26 NC App 486, 358 SE2d 560 (1987)

110. 426 Mich 223, 393 NW2d 847 (1986)

111. Hyde v University of Michigan Board of Regents, 426 Mich 223, 393 NW2d 847 (1986), revised in accord with Ross v Consumer Power Company, 420 Mich 567, 363 NW2d 641 (1986)

112. No 84-674 CA(L)(H) 15th Jud Dist Cir Ct, Palm Beach Cty (Fla April 4, 1986)

113. Soloff P, George A, Nathan R, et al: Progress in pharmacotherapy of borderline disorders: a double-blind study of amitriptyline, haloperidol, and placebo. Arch Gen Psychiatry 43:691–697, 1986

114. 322 NW2d 917 (Iowa Ct App 1982)

115. Barclay v Campbell, 704 SW2d 8 (Tex 1986)

116. Rosenbloom v Goldberg, No 29798 Suffolk Cty Super Ct (May 1984)

117. See, for example, Radank v Heyl, No F4-2316 Wisc Compensation Bd (1986); Frasier v Department of Health and Human Services, 500 So 2d 858 (La Ct App 1986); Rivera v NYC Health and Hospitals, No 27536/82 New York Sup Ct (NY 1988)

118. Clites v State of Iowa, 322 NW2d 917 (Iowa Ct App 1982)

119. Bellamy WA: Malpractice risks confronting the psychiatrist: a nationwide fifteen-year study of the appellate court cases, 1946–1961. Am J Psychiatry 118:769–780, 1962; Slawson PF: Psychiatric malpractice: the California experience. Am J Psychiatry 136:650–654, 1979

120. Kane JM, Woerner M, Weinhold P, et al: A prospective study of tardive dyskinesia development: preliminary results. J Clin Psychopharmacol 2:345–349, 1982

121. Jeste DV: Madness, movements, and malpractice: what a mess! Paper presented at the 21st annual meeting of the American Academy of Psychiatry and the Law, San Diego, CA, October 1990

122. 653 F2d 836 (3d Cir 1981) (en banc), vacated and remanded, 458 US 1119 (1982) on remand, 720 F2d 266 (3d Cir 1983) (en banc)

123. FDA Bulletin, May 1973

124. Schiele BC, Gallant D, Simpson G, et al: A persistent neurological syndrome associated with antipsychotic drug use. Ann Intern Med 79:99–100, 1973

125. American Psychiatric Association: Tardive Dyskinesia (APA Task Force Report No 18). Washington, DC, APA, 1979

126. Singer C: The Pink Sheets. FDC Reports 46(9), 1984

127. Simon RI: Clinical Psychiatry and the Law, 2nd Edition. Washington, DC, American Psychiatric Press, 1992

128. Guttmacher LB: Concise Guide to Somatic Therapies in Psychiatry. Washington, DC, American Psychiatric Press, 1988, pp 1–7

Chapter 6

Suicide ─────────────────────

Understanding Suicide

Definition and Topology

The issue of suicide is a troubling one for most people, including health care professionals. It often stimulates contemplation of the very nature of human existence, the vulnerability and frailty of this existence, and, most of all, a search for some meaning in life. Some people perceive suicide as a sin, while others see it as an act of great courage and resolve. Whether viewed as the ultimate expression of freedom and self-determination or the act of an irrational and deeply troubled individual, most commentators would agree, it is an issue that commands considerable attention.

To fully understand the many nuances of suicide would likely implicate every facet of human emotional, intellectual, and social behavior. It is a common topic of philosophical meditation, the focus of many great theatrical works, and a considerable and increasing medicolegal dilemma in the psychiatric and mental health professions.

Despite centuries of examination and debate, the subject of suicide defies an accepted definition or relatively uniform classification (1). The eminent 19th-century sociologist and philosopher Emil Durkheim described suicide in the following way:

> We may then say conclusively: the term suicide is applied to all cases of death resulting directly or indirectly from a positive or negative act of the victim himself which he knows will produce this result. An attempt is an act thus defined but falling short of actual death. (2)

In any contemporary study of suicide Durkheim's classification remains a fundamental starting point. In his classic treatise *Le Suicide*, he identifies three basic types: altruistic ("self-sacrifice"), egoistic ("lack of close social bonds"), and anomic ("emotional disorientation due to personal disruption") (3). From a clinical perspective, a seemingly more practical taxonomy might include rational (i.e., to escape pain); reactive (i.e., following a

121

loss or trauma); vindictive (i.e., to punish someone else); manipulative (i.e., to thwart others' plans); psychotic (i.e., to fulfill a delusion); and accidental (i.e., reconsidered too late).

Theories regarding the cause of suicide abound. Beginning with Durkheim's postulations—that social forces and social integration heavily influenced suicide rates—clinicians, philosophers, and researchers have struggled to develop an acceptable explanation for this behavior. To Sigmund Freud, for instance, suicide was an internal matter that arose from an unconscious impulse toward self-destruction. Later theories concentrated on the concepts of ambivalence and the role of aggression. Contemporary suicidologists believe that suicide is due to several factors, often in some combination with each other. These include, but are not limited to, familial influences, biochemical factors, medical and psychiatric illness, and environmental traumas.

Common Characteristics

From a clinical perspective, a more important question than classification or etiological theory is, What are the most common features or "characteristics" of suicide? Because suicide is a highly idiosyncratic phenomenon, there can be no absolutes or universal traits. Aptly stated then, the notion of suicide should be discussed in terms of the most frequent characteristics associated with most suicides. Shneidman identifies 10 characteristics or commonalities associated with suicide (4). Each (and taken together as a group) provides much of the substance that sustains contemporary medical, psychiatric, moral, social, and philosophical debates about suicide. The ten commonalities are as follows:

❖ The common *purpose* of suicide is to seek a **solution.**
❖ The common *goal* of suicide is **cessation of consciousness.**
❖ The common *stimulus* in suicide is **intolerable psychological pain.**
❖ The common *stressor* in suicide is **frustrated psychological needs.**
❖ The common *emotions* in suicide are **hopelessness and helplessness.**
❖ The common *internal attitude* in suicide is **ambivalence.**
❖ The most common *cognitive state* in suicide is **constriction.**
❖ The most common *action* in suicide is **escape** (from distress).
❖ The most common *interpersonal act* in suicide is **communication of intention.**
❖ The most common *consistency* in suicide is with **lifelong coping patterns.**

Familiarity with these 10 characteristics can assist the treating clinician in understanding the dynamics of suicide and avoiding the various myths commonly perpetuated about suicidal patients (5). For instance, the conclusion that suicidal persons are completely intent on self-destruction ignores the reality that most suicidal people are *ambivalent* about dying. Similarly, the notion that *once decided upon, suicide is inevitable* fails to reconcile the fact that strong suicidal intent usually represents an acute condition that significantly subsides once the precipitating forces pass or are survived. *People who discuss killing themselves are not generally the ones who actually follow through* is a dangerous myth that even some mental health professionals accept. The fact is that approximately 75% of the people who successfully kill themselves had at some time communicated clear intentions of their desire to die, and about half had seen a doctor in the month before they died (6). Conversely, belief in the myth that *discussing suicidal ideation and plans will more firmly fix the idea of suicide in a person's mind* can naively alienate a person to greater despair. Oftentimes, sensitive and open inquiry into a person's suicidal plans will relieve pent up feelings of desperation and anxious feelings "to do something." However, even the most caring and genuine therapist must guard against being lulled into a false sense of security by believing the myth that *improvement following a suicide crisis means that the period of risk has passed.* Research has shown that most successful suicides occur within 90 days **after** an acute crisis, when the period of "improvement" enables the suicidal person to recoup lost strength (i.e., psychic energy) and put his or her suicidal intentions into effect (7).

Prevalence and Epidemiology

Notwithstanding the numerous epidemiological problems commonly associated with suicide studies, almost every country in the world considers suicide a major public health problem (8). It is estimated that there is a total of 30,000 suicides a year in the United States, although some believe that the actual total is as high as 100,000 (9). Suicide is currently believed to be the 10th leading cause of death in the United States and accounts for *at least* 1% of all deaths (9). A comparative estimate, from two large V.A. hospital studies, revealed that over a 3-year period (1973–1975), there were 150.9 suicides per 100,000 patients (10). *Since 1945, the official suicide rate for the general population has been between 10 and 12 per 100,000!*

Among *neuropsychiatric* patients, the average annual suicide rate in the two studies above swelled to 370.7 per 100,000 patients, with younger neuropsychiatric patients accounting for nearly *double* this rate (10). In terms of pathology, functional psychoses (predominantly schizophrenia) represented nearly three-fourths of the suicides. Alcoholism made up approximately 11% of the total number of suicides (11). For clinicians concerned about preventive psychiatry, as well as reducing the risks of a malpractice claim, the two studies noted that approximately 64% of the suicides occurred *outside* of the hospital, 35% during *authorized* leaves and 30% during *unauthorized* absences.

Farberow reported that the average rate of suicides among *general medical and surgical* patients was about 41.7 per 100,000, or "about three and one-half times that of the general population" (12). Interestingly, he found that 72% of the general medical and surgical suicides occurred *inside* the hospital and 25% occurred outside the hospital (12).

The figures presented are by no means definitive. However, they do provide a viable statistical starting point for putting into focus the significance of suicide among hospital populations, especially in regard to psychiatric patients. Inconsistencies in reporting; vaguely defined accidents, particularly involving car crashes; substance abuse; and a general resistance by family, friends, and public authorities to ascribe suicide as a cause of death—all contribute to this belief of underreporting. It has been consistently demonstrated that more people die of suicide than homicide each year (13).

The risk of suicide is affected by numerous biosocioeconomic and cultural factors. For instance, age, marital status, gender, occupation, physical and mental health, religion, and socioeconomic class are considered important risk factors (see below). Therefore, it behooves the psychiatric clinician who treats patients who are suicidal or potentially suicidal to become familiar with the significance of these factors in order to enhance diagnostic accuracy and reliability.

Assessment of Suicide Risk

Diagnosis

The assessment of suicide potential, like that of any future behavior, raises the much debated point: Is this something that psychiatrists can reasonably be expected to do, and if so, how should they do it? It is well accepted in the law (14), as well as by the governing body of the psychiatric profession (14), that psychiatrists cannot predict future behavior with any high degree of reliability. However, as in many other potentially lethal circumstances, it is the responsibility of the psychiatrist to recognize the significance of the situation (i.e., potential suicide threat) and to respond to it in a *reasonable* manner.

It is important for the treating psychiatrist to recognize that his or her actions will not be held, clinically or legally, to a standard of exactness or 100% accuracy. Instead, the standard of care in assessing suicidal patients, or in any other professional act, will be one of *reasonableness*. This standard, while inherently ambiguous, relieves the psychiatrist of the thorny issue of "prediction" and simply requires that his or her assessment be "reasonable" given the prevailing circumstances at that time. The question of what is reasonable will often turn on the question, Was the suicide or self-destructive behavior *foreseeable?* In the case of a lawsuit, if it is determined that an ordinary psychiatric practitioner would have *foreseen* the patient attempting or committing suicide and done something (e.g., preventive) about it, then it will be very difficult for a defendant who failed to identify the patient's suicidal potential to claim that his or her actions were "reasonable."

The evaluation of a patient's potential for suicide includes a careful evaluation of past history, including past medical and psychiatric records, present mental status, and available resources (i.e., physical and emotional). The medical and psychiatric literature is filled with research and commentary that conclude that the prediction of whether a patient will commit suicide in the foreseeable future is generally questionable, at best (15). A much more realistic and practical approach is to assess suicide risk factors (16). In other words, what and how many factors generally associated with suicide attempts does a patient manifest or represent at the time of the evaluation? It is important to note that "there are no pathognomonic predictors of suicide" (17). The psychiatric literature is replete with studies, empirical and anecdotal, that outline a plethora of risk variables. The fact that these studies or their conclusions are empirically suspect does not necessarily diminish their value to the treating psychiatrist. The operative issue in the assessment of potentially dangerous behavior is the *reasonableness* of the assessment. Both clinically and legally, it is considered reasonable psychiatric practice to be familiar with the professional literature and integrate that which is useful and/or accepted within the profession into one's clinical protocol.

Risk Factors: Suicide Potential

The following list of suicide variables is not intended to be exhaustive. Moreover, because suicide is generally thought to be the product of a complex interaction of many different factors, a case-by-case perspective, rather than rigid reliance on a single set of criteria, is probably the most suitable approach.

Personal Variables

Age. Suicide rates vary with age and gender. Recent research has demonstrated that for men a bimodal distribution of suicide rates occurs, with a peak occurring in the 25–34 year range, followed by a decrease in rates in the 35–44 year range, after which the rates steadily climb (18). In rates for females, the relationship between suicide and age demonstrates a curvilinear pattern. Rates for women steadily increase with age until the 45–54 year range, after which there is a steady decline (19). One exception to this trend is the rise in suicide rates noted among adolescents (see section on special populations below).

Gender.   Men are three times more likely to *commit* suicide than women (20). Women, however, *attempt* suicide two to three times more frequently than men. The mode of suicide also appears to be gender related. Men generally prefer more lethal means, such as with knives and firearms, whereas women indicate a preference for poisoning (21).

Race.   Generally, whites demonstrate a higher frequency of suicide than do nonwhites—as high as 3 to 1 depending upon the age range (22).

Marital status.   Persons who are separated, divorced, or widowed show a higher rate of suicide (23). Married persons demonstrate the lowest rate. In fact, some researchers view marriage as serving as a form of "protective role," especially among white males. Also, suicide rates are noted to be especially low among married persons with children (24).

Employment.   Studies have indicated that there is a corresponding relationship between changes in the national suicide rate and economic conditions (25). The unemployed, especially men between the ages of 35 to 74, suffer a much higher rate of suicide than the employed (26). Interestingly, professionals (e.g., male physicians) have a disproportionally high risk of suicide (27).

Living circumstances.   Persons living alone are at a higher risk of committing suicide than persons who live with others (28).

History of suicide.   It has been estimated that 20% to 65% of individuals who commit suicide have made at least one previous attempt (29). Related variables include lethality of past attempts, time since the last attempt, number of attempts, and reasons for failure (the more external, the greater the potential).

Current suicidal ideation.   An assessment should be made of the following:

❖ Specific plan (30): practicality; lethality (31)
❖ Access to means to carry out the plan
❖ Reason for suicide
❖ Availability of physical and emotional resources (32)
❖ Some form of warning that the patient wishes to or intends to kill himself or herself (33)

Psychiatric / Medical Variables

While it is abundantly clear that suicide is the result of numerous causal factors, the role that psychiatric variables play is a significant one in many cases. For instance, in three separate retrospective studies involving a sample of 100 or more suicide cases, an overwhelming majority of the deaths were by individuals with serious psychiatric illnesses (34). Depressive illness and alcoholism were discovered to be the predominant diagnostic factors in these studies.

The importance of psychiatric variables in assessing suicide risk is aptly described by Roy in his retrospective investigation of 90 suicides:

> [I]t is the psychiatric patient who is admitted to a psychiatric ward during his last episode of psychiatric contact who is a risk for suicide, and the period when changing from inpatient to outpatient care is particularly a time of increased risk. (35)

Several long-term follow-up studies have evaluated suicide risk in specific psychiatric disorders and discovered that, relative to their prevalence in the general population, *affective disorders* and *schizophrenia* are diagnoses carrying the highest risk of suicide, with diagnoses of alcoholism and personality disorders also associated with increased risk (36). In summary:

- ❖ Alcohol and/or substance abuse significantly increases suicide risk (37), especially suicide "accidents."
- ❖ Psychopathology associated with high suicide potential includes schizophrenia (38), major depression (39), manic-depressive illness (40), and certain personality disorders (41) (e.g., borderline).
- ❖ Other related factors such as feelings of helplessness and hopelessness, recent or ongoing life stresses, and interpersonal conflicts with significant others, have been known to increase a person's potential for suicide (42).

In their prospective study of suicide among 954 persons with major affective disorder, Fawcett et al. (43) have identified several statistically significant short-term suicide indicators such as panic attacks, psychic anxiety, anhedonia, alcohol abuse, loss of pleasure or interest, depressive turmoil, diminished concentration, and global insomnia.

The short-term and long-term distinction among suicide risk factors has important clinical implications. For example, the suicide signal-to-noise ratio for short-term risk factors is greater than that for long-term risk factors. Furthermore, as demonstrated by Fawcett et al. (43), the suicide risk factors for individuals with major affective disorder who committed suicide within 1 year of assessment were different from the suicide risk factors found among individuals who committed suicide within 2–10 years of assessment. In the former group, the anxiety-related symptoms of panic attacks, psychic anxiety, global insomnia, diminished concentration, alcohol abuse, and loss of interest and pleasure were significantly more severe. The more traditional suicide risk factors such as hopelessness, suicidal ideation, suicidal intent, and a history of previous suicide attempts were not associated with short-term suicide but were significantly associated with long-term suicide. Thus, clinical interventions directed at treating anxiety-related symptoms in patients with major affective disorder may significantly diminish a number of short-term suicide risk factors.

As noted earlier, the above list of variables is not intended to be exhaustive or scientifically certified. In essence, there is no "magical formula" or fixed set of factors that will *predict* suicide. While other commentators have developed longer lists of suicide factors (44) and even prediction risk instruments (45), the most important task likely confronting the treating psychiatrist is the assessment of the *seriousness* and *imminence* of a patient's current suicidal risk. It is this evaluation that will generally dictate future treatment interventions and discharge or pass decisions and, if later sued, whether the doctor's actions (e.g., decisions) were reasonable.

Risk-Benefit Assessment

A review of the relevant literature regarding *clinical predictions of dangerousness* consistently raises serious doubts about the ability of mental health professionals to make reliable determinations of future behavior (e.g., suicide) (46). Accordingly, many clinicians are concerned that they are sitting targets for malpractice lawsuits if they fail to accurately predict the future behavior of a patient who kills himself or someone else while under their care.

Description.   The legal standard of "reasonableness" in assessing and treating suicidal patients preempts the thorny dilemma of violence prediction by judging professionals not on the absolute accuracy of their determinations but on whether their assessment *process,* which led to their final determination, was clinically reasonable (47). The defensive tension created by concerns of overrestricting a patient's freedom of movement and possibly not providing enough safeguards for the patient's immediate welfare, can be relieved by implementing a suicide "risk-benefit" analysis each time a significant procedural decision is made (e.g., initial determination of risk, consideration for day pass, consideration for more freedom of movement):

> Risk-benefit analysis provides a systematic assessment of the balance of clinical factors favoring or opposing the treatment intervention under consideration. A risk-benefit evaluation also allows the psychiatrist more therapeutic latitude with the suicidal patient in cases in which fears of

malpractice inhibit appropriate therapeutic interventions. It is not unusual for psychiatrists to be so fearful of a malpractice action when treating a suicidal patient that they overly restrict the patient to the latter's therapeutic detriment. If, after reasonable clinical examination and evaluation the clinician feels that the benefits for the patient's recovery outweigh the specific risks of any given psychiatric intervention, then these judgments should be recorded in a risk-benefit note in the patient's chart. . . . Risk benefit notes are decisional road marks. When in doubt about a particular intervention, a risk-benefit analysis should be conducted and recorded. (48)

Procedural considerations. The dire consequences that can occur if a potentially suicidal patient is mismanaged necessitates that a risk-benefit analysis be conducted frequently. This is especially true 1) following any period of absence from the institution; 2) prior to making significant treatment decisions; and 3) whenever there are signs of behavior change in the patient. Accurate, reliable, and thorough information gathering is essential to the risk-benefit analysis process. Data regarding the various risk factors identified and described in the previous section should be carefully assessed and *systematically documented* in a patient's records. This information, coupled with a current mental status examination and direct inquiry into a patient's feelings (e.g., Are you feeling depressed? Helpless? Hopeless?), thoughts (e.g., Do you want to harm yourself or think about hurting yourself?), and immediate and long-term plans (e.g., If given a day pass or if discharged, who do you plan to see? What do you plan to do?), is relevant information that a "reasonable" clinician would likely utilize.

Once this information is assimilated, a considered effort should be made to *assess the patient's risk for suicide in the near future.* A number of assessment scales, risk behavior formulas, and rating charts are available to assist the clinician in making this determination (49). The clinician's treatment decision should be the result of such an analysis. For instance, if after identifying all of the relevant risk factors it is determined that the sum total of the data suggests that the patient has a high *potential* for suicide, then the clinician *must* follow up with appropriate psychiatric intervention (e.g., immediate hospitalization) (50). Lesser degrees of suicide potential will obviously require other, less restrictive or imminent intervention plans. *Reasonable* clinical management requires that the intervention be commensurate with the projected level of suicide risk.

While it is true that "every suicide is a unique event that defies easy analysis, even in retrospect" (51), the application of a risk-benefit assessment process whenever confronted with a potentially suicidal patient will greatly help the clinician in making a "reasonably" appropriate diagnosis or treatment decision.

Inpatient considerations.   Suicides occurring in a hospital raise significant clinical and legal questions about a facility's or unit's general standard of care, fundamental hospital policy, and, of course, legal liability.

Although suicides in an inpatient setting are essentially motivated by the same reasons seen in outpatient practices, other unique factors are likely to exacerbate or add to a patient's existing potential for self-destruction. First of all, the very fact that a person is in the hospital indicates that he or she is in a relatively serious state of physical and/or emotional distress. Second, the more chronic the patient or serious his or her condition is, the greater the likelihood that the patient is without meaningful support resources or relationships outside the hospital. As a consequence, hospital staff and the hospital itself become a form of extended family to the patient.

As previously noted, most individuals are ambivalent about killing themselves (52). For many hospital patients who contemplate suicide, there is a competing desire for self-destruction and self-punishment against a hopeful wish to be saved, reborn, and forgiven (53). A primary goal of the hospital and its staff should be, then, to alter these feelings and increase the patient's will to survive and grow. Not surprisingly, feelings of powerlessness and helplessness are frequently the most salient characteristics found among suicidal patients in mental hospitals (54). For a patient to have some personal control over his or her existence is essential in the development of an adaptive self-concept. In the hospital, however, the opportunity for autonomy and self-determination is greatly limited. Hospital staff, therefore, must make an effort to foster healthy relationships with patients in order to assist them in improving their self-esteem and sense of hope.

Retrospective research on suicidal patients following discharge from inpatient units reveals that many suicides occurred because the patients' sense of self-worth and self-confidence was not sufficiently developed to cope with a significant setback. These patients either did not believe that the hospital could help them any more, or they resigned themselves to the belief that they would never get well again (55). These results underscore the significance that patients' feelings of *hopelessness* play as a suicide risk factor. Moreover, they highlight the need that patients have in maintaining or establishing relationships after discharge, either through outpatient treatment, through outreach efforts, or through informal support by family and community agencies. It is therefore incumbent upon the clinician to ascertain the availability of accessible, reliable, and viable support systems for patients in whatever community to which they are returning. Such a determination should be a part of any risk-benefit analysis in deciding whether a patient is appropriate for discharge or release. This is the one area where there appears to be a conflict between the legal mandate of least-restrictive alternative to treatment (or an open-door policy in the treatment) of the mentally ill and psychiatric considerations. The least-restrictive alternative, which is different in the highly suicidal cases than it is among those who are not highly suicidal, should be considered when making appropriate dispositions for treatment. Some individuals require close observation or even constant observation as part of their treatment, despite the legal concept of least-restrictive alternative. The patient should be treated in the least restrictive alternative consistent with his or her clinical needs. In suicidal cases, the clinical needs will dictate the degree of restriction for appropriate treatment.

Special populations: adolescents and the elderly. Two groups that bear special mention with regard to suicide potential are adolescents and the elderly. Psychiatrists with a pediatric or geriatric focus will attest to the many social, economic, and psychological factors that tend to make these two populations especially prone to suicidal ideation and behavior.

Statistically, people over age 60 comprised only 16% of the United States population in 1980 but accounted for **23%** of those who *committed* suicide. In fact, it has been reported that the highest rates of *completed* suicides are among people between the ages of 55 and 64. There are some commentators who believe, as astounding as this rate might appear, that this figure likely underestimates the number of actual suicides by the elderly. A significant, albeit unknown, percentage of the elderly covertly kill themselves by starvation, by sabotaging needed medical care, or by withdrawal from medical, psychological and social contact (56). In these cases, the cause of the elderly person's death is invariably viewed as something *other than* a suicide. Too often, Simon notes (56), persons close to the decedent (e.g., family members or friends) attribute death to "old age" or standard "medical problems" associated with the aged rather than to an untreated suicidal depression. He cautions that geriatric suicide is a vastly underrated and misunderstood problem to which professionals who treat the elderly need to pay closer attention.

For adolescents in the United States, suicide is the *third* most common cause of death, following accidents and homicide (57). In 1968, it was estimated that 7.1 per 100,000 persons between the ages of 15 to 24 years committed suicide. This total accounted for approximately 12% of the number of suicides nationwide. Since 1977, this number has increased to 20% of the total number of suicides, or 5,000 youth, ages 15 to 25, killing themselves each year. Various studies have reported that suicide attempts outnumber suicide completions in ratios anywhere from 10:1 to 100:1 (58). The comparative rate for adolescents is 25 to 50 suicide attempts for every one completion (59). Adolescents do not necessarily commit suicide for the same reasons as adults. Youths are typically going through a difficult adjustment period that is characterized by conflicting standards, social pressures, and often very little stable guidance. Because of immaturity and impulse, there may be a tendency to overreact to everyday frustrations. In response to a suicide in the community or fictional accounts of suicide, clusters of *contagious* suicides have been reported among adolescents (60). Approximately 2% to 3% of adolescent suicides occur in these clusters (61).

Another area of concern with adolescents, and somewhat similar to the unique suicide crisis concept, is the behavior *parasuicide*. Parasuicide is described as acts of deliberate self-harm that do not result in death. This behavior, which occurs much more frequently in females than in males, appears to be on the increase in the United States and internationally (62).

Suicidal adolescents, like their adult counterparts, are generally thought to be deeply depressed, but, like the elderly, the signs of their pathology may be difficult to recognize. Often their sadness and hopelessness are masked by boredom, apathy, hyperactivity, or physical complaints (63). Also, alcohol, drug abuse, and other forms of maladaptive acting out will frequently disguise the deep depressive feelings they harbor.

Treatment and Management

It should come as no surprise that the rate of suicides in psychiatric facilities is several times greater than that of the general population (64). With this in mind, hospitals and their staffs should assume an added degree of caution and precaution.

It is important to note that patients who are intent on dying will not likely be thwarted by psychiatric or other interventions. In some respects, death becomes their objective while living. These patients, as one might imagine, are as difficult to identify as they are to treat. For these individuals, albeit a small percentage of all suicide casualties, the treating psychiatrist must be prepared for the worst, because it will eventually occur. For the majority of patients, however, their ambivalence about dying gives the treating clinician a realistic chance to intervene with the patient.

Acutely suicidal patients will and do test the physical and psychological limits of an inpatient unit. If the unit is secured, as it will likely be if there are known suicidal patients on it, doors will be tried, windows and screens examined, staff routines studied, and the entire ward thoroughly inspected. It is believed that in a way, the instituting of "suicide precautions," restrictions, and limits invites testing by patients. Also, patients, no matter how depressed or disturbed, are aware that no unit is 100% secure or suicide proof and no professional staff infallible. However, many of these same patients are reassured by the staff's efforts to protect them from hurting themselves. This assurance, for some patients, represents a significant milestone in their ability to confront their internal conflict and hopefully deal with their suicidal impulses. Accordingly, clinically as well as legally, the duty of care owed by hospitals and their staffs to act *reasonably* in their care of vulnerable patients includes the responsibility of providing a reasonably safe environment for the patients in which they can receive needed treatment (65).

Common Methods of Suicide

The variety of ways that hospital patients attempt suicide would likely surprise even the most seasoned staff psychiatrist. The ingenuity and deceptiveness of some patients are astounding. Benensohn and Resnik, in a study of suicide prevention in two prominent psychiatric facilities, identified several of the more common means that patients attempted, completed, or said they would use to commit suicide if adequately compelled (66). The authors acknowledge that this list is not inclusive but it does provide staff psychiatrists some insight into how suicide is commonly committed. This information is especially useful when developing, evaluating, or revising appropriate treatment and management precautions (see section on management issues below).

Hanging.   The most commonly cited means of suicide is by hanging. Materials used included belts from robes, yarn, bed linen, electrical cords, wire hangers, clothing belts, guitar strings, and string. These articles were attached to various fixtures such as door handles, shower rods, bedposts, clothes hooks, and grates.

Jumping.   Another primary means of suicide is by jumping. In fact, a majority of suicide reports from general medical-surgical hospitals list jumping as the most prevalent method (67). Patients participating in the Benensohn and Resnik study indicated that they had independently evaluated the dimensions and security of windows and screens as a future means of suicide and/or escape. Moreover, elevator shafts, heating ducts, and stairwells were also cited as *potential* suicide routes or avenues.

Cutting.   Although acknowledged by professionals as rarely lethal, cutting and stabbing are common means of suicide attempts. The possible implements, frequently referred to by inpatient staffs as "sharps," are too numerous to recite here. Just about any form of glass object, such as light bulbs, mirrors, picture frames, and so forth, could be used. In addition, pointed objects including pens, pencils, and dining room utensils are popular instruments for such purposes.

Ingestion.   This category can be divided into two groups: 1) medication and 2) nonmedical substances. Many patients have attempted or contemplated suicide by drug overdose; therefore, it should come as no surprise that ingestion of medication is a frequently mentioned method. Patients are ingenious in the ways they devise to either "stockpile" their medication or obtain medication that is not prescribed for them. Consumption of non-medical materials often involves substances used by housekeeping staff such as cleansers and other cleaning compounds. Perfumes, lighter fluid, and insect repellents have also been known to be consumed by the suicidal patient.

Other means.   There is a variety of "miscellaneous" methods of suicide tried by patients. For example, drowning in the bathtub, suffocating with a paper or plastic bag, setting oneself on fire, banging one's head into blunt objects to cause trauma—all have been identified as ways that some patients have attempted or committed suicide, or thought of killing themselves while in the hospital.

Management Issues

Hospitals and psychiatric facilities have an inherent responsibility to make their environment as safe and risk free as possible. As a result, careful assessment and inspection of the physical plant, staff procedures, and personnel are required to determine what safeguards can be developed without impairing treatment effectiveness (68).

Suicide precautions generally are directed toward maintaining patients in a safe environment and minimizing their opportunity to harm themselves. For most hospitals and facilities, this would involve frequent, if not constant, supervision of patients by the nursing staff, as well as greatly limiting access to objects or situations in which patients could harm themselves. Some commentators, however, believe that this rigid approach is contrary to basic psychiatric care philosophy (69).

Fundamental to many general psychiatric units is the desire to enhance the patient's ability to function adaptively outside of the hospital. This is frequently accomplished by hospitals encouraging patients to take responsibility for their lives, by expecting patients to enter into treatment offered on the unit, and, in general, by assisting patients to learn more about their psychiatric difficulties and then discover ways of learning how to cope with these difficulties. When suicide precautions or some other restrictive plan is implemented, the patient's freedom of choice and movement is greatly reduced. As a result, the patient assumes less and less control over his or her life and becomes more dependent on the hospital and its staff. This is the *opposite* result of what intervention objectives are for the psychiatric inpatient, especially the suicidal patient whose self-esteem and hopefulness have essentially "bottomed out."

One way to deal with this conflict in approaches is to involve the patients in the setting of their own limits and defining unit protection plans. Benensohn and Resnik believe that involving patients in the "suicide proofing" of the unit reassures them and provides them with a sense of control and with a sense that someone (i.e., staff) cares for and respects them (70).

Probably the best approach for many facilities in addressing the issue of developing a safe *and* therapeutic environment for their patients is to integrate aspects of both approaches—that is, patient involvement coupled with reasonable safety precautions. Some suggested guidelines that incorporate both of these approaches include, but are not limited to, the following:

Patient identification. Admission and intake considerations include the following:

* Specifically inquire about current suicidal behavior or ideation and explore any details.
* Specifically inquire about past suicidal behavior or ideation and explore any details.
* Clearly apprise *all* unit staff of pertinent details.

Following admission:

* Be aware of suspect mood (e.g., hopelessness, helplessness, depression, constant anxiety, excessive guilt and self-blame, severe frustration).
* Be aware of suspect behavior (e.g., refusing nutrition, medication; hoarding medication; talking about death; inquiring about suicide methods; checking ward layout, windows, doors).
* Be aware of personality characteristics or changes (e.g., severe disorganization, schizophrenia diagnosis, recent trauma/object loss, feelings of no future, feelings of no goals and no support outside of the hospital).

Safeguards/precautions. Environmental considerations are as follows:

* Establish a system of checks with vulnerable patients, preferably with their input.
* Install safety glass in windows and mirrors.
* Restrict window openings with frame stops.
* Install durable, nonsharp-edged screens for windows.
* Secure stairwells and access to roof and housekeeping and maintenance areas.
* Use breakaway shower curtains, clothes hooks, and lockers.
* Shroud exposed pipes.

Safety procedures include the following:

* Secure all materials from suicidal patients that are commonly used for self-destruction, including, *but not limited to,* belts, razors, light cords, shoelaces, suspenders, lighters and matches, nail clippers, nail files, and pocket knives.
* Develop a system of observation for suicidal patients using the restroom.

❖ Develop a system for accounting for all dining room instruments used by suicidal patients.

❖ Be aware when suicidal patients are using sharp materials such as pins, scissors, therapy tools, and can opener.

❖ If a seclusion room is available, construct its environment so that the suicidal patient is visible and easily accessible; walls, surface edges, and windows are padded; and no area is capable of supporting the weight of a person.

❖ Develop a rating system for suicidal patients and a corresponding system of active monitoring and involvement with other patients.

❖ Position acutely suicidal patients in rooms with at least one other patient, close and accessible to the nurses' station.

❖ Initiate a system of checking all visitors for bringing in any material that might be used for lethal purposes.

❖ Develop a system of monitoring suicidal patients during staff changes, dining room visits, and any emergencies.

❖ Ensure the continuous availability of staff.

Staff considerations.   Some issues concerning understanding and communication are as follows:

❖ Understand that the great majority of patients want help and want to live.

❖ Accept the fact that suicidal patients, regardless of motive, will test the security of the unit and the resolve of the staff.

❖ Resist preoccupation and fear regarding the possibility that a patient might kill himself or herself or that a lawsuit may result. The documentation of the provision of good clinical care is the best antidote to fears of being sued.

❖ Temper desires to repress patients for "security" and seek to know patients and their motives and real desires.

❖ Strive to help restore the patient's hope and self-esteem by appropriately involving him or her in the treatment process as much as possible, including the establishment and implementation of "suicide precautions."

❖ Accept the reality that sometimes mistakes will be made, and strive to minimize them.

❖ Utilize a risk-benefit analysis with any treatment decision.

❖ Document all decisions.

❖ Ensure that all staff, including the night and weekend staff and any replacement personnel, are aware of relevant patient information.

❖ Regularly assess the progress of suicidal patients involving all of the staff that have primary contact with them. Also, involve the patient in these evaluations. Set concrete objectives regarding physical and emotional changes and improvements.

Summary. There is no way that this or any list of "precautions" can cover all of the circumstances or situations that might occur on an inpatient unit. The above are suggestions based on clinical experience, perusal of the relevant psychiatric literature, and common sense. The "best" plan for any particular unit will have to be tailor made according to the resources available. Whatever that plan or set of precautions is, it is sure to be best understood and implemented if it is formulated as a *standard protocol*. The staff will then have a clear and consistent understanding of the means and procedures for handling the suicidal patient, and the patient will hopefully receive the type of concentrated attention his or her unique emotional needs require.

Legal Issues

Suicide, the Standard of Care, and Liability

It was once thought that psychiatry, probably more than any other medical specialty, was relatively immune to lawsuits. A number of reasons have been cited for this perception (71), and what little relevant data exist would appear to give it credence (72). As psychiatry has grown in professional stature, it has become an increasingly attractive target for malpractice suits, meritorious or not. Couple psychiatry's growth with an increased level of sophistication by the judiciary and greater willingness by society to "publicly air its personal problems," and one has all of the ingredients for an increase in litigation. Of course, this increase must be viewed in its proper context. Psychiatrists still enjoy the "honor" of being one of the least sued groups of all medical specialties (73).

Notwithstanding the statistical "big picture," among all lawsuits alleging psychiatric nonfeasance or malfeasance, those suits alleging liability for patient suicides comprise, by a large margin, the greatest number. This conclusion is supported by insurance data kept by the American Psychiatric Association (74), as well as by unofficial tallies maintained by knowledgeable commentators (75). The increasing number of personal injury cases brought by psychiatric patients reflects a pervasive willingness by the courts to recognize a fairly broad "duty of care" by psychiatrists and hospitals who care for suicidal patients (76).

Negligence committed by psychiatrists is dealt with in exactly the same manner as negligence committed by individuals in any other medical specialty (77). A psychiatrist, like any other physician, owes to the patient the duty "to possess and exercise the degree of skill and learning ordinarily possessed and exercised, under similar circumstances, by the members of his profession in good standing, and to use ordinary and reasonable care and diligence, and his best judgment, in the application of his skill to the case" (78).

Thus, rules of law that apply to other medical malpractice actions apply equally to actions against psychiatrists. As a practical matter, however, they are less easily applied in the field of psychiatry because of the relatively wide discretion afforded psychiatrists as to just what the standard of care (in the profession) is for a given clinical situation (79).

The relatively larger number of "suicide suits" is not surprising given the fact that suicidal patients represent a very vulnerable and unpredictable population. Moreover, the standard of care by which a psychiatrist's actions will be judged makes no specific allowances for the unique situation that these patients create. As one California court aptly described this standard, "[T]he duty requires that those charged with the care and treatment of a patient, who know of facts from which it might reasonably be concluded that a patient would be likely to harm himself in the absence of preclusive measures, use *reasonable care* to prevent such harm" [emphasis added] (80).

In assessing liability in suicide cases, whether it involves an inpatient or an outpatient, the threshold issues are as follows:

1. Did the defendant have or should he or she have had *notice* of the patient's dangerous propensities? (In other words, was the patient's behavior *foreseeable?*)
2. If such notice was known or should have been known, did the defendant act *reasonably* in light of that information?

Accordingly, the duty of care owed to a patient by a psychiatrist or hospital is directly related to the patient's dangerous propensities that are known or discoverable by the exercise of reasonable skill and diligence (81). Therefore, when a hospital or psychiatrist knows or reasonably should have known of the patient's suicidal tendencies, the hospital or psychiatrist must exercise reasonable care to protect the patient from himself or herself (82).

In suicide cases, for instance, the various factors, risk variables, and special diagnosis and treatment considerations identified in previous sections of this chapter *could* be considered relevant "standard of care" facts depending on the case and surrounding circumstances.

It is important to keep in mind that the institution itself also owes a corresponding duty of "reasonable" care. A hospital or clinic owes a duty to its patients to exercise that degree of care commonly provided by other similarly situated hospitals or clinics. The precise degree of care required, or at least the one by which its care will be judged, will depend on the particular circumstances of each case. For instance, in *Wogelius v. Dallas,* the court held that in those cases in which a hospital's care of a patient after a suicide attempt was primarily medical, not psychiatric, it would not be held to the standard of care of a licensed psychiatric facility (83).

Causes of Action

Inpatient

When an injury or death occurs in an inpatient setting because of apparent negligence in the provision of services, there are often several potential defendants. The staff psychiatrist is frequently a prime candidate but not necessarily the *primary* defendant. The hospital or facility in which the patient was being treated is often viewed as the "defendant of choice," because it is most able to pay the damages if a judgment for the plaintiff is handed down. In addition, if a patient uses a physical device or material to inflict self-harm, such as restraints, electric bed, or shower rod (for hanging), the manufacturer of that product may also be sued. In some cases, the plaintiff will name many defendants, generally beginning with the institution and then naming several additional parties (e.g., manufacturer, primary care psychiatrist, and other staff) (84).

Psychiatrists may also be sued in their capacity as *supervisors* if they fail to adequately monitor and intervene, if necessary, in the care provided by a supervisee under their tutelage. For instance, in *Cohen v. State* (85), a first-year psychiatric resident concluded that a psychiatric patient who had a history of suicide could be released. The patient killed himself the day of his release. The court determined that a resident "did not at this point in his medical career possess the requisite skill or trained psychiatric judgment to, essentially unsupervised, provide ordinary and reasonable psychiatric medical treatment and care to this decedent." Thus, because he was permitted to act beyond the scope of his competence, the supervisor could be liable for inadequate supervision.

Psychiatrists have more often been sued when inpatients kill or harm themselves than when outpatients commit suicide. This is because hospitals (and their staff) have the greatest opportunity to observe, treat, and control a patient. As determined in one case, "The degree of care to be observed is measured by the patient's physical and mental ills and deficiencies as known to the officers and employees of the institution" (86). In dealing with hospitalized patients, psychiatrists must balance the need for precautions to prevent suicide against the therapeutic benefits of a more liberalized and open unit. The trend in recent years toward deinstitutionalization has led to a greater use of "open doors" and less restrictive environments, causing a greater tension for clinicians between, on the one hand, restricting activities and, on the other hand, allowing more freedom in the management of the suicidal patient.

Once a suicidal person becomes an inpatient, there is an assumption that control over the suicidal behavior shifts to the institution. A hospital or other facility will be liable for the suicide of its patients whenever its employees (e.g., nurses, staff psychiatrists) are negligent in fulfilling some aspect of their ordinary duties and whenever that negligence results in the suicide death or injury of a patient.

Negligence associated with inpatient suicide can occur in many ways, and therefore there is no exact or single list of "acts of liability." Two commentators have classified the most common areas of negligence that lead to a civil suit for the suicide of an inpatient into three fields: diagnosis, treatment, and discharge (87).

Diagnosis.   Diagnostic errors involving suicidal patients generally occur when a patient is "foreseeably suicidal" but the psychiatrist or staff fails to diagnosis properly his or her condition and treat the patient accordingly. For example, in the case of *Rudy v. Meshorer* (88), relatives on behalf of the decedent patient brought suit against a psychiatrist in his capacity as the admitting and treating physician at a local hospital. Prior to hospitalization by his wife, the decedent had indicated suicidal feelings and hallucinatory experiences. At least one nurse made note of these ideations, but the defendant psychiatrist claimed that he was never apprised of the suicide-related information and at no time did he think the patient was suicidal. Shortly following admission, the patient signed himself out and subsequently killed himself. The court rendered summary judgment in favor of the psychiatrist because of the plaintiff's failure to provide appropriate expert testimony that the defendant's diagnosis (of no suicide) and treatment were negligent. Despite this outcome, the fact that the psychiatrist was supposedly not informed of the patient's suicidal ideation will generally not relieve him of liability. Part of any hospital physician's standard of care is to regularly consult all recorded notes, as well as the treating staff (e.g., ward nurses). Since the demise of the "captain of the ship" doctrine, the psychiatrist will not likely be held legally liable for the acts of all members of a team, but only for those directly under his or her control (89).

The need to communicate relevant history information to the entire treatment staff, especially the primary care physician (e.g., staff psychiatrist), cannot be emphasized enough. In order for appropriate treatment and precautions to be ordered, an *informed* diagnosis of the patient's status must be made. Therefore, it is essential that patient data, whether directly or indirectly gathered, be placed in the patient's record and, whenever possible, personally communicated to necessary care personnel. A failure to do this could result in an unsupervised patient harming himself or herself and a lawsuit being filed. For instance, in *Huntley v. State* (90), an action was brought against a New York State hospital for its failure to properly supervise a foreseeably suicidal patient who had a history of instability and depression. On one occasion, this patient had disclosed to a hospital staff member her specific suicide plan. This information, however, was not communicated to the staff psychiatrist, who ultimately permitted the patient out of the hospital on a pass. The patient subsequently jumped from the roof of a nearby parking garage. In affirming a judgment for the plaintiff, the appellate court noted that the hospital staff's failure to communicate all relevant information to the appropriate decision-making personnel (e.g., staff psychiatrist) was negligent and precluded the ordering of supervision and control of what amounted to a foreseeably suicidal patient.

In determining whether a patient's suicide was foreseeable, the court will typically rely on the opinion of experts. For example, 4 days after a patient underwent a laminectomy, he was found dead beneath his hospital room window. The court concluded that whether the treating physician should have considered the patient as a potential suicide risk was a question requiring expert testimony (91). In another case, *Kanter v. Metropolitan Medical Center,* expert testimony was required to establish that a nurse was negligent in failing to prevent a psychiatric patient from drowning in a hospital bathtub (92).

Treatment.   Suicide cases that allege that the treatment was negligent usually involve patients who were known to be suicidal but for whom the resulting care and intervention were considered substandard. For instance in the case *Texarkana Memorial Hospital v. Firth* (93), a Texas appellate court held that the defendant could be found "grossly negligent" for failing to take appropriate measures in preventing a patient's suicide. The jury concluded that the hospital was indeed negligent for failing to monitor the patient, failing to maintain secure windows in order to prevent patient escape, and failing to staff the psychiatric unit with appropriately trained personnel. The plaintiff was subsequently awarded over $900,000, which the state court of appeals upheld. In its affirmance, the court noted that the public has a right to expect a hospital to maintain safe conditions and to treat patients in accordance with their needs (e.g., suicidality).

The *failure to supervise* a known suicidal patient is one of the most common complaints of negligence made against hospitals when a suicide is involved (94). As noted above, hospitals and their staff have an affirmative duty to safeguard patients with whatever precautions are considered *reasonable* given the particular circumstances. When a staff is on notice that a patient is suicidal, the courts generally hold them to a fairly high standard of care, because they are in a position of control and because they have unique expertise in treating vulnerable patients. For instance, in *Psychiatric Institute v. Allen* (95), the District of Columbia Court of Appeals held that a psychiatric hospital's failure to safeguard a patient who had a history of self-destructive acts was the proximate cause of the patient's suicide. In *Missouri v. St. Mary's Health Center* (96), the court instructed the jury to find for the plaintiff based on three aspects of liability: 1) failure to keep a suicidal patient under reasonable observation; 2) failure to formulate reasonable rules for the observation of such patients; and 3) failure to reasonably restrict access to a plastic bag that the patient used to kill himself.

Courts recognize that there is no one way to intervene in the care of a suicidal patient. Depending on the facts and circumstances, a ward staff might choose any number of intervention strategies, ranging from seclusion and constant observation to periodic observations and open ward movement. However, it is both clinically and legally responsible to adopt an attitude that *the higher the potential risk for self-harm, the more restrictive the precaution.* Similarly, even in situations in which a hospital has not yet assumed control of a patient, a duty to do *some* preventive act might nonetheless be owed. For instance, the suicide of a patient who had been refused emergency services at a hospital because of financial reasons raised issues of negligence that a court concluded a jury would decide (97). In situations involving an emergency or possible emergency, private physicians and hospitals are generally not free to "do nothing." Even if the defendant does not have a duty to accept the patient and provide treatment (98), public policy requires that, at the very least, the patient be referred to someone who is accessible and who can provide the treatment that appears to be needed. In the case of a potentially suicidal patient, notifying the police, in order to detain the patient, and simultaneously facilitating arrangements for transfer to a publicly financed facility would be one viable response.

Discharge.   The other general area of hospital negligence in which suicides sometimes result is when a foreseeably suicidal patient is inappropriately released from the facility. This can occur when a suicidal patient is prematurely released on a pass (99), when he or she is discharged from the hospital (100), or if the patient escapes and the hospital fails to reasonably attempt to retrieve him or her (101). As with any allegation of negligence, the threshold issue will be the *reasonableness* of the decision to release the patient or permit his or her escape. As stated earlier, the standard of reasonableness is not one requiring 100% accuracy or certainty. A mere mistake in diagnosis or judgment is insufficient for liability (102). However, the clinician is still required to conduct a reasonable examination in arriving at his or her clinical judgment even if in error. Therefore, if reasonable care in observing, evaluating, and treating a patient would not have revealed the patient as suicidal, then liability ordinarily will not be found.

Outpatient

Psychiatrists who primarily treat outpatients are less likely to be found liable for patients' self-inflicted injuries and suicides than are hospital staff practitioners. Often the courts have an understanding of the difficulties that psychiatrists and other mental health clinicians have in predicting future behavior such as suicide. As a result, they are less apt to impose liability unless the patient's suicidality is known by the defendant (103). One court aptly addressed this situation when it remarked that "prediction of the future course of mental illness is a professional judgment of high responsibility and in some cases . . . involves a measure of calculated risk" (104). A second reason for the reduced likelihood of outpatient therapists being successfully sued as compared with their inpatient counterparts is because of the greatly reduced amount of control that they exercise over a patient (105).

Notwithstanding this diminished frequency of lawsuits, outpatient suicides do occur and malpractice actions are filed. Psychiatrists and other professionals open themselves up to a lawsuit when they fail to take adequate precautions to manage their vulnerable patients. Courts will not blindly defer to a professional's judgment if it is determined that because of totally unreasonable care, the need for special treatment, considerations, or immediate, affirmative action was underestimated or not followed through (106).

Suits that allege negligence which results in the suicide of an outpatient can generally be categorized into two broad groups: those involving *diagnosis* and those involving *treatment.*

Diagnosis. Part of the duty of care owed by psychiatrists and other regulated mental health professionals is to stay abreast of the current literature. For clinicians treating vulnerable patients, this responsibility should include becoming familiar with contemporaneous, professional literature regarding indicators and symptoms exhibited by potentially suicidal patients. A frequent source of lawsuits against both inpatient and outpatient psychiatrists and hospitals is that they negligently (e.g., unreasonably) failed to recognize that patients were suicidal and thus prevent them from hurting themselves (107).

Proper diagnosis is critical when treating vulnerable or potentially suicidal patients. If a psychiatrist fails to recognize reasonably obvious indicators that would have alerted other competent clinicians to take precautions, the psychiatrist may be sued and found liable. Generally, diagnostically related negligence can occur when the patient is foreseeably suicidal but the therapist fails to conduct a reasonable assessment that could reveal those tendencies. A second scenario arises when the patient is known to be suicidal but the therapist underdiagnoses or underestimates the severity and imminence of the threat (108). In both situations, the question of how reasonable was the defendant's evaluation of the patient, and any resulting precautions, will determine whether he or she is likely liable for any injuries that may have later occurred.

Treatment.   Once a therapist has determined that a patient is a suicide risk, he or she has an affirmative duty to take whatever precautions are reasonable under the circumstances to safeguard the patient's welfare. Therefore, it is incumbent upon clinicians to keep in mind what resources are available to them should this situation arise. Before determining a course of action, it is essential that the therapist have a reasonable idea of the seriousness and imminence of the potential suicide threat. It is this evaluation that will generally dictate the appropriate preventive strategy and action. For instance, clinical judgment might suggest that because a patient's suicidal ideation is poorly defined and halfhearted, and the patient does not indicate serious psychopathology or feelings of hopelessness, a less restrictive course of action is warranted. Of course, if a patient manifests symptoms or expresses desires that suggest a more lethal set of circumstances, then a more immediate and restrictive approach is necessary. General treatment considerations (109) such as use of crisis intervention techniques in therapy, more frequent patient contacts, referral to a crisis or emergency service, initiating or increasing medication, and voluntary or involuntary hospitalization, are all options depending upon the immediate circumstances.

Therapists become vulnerable to a malpractice action when they recognize that a patient is potentially suicidal but they fail to adjust their intervention accordingly (110). For instance, allegations of failing to closely monitor a patient, failing to refer the patient to a specialist or more appropriate professional, or even abandonment of the patient during a potential suicide crisis (e.g., going on vacation without appropriate coverage) can all precipitate a patient suicide and possible lawsuit. Occasionally, therapists will also err by recognizing that a patient is seriously suicidal and thus requires protective custody, such as hospitalization, but will recommend an open-ward placement when a more secure environment is needed.

Defenses: Inpatient and Outpatient

It is important to keep in mind that regardless of whether a "bad result" occurred or even that the defendant was negligent in some way, liability will not be found if the plaintiff does not prove his or her case by a preponderance of the evidence. Like any other medical malpractice action, this requires that the claimant establish that 1) there was *duty of care* owed to the patient by the defendant; 2) there was a *deviation* in the standard of care by the defendant; 3) the claimant suffered an injury or *damages*; and

4) the defendant's deviation or breach in the duty of care was the *direct* cause of the plaintiff's injury (111). The failure by the claimant to prove *any one* of these elements, regardless of the actions of the defendant or the resultant injury, will undermine the success of the lawsuit. For instance, a New York appellate court ruled in *Krapivka v. Maomonides Medical Center* (112) that the failure of a hospital to question a patient's spouse and others about the patient's psychiatric history was not the *cause* of the patient's suicide. In *Gaido v. Weiser* (113), a jury found a psychiatrist negligent for failing to diagnose and adequately treat a patient who committed suicide. The jury, however, did not find that the negligence was the *proximate cause* of the suicide. The psychiatrist had seen the patient on an outpatient basis following release from a psychiatric hospital. After the patient exhibited unusual behavior, the patient's wife communicated this information to the psychiatrist. He prescribed some tranquilizers and then saw the patient the next day. Shortly after the appointment, the patient's body, with a blood alcohol content of .23 percent, was found in a creek.

In *Newton v. Louisiana Department of Health and Human Services* (114), a Louisiana appeals court affirmed a decision that a psychiatrist was not liable to the family of a former patient who had committed suicide. The plaintiff first took his wife to see the defendant at a state mental health center in 1984. The psychiatrist evaluated the patient and determined that she did not meet the criteria for civil commitment. He instead referred her to a private psychiatrist for outpatient treatment. A year later, the husband called the first psychiatrist (defendant) to say that he would bring her in for another evaluation. When the wife refused to come in, the husband declined to have her taken into custody, ostensibly because the defendant could give no assurances that an emergency commitment was warranted. Several days later the wife killed herself. On appeal, the court concluded among other things, that the husband's telephone call did not create a *doctor-patient relationship* (115) and, therefore, the psychiatrist was under no duty to commit the wife, even if it had been appropriate.

In addition to the difficult burden that plaintiffs must meet in order to prove a case of negligence, there are a number of defenses that the defendant can raise that might successfully bar or mitigate a claim of negligence. In most respects these defenses, depending upon the circumstances, can apply to outpatient as well as inpatient scenarios. Again, the defenses described below are *general* theories that are not intended to be all-inclusive.

Professional judgment and compliance with standard of care. In all likelihood, the most frequently raised defense by clinicians sued for negligence resulting in a patient suicide is that the defendant's actions represented *reasonable professional judgment* and did not deviate from the appropriate standard of care (116). Because the courts generally recognize the difficult task clinicians have in diagnosing and treating vulnerable patients, especially those who are outpatients, the standard by which their conduct will be measured tends to reflect those realities. For instance, in *Fiederlein v. City of New York Health & Hospital Corporation* (117), a New York appellate court reversed a lower court's finding of negligence, stating that the mere fact that the plaintiff's expert disagreed with the conclusions of the treating psychiatrist did not provide the basis for a holding that a prima facie case of malpractice was presented requiring jury consideration. Moreover, it noted that the prediction of future illness is a professional judgment that must be *demonstrated* to have been negligently made in order for liability to be found. In a similar vein, the court in *Centano v. New York* (118) ruled that "the decision to release a patient from the hospital and place him on convalescent out-patient status was a medical judgment. Although another physician might disagree as to the form and period of treatment to be followed, liability would not arise."

Accurate determination of suicide not possible.   As long as a professional's decision or assessment is based on reasonable methods, a mere error would not result in liability (119). It is well established that suicide can be a wholly unpredictable act or one in which the vague and confusing signals given by a vulnerable person can easily be misinterpreted. In these and similar situations, the accurate determination of suicide may not be possible, or at least may not be *reasonable* under the prevailing circumstances. If this is the case, liability is not likely to be found. For instance, in *Wilson v. State* (120), the court held that no liability could be imposed for granting grounds privileges to a patient who later committed suicide because there was no evidence that the patient was suicidal and that the defendant knew the patient's history through records of prior treatment.

Justified allowance of movement ("open door policy").   The debate involving inpatient release cases frequently focuses on the question of "predicting dangerousness" and the therapeutic benefits and consequences of providing a patient greater freedom in an "open door" environment. Probably no issue involving the care and treatment of destructive psychiatric patients better represents the tension between the traditional "custodial" treatment approach and the more liberal "open therapy" format. Proponents of the latter contend that successful psychiatric treatment requires considerable collaboration, trust, and rapport between therapist and patient. In this vein, a treatment philosophy that emphasizes freedom of movement and personal responsibility tends to foster the kind of trust and self-esteem development that clinicians working with suicidal patients deem as crucial. Locked doors, rigid restrictions, and diminished privacy tend to convey to patients that they cannot be trusted or that they are not responsible for themselves. These types of messages only serve to increase a patient's self-deprecatory attitudes and reinforce their belief that all is hopeless.

In order to reverse this pattern and try to instill some confidence and trust in a patient, some facilities use what is known as an "open door" policy. In the case of *Meier v. Ross General Hospital,* this policy is described as follows:

> The hospital had adopted an "open door" policy for its psychiatric patients. This method of treatment de-emphasizes physical restraint by providing a "homelike" atmosphere. . . . The patients are free to move about and even to leave the hospital if they are so inclined. No mechanical security devices are regularly used; the doors are not locked; the windows are not barred. The policy rests upon the premise that freedom of movement and personal responsibility of patients, even potential suicides, improve the process of their rehabilitation and reduce possible emotional stress. The proponents of the "open door" policy concede, however, that the lessening of physical security exposes a potentially suicidal patient to greater risk. They assert that no amount of security or physical restraint short of rendering the patient unconscious can effectively prevent suicide. Nevertheless, recognizing the risk of suicide in certain patients, the proponents of "open door" therapy normally enjoy larger staffs to facilitate surveillance, administer chemotherapy to those patients whose symptomatic restlessness and agitation indicate severe depression which may lead to suicide. (121)

Some courts, depending upon the reasonableness of the decision to use the open door policy with certain patients, have accepted this policy as a viable extension of a *professional's judgment* and thus will not impose liability. For instance, in *Johnson v. United States* (122), a discharged patient murdered his brother-in-law, wounded his wife, and then committed suicide. Although the patient had received considerable assessment and treatment procedures prior to his release, the inpatient staff concluded that he did not represent a risk of future violence or dangerousness. The court discussed the issue of dangerousness prediction and the viability of the open door policy in its opinion:

> Modern psychiatry has recognized the importance of making every reasonable effort to return a patient to active and productive life. Thus, the patient is encouraged to develop his self-confidence by adjusting to the demands of everyday existence. . . . Furthermore, all the expert witnesses for both parties agreed that accurate prediction of dangerous behavior, and particularly of suicide and homicide, are [sic] almost never possible. Especially in view of this fact, the Court is persuaded that modern psychiatric practice does not require a patient to be isolated from normal human activities until every possible danger has passed. Because of the virtual impossibility of predicting dangerousness, such an approach would necessarily lead to prolonged incarceration for many patients who would

become useful members of society. It has also been made clear to the Court that constant supervision and restriction will often tend to promote the very disorders which they are designed to control. . . . On the other hand, despite the therapeutic benefits of the "open door" approach, the practice admittedly entails a high potential of danger both for the patient and for those with whom he comes in contact. . . . The Court is aware that some psychiatrists adhere to the older, more custodial approach. However, it has been proved to the Court's satisfaction that the "open door" policy and the *judgmental balancing test* are an accepted method of treatment. **Therefore, no liability can arise merely because a psychiatrist favors the newer over the older approach.** (123)

This judicial view has been accepted in other cases (124), as long as the use of the open door policy was determined to be reasonable. The major issue in such cases, therefore, appears to be whether the psychiatrist's conduct or decision making was "reasonable," meaning the reasonableness of the treatment approach for specific patients at particular times. Not all patients can be treated successfully in this modality (i.e., open door). Proper selection of patients for various treatment settings involves the sound clinical judgment of the psychiatrist and the application of "reasonable" care and treatment.

Intervening acts.   There are situations in which a psychiatrist or hospital exercises reasonable care to safeguard a suicidal or homicidal patient, but because of unforeseen, extraordinary circumstances the patient is able to harm or kill himself or herself, or someone else. When an event or series of events is *unforeseen* and *outside the control of the defendant,* and it serves to *intervene* between the care provided and the act that occurs (e.g., suicide), the court will not find a defendant liable (125). This is because the patient's death was *proximately caused* not by something the defendant did or did not do, but rather by some *other* event. For instance, in *Paddock v. Chacko* (126), a Florida appeals court concluded that a psychiatrist was not liable for the self-inflicted injuries of an adult patient whom the psychiatrist had seen just once. Moreover, the psychiatrist did not have a duty to hospitalize the patient involuntarily, as the parents of the patient contended in a lawsuit regarding the suicide attempt of their daughter. The patient had placed herself under her parents' care and custody, and the parents had disregarded the psychiatrist's recommendation that their daughter be hospitalized. Finally, the court concluded that the failure of the psychiatrist to see the patient was not the proximate cause of death, although the patient had said she was fearful and hallucinating. In *Paddock* the unwillingness of the patient's father to heed the defendant's recommendation of hospitalization served to insulate the defendant from liability because it essentially severed the causal link between the psychiatrist and the patient.

Also, a finding of no liability may occur even if the defendant is negligent in some way as long as his or her negligence was not the direct cause of the patient's injury. For example, in *Weatherly v. State* (127), even though a psychiatrist was negligent in failing to place a patient back on "suicide precaution" following a return from a pass, this omission was determined not to be the proximate cause of the patient's jumping out of a window. At the time of the jump, the court concluded that the patient did not intend to harm himself, but rather was responding to the influence of a drug-induced psychosis: "[I]t is clear that the claimant was not intending to kill himself. . . . This being the case, the risk of attempted suicide was totally irrelevant to the happening of the accident herein, which was occasioned by an *independent intervening cause*" (128).

The courts have generally *not* accepted a patient's voluntary action of committing suicide per se as a defense that severs the chain of causation and exonerates the defendant from liability (129). As a general rule, a psychiatrist will not be relieved of liability if a patient commits suicide, because the suicide would likely be considered a *foreseeable* consequence of the psychiatrist's negligence.

Immunity. Professionals that are employed by state or municipal agencies or facilities such as mental hospitals may be protected from liability by governmental immunity (130). State law and the manner in which the defendant's role is defined will determine whether the defense of immunity is available (131).

Conclusions

It is well accepted in the psychiatric profession that a patient determined to commit suicide will eventually succeed regardless of whether he or she is in the protective confines of a hospital or being treated by the most conscientious private therapist. Even the most well-developed precautionary procedures by a diligent and competent professional cannot forever protect a patient from a self-imposed desire to die. Liability is not a simple determination of whether a suicide was preventable; instead, the pivotal question is whether reasonable care was exercised under the prevailing circumstances. If, after all the relevant facts and testimony are weighed, the answer is "yes," then liability will not be found even if a suicide attempt was successful.

As noted earlier, the courts will not hold a psychiatrist liable for mere honest mistakes, recognizing that "accurate predictions of dangerous behavior, particularly suicide and homicide, are almost never possible" (132). Accordingly, the diligent psychiatrist need not be consumed with thoughts of lawsuits and soaring malpractice premiums every time he or she accepts a vulnerable patient for treatment. Standard clinical practices such as the following are all evidence of *reasonable* professional conduct that not only represents sound treatment procedures but will also serve as strong defense evidence if needed in a lawsuit:

- ❖ Conducting a thorough mental status examination
- ❖ Taking a thorough clinical history
- ❖ Reviewing any past medical and psychiatric records
- ❖ When appropriate, conducting periodic and direct inquiry about suicidal ideation
- ❖ Familiarizing oneself with current professional literature regarding suicide indices and then using these indices to compare them with a patient's personality and history
- ❖ Conducting risk-benefit analysis when dealing with a potentially suicidal patient
- ❖ Consulting with knowledgeable colleagues
- ❖ Considering more secure or emergency placement if a patient's condition deteriorates or becomes overtly suicidal

There is no indication in the legal literature that lawsuits alleging negligence resulting in patient suicide are decreasing or are going to decrease in the near future. Private psychiatrists, staff psychiatrists, and psychiatric hospitals and facilities will likely continue to be sued at a relatively high rate. There is some indication, however, that at least half of all suits are found in favor of the defendant (133).

References

1. Evans G, Farberow NL: The Encyclopedia of Suicide. New York, Facts on File, 1988, p 84
2. Durkheim E: Le Suicide [later republished as "Suicide" by the Free Press, NY, 1897]
3. Levy R: Suicide, homicide, and other psychiatric emergencies, in Comprehensive Textbook of Psychiatry IV, Vol 1. Edited by Kaplan HI, Sadock BJ. Baltimore, MD, Williams & Wilkins, 1985, p 660
4. Shneidman E: Definition of Suicide. New York, John Wiley, 1985, pp123–142
5. Waldinger RJ: Psychiatry for Medical Students, 2nd Edition. Washington DC, American Psychiatric Press, 1990, pp 444–445
6. Suicide, Part II. Harvard Medical School Mental Health Letter 9(March):1, 3, 1986
7. Simon RI: Concise Guide to Psychiatry and Law for Clinicians. Washington, DC, American Psychiatric Press, 1992, citing Roy A (ed): Suicide. Baltimore, MD, Williams & Wilkins, 1986
8. See, e.g., Maxwell SL Jr: Suicide by firearms (letter). N Engl J Med 310:46–47, 1984

9. Suicide, Part I. Harvard Medical School Mental Health Letter 9(February):1–4, 1986

10. Farberow NL: Suicide prevention in the hospital. Hosp Community Psychiatry 32:99, 100, 104, 1981, citing Sletten IW, Brown ML, Evenson RC, et al: Suicide in mental hospital patients. Diseases of the Nervous System, May 1972, pp 328–334; Farberow NL, Williams JL: Status of suicide in Veterans Administration Hospitals: Report IV. Washington DC, Veterans Administration, January 1978

11. Farberow NL: Suicide prevention in the hospital. Hosp Community Psychiatry 32:99, 100, 104, 1981

12. Ibid, p 100

13. National Center for Health Statistics: Unpublished data, 1933–1953, 1961–1979, 1980–1982

14. See, e.g., Barefoot v Estelle, 463 U.S. 880, 899, 901 (1983)

15. See, e.g., Greenberg DF: Involuntary psychiatric commitment to prevent suicide, 1974. NYU Law Review 49:227; Schwartz DA, Flinn DE, Slawson PF: Suicide in the psychiatric hospital. Am J Psychiatry 132:150–153, 1975

16. Simon RI: Clinical management of suicidal patients: assessing the unpredictable, in American Psychiatric Press Review of Clinical Psychiatry and the Law, Vol 3. Edited by Simon RI. Washington, DC, American Psychiatric Press, 1992, pp 3–63

17. Simon RI: Concise Guide to Psychiatry and Law for the Clinician. Washington, DC, American Psychiatric Press, 1992

18. Cross CK, Hirschfeld RM: Epidemiology of disorders in adulthood: suicide, in Social, Epidemiologic, and Legal Psychiatry. Edited by Klerman GL, Weissman MM, Appelbaum PS, et al. Philadelphia, PA, JP Lippincott, 1986, p 248

19. Ibid, pp 247–248

20. Ibid, p 246

21. Ibid, pp 247–49

22. Ibid, p 248, citing 1978 U.S. suicide rates by sex and age groups (race combined), National Center for Health Statistics, 1978

23. Ibid, p 249

24. Kozak CM, Gibb JO: Dependent children and suicide of married parents. Suicide Life Threat Behav 9:67–75, 1979

25. See, e.g., MacMahon B, Johnson S, Pugh TF: Relation of suicide rates to social conditions: evidence from U.S. Vital Statistics. Public Health Rep 78:285–293, 1963

26. See, e.g., Breed W: Occupational mobility and suicide among white males. American Sociological Review 28:179–188, 1963; Sanborn DE, Sanborn CJ, Cimbolic P: Occupation and suicide. Diseases of the Nervous System 35:7–12, 1974; Shepherd DM, Barraclough BM: Work and suicide: an empirical investigation: Br J Psychiatry 136:469–478, 1980

27. Powell EH: Occupation, status, and suicide: toward a redefinition of anomie. American Sociological Review 23:133–139, 1958; Rich CL, Pitts FN: Suicide by male physicians during a five-year period. Am J Psychiatry 136:1089–1090, 1979; Pitts FN, Schuller AB, Rich CL, et al: Suicide among U.S. women physicians, 1967–1972. Am J Psychiatry 136:694–696, 1979

28. Beck AT, Kovacs M, Weissman A: Assessment of suicidal intention: the scale for suicide ideation. J Consult Clin Psychol 47:343–352, 1979

29. Dorpat TL, Ripley HS: The relationship between attempted suicide and committed suicide. Compr Psychiatry 8:74–79, 1967

30. Beck AT, et al: Assessment of suicide intention: the scale for suicide ideation. J Consult Clin Psychol 47:343–352, 1979; Ludwig AM: Principles of Clinical Psychiatry. London, Free Press, 1986

31. Weisman AD, Worden JW: Risk-rescue rating in suicide assessment. Arch Gen Psychiatry 26:553–560, 1972

32. Beck AT, Kovacs M, Weissman A: Assessment of suicidal intention: the scale for suicide ideation. J Consult Clin Psychol 47:343–352, 1979

33. Shneidman ES: Suicide among the gifted, in Suicidology: Contemporary Developments. Edited by Shneidman ES. New York, Grune & Stratton, 1976, pp 341–368

34. Robins E, Murphy GE, Wilkinson RH, et al: Some clinical considerations in the prevention of suicide based on a study of 134 successful suicides. Am J Public Health 49:888–899, 1959; Dorpat TL, Ripley HS: A study of suicide in the Seattle area. Compr Psychiatry 1:349–359, 1960; Barraclough B, Bunch J, Nelson B, et al: A hundred cases of suicide: clinical aspects. Br J Psychiatry 125:355–373, 1974

35. Roy A: Risk factors for suicide in psychiatric patients. Arch Gen Psychiatry 39:1089–1095, 1982

36. Roy A: Risk factors for suicide in psychiatric patients. Arch Gen Psychiatry 39:1089–1095, 1982; Morrison JR: Suicide in a psychiatric population. J Clin Psychiatry 43:348–352, 1982

37. See, e.g., Goodwin DW: Alcoholism and suicide: association factors, in Encyclopedic Handbook of Alcoholism. Edited by Pattison EM, Kaufman E. New York, Gardner, 1982, pp 655–660

38. Tsuang MT: Suicide in schizophrenics, manics, depressives, and surgical controls: a comparison with general population suicide mortality. Arch Gen Psychiatry 35:153–155, 1978; Wilkinson DG: The suicide rate in schizophrenia. Br J Psychiatry 140:138–141, 1982

39. Robins E, Guze SB: Classification of affective disorders: the primary-secondary, the endogenous-reactive, and the neurotic-psychotic concepts, in Recent Advances in the Psychobiology of the Depressive Illnesses. Edited by Williams TA, Katz MM, Shields JA. Washington, DC, U.S. Government Printing Office, 1972

40. Tsuang MT: Suicide in schizophrenics, manics, depressives, and surgical controls: a comparison with general population suicide mortality. Arch Gen Psychiatry 35:153–155, 1978; Guze SB, Robins E: Suicide and primary affective disorders. Br J Psychiatry 117:437–438, 1970

41. Pokorny AD: Suicide rates in various psychiatric disorders. J Nerv Ment Dis 139:499–506, 1964

42. Paykel ES, Prosoff BA, Myers JK: Suicide attempts and recent life events: a controlled comparison. Arch Gen Psychiatry 32:327–333, 1975

43. Fawcett J, Scheptner WA, et al: Time-related predictors of suicide in major affective disorder. Am J Psychiatry 147:1189–1194, 1990

44. See National Institute of Mental Health: Useful Information on Suicide. Rockville, MD, NIMH, 1986, pp 15–17; Simon SI: Concise Guide to Psychiatry and Law for Clinicians. Washington, DC, American Psychiatric Press, 1992

45. See, e.g., Motto JA, Heilbron DC, Juster RP: Development of a clinical instrument to estimate suicide risk. Am J Psychiatry 142:680–686, 1985; Weisman AD, Worden JW: Risk-rescue rating in suicide assessment. Arch Gen Psychiatry 26:553–560, 1972

46. See, e.g., Barefoot v Estelle, 463 US 880 (1983); Monahan J: The prediction of violent behavior: developments in psychology and law, in Psychology and the Law, Vol 2 (Master Lecture Series). Edited by Schreirer J, Hammonds B. Washington DC, American Psychological Association, 1982; Slobogin C: Dangerousness and expertise. University of Pennsylvania Law Review 133:97, 1984

47. Simon RI: Concise Guide to Psychiatry and Law for Clinicians. Washington, DC, American Psychiatric Press, 1992

48 Ibid, p 87

49. Simon RI: Concise Guide to Psychiatry and Law for Clinicians. Washington, DC, American Psychiatric Press, 1992; Weisman AD, Worden JW: Risk-rescue rating in suicide assessment. Arch Gen Psychiatry 26:553–560, 1972; Motto JA, Heilbron DC, Juster RP: Development of a clinical instrument to estimate suicide risk. Am J Psychiatry 142:680–686, 1985

50. Simon RI: Concise Guide to Psychiatry and Law for Clinicians. Washington, DC, American Psychiatric Press, 1992

51. Ibid, p 91

52. Shneidman ES: Suicide among the gifted, in Suicidology: Contemporary Developments. Edited by Shneidman ES. New York, Grune & Stratton, 1976, pp 341–368

53. See, for example, Robins E: The Final Months: A Study of the Lives of 134 Persons Who Committed Suicide. New York, Oxford University Press, 1981

54. See, for example, Reynolds DK, Farberow NL: Suicide Inside and Out. Berkeley, CA, University of California Press, 1976

55. Miller DH: Suicidal careers: case analysis of suicidal mental patients. Social Work 15:27–36, 1970; Farberow NL, MacKinnon DR: Follow-up of High Risk Suicidal Neuropsychiatric Patients: A Pilot Study. Washington, DC, Veterans Administration, 1974

56. Simon RI: Silent suicide in the elderly. Bull Am Acad Psychiatry Law 17:83–95, 1989

57. National Institute of Mental Health: Useful Information on Suicide. Rockville, MD, NIMH, 1986, p 4

58. Earls F: Epidemiology of psychiatric disorders in children and adolescents, in Social, Epidemiologic, and Legal Psychiatry. Edited by Klerman GL, Weissman MM, Appelbaum PS, et al. Philadelphia, PA, JP Lippincott, 1988, pp 123–152 (140)

59. National Institute of Mental Health: Useful Information on Suicide. Rockville, MD, NIMH, 1986, pp 4–5

60. Brent DA, Kerr MM, Goldstein C, et al: An outbreak of suicide and suicidal behavior in a high school. J Am Acad Child Adolesc Psychiatry 6:918–924, 1989

61. Gould MS, Wallerstein S, Kleinman M: Time-space clustering of teenage suicide. Am J Epidemiol 131:871–878, 1990

62. Eisenberg L: Adolescent suicide: on taking arms against a sea of troubles. Pediatrics 66:315–320, 1980

63. Shaffer D: Suicide in childhood and early adolescence. J Child Psychol Psychiatry 15:275–291, 1974

64. Sletten IW: Suicide in mental hospital patients. Diseases of the Nervous System 33:328–334, 1972

65. Mounds Park Hospital v Von Eye, 245 F2d 756 (8th Cir 1958)

66. Benensohn HS, Resnik HL: Guidelines for "suicide proofing" a psychiatric unit. Am J Psychotherapy 27:204–212, 1973

67. Polack S: Suicide in a general hospital, in Clues to Suicide. Edited by Shneidman ES, Farberow NL. New York, McGraw–Hill, 1957

68. Joint Commission on Accreditation of Healthcare Organizations: Consolidated Standards Manual. Chicago, IL, Joint Commission on Accreditation of Healthcare Organizations, 1988

69. See, e.g., Margolis PM, Meyer GG, Louw JC: Suicide precautions: a dilemma in the therapeutic community. Arch Gen Psychiatry 13:224–231, 1965; Perr W: Suicide responsibility of the hospital and psychiatrist. Cleveland-Marshall Law Review 9:427, 1960; Meier v Ross General Hospital, 67 Cal 2d 420, 445 P2d 519, 71 Cal Rptr 903 (1968)

70. Benensohn HS, Resnik HL: Guidelines for "suicide proofing" a psychiatric unit. Am J Psychotherapy 27:204–212, 1973

71. Robertson J: Psychiatric Malpractice. New York, John Wiley, 1988, p 4

72. Hogan D: Regulation of Psychotherapists, Vol 1–3. Cambridge, MA, Ballinger, 1979; Bellamy WA: Malpractice risks confronting the psychiatrist: a nationwide fifteen-year study of appellate court cases, 1946–1961. Am J Psychiatry 118:769–780, 1962

73. Malpractice claims per 100 physicians. U.S. News & World Report, December 14, 1987, p 66

74. Psychiatry claims closed 1980–1985. Psychiatric News, Vol 22, April 3, 1987, p 11

75. Most lawsuits in psychiatry involve suicide. Clinical Psychiatry News 17(January):1, 13, 1989

76. See, for example, Kent v Whitaker, 58 Wash 2d 569, 364 P2d 556 (1961); Vistica v Presbyterian Hospital and Medical Center, Inc, 67 Cal 2d 465, 432 P2d 193, 62 Cal Rptr 577 (1967)

77. Smith JT: Medical Malpractice: Psychiatric Care. Colorado Springs, CO, Shepard's/McGraw-Hill, 1986

78. Titchnell v United States, 681 F2d 165 (3rd Cir 1982)

79. See, e.g., White v United States, 244 F Supp 127, 134 (ED Va 1965), affirmed, 359 F2d 989 (4th Cir 1966)

80. Meier v Ross General Hospital, 69 Cal App 2d 420, 526, 445 P2d 519, 525, 71 Cal Rptr 903, 909 (1968)

81. See, e.g., Emory University v Lee, 97 Ga App 680, 104 SE2d 248 (1958); Weglarz v State, 311 App Div 2d 595, 295 NYS2d 152 (1968)

82. Annotation: Suicide—liability of mental care facility for suicide of patient or former patient, 19 ALR4th 7 (1983)

83. 152 Ill App 3d 631, 504 NE2d 791 (1987)

84. Fed R Civ P 18-25

85. 382 NYS2d 128 (App Div 1976)

86. Zajaczkowski v State, 71 NYS2d 261 (Ct Cl 1947)

87. Bisbing SB, Smith JT: Suicide: psychiatry's greatest malpractice threat. Course presentation at the 141st annual meeting of the American Psychiatric Association, May 11, 1987
88. Rudy v Meshorer, 146 Ariz 467, 706 P2d 1234 (1985)
89. Price SH: The sinking of the "captain of the ship": reexamining the vicarious liability of an operating surgeon for the negligence of assisting hospital personnel. J Leg Med 10:323–356, 1989
90. 476 NYS2d 99, 464 NE2d 467 (1984)
91. Biundo v Christ Community Hospital, 104 Ill App3d 670, 432 NE2d 1293 (1982)
92. 384 NW2d 914 (Minn Ct App 1986)
93. 746 SW2d 494 (Tex Ct App 1988)
94. See, e.g., Abille v United States, 482 F Supp 703 (ND Cal 1980); Adams v Carter County Memorial Hospital, 548 SW2d 307 (Tenn 1977), Adams v State, 71 Wash 2d 414, 429 P2d 109 (1967); in re Apicella's Estate, 207 Misc 743, 140 NY2d 634 (Ct Cl 1955) Arlington Heights Sanitarium v Deaderick, 272 SW 497 (Tex Civ App 1925); Brown v State, 84 AD2d 644, 444 NYS2d 304 (1981); Brown v St Mary's Health Center, 713 SW2d 15 (Mo App 1986)
95. 509 A2d 619 (DC 1986)
96. 713 SW2d 15 (Mo Ct App 1986)
97. Tabor v Doctors Memorial Hospital, 501 So 2d 243 (La Ct App 1986)
98. Simon RI: Clinical Psychiatry and the Law, 2nd Edition. Washington, DC, American Psychiatric Press, 1992
99. See, e.g., Uphoff v DePaul Hospital, CD 83-18047 New Orleans Dist Ct (La 1987)
100. See, e.g., Bell v New York City Health & Hospital, 90 AD2d 270, 456 NYS2d 787 (1982)
101. See, e.g., Lando v State, 47 AD2d 972, 366 NYS2d 679 (1975), modified 39 NY2d 803, 385 NYS2d 759, 351 NE2d 426 (1976)
102. See, e.g., Dimitrijevic v Chicago Wesley Memorial Hospital, 92 Ill App 2d 251, 236 NE2d 309 (1968)
103. See Leverette v State, 54 Ill App 3d 7, 369 NE2d 106 (1978); Ross v Central Louisiana State Hospital, 392 So 2d 698 (La App 1980)
104. Taig v State, 19 AD2d 182, 241 NYS2d 495 (1963)
105. Speer v United States, 512 F Supp 670 (ND Tex 1981); Runyon v Reid, 510 P2d 943 (Okla 1973)
106. See Weatherly v State, 109 Misc 2d 1024, 441 NYS2d 319 (1981); Abille v United States, 482 F Supp 703 (ND Cal 1980)
107. Barrett v State, No 65243 NY Cty Sup Ct (NY March 1985); Behrems v Raleigh Hills Hospital, 675 P2d 1179 (Utah 1983); Coltraine v Pitt County Memorial Hospital, 35 NC App 755, 242 SE2d 538 (1978)
108. See, e.g., Jackson v United States, 577 F Supp 1377 (ED Mo), affirmed 750 F2d 55 (8th Cir 1984)
109. See, e.g., Schultz B: Legal Liability in Psychotherapy. Washington, DC, Jossey-Bass, 1982, pp 72–73
110. See Bellah v Greenson, 81 Cal App 3d 614, 146 Cal Rptr 535 (1978)
111. Simon RI: Clinical Psychiatry and the Law, 2nd Edition. Washington, DC, American Psychiatric Press, 1992; Sadoff RL: Forensic Psychiatry, 2nd Edition. Springfield, IL, Charles C Thomas, 1988, p 195

112. 119 AD2d 801, 501 NYS2d 429 (1986)
113. 227 NJ Super 175, 545 A2d 1350 (1988)
114. 536 So 2d 560 (La Ct App 1988)
115. Also see King v Smith, 539 So 2d 262 (Ala 1989)
116. Bisbing SB, Smith JT: Suicide: caselaw summary and analysis. Unpublished manuscript, 1989 [reviewing over 300 settled and adjudicated cases involving suicide]
117. 450 NYS2d 181, 56 AD 245 (1982)
118. 48 AD2d 812, 369 NYS2d 710 (1975), affirmed, 40 NY2d 932, 389 NYS2d 837, 258 NE2d 520 (1976)
119. St George v State, 127 NYS2d 147, 283 AD 245, affirmed, 124 NE2d 320 (1954)
120. 112 AD2d 366, 491 NYS2d 818 (1985)
121. 67 Cal 2d 420, 425, 445 P2d 519, 523, 71 Cal Rptr 903, 907 (1968)
122. 409 F Supp 1283 (MD Fla 1976)
123. Ibid
124. See, e.g., Broussard v State Division of Hospitals, 356 So 2d 94 (La Ct App), cert denied 358 So 2d 639 (La 1978); Baker v United States, 343 F2d 222 (8th Cir 1965); James v Turner, 184 Tenn 563, 201 SW2d 691 (1941). But see Perr I: Suicide responsibility of hospitals and psychiatrists. Cleveland-Marshall Law Review 9:427, 1960
125. See, e.g., Kates v State, 47 Misc 2d 176, 261 NYS2d 988 (1965); Nieves v State, 91 AD2d 938, 458 NYS2d 548 (1983)
126. 522 So 2d 410 (Fla App 1988)
127. 109 Misc 2d 1024, 441 NYS2d 319 (Ct Cl 1981)
128. 441 NYS2d 322
129. See, e.g., Riesbeck Drug Co v Wray, 111 Ind App 467, 39 NE2d 776 (1942); Runyan v Reid, 510 P2d 943 (Okla 1973); Farrow v Health Services Corporation, 604 P2d 474 (Utah 1979)
130. See, e.g., Miller v State, 731 SW2d 885 (Mo Ct App 1987)
131. Smith JT: Medical Malpractice: Psychiatric Care. Colorado Springs, CO, Shepard's/McGraw-Hill, 1986, pp 518–522
132. Paradies v Benedictine Hospital, 431 NYS2d 175, 77 AD2d 757 (1980); Fiederlein v New York Health and Hospital Corporation, 56 NY2d 573, 437 NYS2d 321 (1981)
133. Bisbing SB, Smith JT: Suicide: psychiatry's greatest malpractice threat. Course presentation at the 141st annual meeting of the American Psychiatric Association, May 1987

❖ Chapter 7 ❖

Sexual Exploitation of Patients ─────────────

Doctor-Patient Relationship

Development and Value to Therapy

The doctor-patient relationship forms the basis for any duty or responsibility and potential liability between psychiatrist (physician) and patient (1). For purposes of a malpractice action, there must be evidence of this relationship, or no legally enforceable cause of action can exist, regardless of any harm that might have resulted (2).

From a clinical perspective, the therapeutic relationship is considered by many practitioners the single most essential element associated with successful treatment. For example, Marziali and his colleagues, in their study of brief psychodynamic therapy, concluded that "patients who developed and maintained positive attitudes toward the therapist and the work of therapy achieved the greatest gains" (3).

All psychiatric therapies, regardless of their philosophical, theoretical, or social origin, can be traced to the fundamental premise that interaction with another human being can alleviate feelings of distress, change behavior, and alter a person's feeling and perspective of the world. Moreover, by analyzing the infinitely complex ways in which people interact, behavioral scientists attempt to discriminate the factors that seem to promote emotional well-being from those that maintain unstable, maladaptive life patterns and ill health (4).

Psychotherapy is defined as

a form of treatment for problems of an emotional nature in which a trained person deliberately establishes a professional relationship with a patient with the object of removing, modifying or retarding existing symptoms, of mediating disturbed patterns of behavior, and of promoting positive personality growth and development. (5)

In essence, psychotherapy is a means by which a trained professional (e.g., a psychiatrist) and a person in need of psychological help (e.g., psychotherapy patient) strive to explore the various levels of the patient's character, life-style, and manner of being. One purpose of psychotherapy and the doctor-patient relationship, therefore, is to assist the patient to develop a more effective and fulfilling means of experiencing and interacting with the world (6). This rather broad and ambitious objective is in many ways no different from that of the medical doctor who treats a broken limb or internal disease. The ultimate purpose of all therapeutics is to enhance and improve a patient's quality of life. Interestingly, despite the obvious quantitative and procedural differences between the somatic and psychotherapeutic forms of treatment, veteran practitioners of both will invariably attest to the positive value and essential need for developing a strong, working relationship with their patients (7).

The interaction or process between psychiatrist and patient represents the very mechanism by which the effects of psychotherapy are brought about. Regardless of a therapist's "style" or the nature of treatment, the primary variable in promoting change or patient growth is the relationship that is developed with patients over time:

> The therapeutic relationship involves characteristics of both the therapist and client. The therapist's degree of caring, his or her interest and ability in helping the client, and his or her genuineness are factors that influence the relationship. . . . Counseling or psychotherapy is a personal matter that involves a personal relationship, and evidence indicates that honesty, sincerity, acceptance, understanding, and spontaneity are basic ingredients of a successful outcome. (8)

The psychotherapeutic relationship is a very special, unique, and powerful union. The process that develops from this relationship serves an important dual purpose: as a basis for patient growth and as a framework for establishing the boundaries in which that growth is made possible. The patient generally brings to therapy, consciously or unconsciously, the basic expectation that help is possible (9). Accordingly, psychotherapy inherently prescribes that the psychiatrist and patient work together in ways that will be curative and beneficial. One of the ways that this is accomplished is through the psychiatrist's guidance in establishing a conceptual scheme for making sense of the patient's confusing and subjective feelings. Patients are thus given an opportunity to establish a sense of control over their problems and develop a relative sense of security in taking certain risks they might not otherwise take. One of those risks is the disclosure of intimate feelings, attitudes, and experiences. In order for this "security to disclose" to occur, the psychiatrist must create a psychological environment of unconditional trust, openness, and acceptance of the patient. In addition, therapeutic security emanates from more practical factors such as the establishment of boundaries—of conduct and logistics. For instance, the time, setting, and duration of treatment are articulated to the patient and carried out in a consistent manner; the psychiatrist conducts the therapy session in a restrained and professional manner, and the activities between patient and therapist are essentially limited to verbal interaction and listening. These parameters can at times be frustrating for both the psychiatrist and the patient, but they are also reassuring in the sense that the boundaries of the relationship are out in the open, well-defined, and consistently applied.

Ethical Considerations

Ethics are the "rules or standards governing the conduct of a profession, . . . [or] any set of moral principles or values" (10). One aspect of ethical standards is philosophical; in it, individuals strive to synthesize ultimate "truths and realities" in order to determine a sense of values. From a practical perspective, ethics assume a more pragmatic posture and represent a system of guidance and rules in which to address specific problems and issues. These regulations provide a practical means of achieving limited and selected objectives rather than furnishing "insights" and philosophical principles. Hopefully, the practical aspects of ethics reflect or represent a general philosophical underpinning, such as safeguarding the welfare of patients.

The basic themes of medical ethics and morality, from which the fundamental tenets of psychotherapy ultimately originate, are quite old and established. Their genesis can be traced to the Code of Hammurabi, developed around 2000 B.C., and in the oath attributed to Hippocrates 2,400 years ago.

Despite these early vestiges of medical morality, today's ethical codes stem more directly from the insights of Thomas Percival in his seminal work *Medical Ethics; or, a Code of Institutes and Precepts Adapted to the Professional Conduct of Physicians and Surgeons* (1803) (11). Even before Percival's work, the history of medical ethics is replete with references to admonitions and declarations regarding the rightness and wrongness of various acts by physicians. For example, commentators in the 17th century explicitly frowned on the practice of laying hands on female patients for nonsurgical purposes (12). As noted earlier, the oath of Hippocrates specifically cautioned physicians to guard their position of trust with patients and to refrain from doing anything that might endanger their welfare or best interests:

> . . . I will preserve the purity of my life and my art. . . . In every house where I come I will enter only for the good of my patients, keeping myself far from all intentional ill-doing and all seduction, and especially

from the pleasures of love with *women* or with men, be they free or slaves [emphasis added]. (13)

These early warnings to physicians to refrain from social or sexual contact with a patient provide ample illustrations of the consistent view of the medical profession and its progeny that such activity is unethical and contrary to the fundamental precepts of medical practice. In one form or another, a review of the standards of ethics of *every* major mental health organization reveals a clear and consistent prohibition to sexual activity between professional and patient (14). For example, *The Principles of Medical Ethics, With Annotations Especially Applicable to Psychiatry* states:

> The requirement that the physician conduct himself [or herself] with propriety in his/her profession and in all actions of his/her life is especially important in the case of the psychiatrist because the patient tends to model his/her behavior after that of his/her therapist by identification. Further, the necessary intensity of the therapeutic relationship may tend to activate sexual and other needs and fantasies on the part of both patient and therapist, while weakening the objectivity necessary for control. *Sexual activity with a patient is unethical* [emphasis added]. (15)

In light of this brief summary of modern as well as historical ethics, it is abundantly clear that the psychiatric and other mental health professions unequivocally condemn and forbid their members to engage in sexual activity with patients.

Transference and the Potential for Abuse

Description

It is rare that a psychotherapy patient does not initially enter treatment with feelings of insecurity, emotional instability, and a desire to "get better." Couple this with the general offering of a sincere, attentive, and reliable presence by the therapist and it is not difficult to understand how many patients harbor the perception that the psychiatrist is a benign and omnipotent presence. These feelings can translate into a form of unconscious hope or expectation that the patient is safe and in "good hands." The psychotherapist serves as both a role model and a reinforcer, because patients are often significantly influenced by a psychiatrist's unconditional respect and concern for them (16).

What is the source of this "cure" and unconditional trust that patients commonly feel, thereby creating a pervasive, albeit unconscious, sense of influence by and attraction for their therapists? As children growing up, humans spend many influential years in dependent relationships with their parents or other caregivers. Throughout infancy and childhood, children learn that their needs are satisfied, their fears allayed, and their pains eased by the care and attention of adults. This "learned expectation" of parental help eventually becomes activated in various situations during adult life, especially when a psychiatrist is consulted. These unconscious hopes and expectations serve as the cornerstone of effective psychotherapy.

The "transference effect"—the unconscious hope and expectations of patients' early life experiences with their parents and other significant adults directed toward the psychiatrist or psychotherapist—is regarded as one of the most significant aspects of Freudian psychoanalytic theory (17).

Generally speaking, transference is the unconscious shifting or projection of emotions and reactions from one person to another. The transference effect may be manifested in a positive manner, such as through friendliness and affectionate or loving feelings, or it may be expressed negatively, when the feeling is one of disappointment, anger, or hostility. The development of the transference is an eventual consequence of the psychotherapeutic relationship (18) and thus forms a basic element of many types of psychologically related interventions. In traditional psychoanalysis and most contemporary psychotherapies, the transference phenomenon provides the psychiatrist-therapist with a valuable mechanism with which to help the patient "understand in a very real way how he [or she] misperceives, misinterprets, and misresponds to the present in terms of the past" (19).

Feelings of attraction by a patient for his or her psychiatrist-therapist comprise a natural and common transference reaction (20). Equally, it is not unusual for the psychiatrist-therapist to experience a similar unconscious reaction toward the patient. This experience is referred to as *countertransference* (21), and it too can be positive or negative.

Potential for Abuse and Misuse

The critical but seemingly obvious distinction between the transference experience of the patient and that of the therapist is that it is the *sole* responsibility of the psychiatrist-therapist to actively manage the patient's transference feelings as well as any feelings the therapist may have. The management of these experiences must be conducted within the boundaries of professional objectivity and integrity.

It is an implied aspect of a psychiatrist's duty of care to "first do no harm." It is therefore reasonable to expect that any psychiatrist-therapist should know that an emotionally troubled patient is inherently vulnerable when seeking psychotherapeutic help. It should go without saying that the warm, secure environment of the therapy relationship creates a powerful aura of influence and suggestibility. This "natural" vulnerability is further enhanced by the transference feelings that develop between patient and psychiatrist-therapist.

Feelings of positive transference, countertransference, patient seductiveness, and attempts by patients to induce the therapist to engage in extratherapeutic social activities are experiences that *all* psychiatrists-therapists must regularly and commonly deal with (22). Unfortunately, addressing impulses and emotions aroused by a sexually or physically attractive patient is not something that a psychiatrist learns in medical school or during residency (22). Yet, for a psychiatrist-therapist to succumb to these feelings or take advantage of a patient's vulnerabilities would be a clear ethical violation of the trust and care that underlies the therapeutic process and fiduciary relationship. Moreover, the courts have continually concluded that sexual activity between a psychiatrist and his or her patient is an abridgement of the fundamental duty of care owed to all patients and an unacceptable deviation in practice under *any* circumstances (23).

In brief, the transference phenomenon can be viewed as a powerful double-edged sword. If properly managed through the process of active listening, interpretation, and appropriate verbal feedback, it can serve as the single most helpful therapeutic resource. However, it also *can* represent an opportunity for nearly unbridled misuse and abuse that are only likely to result in unpleasant, countertherapeutic, and potentially harmful consequences for both the patient (24) and the therapist (25).

The Psychiatrist as a Fiduciary

The psychiatrist-patient relationship is fiducial in nature. Because of the special training and knowledge of the psychiatrist and the trust reposed in the psychiatrist by the patient, the psychiatrist is required to act in good faith and in the best interest of the patient (26).

In explaining therapist-patient sex, the concepts of transference and countertransference mismanagement have limitations. Psychotherapists with malignant character disorders or paraphilias manifesting severe narcissistic, antisocial, and perverse character traits sexually exploit patients quite apart from the mismanagement of transference and countertransference feelings.

Biologically or behaviorally trained psychiatrists and psychotherapists may not place much emphasis on transference issues in treatment. For therapists not trained in the management of transference and countertransference, the legal concepts of undue influence and breach of fiduciary trust may have greater applicability in the civil litigation of sexual misconduct cases (27). The presence of transference in both the therapist and the patient is such a basic psychological phenomenon, however, that no mental health professional can legitimately claim ignorance of its existence or of its significant influence on the therapist-patient relationship.

Sexual Exploitation

How It Begins

Psychotherapeutic treatment is a relative term. There are over 450 schools or approaches currently being used (28). In part, the reason for this diversity of treatments is that there is no one way of treating psychopathology, and many times a psychiatrist will have to adapt his or her methods to the unique needs or experiences of the patient. As a result, variations of previously used or more traditional therapies are developed. There is nothing wrong with this therapeutic flexibility; in fact, in some situations, clinical ingenuity may be required to treat a patient. Regardless of a therapist's approach, however, one constant that should underlie every treatment is that the psychiatrist will assume a position of neutrality striving to meet the patient's needs.

This standard approach is, however, not always so easy to attain. Treatment boundaries are always ready to be tested and are sometimes crossed. Crossing or going beyond the position of neutrality occurs whenever the primary source of a psychiatrist's gratification is achieved directly *from* the patient rather than from involvement in the treatment process *with* the patient (29). The process that likely occurs when boundaries are crossed is an acting out of the countertransference on the part of the therapist.

Some clinicians worry that when they give a hug or a reassuring touch to a patient during a time of crisis, they may be giving the wrong signal or initiating an unethical form of intimacy. In situations in which the touching is in a nonerotic, appropriately supportive manner, the contact is quite likely to be therapeutic as well as ethically proper. (There are some commentators, however, who believe that any touching is inherently improper, inevitably countertherapeutic, and potentially exploitative.) It is only when the touching of the patient "becomes part of a progressive pattern of intimacy serving primarily the therapist's needs that exploitation and misconduct occur. In this regard, exploitation of the patient may occur even if overt sexual relations . . . do not occur" (29). Precursor boundary violations to therapist-patient sex often cause serious psychological injury by interfering with proper diagnosis and treatment. Although attorneys and even most courts focus almost exclusively on the sexual relationship between therapist and patient, the precursor violations may be as damaging, if not more so, than the actual sexual misconduct itself (30).

There are numerous ways to exploit a patient other than through seductive manipulation and sexual activity. The following is a sample of some activities and practices that are inconsistent with a psychiatrist-therapist's position of neutrality and likely to lead to an exploitation of the doctor-patient relationship:

❖ Arranging for and engaging in social contact with the patient outside of clinically scheduled appointments

❖ Regular or even periodic disclosures of personal information about the therapist or his or her private relationships

❖ Acceptance of services, gifts, and nonmonetarial goods in exchange for treatment or in lieu of payment

❖ Talking about the therapist's personal problems to the patient and soliciting his or her sympathy and input

❖ Asking the patient to do personal favors for the therapist

❖ Engaging in extratherapy ventures with the patient such as joint-business arrangements

❖ Soliciting or using information from the patient for personal, financial, or career advancement (e.g., stock tip, business advice)

❖ Recommending treatment procedures or referrals that are not believed to be therapeutic or in the patient's best interest but that may be to the therapist's direct or indirect financial, personal, or professional interest (e.g., research)

❖ Making exceptions for a patient that are not regularly done for other patients (e.g., lowering of fee or charging no fee, providing special scheduling, except in appropriate cases in which special considerations because of physical handicap or emotionally disadvantaged patients occur)

❖ Joining in activities "for the patient" that are unethical or illegal (e.g., deceiving an insurance company regarding fee schedule and payment)

Psychiatrists and other therapists must recognize the position of extreme power, authority, and trust that they assume with their patients. Accordingly, it is an affirmative part of their duty of care to every patient to not exploit that position in any manner. Exploitation of the patient is usually a gradual process involving a series of precursor boundary violations to therapist-patient sex (28). Decreasing the incidence and frequency of patient exploitation is possible through education of both therapist and patient (31), active attention by other therapists to signs of exploitation and impairment in colleagues, and a willingness of exploitative therapists to seek appropriate supervision and/or treatment when treatment boundaries are threatened.

Scope of the Problem: Research

It is unanimously accepted among mental health commentators that erotic touching in treatment is inappropriate and has no empirically established therapeutic value. As noted earlier, every major mental health organization considers sexual activity between practitioner and patient to be unethical, and the courts have regularly held that this activity represents a deviation in the standard of care and is civilly, and sometimes criminally, actionable. Yet, despite all of these prohibitions and unfavorable commentary, a relatively significant number of health care professionals sexually exploit their patients.

Despite increasing attention paid to this problem by the media as well as by professional organizations, obtaining some reasonably reliable data on the scope of this problem remains elusive. For example, the results of a nationwide survey of psychiatrists regarding their sexual involvement with patients indicated that 7.1% of the male respondents and 3.1% of the female respondents acknowledged sexual conduct with their own patients (32). This study is often used to represent an accurate estimate of the scope of this issue. Unfortunately, like the studies preceding and following it, this study is too methodologically flawed to be relied on for an accurate estimate of the extent of sexual exploitation among psychotherapists.

Common problems associated with all studies of the prevalence of sexual exploitation include the following: 1) the return rate of professionals responding to the survey (e.g., actual sample size) is generally quite low; 2) there is no reliable means for evaluating the honesty and accuracy of the responses that are received; 3) erotic contact often is not adequately defined; and 4) multiple exploitations are either not accounted for or are poorly collected. Based on the current body of research, notwithstanding its low empirical reliability, the prevalence of sexual exploitation between health care providers and their patients has been estimated at a high of 13.7% for males (33) and 3.1% for females (30). It is strongly suspected that these figures actually *underrepresent* the problem in light of the annual rise in licensing complaints involving sex (34), the frequency and rise in civil litigation (35), the number of sexual exploitation legal cases that are settled (36), and the rise in the number of patients seeking treatment for emotional injuries stemming from sexual abuse by a former therapist (37).

Consequences for Sexual Exploitation

There are essentially five distinct consequences that a psychiatrist-therapist might face for engaging in sexual exploitation with a patient: 1) criminal prosecution, 2) licensure revocation, 3) expulsion from professional organizations (such as the American Psychiatric Association [APA]), 4) civil lawsuit, and 5) the refusal of a malpractice carrier to pay for civil damages or defend the claim. Depending upon the facts of the case, an exploitative practitioner could face any combination of these sanctions.

Civil Action

Theories of liability.   Depending upon the circumstances and nature of the exploitation, civil law provides a patient with a variety of causes of action in which to seek damages from an abusive therapist. The cause of action most commonly pursued is a suit alleging malpractice or professional negligence. Establishing a cause of action for malpractice or professional negligence requires that the plaintiff (e.g., complaining patient) establish four elements:

1. *Duty:* an obligation of care owed to the plaintiff (i.e., patient) by the defendant (i.e., doctor)
2. *Breach of duty:* failure of the doctor to meet the duty of care owed to the patient
3. *Proximate causation:* a causal link between the breach in the duty of care owed to the patient and the injury suffered by the patient
4. *Damages:* compensable injury sustained by the patient as a result of the doctor's breach of the duty owed

For purposes of establishing malpractice, if the psychiatrist-therapist dupes the patient into engaging in sexual relations under the pretext that it is a part of treatment, or if the relationship is manipulated so that the sexual activity evolves from the treatment, then a cause of action for professional negligence or some other sanction is more likely to be considered. From a factual perspective, sexual exploitation cases are generally difficult to litigate and win, because the plaintiff assumes the difficult burden of establishing, by a preponderance of the evidence, the four elements cited above. Typically, the most difficult element to establish is that the exploitation took place. Assuming that the defendant denies that any sexual activity ever occurred, which many doctors will claim, the patient must then present reliable evidence indicating that indeed there was sexual activity. This is not an easy task, but it is not insurmountable. For example, in the case of *Andrews v. United States,* a patient was able to successfully present circumstantial evidence in the form of testimony from a neighbor, in whom she had confided about her sexual relations with a therapist (38). This circumstantial evidence alone was not dispositive, but it did support the contention of the plaintiff that the sexual behavior in fact occurred.

Often, suits claiming sexual exploitation by a therapist allege that the deviation in the standard of care was the doctor's "mishandling of the transference phenomenon" (39). Two sexual exploitation cases cited most often provide excellent illustrations. In *Anclote Manor Foundation v. Wilkinson,* a psychiatrist was found civilly liable for manipulating the transference because he told his patient that he "loved her" and would divorce his wife if she married him (40). A more recent and particularly egregious example of the potential for gross abuse by malevolent psychotherapists is illustrated by the case *Walker v. Parzen* (41). In *Walker,* a psychiatrist was found to have given his patient unnecessary and clinically contraindicated medications, regularly engaged in sexual relations with her, and ordered her to leave her husband and children. Following a jury finding of "gross professional negligence," partly based on the admissions of Dr. Parzen, a landmark award of 4.6 million dollars in compensatory and punitive damages was made to the plaintiff. She ultimately agreed to a settlement of 2.5 million dollars to avoid further litigation on appeal.

While the fact of sexual exploitation is typically the most difficult element for a plaintiff to establish, occasionally the other elements will present some problems. For instance, in *Govar v. Hiett,* the defendant therapist admitted to having an *affair* with the plaintiff, whom he was treating for childhood sexual abuse, but claimed that his actions did not constitute malpractice (42). Three psychologist-experts independently testified for the plaintiff that the defendant knew or should have known that his "maltreatment of the plaintiff could result in serious and permanent damage"; that sexual intimacies between therapist and client are unethical; and that a person in therapy cannot be considered competent to consent to engage in sexual relations with the therapist (42). The jury agreed and awarded the plaintiff $342,465.

It is currently accepted that "sex between [a] psychiatrist (or therapist) and his or her patient is negligence per se" (43). In other words, sexual activity is presumed to be a deviation from the standard of care. Whether a patient can successfully sue the exploitative doctor depends upon proving causation and injury.

Another malpractice element that occasionally is used by defendants as an affirmative defense theory is the claim that the sexual activity did not injure or damage the plaintiff. While it is true that the plaintiff bears the burden of proving that he or she was injured by the defendant's manipulation of the transference and eventual sexual exploitation, this is generally not too difficult to accomplish. Some of the more common destructive consequences that are reported by exploited patients include mistrust of male figures (44), aggravation of preexisting psychiatric problems (45), breakup of marriage (38), and increased deterioration of emotional stability and medication addiction (46). Pope describes a "therapist-patient sex syndrome" that is characterized by the following (47):

❖ Ambivalence about the exploitative therapist and the exploitation
❖ Guilt feelings about responsibility for the sexual activity
❖ Emptiness and isolation
❖ Sexual confusion
❖ Inability to trust
❖ Identity and role reversal
❖ Emotional lability or dyscontrol
❖ Suppressed rage
❖ Increased suicidal risk

❖ Cognitive dysfunction

While there is little in the way of statistically reliable empirical support for this "syndrome," therapists who work with sexually exploited patients should find these characteristics a starting point in understanding what emotional damage the victim may suffer.

The vast majority of lawsuits involving claims of sexual exploitation are brought under the theory of professional negligence or malpractice (48). However, other theories have been applied, with some limited success. For instance, two theories that were popular before suits in malpractice became more regularly recognized were 1) that the sexual relationship amounted to "criminal conversation" (49) by interfering with the patient's marital relationship (50), or 2) that the sexual relationship resulted in an "alienation of affections" (51). As their terminology suggests, these theories are quite outdated and have been statutorily abolished in nearly every jurisdiction, if not every state (52). It should be noted, however, that even though both of these theories have been abandoned, this does not preclude an action for professional negligence. For example, in *Richard F.H. v. Larry H.D.*, a California appellate court concluded that the abolition of causes of action for criminal conversation and alienation of affection did not bar a negligence claim against a psychiatrist who had sex with the wife of a patient with whom he was conducting marital counseling (53).

Other theories, in lieu of malpractice or negligence, that have been asserted by plaintiffs include breach of contract (54), breach of implied warranty to adhere to professional ethics (55), negligent infliction of emotional distress (56), and nuisance (57).

Relevant statutes.   To date, California (58), Illinois (59), Minnesota (60), and Wisconsin (61) have *statutorily* made sexual exploitation between a patient and physician, psychotherapist, or other health care provider grounds for a civil lawsuit. By statutorily acknowledging sexual exploitation as an actionable offense, a state is explicitly declaring that this exploitation *is* a recognized deviation from the standard of care. Of course, in order to pursue a lawsuit against a therapist, a plaintiff will still have to prove that a doctor-patient relationship existed, that some sexual activity did take place, and that the plaintiff sustained harm because of the sexual activity. As far as patient-rights activists are concerned, states that have enacted legislation have explicitly acknowledged the severity of the problem, and the legislation represents a social commitment to deal with the problem.

By far, the legislation enacted by the state of Minnesota is the clearest and most comprehensive. For example, such issues as the scope of those parties potentially liable (i.e., psychotherapists and employers), the definition of the types of contact that are actionable, penalties for professionals who fail to report suspected sexually exploitative practitioners, and even the scope of document discovery for trial, are clearly articulated. Another unique aspect of the Minnesota criminal statute is the inclusion of an *extradition* passage that enables state officials to go after exploitative practitioners that have left the state and to bring them back to Minnesota for trial. For instance, this provision of the statute was applied to a psychologist who had fled to Nevada and, with that state's cooperation, was successfully returned to Minnesota for adjudication of the allegations against him (62).

It is unfortunate that so few states, to date, have chosen to statutorily address this issue. This lack of legislation is especially tragic because the number of psychotherapy patients that are sexually exploited seems to be increasing each year, or at least the number of lawsuits claiming sexual exploitation of psychotherapy patients appears to be on the rise.

Defenses. In the landmark case *Roy v. Hartogs* (63), one of the experts for the plaintiff testified that "there is absolutely no circumstance which permits a psychiatrist to engage in sex with a patient" (64).

This conclusion would seem to be both obvious and well documented in light of the clear ethical positions of each of the major mental health organizations and the overwhelming amount of research and commentary that has been generated on this subject (65). Yet, despite this information, psychiatrists and other professionals who have been sued for sexual exploitation have asserted a number of rationales in an effort to defend their actions.

Because sexual exploitation cases are generally quite difficult to win, only the most blatant cases usually reach the trial stage. A defendant being sued will almost always deny the claim, thereby forcing the plaintiff to prove his or her allegations. Of course, depending upon the reality of the allegations and the available evidence to corroborate the plaintiff's claim, some defendants will assert reasons or defenses to justify their actions. This is done with the hope that the claim against them will somehow be mitigated or lessened. As a general rule, if the claim of exploitation is admitted by the defendant or there is strong evidence to corroborate it, no defense will likely be successful.

The following points highlight some of the defenses that have been asserted; none of them served as a complete defense to the plaintiff's claims:

❖ The patient "consented" to the sexual acts (66).
❖ The treating psychiatrist was "emotionally disturbed" and therefore not accountable for his actions (67).
❖ The plaintiff was not "injured" by the sexual activity (68).
❖ The sexual activity was therapeutic (i.e., "a means of alleviating the patient's feelings of depression and inadequacy") (69).

❖ The plaintiff had a rich fantasy life, and the claim of sexual activity was just a part of her mental illness (70). (This defense can be a viable one *if* the therapist can both corroborate the claim of an active fantasy life and defend against the plaintiff's evidence that the sex actually took place.)
❖ Sex was part of therapy (71).
❖ The plaintiff "seduced" the therapist into the sexual activity. (This assertion parallels the reasoning and typical results associated with the "patient consent" defense.)

It is important to distinguish between the above defenses, which are essentially fact oriented, and those that have a more legal-technical basis. In the latter situation, a defendant may successfully have a case dismissed or reversed on appeal if the plaintiff's claim is technically flawed. For instance, in *Lenhard v. Butler,* a Texas appeals court dismissed a patient's medical malpractice action against her psychologist because psychologists were not covered by the statute covering health care providers (72). In other cases, plaintiffs pled the wrong theory for recovery and their claims were disallowed (73). Claims may also be barred by government or statutory immunity (74). Finally, a claim for sexual exploitation, like any tort action, may be barred if the plaintiff waits too long to file the action and the statute of limitation runs out. A good example of this situation is the matter of *Decker v. Fink* (75). In *Decker,* the Maryland Special Court of Appeals ruled that the plaintiff's impaired judgment, presumably because of the effects of transference, was not "sufficient legal justification for failing to timely file [a] medical malpractice action, and evidence established that [the] plaintiff knew or should have known [of the] existence of her alleged cause of action . . ." (75). However, in *Riley vs. Presnell* (76), the Massachusetts Supreme Judicial Court invoked the discovery rule that tolled (i.e., stopped) the statute of limitations from running. It rejected the defendant's defense that it was too late to bring a malpractice suit 7 years after the alleged sexual misconduct. The plaintiff successfully contended that he was unable to discover the psychological injuries resulting from the sexual misconduct because of the harm caused by the psychiatrist's behavior.

The fact that a claim is dismissed or reversed on legal grounds, of course, has no bearing on the veracity of the claim. This knowledge, while little consolation for plaintiffs who are barred from pursuing their claims further using their original theory of action (e.g., malpractice), may prove to be useful in later actions against the same doctor. For instance, the defendant in the dismissed *Decker* case was later successfully sued for sexual exploitation by another patient (77).

Post-therapy sex.   One defense that has begun to generate much interest among psychiatric and mental health commentators, as well as lawyers and their clients, is the assertion that the sexual activity did not begin until *after* the doctor-patient relationship had terminated. From a legal and clinical perspective, the post-therapy sex argument does merit a moment of reflection. From a legal posture, the technical requirements of a malpractice action (see above) would seem to be defeated. Recall that the first element requires that there be a doctor-patient relationship. Technically, if treatment had ended before the "alleged harm" began (i.e., sexual exploitation), then the first element is not met and a lawsuit for malpractice cannot go forward. Somewhat analogous reasoning was found in the nationwide study of psychiatrists in 1986 in which approximately 27% of the respondents felt that sex with a patient after termination was permissible because they "were no longer their patients," and 17.4% thought the APA ethics allowed it (32).

The problem with this reasoning is the same as can be found in the assertion that the patient "consented" or "seduced" the therapist. The strong dependence, lure, and trust created by the transference phenomenon *during* therapy does not automatically end once therapy is terminated. Instead, there is an indefinite carry-over effect that can impair a patient or former patient's judgment about his or her therapist. *The Principles of Medical Ethics* states that it is basically unethical for psychiatrists to have sex with former patients: "Sexual involvement with former patients *generally* exploits emotions deriving from treatment and therefore *almost always* is unethical [emphasis added]" (78).

From the smattering of cases that have addressed this issue, the courts have consistently concluded that the mere fact that the sex occurred after the treatment ended was not a bar to a malpractice action. For instance, in the oft-cited case of *Whitesell v. Green,* the plaintiff and his wife consulted a psychologist for marital counseling (79). Two weeks after the termination of treatment, the therapist and wife began a sexual relationship. The husband sued on the ground of professional negligence, but the therapist argued that because no professional relationship existed, no duty was owed. The court upheld the plaintiff's claim and awarded him $18,000. In *Barnett v. Wendt,* an Ohio appellate court concluded that a psychologist's license was properly denied based on his violation of state licensure law forbidding sexual involvement with "immediate ex-clients" when it was learned that he had had sex with a client 3 or 4 weeks after treatment had ended (80). Other cases involving post-therapy sex have arrived at similar conclusions based on a variety of lengths of time in which the sex was initiated after the treatment ended (81).

All three states with sexual exploitation civil statutes make allowances for post-therapy sex by indicating that a therapist can still be sued for any sexual activity that later occurs during a proscribed period (usually 2 years) (82).

In summary, the defendant's claim that the lawsuit is not viable because the sexual activity occurred following termination of treatment is often not acceptable in many jurisdictions. Proper expert psychiatric testimony on the nature of the transference phenomenon and its long-term effect on patients, provides ample evidence to support the claim against the psychiatrist. There is no established time after which it is appropriate to have social or sexual relations with a former patient. However, there is statutory (83) and case law specifically prohibiting this type of behavior. The safest course of action is to avoid any sexual contact with a former patient, because the power asymmetry between therapist and patient that arose from the previous treatment may nevertheless continue to significantly influence the patient's free exercise of judgment and discretion. Such a process must affect the nature of the relationship between therapist and former patient.

Criminal Prosecution

Overview and applicable case law.   Under some circumstances, a psychiatrist or psychotherapist who sexually exploits a patient in treatment may be criminally prosecuted. This avenue of redress is generally consistent with the elements of criminal sexual assault or second-degree rape, and as a result it is usually the most difficult to try and often the most emotionally upsetting to the victim. Consistent with the general laws governing crimes of sexual assault with adults, states generally require that there be some evidence that coercion was used either to induce compliance, to minimize resistance, or to overcome the will of the victim.

Criminal cases involving health care providers such as psychiatrists and other physicians consistently have required as a factual element evidence that there be some form of coercion (e.g., typically medication). For example, in *State v. Sway,* an indictment against a physician who was selling controlled substances to female patients in exchange for sexual favors was upheld by the Ohio Supreme Court (84). In an even more egregious case, a physician was charged with the rape of a patient to whom he administered tranquilizing medication in order to prevent the patient from resisting his advances (85). In *People v. Middleton,* a physician was found guilty of deviant sexual assault and aggravated battery and sentenced to 5 to 10 years in prison when it was found that he had rendered a patient helpless with the use of medication and then committed oral sex on her (86).

In one case, a physician who was charged with, among other things, indecent assault and battery upon a woman who consulted him, attempted to defend his actions by claiming that the state statute was unconstitutionally vague because "it failed to give him clear notice that his touching of the woman was indecent and therefore a criminal act" (87). The Massachusetts Court of Appeals rejected the doctor's claim and upheld his conviction.

A particularly alarming and egregious situation arises when health care providers sexually assault their minor patients. In situations where the patient is either underage or considered incompetent, the law requires only that proof of the act be demonstrated. There is no requirement of coercion, force, or manipulation as with adult cases. Several cases illustrate the law in this area. In the case *State v. Von Klock,* a licensed psychologist was convicted of aggravated felonious sexual assault when, during weekly therapy sessions, he verbally induced a 14-year-old mildly retarded boy to engage in mutual masturbation and oral sex (88). In another case, a 14-year-old girl was being treated over a 6-month period by a psychiatrist, whose office was in the basement of his home (89). During every visit, the girl alleged that she had sex with the doctor and was given illegal drugs and medications. Following the last visit, the patient was reported to have overdosed on the drugs allegedly supplied by the doctor. At his criminal trial, the doctor claimed that the patient was a prostitute taking drugs as payment. The court rejected this argument and convicted the psychiatrist of statutory rape and the illegal sale of controlled substances.

In one of the most extraordinary and grossest abuses of the doctor-patient relationship, a general physician was convicted of the forcible rape of five of six female patients, some as young as 15. Supposedly, the doctor was conducting pelvic examinations, but instead, out of the direct view of the patients because of their position on the examination table, he would insert his penis into their vagina (90). In a lengthy analysis of the facts and relevant law, the Wyoming Supreme Court held that the defendant could be charged with rapes that were alleged to have occurred as much as 17 years earlier because there was no applicable statute of limitations for the crimes charged. What makes this case particularly instructive is the fact that despite overwhelming town pressure to not pursue the case and the fact that the complainants only had circumstantial evidence to support their claims, guilty verdicts were entered on six separate charges, with five being upheld on appeal. As a result of the five convictions, the physician was sentenced to at least 15 to 20 years in prison. It was later reported in a book that accounted in detail the events, politics, and various town sentiment surrounding this case that the defendant, a "respected physician and founder of a fundamentalist Baptist church, methodically raped the town's Mormon mothers and daughters on the examining table" (91). This case, if not for anything else, provides in graphic detail what many therapists and psychiatric consultants who work with these types of cases already know: Where there is evidence of one assault, there are likely others.

Specific statutes. The criminalization of sexual exploitation by health care and mental health providers is generally going to be determined by how the facts of a case fit within the applicable criminal statutes for rape, sexual assault, or some similar offense. Several states—Florida (92), Minnesota (93), New Hampshire (94), Wisconsin (95), Colorado (96), North Dakota (97), and Maine (98)—have criminal statutes particularly tailored for psychotherapists who engage in sexual activity with a patient during the course of treatment.

Unlike the general content of the majority of state statutes, the Minnesota and Wisconsin statutes, for example, reflect a more contemporary view of this therapeutic problem. Their provisions specifically include psychotherapists and psychotherapy as applicable parties and events. States like New Hampshire and Michigan continue to construe sexual exploitation under their generic "sexual offense" laws and thus subject its prosecution to the same ambiguities that plague most criminal code sections.

One additional state, Massachusetts, presently has legislation pending that would make doctor-patient sexual activity a criminal offense (99). This development is the result of recent media disclosures of repeated patient exploitations by a Boston psychoanalyst and a physician practicing holistic medicine. According to the *Psychiatric News,* one of the bills before the Massachusetts legislature, House Bill 936, would "alter the state's sex crime statutes to make 'a psychotherapist who engages in sexual intercourse with a patient under certain circumstances . . . guilty of rape,' a crime punishable by a life sentence or 'any term of years' in the state prison" (100).

According to the Massachusetts bill, three sets of circumstances would constitute an actionable crime: 1) when therapists have intercourse with a patient or former patient who is emotionally dependent on them; 2) when therapists persuade patients that sexual intercourse is integral to therapy; or 3) when the intercourse occurs "during the therapy session and/or at any time outside the actual session until three months after the actual sessions cease." It is notable that the bill also provides that psychotherapists that have sexual contact with a patient other than intercourse under any of the above stated circumstances would face a charge of sexual assault.

Professional Sanctions

Ethical codes/traditional considerations.   A review of the current mental health literature, popular press, relevant research, and case law would appear to suggest that a significant number of psychiatrists and other mental health professionals are engaging in some form of sexual activity with their patients. Interestingly, this practice persists despite a long history of warnings, condemnation, and ridicule by licensing boards, professional organizations, the legal system, and most commentators who have written on the subject (101).

While the subject of doctor-patient sex did not actually begin to gain attention in the professional literature until the early to middle 1970s (102), the conventional wisdom regarding the involvement of physicians and other similar professionals with their patients is clearly spelled out in the Hippocratic oath (13) and other similar historical passages (103).

Although these inscriptions do not represent a basis for liability per se, they are clear indications of the medical profession's historic recognition and concern regarding the potential for doctors to exploit a patient's trust in them.

Consequences: duty to report abuse.   *The Principles of Medical Ethics* states:

> A physician shall deal honestly with patients and colleagues, and strive to expose those physicians deficient in character or competence, or who engage in fraud or deception . . .

> When a member has been found to have behaved unethically by the American Psychiatric Association or one of its constituent district branches, there should not be automatic reporting to the local authorities responsible for medical licensure, but the decision to report should be decided upon the merits of the case. (104)

These provisions clearly indicate that psychiatrists have an ethical duty to help the profession police itself. From a legal perspective, however, there is generally no corresponding responsibility per se. Many states do have provisions, often in their licensing laws, that require doctors to report other physicians who are or appear to be "impaired" (105). Unfortunately, like many laws in which there is little or no regulatory oversight, these provisions are extremely difficult to monitor and enforce. However, in at least three states—Minnesota (106), California (107), and Wisconsin (108)—the provisions for reporting are clearer. In Minnesota, for example, therapists *and* employers have an affirmative duty to report any reasonable indication that another therapist is or has engaged in sexual relations with a treatment patient. A pertinent part of this statute states:

> An employer of a psychotherapist may be liable . . . if:

> (1) the employer fails or refuses to take reasonable action when the employer knows or has reason to know that the psychotherapist [is] engaged in sexual contact with the plaintiff or any other patient or former patient of the psychotherapist; or

> (2) the employer fails or refuses to make inquires of an employee or former employee, whose name and address have been disclosed to the employer and who employed the psychotherapist as a psychotherapist within the last five years, concerning the occurrence of sexual contacts by the psychotherapist with patients or former patients of the psychotherapist.

In states other than these three, it is not clear what legal duty, if any, a psychiatrist or other therapist has with regard to knowledge or reports of sexual exploitation by other professionals. To date, there has been no reported appellate case in which a professional was sued for failing to report knowledge of past or active sexual activity by a fellow therapist. Notwithstanding this finding, the position of the APA seems quite clear. When asked what should a psychiatrist do if he or she learns that a colleague is having, or has had, sexual relations with a patient, an official on the APA Ethics Committee responded, "[W]e strongly encourage psychiatrists to report colleagues who they [believe] are engaging in unethical practices."

At the end of *The Principles of Medical Ethics* is an appendix entitled "Procedures for Handling Complaints of Unethical Conduct." These procedures provide reporting psychiatrists with some guidance to the requirements and method for filing an ethical grievance with a local district branch. It is further noted by the same APA official quoted above, "[A]ny fear of being sued for reporting an unethical practice should be lessened by the knowledge that no lawsuits have been brought against psychiatrist complainants in APA ethics procedures."

Licensure revocation.   The application and provision of mental health services are relatively new and constantly changing aspects of the total health care industry. In comparison with conventional medicine, the mental health field lacks considerable definiteness in terms of diagnosis, treatment, methodology, and general acceptance in and out of its own profession. For example, as mentioned above, there are estimated to be over 450 types of psychotherapy in existence. Moreover, the number of variations of "therapists" and persons calling themselves "mental health professionals" is overwhelming. How can the consumer public make informed decisions about "who, what, where, and how" when seeking mental health services with so many differences and apparent choices? More importantly, how can the public be protected against incompetent, useless, or even destructive practitioners? Who determines the competent from the incompetent, the qualified from the unqualified, or frauds and cheats from the otherwise ordinary and reasonable professionals?

These questions underscore the critical issue of professional regulation, which for years has often been either an afterthought that was not taken very seriously or considered an internal concern to be solely addressed by the various professions. Not surprisingly, these sentiments indirectly paralleled the lack of legal accountability (e.g., litigation) that involved psychiatrists, psychologists, and other mental health professionals for years. Mental health professionals had been, in effect, generally immune from both legal liability and regulatory intervention because of a variety of difficulties in pursuing claims against them. In the past decade, this phenomenon has gradually changed, and certain mental health practices have come under increasing regulatory control.

The general objective of the legislature in formulating licensing statutes, with regard to the provision of health and mental health care, is essentially to protect the public through 1) the establishment of quality care standards (e.g., minimum requirements governing the identification and promotion of services to the public via licensing and certification laws); 2) control of the supply distribution of services; and 3) enactment of cost containment measures of mental health care.

These objectives are essentially met by the establishment of minimum requirements for licensure to practice; the development of processes and procedures for settling disputes and alleged violations of the statutes; and the determination of appropriate sanctions when a violation has been established. This latter function is of particular importance because it serves as one mechanism for ridding the psychiatric profession and the public of corrupt and dangerous practitioners who sexually exploit their patients.

Numerous cases over the past 10 years have illustrated the role and effect of the licensure disciplinary process as another consequence that doctors can face if they sexually exploit their patients. For example, in *Dorsey v. Board of Regents,* a psychiatrist had his license revoked for, among other things, having sexual intercourse with two female patients (109). His appeal, based on the argument that the board failed to afford him certain due-process rights, was denied. While it is true that a medical license constitutes a liberty interest that cannot normally be taken away without certain due-process protections, those rights are more limited than would be granted in a criminal (or even a civil) trial. Accordingly, the court in *Dorsey* concluded that New York law only required notification of the charges against him and an opportunity to be heard (109).

In addition to the strong presumption of authority that state licensing agencies have to discipline their members, there is also an inherent assumption that licensing is a constitutionally valid means of regulating a profession. For instance, in a Florida case, a psychiatrist was charged with engaging in sexual relations with a 22-year-old patient during the course of treatment (110). The Board of Examiners held a hearing and subsequently revoked his license. On appeal, the defendant claimed that the applicable statute and disciplinary process were unconstitutional, in part, because the board had failed to articulate the standards by which it found his conduct to be unprofessional. The Florida District Court of Appeals found no merit in either argument, holding that sexual activity with a patient fell within the definition of applicable conduct for revocation and thus the board's actions were appropriate.

While a licensing board's decision carries considerable weight, it too must respect the system that the state legislature has established. For instance, in *Yero v. Department of Professional Regulation,* a psychiatrist appealed the 3-month suspension of his license based on sexual relations in which he admitted engaging with a patient (111). The court of appeals reversed the suspension, stating that the board of medical examiners could not reweigh a hearing officer's findings that the sexual act occurred after termination of the professional relationship, and that there was no evidence showing that the psychiatrist used the doctor-patient relationship to influence the patient to have sex with him. Two observations are notable about this decision. First, the fact that no evidence was offered to demonstrate the psychiatrist's influence in precipitating the sexual relation does not mean that there was no transference effect. In many cases involving sexual exploitation, such as this one, expert testimony is not developed adequately and fully to show this psychological fact. Second, Florida, the jurisdiction in which the *Yero* decision was made, has two statutory provisions that would appear to be appropriate in deciding this case *against* the defendant, but they were not applied. The statutory provisions state the following:

> For purposes of determining the existence of sexual misconduct as defined herein, the psychologist-client relationship is deemed to continue in perpetuity. (112)

> The following acts shall constitute grounds for which disciplinary actions specified in subsection (2) [not shown] may be taken: . . . .

> (d) Exercising influence within the patient-physician relationship for purposes of engaging a patient in sexual activity. A patient shall be presumed to be incapable of giving free, full, and informed consent to sexual activity with his or her physician. (113)

It is well agreed that the sexual exploitation of a patient is an egregious act that requires direct accountability and significant consequences for the unethical professional. While the forfeiture or revocation of a medical license is likely the harshest consequence a physician might face, boards generally have considerable discretion in determining an appropriate penalty (114). For instance, the board can decide to suspend a physician's license for an indefinite period (115); suspend the license for a specific period of time (111); or condition the return of the practitioner's license on some form of rehabilitation such as personal psychotherapy (116) or restriction of the doctor's future therapy practice (e.g., same-sex patients only) (117). Sometimes a defendant in exercising his or her right to be heard will seek to retain his or her license or have the final punishment lightened by offering to seek treatment. The board has the authority to consider any recommendation made by a defendant, but it is not required to accept it (118).

Because licensure disciplinary proceedings are statutorily created, they are considered independent forums. In other words, the fact that a defendant is acquitted of criminal charges or unsuccessfully sued has no dispositive value in terms of how a licensing board might rule (119). Finally, as was noted in a previous section, a practitioner who sexually exploits a patient may be subject to more than one punitive consequence. For example, an exploitative doctor could be civilly sued and then criminally prosecuted (120); be sued and then be subject to a licensure revocation hearing (117); or be sued by the patient and then be denied coverage by the malpractice carrier (121).

Malpractice Insurance

Scope of the law. In addition to other consequences, the exploitative practitioner who gets sued is also likely to experience resistance from his or her insurance carrier either to defend the claim or to pay the award if the defendant loses at trial. Generally, the most common and simplest explanation for this response by the insurance industry is that sex is not a part of treatment and, therefore, it is not an insurable act. A clear explanation of this reasoning is provided by the case *St. Paul Fire & Marine Insurance Co. v. Mitchell* (122). In *Mitchell,* the insurer claimed that sexual activity during treatment did not fall within the scope of its coverage *as indicated by the language of its contract.* The contract stated:

> The insurer will pay all sums which the insured shall be legally obligated to pay *as damages arising out of the performance of services rendered or which should have been rendered* during the policy period by the insured . . . and the company shall have the right and duty to defend in his name and on his behalf any suit against the insured alleging damages, even if such suit is groundless, false, or fraudulent [emphasis added]. (122)

The threshold issue then requires determining whether manipulation of the transference, resulting in sexual activity, is the type of conduct and "damages arising out of the performance of professional services rendered" that the insurer must pay. This *can* be a difficult issue with no conclusive resolution. What some insurers have done, particularly in the past 5 years, is to specifically exclude or limit coverage for claims alleging sexual misconduct. For instance, since May 1985, a major insurer for the American Psychiatric Association is reported to no longer pay claims for "undue familiarity," but will continue to provide up to $100,000 for a legal defense "as long as" the charge of sexual activity is denied (123). Similarly, the American Home Assurance Company, a major insurer of psychologists in the United States, includes the following exception: "Further note that amounts incurred for legal defense shall be applied against the deductible amount. Also note that a smaller limit of liability applies to judgments or settlements when there are allegations of sexual misconduct . . ." (124).

In situations where an insurance policy does not have a defined exclusionary or restrictive clause for sexual exploitation, disputes over construction of whether such coverage exists often wind up in court. The court will strictly construe any ambiguity of coverage against the insurer (125). Depending upon the jurisdiction or court, judicial interpretation of whether a policy covers sexual activity has been mixed. Some courts have concluded that sex between a doctor and patient is a deviation from the standard of care and an act of negligence, no different from the case of a patient who commits suicide because of poor supervision and inadequate protection. Consistent with this reasoning, courts have ruled that sex is within the scope of the insurance policy and therefore must be defended, and any judgment paid (126).

Other courts, however, beginning with the now infamous *Hartogs* decision, have stated that a physician's sexual exploitation of his or her patient is purely a self-indulgent act and has no place in professional practice, and therefore is not covered. In *Hartogs v. Employers Mutual Liability Insurance Company of Wisconsin,* the defendant psychiatrist sued his malpractice insurer to recover his costs in defending an earlier civil action (63) brought by one of his patients (127). In rejecting Dr. Hartogs' motion, a New York appeals court concluded that the doctor knew that his conduct was for his own pleasure and therefore did not constitute malpractice within the meaning of the insurance policy. In addition, the court noted that public policy prohibited the "indemnification of the plaintiff's conduct, since to do so would have been tantamount to insuring morality" (127).

It is apparent that the *Hartogs* court was not going to aid the doctor in any way by relieving him of his responsibility for his acts. Yet the flip side of the decision was to (unwittingly) penalize the patient who had been victimized. It is doubtful that many psychiatrists or physicians have sufficient personal assets to cover a six- or seven-figure award if they are successfully sued. Besides placing the doctor in deep debt, if not bankruptcy, this reasoning also leaves the victorious patient-plaintiff with no source from which to collect the damages that have been awarded him or her. This renders a patient's painful and hard fought trial success a somewhat hollow victory. Despite this consequence, several courts have either adopted this reasoning or produced the same result through other analyses (128).

A third line of reasoning has evolved that straddles the line in an attempt to hear both sides. For instance, in *Vigilant Insurance Co. v. Kambly,* an insurer sought absolution from liability under its malpractice policy claiming that the defendant psychiatrist's sexual exploitation was not within the wording or spirit of its policy (129). The Michigan Court of Appeals held that the doctor's acts were neither criminal nor an intentional tort and were not explicitly barred by the policy's language. Therefore, if a jury concluded that the defendant's conduct amounted to malpractice, then coverage was required, including any legal fees incurred in defending the claim. In a somewhat similar case, the Idaho Supreme Court concluded in *Standlee v. St. Paul Fire & Marine Insurance Co.* that the duty to defend a claim was broader than the duty to pay damages (130). As a result, it upheld a district court's ruling that the insurer's professional liability policy did not provide coverage for "sexual torts," but ruled that "if the petitioner's complaint alleged facts which, if true, created potential liability within the language of the liability policy, then the insurer had an initial duty to *defend* the claim" [emphasis added].

This reasoning serves as a kind of harbinger of the latest strategy by doctor-plaintiffs seeking to have their malpractice insurers provide coverage. One way the lawyers of exploitative doctors are attempting to avoid this problem of coverage for sex-related claims is to frame their pleadings in terms of general negligence, rather than emphasizing or confining the cause of action to the sexual activity. In other words, some lawyers will note the occurrence of the sexual exploitation as simply one *example* of a number of deviations from the standard of care, or will cite other instances of professional negligence. The idea is to project a more traditional picture of malpractice (which the insurers will have to defend) rather than run the risk of falling outside the scope of the policy (131).

Conclusions

Medicolegal Trends and Concerns

The position of the American Psychiatric Association and all other major mental health professional organizations regarding doctor-patient sex is clear: it is unethical; countertherapeutic; destructive to the patient, to the professional, and to the profession; and a violation of a therapist's fiduciary duty of care. These views have a long and consistent history in the development of modern medicine. A psychiatrist failing to remain a neutral participant in the psychotherapeutic process must be prepared to accept a number of potential consequences. A civil lawsuit or criminal prosecution, loss of licensure, censure from local and national organizations, and sole responsibility for all fees, litigation expenses, and any trial judgment are more than most people could emotionally or physically handle. Yet, despite this knowledge, reports of sexual exploitation of patients increase at an alarming rate. Research estimates of the prevalence of this problem should be considered a *minimum* figure, because countless allegations never get reported and many cases are settled and are never reported. Moreover, it is likely that a significant number of offenders have abused more than one patient.

It is a relatively common experience that many psychiatrists are *aware* of colleagues who are having or have had sex with a patient. Despite having an ethical as well as a professional obligation to "strive to expose those physicians deficient in character or competence," the great majority of doctors, who *are* ethical and competent, tend to ignore the problem. It is not enough to simply keep one's own house clean. When a patient is exploited, more than just that person suffers. The profession's image comes under attack (132), and the public begins to lose faith and trust in psychiatrists and other mental health professionals.

It is predicted that the percentage of practitioners currently exploiting patients will not diminish. It is important to note, however, that this problem is *not* limited to psychiatrists or other mental health professionals. Reports of adjudicated and settled cases involving the exploitation of the fiduciary relationship resulting in sex have included a variety of mental health and other professional groups: pastoral counselors (133), chiropractors (134), dentists (135), lawyers (136), judges (137), social workers (138), psychologists (139), and teachers (140). However, as one commentator put it, "[W]hile sexual abuse is hardly limited to therapists, the problem is considered especially grave when it concerns professionals dealing with emotionally dependent patients. In these cases, therapists define abuse not only as rape or molestation but as seduction" (141).

There are no quick, easy, or even clear solutions for this problem. There are reports that both the American Psychological Association and the American Psychiatric Association are stepping up their efforts to focus more attention on this matter and to develop possible solutions (141). However, much needs to be done on many fronts (142). Professional organizations, like both the APAs, must promulgate clearer and more affirmative policies about such measures and situations as the duty of psychiatrists to report unethical colleagues, the impropriety of post-termination sex, the reporting of unethical members to state licensing boards, increased education about the scope of sexual activity and its impact on patients, and finding ways to help the impaired physician. Moreover, licensing boards, which are notoriously slow, ineffective, and nonpunitive in most jurisdictions (143), must be given greater priority by state legislatures so they can respond more quickly and thoroughly to disciplinary complaints. Individual practitioners *must* become more invested in addressing this problem. For clinicians who regularly treat patients, there must be an added vigilance to patient complaints of past exploitation as well as to their own personal acts that might stray from a position of neutrality.

The Role of the Plaintiff's Expert Witness

Psychiatrists who act as plaintiff's experts in these cases should exercise a reasonable caution in giving expert opinion testimony. Very often, a psychiatrist retained by the plaintiff believes the plaintiff's account and testifies that the defendant psychiatrist deviated from the standard of care in his or her work with the plaintiff. It is not uncommon for this opinion to be given prior to any testimony, deposition, or input by the defendant. It may be based solely on the plaintiff's allegations that are not verified or documented. Defendant psychiatrists may deny their involvement and may be able to prove their defense in a more credible manner than plaintiffs can prove their accusations and allegations against the psychiatrists. Therefore, it is suggested that in the name of responsible advocacy, the expert give his opinion in a conditional form such as, "If the accusations of the plaintiff are correct, then the defendant has deviated from the standard of care." This is much more responsible than the declarative statement of an adversarial expert who gives the opinion, based on insufficient data, that the defendant *has* deviated from the standard of care.

References

1. Smith JT: Medical Malpractice: Psychiatric Care. Colorado Springs, CO, Shepard's/McGraw-Hill, 1986, p 6
2. Halverson v Zimmerman, 60 ND 113, 232 NW 754 (1930); Oliver v Brock, 342 So 2d 1 (1977)
3. Marziali EM, Marmar C, Krupnick J: Therapeutic alliance scales: development and relationship to psychotherapy outcome. Am J Psychiatry 138:361–364, 1981
4. Corey G: Theory and Practice of Counseling and Psychotherapy. Belmont, CA, Wadsworth Publishing, 1977, pp 4–9
5. Wolberg LR: The Techniques of Psychotherapy, Vol 1. New York, Grune & Stratton, 1967, p 3
6. Rogers C: Client-Centered Therapy. Boston, MA, Houghton-Mifflin, 1965
7. Caplan G: Principles of Preventive Psychiatry. New York, Basic Books, 1964
8. Corey G: Theory and Practice of Counseling and Psychotherapy. Belmont, CA, Wadsworth Publishing, 1977, p 199
9. Yalom I: The Theory and Practice of Group Psychotherapy. New York, Basic Books, 1975, pp 6–7
10. American Heritage Dictionary of the English Language, New College Edition. Boston, MA, Houghton-Mifflin, 1979
11. Leake A: Codifiers of medical ethics. JAMA 194:1319, 1965
12. Braceland F: Historical perspectives of the ethical practice of psychiatry. Am J Psychiatry 126:230–237, 1969; see pp 230, 237
13. Stedman's Medical Dictionary, 25th Edition. Baltimore, MD, Williams & Wilkins, 1990, pp 716–717

14. American Association of Marriage and Family Therapy: Ethical Principles for Family Therapists. § 1.2. Washington, DC, AAMFT, 1985; American Association of Sex Educators, Counselors and Therapists: Code of Ethics. Ethical Standard 4. Washington, DC, AASECT, 1980; American Psychological Association: Ethical Principles of Psychologists. § 7(g). Washington, DC, American Psychological Association, 1981; American Psychoanalytic Association: Principles of Ethics for Psychoanalysts. § 10. New York, American Psychoanalytic Association, 1983; National Association of Social Workers: Code of Ethics. § II.F.5. Silver Spring, MD, NASW, 1980

15. American Psychiatric Association: The Principles of Medical Ethics With Annotations Especially Applicable to Psychiatry. Section 2, Annot 1. Washington, DC, American Psychiatric Association, 1989

16. Yalom I: The Theory and Practice of Group Psychotherapy. New York, Basic Books, 1975; also see Corey G: Theory and Practice of Counseling and Psychotherapy. Belmont, MA, Houghton-Mifflin, 1977

17. Schaffer T: Undue influence, confidential relationship, and the psychology of transference. Notre Dame Lawyer 45:197–198, 1970

18. Freud S: Lines of advance in psycho-analytic theory (1919 [1918]), in The Standard Edition of the Complete Psychological Works of Sigmund Freud, Vol 17. Translated and edited by Strachey J. London, Hogarth Press, 1955, pp 157–168; see pp 157, 164

19. Arlow JA: Psychoanalysis, in Current Personality Theories. Edited by Corsini R. Itasca, IL, FE Peacock, 1977

20. Freud S: The case of Schreber, papers on technique and other works (1911–1913), in The Standard Edition of the Complete Psychological Works of Sigmund Freud, Vol 12. Translated and edited by Strachey J. London, Hogarth Press, 1955

21. Ibid, p 160

22. See, e.g., Pope KS, Keith-Speigel P, Tabachnick BG: Sexual attractions to clients. Am Psychol 41:147–158, 1986

23. See, e.g., Mazza v Huffaker, 61 NC App 170, 300 SE2d 833 (1983); Roy v Hartogs, 85 Misc 2d 891, 381 NYS2d 587 (App Term 1976); Decker v Fink, 422 A2d 389 (Md Spec Ct App 1980); Combs v Silverman, No LE 596 Richmond Cty Cir Ct (Va February 2, 1982), cited in American Trial Lawyers Association Law Reporter 25:98 (1982); Cotton v Kambly, 300 NW2d 627 (Mich 1981); Omer v Edgren, 38 Wn App 376, 685 P2d 635 (1984); Osborne v Leonard, No 21788/77 NY Cty Sup Ct (NY November 5, 1982), cited in American Trial Lawyers Association Law Reporter 26:188 (May 1983)

24. See, e.g., Burgess AW: Physician sexual misconduct and patients' responses. Am J Psychiatry 138:1335–1342, 1981; Sonne J, Meyer CB, Borys D, et al: Clients' reactions to sexual intimacy in therapy. Am J Orthopsychiatry 55:183–189, 1985

25. See generally Feldman-Summers S, Jones G: Psychological impacts of sexual contact between therapists or other health care practitioners and their clients. J Consult Clin Psychol 52:1054–1061, 1984

26. Simon RI: The psychiatrist as a fiduciary: avoiding the double agent role. Psychiatric Annals 17:622–626, 1987

27. Simon RI: The practice of psychotherapy: legal liabilities of an "impossible" profession, in American Psychiatric Press Review of Clinical Psychiatry and the Law, Vol 2. Edited by Simon RI. Washington, DC, American Psychiatric Press, 1991, pp 3–91

28. Simon RI: Sexual exploitation of patients: how it begins before it happens. Psychiatric Annals 19:104–112, 1989

29. Ibid, p 105

30. Simon RI: Psychological injury caused by boundary violation precursors to therapist-patient sex. Psychiatric Annals 21:614–619, 1991

31. APA board sets up work group to assess sex problem between professionals, patients. Psychiatric News, Vol 19, August 3, 1984, p 4; Pope KS: Preventing therapist-patient sexual intimacy: therapy for a therapist at risk. Professional Psychology 18:624–628, 1987

32. Gartrell N, Herman J, Olarte S, et al: Psychiatrist-patient sexual contact—results of a national survey, I: prevalence. Am J Psychiatry 143:1126–1131, 1986

33. Forer BR: The therapeutic relationship: 1968. Paper presented at the annual meeting of the California State Psychological Association, Pasadena, CA, February 1980, cited in Pope KS, Bouhoutsos JC: Sexual Intimacy Between Therapists and Patients. New York, Praeger, 1986, p 34

34. See, e.g., Gottlieb MC, Sell JM, Schoenfeld LS: Social/romantic relationships with present and former clients: state licensing board actions. Professional Psychology 19:459–462, 1988

35. See, e.g., Smith JT, Bisbing SB: Sexual Exploitation by Health Care Professionals, 2nd Edition. Potomac, MD, Legal Medicine Press, 1987

36. Walsh E, Weiser B: Hundreds of cases shrouded in secrecy. Washington Post, October 24, 1988, A1, 20

37. Gary Schoener, Executive Director, Walk-In Counseling Center, Minneapolis, MN, personal communication, December 1989

38. 723 F2d 366 (4th Cir 1984)

39. Anonymous v Berry, No 78-8182-CA Duval Cty Cir Ct, (Fla March 14, 1979), cited in American Trial Lawyers Association Law Reporter 22:473 (1979); Landau v Werner, 105 Sol J 527, affirmed, 105 Sol J 1008 (Court of Appeal 1961); Martz v Horowitz, HLA 83-345 (nd), cited in Medical Malpractice: Verdicts, Settlements, and Experts 2(March):29, 1986; Maxwell v United States, No C-3-86-0090 USDC (SD Ohio 1986); Mazza v Huffaker, 61 NC App 170, 300 SE2d 833 (1983); Walker v Parzen, 24 ATLA L Rep 295 (1984); Trout v Boyd, Douglas Cty Dist Ct (Neb nd), cited in American Trial Lawyers Association Law Reporter 32:117 (April 1989)

40. 263 So 2d 256 (Fla Dist Ct App 1972)

41. 24 ATLA L Rep 295 (1984); for other cases of gross exploitation of the transference phenomenon, see Roy v Hartogs, 81 Misc 2d 350, 366 NYS2d 297 (Civ Ct 1975), affirmed, 85 Misc 2d 891, 381 NYS2d 587 (App Term 1976); Lackey v Bressler, 86 NC App 486, 358 SE2d 560 (1987); Evans on behalf of "JB" et al v Rippy, 23 ATLA L Rep 62 (1980)

42. No 85-480, Independence Cty Cir Ct (Ark nd), cited in Medical Malpractice: Verdicts, Settlements and Experts 3(October):43, 1987

43. Simon RI: Concise Guide to Psychiatry and Law for Clinicians. Washington, DC, American Psychiatric Press, 1992

44. See, e.g., Thompson v Nevels, No 80-CV-1031, Shawnee County Dist Ct (Mo June 30, 1983)

45. See, e.g., Doe et al v Wang, No 691,869 and 691, 151, San Francisco Dist Ct (Ca March & June 1977)

46. See, e.g., Barton v Achar, No 86-0873, Portland Cir Ct (Ore October 1986), cited in Personal Injury: Verdicts and Research, Vol 18, January 11, 1988, p 4

47. Pope KS: Therapist-patient sex syndrome: a guide for attorneys and subsequent therapists to assessing damages, in Sexual Exploitation in Professional Relationships. Edited by Gabbard GO. Washington, DC, American Psychiatric Press, 1989, pp 40–45

48. Frankenmuth Mutual Insurance Co v Kompus, 135 Mich App 667, 354 NW2d 303 (1984)

49. Keeton WP, Dobbs DB, Keeton RE, et al: Prosser and Keeton on Torts, 5th Edition. St Paul, MN, West Publishing, 1984, p 917

50. See, e.g., Nicholson v Han, 12 Mich App 35, 162 NW2d 313 (1968)

51. See, e.g., Weaver v Union Carbide Corp, 378 SE2d 105 (WVa 1989). But also see Mazza v Huffaker, 61 NC App 170, 300 SE2d 833 (1983) [awarding damages in part for alienation of affection]

52. See, e.g., Keeton WP, Dobbs DB, Keeton RE, et al: Prosser and Keeton on Torts, 5th Edition. St Paul, MN, West Publishing, 1984, pp 929–931

53. 198 Cal 3d 591, 243 Cal Rptr 807 (1988)

54. Anclote Manor Foundation v Wilkinson, 263 So 2d 256 (Fla Dist Ct App 1972); Spiess v Johnson, 89 Or App 289, 748 P2d 1020 (1988)

55. Dennis v Allison, 698 SW2d 94 (Tex 1985)

56. Marlene F v Affiliated Psychiatric Medical Clinic, Inc, 48 Cal 3d 583, 257 Cal Rptr 98, 770 P2d 278 (1989)

57. Corgan v Muehling, 167 Ill App 3d 1093, 118 Ill Dec 698, 522 NE2d 153 (1988)

58. Cal Civ Code § 43.93 (West Supp 1991)

59. Ill Stat Ann ch 70 §§ 801–807 (Smith-Hurd 1989)

60. Minn Stat Ann §§ 148A.01-.06 (West Supp 1989)

61. Wis Stat Ann §§ 893.585, 895.70, 940.22 (West Supp 1990)

62. Minnesota v Nevers, SJIS No 21-31-1-000004, Douglas Cty Dist Ct (MN filed July 30, 1987)

63. 81 Misc 2d 350, 366 NYS2d 297 (Civ Ct 1975), affirmed, 85 Misc 2d 891, 381 NYS2d 587 (App Term 1976)

64. Stone A: Law, Psychiatry, and Morality. Washington, DC, American Psychiatric Press, 1984, p 199

65. Smith JT, Bisbing SB: Sexual Exploitation by Health Care Professionals. Potomac, MD, Legal Medicine Press, 1987, pp 318–330

66. Breitbart v Leonard, No 8205/78 NY Cty Sup Ct (NY November 28, 1982), cited in American Trial Lawyers Association Law Reporter 26:187 (May 1983); Roy v Hartogs, 81 Misc 2d 350, 366 NYS2d 297 (Civ Ct 1975), affirmed, 85 Misc 2d 891, 381 NYS2d 587 (App Term 1976) (Riccobono J, dissent)

67. Anonymous v Berry, No 78-8182-CA Duval Cty Cir Ct (Fla March 14, 1979)

68. Benetin v Carney, No 82-2-02722-7 Seattle Dist Ct (Wash January 1984); Combs v Silverman, No LE 596 Richmond Cty Cir Ct (Va February 2, 1982)

69. Postmanier v Leonard, No 21789-77 NY Cty Sup Ct (NY November 5, 1982)

70. Bomyea v Berent, No NWC-1482, Van Nuys Superior Ct (Cal nd), cited in Medical Malpractice: Verdicts, Settlements, and Experts 5(January):59, 1989

71. See, e.g., Rotenberry v Wilhoit, No 78-1233-B Escambia Cty Cir Ct (Fla May 10, 1980)

72. 745 SW2d 101 (Tex App 1988)

73. See, e.g., Hammond v Lane, 162 Ill App 3d 17, 515 NE2d 828 (1987); Dennis v Allison, 698 SW2d 94 (Tex 1985)

74. Dockweiler v Wentzell, 425 NW2d 468 (Mich App 1988)

75. 47 Md App 202, 422 A2d 389 (1980)

76. 565 NE2d 780 (Mass 1991)

77. See, e.g., Dawson v Fink, HCAB No 83,283 (Md 1985), cited in Medical Malpractice: Verdicts, Settlements, and Experts 2(February):32, 1986

78. Assembly endorses adversarial ethics hearing rules. Psychiatric News, Vol 23, December 2, 1988, pp 1, 12

79. No 38745 Honolulu Dist Ct (Haw November 19, 1973)

80. 330 Ohio App 3d 124, 514 NE2d 739 (1986)

81. Stark v Muehling, No 78-3760 Cook Cty Cir Ct (Ill May 1982); Doe v Roe, No 344,601 Norwalk Dist Ct (CA 1987); Dawson v Fink, HCAB No 83,283 (Md 1985); Gray v Wood, No F2-1670 Dane Cty Patients Compensation Panel (Wisc February 1, 1984); Noto v St Vincent Hospital, New York Law Journal, January 10, 1989, p 22; Lovelace v York-Adams MH-MR Program, York Cty Ct Comm Pleas No 9 (Pa nd), cited in Medical Malpractice: Verdicts, Settlements, and Experts 2(October):30, 1986

82. Cal Civ Code § 43.92 (West Supp 1991); Minn Stat Ann §§ 148A.01–.06 (West Supp 1989); Wis Stat Ann §§ 893.585, 895.70, 940.22 (West Supp 1990)

83. See, e.g., Cal Civ Code § 43.93(b) (West 1987); Fla Admin Code 21U-15.004(5)(a) (1986)

84. 15 Ohio St 112, 472 NE2d 1065 (1984)

85. Ballard v Superior Court of San Diego County, 64 Cal 2d 159, 49 Cal Rptr 202, 410 P2d 838 (1966)

86. 38 Ill App 3d 984, 350 NE2d 233 (1976)

87. Commonwealth v De La Cruz, 15 Mass Ct App 52, 443 NE2d 427 (1982)

88. 121 NH 697, 433 A2d 1299 (1981)

89. Doe v Salama, No 38814 Arlington Cty Cir Ct (Va May 1979)

90. Story v State, 721 P2d 1020 (Wyo 1986)

91. Story (the defendant) was not the first town physician to sexually assault his patients. W. W. Horsely, who died in 1971, had for years allegedly indulged himself with young male patients. See Burns R: Anatomy of a town torn by rape. Washington Post, August 1990, reviewing Olsen J: "Doc": The Rape of the Town of Lovell. New York, Atheneum, 1989

92. 1990 Fla Sess Law Serv ch 90-70 § 1(4)(a) (West 1991)

93. Minn Crim Code §§ 609.341(17)–(20), 609.344(g)(v), (h)–(j), 609.344 (1987) (Supp 1991)

94. NH Rev Stat Ann § 632-A:2 Part VII (Supp 1986)

95. Wis Stat Ann §§ 940.22(2), 940.255(2)(b) (West Supp 1990)

96. Colo Rev Stat § 18-3-405.5 (Supp 1990)

97. ND Cent Code § 12.1-20-06.1 (1987)

98. Me Rev Stat Ann tit 17-A § 253(2)(I), 2255 (Supp 1990)
99. Patient-therapist sex in Mass[achusetts] could lead to rape charges. Psychiatric News, Vol 24, May 5, 1989, pp 1, 34
100. Ibid, p 34
101. Sadoff R: New malpractice concerns for the psychiatrist. Legal Aspects of Medical Practice, March 1978, pp 31–35; Sadoff R: Physician-patient sexual indiscretion. International Journal of Medicine and Law 1980
102. See, e.g., Boas CVE: The doctor-patient relationship: some reflections on sex relations between physician and patient. Journal of Sex Research 2:215–218, 1966; Brodsky A: Counter-transference issues and the female therapist: sex and the student therapist. Clinical Psychologist 30:12–18, 1977; Cohn RC: The sexual fantasies of the psychotherapist and their use in psychotherapy. Journal of Sex Research 2:219–226, 1966
103. Braceland F: Historical perspectives of the ethical practice of psychiatry. Am J Psychiatry 126:230–237, 1969 [citing Arnald of Villanova]
104. American Psychiatric Association: The Principles of Medical Ethics With Annotations Especially Applicable to Psychiatry. Section 2. Washington, DC, American Psychiatric Association, 1989
105. Petty S: The impaired physician. Legal Aspects of Medical Practice 12:5–8, 1984
106. Minn Stat § 147.111 (1985)
107. Cal Bus & Prof § 728 (West 1990)
108. Wis Stat Ann § 940.22(3)(d) (West Supp 1990)
109. 449 NYS2d 337 (AD 1982)
110. Solloway v Department of Professional Regulations, 421 So 2d 573 (Fla App 1982)
111. 481 So 2d 61 (Fla App 1 Dist 1985)
112. Fla Admin Code 25U-15.004 (1986)
113. Fla Stat Ann §§ 458.329, 458.331 (West 1991)
114. See, e.g., McWilliams v Haveliwala, 61 AD2d 1031, 403 NYS2d 103 (1978)
115. Ewing v State Board of Medical Examiners, 290 SC 89, 348 SE2d 361 (1986)
116. Hening v Ambach, 517 NYS2d 331 (AD 1987)
117. Walker v Parzen, American Trial Lawyers Association Law Reporter 24:295 (1984)
118. See, e.g., Mancini v Board of Registration in Medicine, 390 Mass 1002, 456 NE2d 1136 (1983)
119. See, e.g., Thangavelu v Department of Licensing & Regulation, 149 Mich App 546, 386 NW2d 584 (1986)
120. Worsham v United States, No 85-0145 (SD Ga nd), cited in Medical Malpractice: Verdicts, Settlements, and Experts 3(February):42, 1987
121. Roy v Hartogs, 81 Misc 2d 350, 366 NYS2d 297 (Civ Ct 1975), affirmed 85 Misc 2d 891, 381 NYS2d 587 (App Term 1976); Hartogs v Employers Mutual Liability Insurance Co of Wisconsin, 391 NYS2d 962 (1977)
122. 164 Ga App 215, 296 SE2d 126 (1982)
123. Simon RI: Clinical Psychiatry and the Law, 2nd Edition. Washington, DC, American Psychiatric Press, 1992
124. American Home Assurance Company: Psychologist's Professional Liability, Form No 43274, December 1985

125. Stroemann v Mutual Life Insurance Co, 300 US 435 (1937)
126. See, e.g., LL v Medical Protective Co, 122 Wis 2d 455, 362 NW2d 174 (1984); Mazza v Medical Mutual Insurance Co of North America, 311 NC 621, 319 SE2d 217 (1984)
127. 89 Misc 2d 468, 391 NYS2d 962 (1977)
128. See, e.g., Frankenmuth Mutual Insurance Co v Kompus, 135 Mich App 667, 354 NW2d 303 (1984); Security Insurance Group v Wilkinson, 297 So 2d 113 (Dist Ct App Fla 1974); Smith v St Paul Fire & Marine Insurance Co, 353 NW2d 130 (Minn 1984)
129. 114 Mich App 683, 319 NW2d 382 (1982)
130. 107 Idaho 899, 693 P2d 1101 (1984)
131. See South Carolina Medical Malpractice Liability Insurance v Ferry, 291 SC 460, 354 SE2d 378 (1987)
132. Taylor E: Living by the letter: interview with Ann Landers. Time, August 21, 1989, pp 62–64
133. Destefano v Grabrian, 729 P2d 1018 (Colo App 1986), cert granted (Colo December 2, 1986)
134. Davidson v State, 33 Wash App 783, 657 P2d 810 (1983)
135. Hubin v Shira, 563 P2d 1079 (Kan Ct App 1977)
136. Barbara A v John G, 145 Cal 3d 369, 193 Cal Rptr 422 (1983)
137. Geiler v Commission on Judicial Qualifications, 10 Cal 3d 270, 110 Cal Rptr 201, 515 P2d 1 (1972), cert denied, 417 U.S. 932 (1973)
138. Horak v Biris, 130 Ill App 3d 140, 474 NE2d 13 (1985)
139. Rudner v Board of Regulations of NY State Board of Education, 105 AD2d 555, 481 NYS2d 502 (1984)
140. Reid v Lukens, No 77-719 848 NO Wayne Cty Cir Ct (Mich December 3, 1980)
141. Diesenhouse S: Therapists start to address damages done by therapists. New York Times, August 20, 1989, E4–5
142. Survey results on psychiatrist-patient sex underscore great need for ethical guidelines. Psychiatric News, Vol 21, September 19, 1986, p 14
143. See, e.g., Licenses valid despite crimes: many convicted doctors given probation by panel. Washington Post, January 10, 1988, A17

Chapter 8

Violent Behavior
Toward Others ─────────

A recent upsurge in cases involving patients' violent behavior toward others can be divided into two general categories: 1) those cases involving negligent discharge from psychiatric hospitals, and 2) those cases construing the limits of a duty to warn or to protect. These distinctions are somewhat arbitrary, because many of the variables in these cases overlap. As will be noted below, in a number of cases that, on the surface, appear to involve negligent discharge, courts have utilized "duty to warn" or "duty to protect" language in assessing liability and damages.

These cases are complex and the issues at times confusing. The courts have imposed a duty on psychiatrists to assess foreseeable danger in patients who are released from hospitals and in those who are treated in outpatient facilities. The difficulty of assessing the risk of violence is discussed and suggestions provided for meeting the applicable standards of care.

Confusion often arises in using the terms *dangerousness* and *violence* interchangeably. A distinction between dangerousness and the potential for violence is made in this chapter. Dangerousness ordinarily refers to legal status rather than a psychiatric disposition. Whenever psychiatric assessments are discussed, the term violence is used throughout instead of dangerousness.

The landmark opinion *Palsgraf v. Long Island Railroad Co.* (1) was the first case to address the relationship between a foreseeable victim (plaintiff) and a corresponding duty of some action. In *Palsgraf,* a train attendant was assisting a passenger to board a train. The passenger was carrying a package that, unknown to the attendant, contained explosives. Because of the negligence of the attendant, the package slipped from the attendant's arms, striking the ground and exploding. The explosion caused hanging scales many feet away to fall on another person. The court, in a ground-breaking decision, held that the passenger, as well as the person several feet away, was a foreseeable victim of the attendant's negligence. Judge Cordozo described determination of a "foreseeable plaintiff" as being relative to the potential risk created by the negligent conduct, specifically noting that "the risk reasonably to be perceived defines the duty to be obeyed, and the risk imports relation; it is risk to another or to others within the range of apprehension" (2). Thus, those who can reasonably be anticipated to be at risk because of the actions of others may be owed a corresponding duty of care by the original party.

The opinions in *Palsgraf* have served as the foundation paving the way for the development of several theories of liability regarding bystanders who are injured as a result of the acts of some unrelated party (3). Two critical questions emerge from this early law that have a marked impact on those persons (e.g., psychiatrists) assuming a degree of responsibility for the care of another (e.g., patients). First, what, if any, relationship does one party (i.e., psychiatrist) have with a foreseeably injured stranger that might give rise to some "duty" on his or her part? Second, if such a duty exists, what "care" or actions are sufficient to discharge that duty?

This historic case and these two issues serve as the general background underlying the primary theories of liability that have developed involving psychiatrists, other mental health professionals, and third parties for the injuries caused by foreseeably violent patients in their care. Two distinct scenarios emerge in which liability may be incurred. The first situation is one in which a foreseeably dangerous inpatient is negligently released and the patient later injures someone. This case, frequently described in the case law and medicolegal literature as a "negligent discharge" or "negligent release" case, is fairly common and theoretically straightforward.

The second situation, which is a much more recent legal doctrinal development, is the case in which the mental health professional is treating an outpatient and becomes aware (or should have become aware) of the risk of danger to others that the patient represents. In negligence law, this scenario addresses the issue of patients who are "foreseeably dangerous." Accordingly, the duty that might arise is far less clear and clinically accepted than that for negligent discharge. Often referred to as "duty to warn" or as *Tarasoff* cases (named for the seminal legal opinion that established this new duty [4]), this doctrine is far more controversial and misunderstood than discharge or release cases. Interestingly, despite all of the attention that the latter "duty to warn" cases have drawn since the original *Tarasoff* decision (4), actual adjudicated cases are far fewer than most commentators originally predicted.

Duty to Warn and/or Protect

Pre-*Tarasoff*: Medicolegal Status

From a psychiatric-medical perspective, ethical considerations regarding the maintenance of confidentiality have historically preempted nearly every consideration that might require unauthorized disclosure of information obtained in treatment. While few data exist concerning the frequency and/or situations in which confidentiality was breached by practitioners (whether to courts, police officers, relatives of patients, or others), anecdotal reports indicate that when unauthorized disclosures were made, there was usually little damage to the psychiatrist-patient relationship and treatment was rarely disrupted. Historically, if a threat of danger existed, the most common clinical course was either to seek hospitalization (voluntary or involuntary) or to attempt other treatment measures (e.g., initiate or increase medication). In terms of specific patient threats of violence (e.g., intended homicide), no reliable data exist regarding an estimate of how often these threats occurred with outpatient therapists. Some commentators believed that however a threat of violence was handled by treating psychiatrists (e.g., in therapy, limited warning to the victim), it neither caused a significant disruption in the therapeutic relationship nor created a major clinical-ethical problem for doctors (5).

Any changes in addressing the apparent conflict between maintaining confidentiality and safeguarding a third party tended to develop through the law rather than through the procedures of the medical or psychiatric profession.

Under common law, a person had no legal duty to warn of danger or prevent a third party (e.g., patient) from causing physical injury to another (6). Over the years, however, a number of courts have recognized an exception to this rule of nonliability when a special relationship exists between defendant (e.g., psychiatrist) and either the third party (e.g., patient) or the defendant and the victim of the third party's conduct (7). The key component to this exception is the right or ability of the defendant to control the conduct of the potentially dangerous party. The general rules of nonliability and its exception are best reflected in Section 315 of the *Second Restatement of Torts*:

> There is no duty to control the conduct of a third party as to prevent him from causing physical harm to another unless:
>
> (a) a special relationship exists between the actor and the third person which imposes a duty upon the actor to control the third person's conduct, or
> (b) a special relationship exists between the actor and the other which gives to the other a right to protection.

Section 315(a), which refers to the "special relation" between the actor (i.e., outpatient psychiatrist) and the third person (i.e., patient), usually serves as the legal basis for imposing liability upon psychiatrists, rather than Section 315(b).

(The legal language in the *Restatement of Torts* is confusing regarding use of the terms *third person* or *third party*. According to the *Restatement,* third person or third party as applied to the psychiatric context refers to the patient, not to the victim of the patient. Everywhere else in this text, third person or third party refers to the victim of a violent patient.)

Section 319 of the *Restatement* further delineates the relation between an actor (e.g., inpatient psychiatrist) and a third person (patient) that requires the actor to control the third person's conduct (8). Specifically, this section holds that "[o]ne who takes charge of a third person whom he knows or should know to be likely to cause bodily harm to others if not controlled is under a duty to exercise reasonable care to control the third person to prevent him from doing such harm."

The illustrations to Section 319, comment (a), of the *Restatement* specifically provide that the section applies to those who are in a position to protect others from persons with contagious disease and to those who are in a position to protect others from the dangerous activities of a mentally ill person who is permitted to escape from an institution (9).

Consistent with Section 319 of the Restatement, courts prior to 1976 held that a doctor may be liable to persons infected by his or her patient if he or she negligently failed to diagnose a contagious disease (10). A doctor could also face liability if, after having diagnosed an illness, he or she failed to warn the patient's family members of the contagious nature of the illness (11). Finally, some courts also held that hospitals had to exercise a reasonable care to control the behavior of their patients who might endanger other persons (12). Such cases relied heavily on the theory that the relationship of a doctor or hospital to a patient is sufficient to support the duty to exercise reasonable care so as to protect others against dangers emanating from a patient's illness.

Merchants National Bank and Trust Co. of Fargo v. United States (13), cited often as a primary precursor to *Tarasoff* and its progeny (14), illustrates the law's willingness to impose continued duty upon physicians and hospitals to exercise reasonable care to third parties to safeguard against the violent propensities of a mental patient. In *Merchants,* an involuntarily committed patient had repeatedly threatened to kill his wife. Despite these threats, the patient's physician released him from the V.A. hospital on work leave to help out on a ranch. The ranch's owner was provided very little information about the patient's emotional problems, especially his violent inclinations. Following a period of working at the ranch, the owner permitted the patient to leave it, and shortly thereafter the patient murdered his wife.

The federal district court, in ruling on the wrongful death claim by the wife's estate, did not specifically refer to a "special relationship" between the patient and the physician who had released the patient in the first place. Nor did the court expressly mention any duty to warn the rancher or his wife of the patient's potentially dangerous tendencies. Nonetheless, it found that the hospital and the releasing physician were liable for the wrongful death of the patient's wife. In so holding, the court recognized a general duty on the part of the physician to exercise reasonable care in determining a patient's suitability for release from the hospital, because the patient was still under the physician's control (15). Such precautions should have included giving the ranch owner specific instructions about the patient (e.g., his mental condition, hostile expressions).

It is interesting to note that the facts of the *Merchants* case illustrate a typical "negligent release or discharge" case. Accordingly, liability was premised on the defendant's failure to *control* the conduct of someone (the patient) with whom he had a relationship and whose actions the defendant had the ability to manage (e.g., continued confinement). These factors significantly differ from the normal circumstances involving outpatient treatment, especially if the patient does not meet the requirements for civil commitment. Nonetheless, the *Merchants* court holding, coupled with the theoretical underpinnings of Sections 315 and 319 of the *Second Restatement of Torts* (see above), provided the legal foundation for the later development of the duty-to-warn doctrine enunciated in *Tarasoff* and the cases that followed.

Tarasoff v. Regents of the University *of California*

Probably no concept in forensic psychiatry is as perplexing and misunderstood as the *Tarasoff* decision and the litany of duty-to-warn decisions that it brought forth. As an illustration, Givelber and his colleagues conducted an empirical study of over 2,800 therapists nationwide to determine their awareness of the *Tarasoff* holding and their understanding of its conclusions and agreement with its findings with regard to assessing dangerousness, impact on confidentiality, and effect on the treatment of dangerous patients (16). Approximately 90% of the respondents indicated that they had heard of *Tarasoff,* yet nearly all believed that the legal obligations arising from its holding could be discharged by warning the intended victim that a patient had, in the course of an evaluation or in psychotherapy, threatened to harm the victim (17). For better or worse, that is not an accurate assessment of the court's opinion.

The commentary and analysis generated by the original *Tarasoff* opinion and its reargued version (*Tarasoff II*) are enough to fill several encyclopedic volumes (18). A brief review of the pertinent facts is therefore instructive.

Prosenjit Poddar, a student at the University of California, Berkeley, was a voluntary outpatient at the University's Cowell Memorial Hospital. He sought psychotherapy at the insistence of a close friend who believed, quite accurately in retrospect, that Mr. Poddar had literally become obsessed with a young woman, Tatiana Tarasoff, whom he had briefly met at a dance. As evidence of this obsession, Mr. Poddar had tape-recorded several conversations with her and then spent hours mentally dissecting those conversations with his roommate in order to evaluate how Ms. Tarasoff may have felt about him.

Mr. Poddar was initially evaluated by a psychiatrist, Dr. Gold, who, contrary to his usual practice, informed the patient during their initial interview that he was quite disturbed, prescribed a major tranquilizer, and established a series of weekly appointments. Because Dr. Gold was a hospital psychiatrist, and because he felt that Mr. Poddar did not require hospitalization, Mr. Poddar's case was referred to a member of the outpatient staff, Dr. Moore, a clinical psychologist. During therapy with Dr. Moore, Mr. Poddar verbalized fantasies of harming, or perhaps even killing, Ms. Tarasoff. Also, Dr. Moore learned from a friend of Mr. Poddar that his patient had recently purchased a gun. The psychologist was deeply concerned about these developments, and when his patient discontinued psychotherapy, he promptly consulted Dr. Gold. They concluded that Mr. Poddar required hospitalization, and wrote the campus police, indicating that the patient's behavior and apparent dangerousness met the requirements of the state's newly enacted civil commitment statute (19). They requested that the campus police assist them in having Mr. Poddar committed.

In light of the relatively recent enactment of California's commitment act, neither the doctors nor campus police were clear about how this new commitment process worked. As a result, instead of the campus police being notified, the city police should have been contacted. The city police would have then transported the named committee (i.e., Mr. Poddar) to a county facility for an emergency psychiatric evaluation of his (alleged) mental illness and dangerousness potential. What instead happened was that the campus police went to Mr. Poddar's apartment and questioned him about his intended behavior toward Ms. Tarasoff. He denied any violent intentions and persuaded the campus police that he was not ill. The campus police left after warning him to keep away from Ms. Tarasoff. Two months later, Mr. Poddar stabbed Ms. Tarasoff to death.

Following the killing, the state sought criminal prosecution, charging Mr. Poddar with first-degree murder (20). Subsequently, the family of Ms. Tarasoff filed a civil suit against the University of California, the campus police, and both Dr. Gold and Dr. Moore. It is this civil suit that became *Tarasoff* (*v. Regents of University of California*) (21). Among other charges, Ms. Tarasoff's parents asserted that the police had been negligent in not properly detaining Mr. Poddar, and that Drs. Gold and Moore had been negligent in not warning Ms. Tarasoff of Poddar's threats and in not properly confining him (22).

The defendants, through the University of California, argued that even if the plaintiff's allegations were true, there was no legal duty on the part of either the campus police or the psychotherapists to warn or protect Ms. Tarasoff. It is this argument that became the threshold issue that was appealed to the California Supreme Court. Furthermore, it was this issue that led the California high court in its 1974 decision to rule that if the facts were as alleged in the plaintiff's complaint, then there was a legal duty on the part of the psychotherapists to warn (the intended victim) (23). In essence, the court concluded that "where a psychotherapist had reason, arising out of a professional relationship with a patient, to believe or reasonably should have believed, that the patient was intending to harm a specific victim, then a duty existed to warn that victim" (24).

However, the court found the defendant psychotherapists immune from liability for failing to confine Mr. Poddar on statutory grounds (25). The court also concluded that the University police were immune from liability because California's involuntary commitment statute provided broad immunity to those releasing civil commitment detainees (26).

Following this holding of a "duty to warn" by the state supreme court, the American Psychiatric Association (APA) and other mental health organizations, alarmed by this expansive and novel responsibility placed on clinicians, sought to intervene (27). In light of the infrequency of patient violent acts and concern that confidentiality would frequently be breached, the APA felt that the new ruling would serve no constructive purpose but instead would generate undue anxiety on the part of "potential victims" and/or the so-called "dangerous patient." In addition, some therapists were concerned that this duty would be expanded to include a therapeutic duty to warn patients about the possible duty to breach confidentiality and warn potential victims (28). These same psychotherapists were therefore concerned about a possible "chilling effect" that such warnings would have on a patient's motivation to reveal highly emotionally laden fantasies and concerns, the disclosure of which might be considered extremely therapeutic for some patients (29). In light of the historic value placed on maintaining confidentiality and also the view that emotionally laden verbalizations are to be addressed as a therapeutic issue, these concerns were not without clinical value or basis.

The APA and other groups sought to have the California Supreme Court rehear the *Tarasoff* case, and the state high court agreed to a rehearing. Unfortunately for psychotherapists, the rehearing opinion in 1976, commonly referred to as *Tarasoff II* (30), not only failed to clarify the many issues raised by the APA but recast the first court's original opinion in several important ways (31).

First and foremost, the court in *Tarasoff II* expanded the original duty to warn to a "duty to protect" (32). Second, the rehearing opinion was uncommonly vague and ambiguous about how psychotherapists, if faced with an applicable situation, might discharge the duty to protect. In its opinion (*Tarasoff II*), the court suggested that the duty might be discharged by warning the victim or calling the police, but it left open the possibility of various conventional clinical interventions used in handling potentially violent patients (33). For example, implementing or increasing an existing medication regimen or hospitalizing the patient might be appropriate discharge options. Other questions or issues left unspecified by the court in both *Tarasoff I* and *II* included the following:

1. Who precisely was a "psychotherapist" with the corresponding duty to protect? Recall that in *Tarasoff* the two psychotherapists were a psychiatrist and a psychologist. Are these the only applicable professions? What about clinical social workers, psychiatric nurse therapists, and marriage and family therapists?

2. What procedures or steps are "sufficient" in attempting to discharge the duty to protect? For example, if a therapist attempted to warn the intended victim by telephone and there was no answer, how many follow-up calls would be necessary? Would a follow-up registered letter be adequate, or a subsequent call to the police? If the victim was not home but a roommate, family member, or spouse was, would it be a breach of confidentiality or outside the scope of *Tarasoff II* to leave a warning message with them, even if done with discretion and sensitivity?

3. Most importantly, what steps would a psychotherapist take to reasonably determine that a patient was indeed dangerous? For example, notwithstanding explicit statements that the patient is going to "kill person A," how does the conscientious psychotherapist adequately assess especially graphic dreams or fantasies that manifest no intention to be acted out?

4. How does a therapist handle an expression of violence that does not include an identified victim? Is there a duty to protect the unidentified victim? If so, who is to be protected?

5. Also, for what period of time following an expression or indication of "apparent dangerousness" is a psychotherapist to be potentially liable for a patient's subsequent acts? For example, what if a patient indicates some sense of potential violence to an unidentified person but does not act on it until 6 months later? Is the duty to protect to be maintained indefinitely?

Tarasoff I and *II* both created a great deal of concern and misunderstanding. Interestingly, but not at all surprisingly, it is the litany of cases that have been decided since the *Tarasoff* decisions that have caused even greater concern and confusion. Since *Tarasoff II* in 1976, no less than 48 case opinions and 17 statutes in 32 jurisdictions have been decided and/or promulgated (see Appendix 1). Using those cases and statutes as a foundation, this section will explain how some states and the professional mental health community have addressed many of the issues left unanswered by *Tarasoff.*

Appelbaum notes that "*Tarasoff* and the decisions that have relied on it as a precedent appear to require clinicians treating potentially dangerous patients to undertake a three-stage process of assessment, selection of a course of action, and implementation" (34). The first part of this triad, assessment, refers to the assessment of a threat of harm or risk of violence and then an assessment of the object of that threat (i.e., victim), as discussed in the following.

When Does the Duty To Protect Arise?

Evaluation of the Threat

The California Supreme Court, in *Tarasoff II,* enunciated a two-step process that psychotherapists must follow to discharge their duty of care to an intended victim of potential violence. First, the psychotherapist "must reasonably determine, according to the standards of his profession, whether his patient presents a serious danger of violence to another" (35). This requirement obviously implies some degree of ability, on the part of psychotherapists, to predict future behavior (e.g., risk of violence). In an attempt to recognize and assuage the psychiatric community's rejection of this requirement, the court noted that the therapist need not "render a perfect performance" in making an assessment of dangerousness (36). Rather, the therapist need only exercise the degree of skill and knowledge possessed and exercised by members of his or her profession under similar circumstances:

> [W]ithin the broad range of reasonable practice and treatment, in which professional opinion and judgment may differ, the therapist is free to exercise his or her own best judgment without liability; proof, aided by hindsight, that he or she is judged wrongly is insufficient to establish negligence. (37)

While this statement seems to allow therapists some professional latitude in assessing dangerousness, it does little in the way of providing guidance regarding the assessment of "foreseeable" violence in situations in which there is no specific or direct threat. For example, the issue of what is "reasonable" professional judgment in terms of assessing a threat seemingly defies both clinical capacity and majority agreement among those professionals required to make such a determination. As argued in their *amicus* brief to the California Supreme Court following *Tarasoff I,* the American Psychiatric Association and other commentators argued that the present state of the profession was that future violent acts could not be reliably predicted (38). Notwithstanding these objections, the court in *Tarasoff* and those courts that have followed it still require that a determination of future dangerousness be made. With that fact in mind, it is instructive to summarize some of the findings and factors associated with the field of psychiatric prediction in order to understand the problem and ensure the best possible assessment under the circumstances.

State of the profession: overprediction.   A review of the research reveals that one of the most consistent findings is the tendency on the part of mental health professionals to overpredict the likelihood of future violence. Rubin's finding in 1972 still rings true today: "[E]ven in the most careful, painstaking, laborious and lengthy clinical approach to the prediction of dangerousness, false positives (persons concluded to be dangerous but are really not) may be at a minimum of 60% to 70%" (39). Numerous factors have been associated with the problem of overprediction, among them political influences, illusory correlations, low base rates for violence, cultural differences, and conceptual/contextual problems (40).

"Political influence" refers to the possibility of different consequences for the predictor, depending on whether the offender actually commits another violent act (41). For example, if a clinician predicts that a patient will not be dangerous and no subsequent violent act is committed, then there is no negative consequence associated with the assessment. If, however, a patient is released on the basis of an assessment of "non-dangerous" and subsequently commits a violent act, the clinician is subject to a number of repercussions including bad publicity and a possible lawsuit. This negative situation can and sometimes is avoided by simply *finding* the patient dangerous and maintaining his or her presence at the hospital. These determinations usually lead to what is known as "preventive detentions" (42). Such factors may influence inpatient clinicians to assess a greater number of patients as potentially violent.

An "illusory correlation" refers to the assumption that a relationship between variables is believed to exist, when indeed the empirical support for this assumption is not available. For instance, some examining clinicians may assume that a patient is dangerous on the basis of the existence of some other factor, thought to be associated with violence. A good example occurs in situations involving civil commitment. It is not unusual for certifying psychiatrists to conclude that a patient is potentially dangerous on the basis of evidence of mental illness—an erroneous belief that mental illness, especially if florid or seemingly severe, is correlated with dangerousness (43).

Another large part of the problem of false-positive predictions of dangerousness that is frequently cited by prediction researchers is that actual patient violent acts are relatively low in frequency. Levinson and Ramsey conclude that an important variable to be considered in studying false-positive dangerousness predictions is the difference in culture between the examining clinician and the patient (44). The majority of clinicians are male psychiatrists from middle- to high-income backgrounds, whereas the most common patient population is predominantly males from low socioeconomic backgrounds. This difference in upbringing and status can create interpersonal hostility, tension, and resentment that consciously or unconsciously can be interpreted by the examining clinician as signs of violence potential. Moreover, even when rapport is reasonably established, the patient's experiences may be too foreign to the clinician and their relevance for future dangerousness poorly understood by the clinician, if at all.

Mental health professionals are inclined to look for dispositional explanations for violent behavior, typically focusing on clinical signs, symptoms, or diagnostic labels as "dangerousness predictors" (45). This focus on dangerousness as a trait creates a significant conceptual problem because it has the tendency to reduce the nature and scope of violence proneness. Critics of this narrow approach (40) discourage the dichotomous categorization of individuals as "dangerous" or "nondangerous" and instead support evaluations that result in probability statements regarding the likelihood of aggressiveness, under what circumstances, and toward what kinds of people. This approach incorporates social and situational variables, in addition to any relevant personal qualities of the patient, in understanding violence.

Risk variables.   Monahan, in reviewing many of the current prediction studies, concludes that long-range predictions of violence are accurate in no more than one out of three cases, or approximately 33% (46). In light of these poor findings, it is difficult to support or accept the requirements of the court for clinicians to make these long-term predictions in cases of potential future violence. However, given the reality that the law and clinical circumstances will continue to need psychiatric input into assessing a patient's future dangerousness, Melton and colleagues have identified the nature of inquiry regarding violence assessment that is most consistent with the current research on the subject:

> [I]f a clinician is going to make statements about an individual's violence potential, he or she may do so either by describing the risk factors with a particular class of individuals whose violence potential is known and to which the subject belongs, or by conducting a careful inquiry into the personal and situational factors that have contributed to the individual's violent behavior in the past, in an effort to identify those conditions under which the likelihood of a future aggressive act is increased. (47)

Some factors that may assist a clinician in generating useful information about potential dangerousness are listed in Table 8-1. There is presently no equation that permits the clinician to systematically integrate all of these factors in a reliable manner. Monahan (48), in fact, warns that some factors may be of little predictive value, depending on the absence or presence of others.

The examining clinician may be able to discern particular personality dynamics (e.g., male paranoid patient responds aggressively to anyone who challenges the reality of his delusions) or situational factors (e.g., a patient is only violent when around an ex-spouse) that may affect the over-

Table 8-1. Factors in assessing the risk of violence

Factor	Association with violence (50)
Prior arrest for violent crime	Probability of future violence increases with each prior violent act and subsequent act
Current age	Strong association between youth and criminal activity and similar acting out
Age at first serious offense	Violence potential greater for offenders who were juveniles when first offense committed
Sex	Males at significantly higher risk than females
Race	Blacks at higher risk than other races; however, race as a violence risk factor disputed by others (51)
Socioeconomic status and employment stability	Lower socioeconomic status and job instability associated with increased incidence of violence and crime
Opiate and alcohol abuse	Abusers at higher risk than nonabusers
Family environment	Stable, supportive family environment associated with relatively lower risk
Peer environment	Higher risk associated with "bad company" (peer relations)
Availability of victims	Higher risk if offender's prior violence has been toward a broad range of victims, or if there is a history of multiple assaults on a narrow class of victims (e.g., spouse, girlfriend) who remain accessible to the abuser
Availability of alcohol or weapon	Risk increases with heavy drinking and ready access to weapons

all assessment of future violence. It is important for the assessing psychiatrist to individualize the assessment to the particular psychodynamics, clinical conditions, and specific history of the person examined, rather than utilizing generalizations applicable to others. The clinician should attempt to assess the risk of potential violence (e.g., low, moderate, high) by evaluating risk factors associated with violence rather than trying to predict the actual occurrence of a violent act (49).

When using this information in determining whether a duty to warn and/or protect might arise, it is important to emphasize that it is the *reasonableness* of the clinician's determination and not its accuracy that will be evaluated by the court. For example, it has been reported that one common misunderstanding among examining clinicians is the belief that the mere utterance of a threat, contemporaneously or in the past, raises the obligation to protect (usually to warn) the potential victim (16). This overvaluation of a "threat" is not likely to be considered reasonable in all circumstances. Patients' threats are but one element to be taken into consideration when assessing the likelihood of future violence. It is the duty of the examining psychiatrist, in an effort to act in a reasonable manner, that sufficient, relevant information is gathered. The courts have criticized psychotherapists for failing to obtain enough information with which to make an appropriate assessment (52). Similarly, psychotherapists should take care in inquiring into the information they gather. A related problem can occur when a therapist acts (e.g., warns or protects) on vague or ambiguous information. The consequence of "erring on the side of public protection" based on flimsy evidence is not ethically sound nor therapeutically prudent.

Assessing the Object of the Threat: Reasonableness

Concomitant with any assessment of dangerousness in terms of a duty to warn and/or protect is the need to extend the evaluation one step further, identifying, if possible, the object of the patient's potential threat of violence. The court's holding in *Tarasoff II* required that a determination of violence potential be made and then "he [the clinician] bears a duty to exercise reasonable care to protect the *foreseeable* victim of danger . . ." (53).

Part of the reasonable care that is owed, and what should be a natural extension of *any* inquiry into utterances or a direct threat by a patient suggestive of future violence, is to whom or what is that violence going to be directed. Because every patient and assessment situation is different, there is no one way to obtain this information. However, the examining clinician, in gathering relevant data, should be as direct and clear as possible so as not to misunderstand, ignore, or give a false impression about the gravity and necessity of the information being sought.

One situation that examining clinicians are likely to encounter is when a patient expresses a statement that initially appears to suggest future dangerousness but on further inquiry seems to be more of a fantasy or dream restatement. How should a statement such as this be handled, and how might the courts evaluate the "reasonableness" of a clinician's conduct in this situation?

An excellent illustration of this scenario is presented in the case of *White v. United States* (54). On December 7, 1979, Dwayne White, a court-ordered committee at St. Elizabeth's Hospital in Washington, D.C., left the hospital's grounds, went home, and repeatedly stabbed his wife with a pair of scissors. At the time of the assault, Mr. White had "grounds privileges," which permitted him to go anywhere on the hospital premises from 9:00 A.M. until 9:00 P.M. Although these privileges did not permit him to leave hospital grounds, at least three of the hospital exits were open and the entire hospital grounds were not considered secure. Mrs. White, the appellant, had brought a Federal Tort Claim Act action against the hospital and the U.S. Government (which operated the hospital) on two theories of liability. First, she alleged that her husband had related a fantasy about harming her to his psychotherapist, and therefore the hospital owed a duty to warn her that she might be in danger. Second, she alleged that the hospital was negligent in failing to take necessary precautions to ensure that Mr. White did not leave the hospital's grounds.

The district court concluded that the psychotherapist had acted within the scope of his professional competence in assessing and ultimately concluding that his client's fantasy did not represent a reasonable threat of harm to the appellant. The lower court further concluded that the hospital was not negligent in granting Mr. White unsupervised access to the hospital grounds because it was not foreseeable that he would leave the grounds and attack his wife.

In addressing the first issue regarding the therapist's duty to warn, the appellate court agreed. In assessing the holding of *Tarasoff II,* the court acknowledged that a mere threatening statement does not trigger the duty to protect (e.g., warn). Applying an objective analysis, the court, in particular, looked at the "detailed and persuasive" explanation given by the psychotherapist of why a single fantasy did not reflect a danger to the patient's wife. For example, the therapist considered the following factors: 1) the patient could distinguish between a fantasy and acting on a fantasy; 2) the patient himself considered the fantasy to be a fantasy; 3) the patient had not had any violent inclinations for almost a year; and 4) none of his known violent inclinations prior to that time involved women. The therapist's conclusions were buttressed by the hospital's expert witness who stated that the therapist's assessment was a reasonable one under the standards of the profession.

This case, unlike some of the duty-to-warn cases, provides an excellent illustration of a reasonable judicial analysis of medical-psychiatric decision making. The application of the court's quasi-objective analysis of the therapist's reasoning not only gives substance to the court's ruling but provides some guidance to clinicians and future court opinions regarding the type of information relevant to the assessment of "professional judgment" in duty-to-protect situations.

Perspectives on the Duty to Protect

Broad View: Foreseeable Victim—Public at Large

Following the decision in *Tarasoff II*, a concern on the minds of many clinicians was how broadly or narrowly would subsequent courts and legislatures interpret the duty to protect. In *Tarasoff*, the object of Mr. Poddar's violent fantasies had been clearly expressed and identified. He indicated fantasies of wanting to harm Ms. Tarasoff, and ultimately he did.

In the second major court decision to impose a duty to warn, the 1979 New Jersey case of *McIntosh v. Milano* (55), the dangerous proclivities of a patient were also directed toward an identifiable victim. In this case, it was the ex-girlfriend of the patient. In finding that a duty to warn existed in New Jersey, the court relied on both the "special relation" section (315) of the *Second Restatement of Torts* and on a state statute requiring notice to be given to third parties who are at risk of getting an infectious disease from a known carrier (56). The New Jersey court held:

> A psychiatrist or therapist may have a duty to take whatever steps are reasonably necessary to protect an intended or *potential victim* of his patient when he determines, or should determine, in the appropriate factual setting and in accordance with the standards of his profession established at trial, that the patient is or may present a probability of danger to that person. The relationship giving rise to that duty may be found either in that existing between the therapist and the patient, as was alluded to in **Tarasoff** . . . or in the more broadly based obligation as a practitioner may have to *protect the welfare of the community,* which is analogous to the obligation a physician has to warn third persons of infectious or contagious disease (57).

It should be clear from this holding that while the facts of the *McIntosh* case did involve a clearly identifiable victim, the New Jersey court, by invoking the state statute regarding infectious disease warning, obviously contemplated a broader expansion of the duty to protect than what the court in *Tarasoff* originally held. By basing a duty to protect on a broad-based obligation to "protect the welfare of the community" as well as on the *Restatement,* the court appeared to expand the responsibility of psychotherapists to protect all parties that could be reasonably foreseen to be in danger.

The element of foreseeability of danger between a patient's utterances and the manifestation of violence and eventual harm to a third party provided the requisite link in determining the "special relation" addressed in the *Restatement*. It is also this element of foreseeability that established a whole second line of duty-to-warn/protect cases that broadened *Tarasoff* and added an extra burden on psychiatrists and other mental health professionals regarding their already suspect ability to predict future behavior.

No case probably better represents the "broad view" of the duty to warn and/or protect and the application of the foreseeability requirement than the third major *"Tarasoff* case," *Lipari v. Sears, Roebuck & Co.* (58). This case was a 1980 federal court decision involving the shooting by a V.A. outpatient of complete strangers in a crowded nightclub area. There was no indication in the facts, nor was it alleged, that the patient had made at any time any specific threats against any reasonably identifiable victim. What actually transpired was that the patient purchased a shotgun from a Sears & Roebuck store, entered a crowded nightclub, and randomly discharged the gun, injuring several customers. The plaintiffs claimed that the V.A. "knew or should have known that the patient was dangerous to himself and others" and failed to properly treat him or hospitalize him. The federal district court framed the issue as "whether Nebraska law would impose a duty on a psychotherapist to take reasonable precautions to *protect potential victims* of his patient, when the psychotherapist knows or should know that his patient presents a danger to *others . . .*" (59).

Significantly, the *Lipari* court rejected the requirement that the duty only arises if the victim is reasonably identifiable. In so doing, the court particularly did not limit the duty incurred by psychotherapists to simply one of "warning," but instead spoke in terms of a "duty to *protect*." In shifting emphasis to the broader notion of protection, the *Lipari* court focused on the *reasonable likelihood of danger* rather than the identity of the victim. The court cited state (i.e., Nebraska) negligence and product liability cases, which in the court's perspective "illustrates the importance of foreseeability [of an injury] in defining the scope of a person's duty to exercise due care" (60).

It does not appear reasonable that when a psychotherapist is not aware of the identity of a potential victim that he or she would have a duty to warn such a person. However, the *Lipari* court and the few others that followed its reasoning require that the psychotherapist initiate "whatever reasonable precautions are reasonably necessary" to protect any potential victim, regardless of his or her identifiability. This broad expansion of a duty to protect the "public at large" was not a welcome legal development to treating psychotherapists. Fortunately for therapists, the reliance on foreseeability is a minority position accepted by only a few courts and state statutes. The following is a summary of some of those holdings.

In a 1983 decision, *Peterson v. State* (61), the plaintiff was injured when her automobile was struck by a car of a patient that had recently been discharged from the state hospital. The plaintiff alleged in her lawsuit that the psychiatrists who released the patient were negligent in not protecting her from the dangerous propensities of the patient. The patient, 5 days after his discharge, struck the plaintiff after he had run a red light, apparently traveling between 50 to 60 miles per hour and under the influence of drugs. Four weeks earlier the patient had cut off one of his testicles and had been admitted to the state hospital. He was known to have a history of taking PCP. Despite what appeared to be a complete resolution of his drug-induced psychosis, just prior to his last discharge, he was apprehended by hospital security for reckless driving while out on a hospital pass. Nonetheless, the psychiatrist chose not to seek involuntary commitment but instead discharged him.

Sometime following discharge, the patient raped a woman and murdered her parents. At the criminal trial, two examining psychiatrists diagnosed his condition as schizophrenia. This information was admitted into evidence at the civil trial. At that trial, the treating psychiatrist testified that the patient was potentially dangerous, and acknowledged that he was likely to use PCP again and was not reliable in taking his medication.

In affirming a judgment for the plaintiff, a Washington appeals court cited *Tarasoff* but chose to follow the more expansive holding of *Lipari*. The court specifically held that the doctor "incurred a duty to take reasonable precautions to *protect anyone who might be foreseeably endangered* by the patient's drug-related mental problems" (62).

In a much more recent case, and one of the most expansive *Tarasoff*-like decisions to date, the Wisconsin Supreme Court concluded in *Schuster v. Altenberg* that once negligence is established, liability will attach for the *unforeseeable consequences of a defendant's actions and to unforeseeable plaintiffs*. The court expressly rejected the relatively common rule that when "absent a readily identifiable victim, no duty exists on the part of a psychiatrist to warn a third party or protect a third party," stating instead that this formulation was inconsistent with state tort law (63). Few facts were actually available to the state supreme court in making its ruling, because the trial court granted the defendant's motion for summary judgment solely on the facts summarized in the pleadings. What was factually established was that Mrs. Schuster was involved in an auto accident when she drove her car into a tree at 60 miles per hour within an hour of a therapy session. The patient, diagnosed as suffering from manic-depressive disorder, was taking alprazolam and phenelzine. Mrs. Schuster was fatally injured, and her daughter was paralyzed. Responding to a request from the state court of appeals for a clarification of state law on this issue (i.e., duty to warn), the supreme court concluded that a psychiatrist may be held liable in negligence for the failure to warn of the side effects of medication if it was foreseeable that an accident might occur because of the driver's medicated state. The Wisconsin high court reversed the original dismissal of this case and remanded the matter back to the lower court for a trial on the merits. The trial court, however, found for the defendant psychiatrist (64).

In a Kentucky case, also the first in the state to address the duty-to-warn issue, the Court of Appeals determined in *Evans v. Morehead Clinic* (65) that a psychiatrist has a duty of "ordinary care to protect a reasonably foreseeable victim of danger from an assault by defendant's patient." A 1987 state statute (66) that specifically addressed the duty-to-warn/protect issue was found by the court to be irrelevant to the *Evans* case because the assault had occurred *before* the statute's effective date and therefore could not be applied retroactively.

Three opinions, adjudicated recently, indicate that while the "foreseeability," or broad view, is a minority approach among courts and statutes addressing the duty to protect, it still remains a viable view. In the earliest of the three, *Littleton v. Good Samaritan Hospital & Health Center* (67) (1988), the Ohio Supreme Court addressed the issue of when an *inpatient* psychiatrist might be held liable for releasing a patient who harms another person. The court determined that such decisions must be evaluated according to the "professional judgment" exercised by the defendants in the case. In other words, if after carefully reviewing all relevant information, a psychiatrist, in good faith, concludes that the patient does not pose an immediate danger to others, no liability will arise. This opinion highlights two notable distinctions. First, the court expressly stated that this finding was inapplicable to outpatient situations (68). Second, although this case was technically a "negligent discharge" or "failure to control" matter, with no allegation that a "duty to warn" was involved, the duty to protect could theoretically have arisen if a patient warning was, or should have been, part of a doctor's discharge plan but was not exercised. Pursuant to the "professional judgment rule," however, liability for failing to warn would only occur in the absence of good faith or failure to exercise reasonable professional judgment in carrying out the plan.

In other cases, the expansive "foreseeability" rule is much more evident. For instance, in the 1989 Arizona case *Hamman v. County of Maricopa,* the state supreme court, as in *Schuster,* refused to confine a psychiatrist's duty to protect third parties to only those situations in which a specific threat was made (69). Borrowing a theory of negligence typically applied to "bystander recovery" cases (70), the court indicated that persons were considered foreseeable victims if they were in the "zone of danger" of probable risk that was created by the patient's violent conduct. This case was sent back down to a lower court for further proceedings to determine whether the defendant psychiatrist owed a duty to protect to the patient's stepfather from an attack by the patient 2 days after being sent home by the defendant.

In the matter *Perriera v. Colorado* (71), the state supreme court also rejected the relatively narrow "identifiable threat–identifiable victim" standard and held that a duty of care is owed when determining whether an involuntarily hospitalized patient has a tendency for violence and would present an unreasonable risk of danger to *others* if released. This court's opinion appears to expand the duty to protect not only to identifiable victims but to the much broader, foreseeable public if it is determined that the patient poses an "unreasonable risk of serious bodily harm" in general. This opinion, like several others (72), overlooks or rejects the well-established fact that psychiatrists *cannot* reliably determine future behavior (e.g., violence). This is especially true as time passes following a patient's discharge. Moreover, inpatient clinicians have an ethical, clinical, and legal duty not to unreasonably maintain a patient in the hospital if treatment is no longer effective or statutorily required. The court in *Perriera* further stated that "due weight should be given to extending the term of a patient's commitment or placing appropriate conditions and restrictions on the patient's release" (71). This requirement ignores the pervasive reality that if a patient is no longer committable, pursuant to state statute, then he or she usually is required to be released.

States that have statutorily embraced a duty to protect the public at large from the foreseeable danger posed by a potentially dangerous patient include Indiana ("threat to others") (73), Minnesota (74), Kentucky ("actual threat of some specific violent act") (75), and Florida ("threat to person or society") (76).

It is clear that the application of the foreseeability rule to duty-to-protect situations places a difficult clinical as well as legal burden on therapists. In the states that do have such a statutory requirement, there is some consolation that these same statutes also prescribe what precautions or actions are legally suitable. Of course, what is factually practical and clinically appropriate remains the decision of the professional. Merely following statutory requirements solely for the purposes of gaining immunity from liability may not necessarily meet the real clinical needs of the patient. In states in which no law is presently on the books (see Appendix 2) and there is a perceivable threat but no identified victim, the professional must assess the threat of potential violence carefully, seek professional consultation if necessary, and pursue the matter assertively with the same clinical consideration as in any other situation involving similar dire circumstances.

Narrow View: Specificity of Threat—Identifiable Victim

Just prior to the *Lipari* decision (see above) being announced, the California Supreme Court issued its decision in the matter *Thompson v. County of*

Alameda (77). This decision was heralded by many psychotherapists and commentators as a reasonable compromise to the vague and ambiguous *Tarasoff II* decision because it appeared to place some limits on the original duty-to-warn requirements. The plaintiffs in *Thompson* sued the county for the wrongful death of their 5-year-old son who was killed within 24 hours after a juvenile delinquent was released on temporary leave from a county detention facility. Their complaint alleged that the county knew that the delinquent had violent propensities toward children and that sexual assaults were likely, and the delinquent had stated that if he was released, he would kill a young child living in the neighborhood. The court in *Thompson* rejected the plaintiff's contentions and ruled that the county had no affirmative duty to warn of the release of an inmate with a violent history who had made "nonspecific threats of harm directed at nonspecific victims" (78). This case established the precedent for "narrowing" the duty to warn and/or protect to a standard much more consistent with the acknowledged capabilities of mental health professionals in what all agrees is a clinically difficult situation. Numerous other courts (79) and statutes (80) have accepted, with some variation, the specificity or "identifiable victim" rule.

For example, a state psychiatrist was concluded by a South Carolina appeals court to not owe a duty to warn a hospital patient's sister that the patient posed a risk to her. In the case *Rogers v. South Carolina Department of Mental Health* (81), a patient was admitted to the state hospital in July 1980 after she had had a hostile argument with her sister. She was subsequently released 5 months later and was thought to be doing well until August 1982, when her paranoid delusions reemerged. At that time she was insisting that her sister was trying to poison her. Approximately 14 days following the paranoid allegation she fatally shot her sister. A wrongful death lawsuit was filed against the treating psychiatrist, alleging that he was negligent in failing to warn the decedent that the patient might harm her. This claim was rejected by the appellate court. The court held that the decedent was aware of her sister's psychological problems and proclivity for hostility and violence. Moreover, the court noted that there was no evidence that the patient had ever made "specific threats" against her sister. *Rogers* is the second duty-to-warn–type case heard by the South Carolina appellate court (82). In both cases, it was held that no duty to warn or protect was owed. Also, the court in each opinion expressly stated that "South Carolina law does not recognize a general duty to warn of the dangerous propensities of others" (83). Despite this conclusion, a careful reading of both cases seems to imply that South Carolina would likely render a clear decision on the duty to warn if the facts involved "a specific threat against a specific victim."

In the 1989 case *Sellers v. United States*, (84) the Court of Appeals for the Sixth Circuit, interpreting Michigan law, concluded that a V.A. psychiatrist owed no duty of care to a third party injured by a patient with manic depression. Adhering to past Michigan precedents on the issue (85), the court held that the defendant had no duty to compel a voluntary patient to remain in the hospital, nor did the defendant have a duty to warn the general public. Michigan, like the majority of jurisdictions recognizing the duty to warn and/or protect, requires that there be a *readily identifiable (potential) victim* before the duty is owed. As in *Rogers,* the court in *Sellers* noted that the patient had never threatened or mentioned harming the victim before the assault.

There has been a minimum of 53 published case opinions and 17 statutes concerning the duty to warn and/or protect since *Tarasoff II* (86). From this body of law, a few conclusions are apparent. Despite initial concerns and even relatively recent predictions (87) that the *Tarasoff* ruling would create an avalanche of cases nationwide, an analysis of the development of the case law and legislative activity reveals about three or four new cases or statutes each year. This number is far less than the number of psychiatric malpractice cases involving suicide (88), sexual exploitation (89), medication-related injuries (90), or negligent discharge cases (91). While it is probable that some duty-to-warn cases are never published because they are settled before trial or are not appealed, and therefore not identified by a state or commercial case reporter, the "total" number of cases is still likely to be far fewer than originally projected. However, the duty to warn and/or protect is a topic of such intense interest that almost all cases see the light of day somewhere (even if only in unofficially reported accounts).

Notwithstanding the actual number of cases involving the duty to warn, the duty to warn and/or protect has become an accepted theory of civil liability involving mental health professionals in the majority of states in this country (see Appendixes 1 and 2). Finally, the narrow rule of requiring a specific or foreseeable threat of violence against a specific or identifiable victim is the standard threshold or trigger element in the majority of states (see Appendix 2).

Discharging the Duty

Clinical-Legal Balance: Considerations

Once a clinician has determined that a patient represents a danger to a third party, the next step should be to select a course of action that will appropriately protect the potential victims by the least restrictive means. Before discharging the duty, whatever means that are exercised should be according to the least intrusive means of protecting the potentially endangered party. In other words, if the duty to protect can be effectively exercised by working with the patient in diminishing his or her violence potential (e.g., voluntary hospitalization for treatment), then this should be considered in lieu of warning the potential victim or contacting the police. While all three means are generally acceptable ways of exercising the duty to protect, the latter two require breaching confidentiality and possibly upsetting the victim, while hospitalization and other less-intrusive clinical courses of action accomplish the duty to protect without these additional problems.

Not only is this consideration for the therapeutic benefit of the patient and existing psychotherapy relationship, but it also reduces the chance of causing any undue emotional problems for the intended victim. This and other considerations underscore the need for therapists to proceed in a clinical manner in both managing the potentially violent patient and discharging the duty to protect (92).

Affirmative Action

Possible courses of action.   When a psychotherapist reasonably concludes that a duty to protect exists, whatever course of action is chosen must be implemented affirmatively and appropriately. Several commentators have already observed that the *Tarasoff* doctrine grants considerable latitude to psychotherapists in the selection of a course of action that might protect a potential victim (93). Many clinicians nonetheless continue to think only in terms of issuing a warning, a procedure on its own that is of questionable value (16). Mills believes that "where the psychotherapist makes a prediction of dangerousness, the psychotherapist should pursue actions designed to reduce the patient's potential for violence" (94).

In general, the range of possible actions to be taken after an assessment of serious danger to another has been vigorously debated. Flemming and Maximov (95), as well as the California Supreme Court in *Tarasoff II*, recommended a case-by-case consideration of a wide range of possible clinical interventions. To some degree, a case-by-case approach makes the most sense clinically and legally. Because it is the therapist's implicit obligation to discharge the duty to protect by balancing the need to protect the potentially endangered third party with the sensitivity of its impact on the patient, the imminence of the danger and the accessibility and identifiability of the victim will generally dictate the choice(s) of intervention. Thus, later in this chapter, the discussion will center on the legal and clinical ramifications of exercising the duty to protect when the endangered victim is identifiable and when the threat is aimed at the public at large.

Other commentators have broken with the case-by-case approach of *Tarasoff II* and Flemming and Maximov and advocated other approaches. For instance, Stone recommends increased reliance upon civil commitment (28). Wexler has proposed conjoint counseling in situations involving intimates or family members (96). Leonard has suggested analyzing cases resembling *Tarasoff* as to whether the patient remains in treatment. In those cases in which the therapist believes that danger exists—as in the actual *Tarasoff* case in which the patient left treatment—the options for discharging the duty to protect are very limited, consisting of a warning to the victim (and/or the police) or commitment (97).

Because the courts will evaluate a psychotherapist's efforts based on a "reasonableness" standard as measured by his or her profession, the alternatives available for discharging the duty to protect should reflect responsive clinical procedures and strategies. The following alternatives are not necessarily in the order of action and are not mutually exclusive. Many of the following may be considered simultaneously:

❖ Maintain careful history taking, perform updated mental status examination, reconsider diagnostic formulation (DSM-III-R, Axis I–V), and update treatment plan (98).

❖ Intensify therapy by increasing the frequency of treatment contacts. This may include periodic telephone contacts.

❖ Have the patient evaluated for appropriate psychotropic medications. If the patient is already on medication, consider if the dose is in its therapeutic range.

❖ As an *adjunct* measure, encourage the patient to contact the therapist if he or she fears a possible loss of control.

❖ Discuss openly and directly concerns about the patient's expressed hostilities and possible impact on his or her welfare and the welfare of others. Focus therapy on the patient's motives and underlying violent intent.

❖ If the patient's potential for violence is mediated by certain circumstances (e.g., potentially violent only when drunk), specialized forms of treatment, such as treatment for alcohol abuse, may be employed.

❖ Suggest voluntary hospitalization, stressing its value in helping the patient maintain control and diminish any potential for violence.

❖ Request that the patient turn over to the police or some other suitable custodial agency his or her planned weapon.

❖ Confront the patient with the fact that the law has imposed a special duty on psychotherapists, the result of which is that they—the psychiatrist and the patient—have to formulate a plan that will be successful in discharging the therapist's duty to protect the public (99).

❖ Confer with the patient about the possibility of bringing into the treatment a third party (e.g., close friend, spouse) who is aware of the patient's potential for violence and is accessible, and whom the patient trusts. A second possibility is to involve the potential victim in the psychotherapy with the patient. **This option is clinically very delicate and therefore must be handled with great care.**

❖ Institute involuntary commitment, especially if the threat of violence appears imminent, the mentally ill patient refuses voluntary hospitalization, and the patient appears likely to benefit from hospitalization.

❖ If commitment is not possible and the threat of violence is imminent, notify the police station that is closest to the intended victim or that is in the best position to respond to the potential threat (e.g., police who are closest to the residence of the patient).

❖ If notifying the police is impractical or likely to be ineffective, notify the potential victim, if and when the victim can be identified and located.

Three factors generally play a significant role in the determination of the appropriate clinical response if the duty to protect must be exercised. The first factor is the relative imminence of the threat of danger. The more likely that the potential threat will be carried out in the immediate future, the more aggressive and invasive the response must be. The second factor involves the identified object of the threat. If the threat is directed toward an identifiable victim, then as the imminence of the threat increases, efforts should be directed toward protecting that particular individual. If, however, the patient makes a threat that the psychotherapist deems is real but there is no identifiable victim (e.g., a patient threatens convincingly that once the session is over, he or she is going to purchase a gun and hurt somebody), the response options are less clear. As is noted later in this chapter (see section below on specificity of threat), in some jurisdictions there may be a legal duty to address this situation.

The third factor may be dictated by the law of the jurisdiction in which the psychotherapist is practicing. Except in states with immunity statutes limiting the responsibility of therapists for their patients' violent acts, no hard and fast rules have been applied. In jurisdictions in which no duty to warn or protect currently exists, case decisions from other states may be applied in deciding lawsuits alleging such a duty. Appendix 1 outlines the 32 jurisdictions that have addressed at least one duty-to-warn scenario. In 17 states, the discharge options are outlined by statute, while in the other 15 states, case law, which is sometimes contradictory, provides relative guidance regarding what is considered appropriate action. Appendix 2 summarizes the scope of the law or what appears to be the current law in all 31 jurisdictions.

Special Considerations

Time Parameters

A critical consideration in the evaluation of the risk of violence is "temporality," or the time frame in which such an assessment is to be made. Assessment accuracy is in part determined by the length of time within which the assessment is to be made. In other words, assessment accuracy diminishes as time increases because of the increasing opportunity for the predicted behavior (e.g., violent act) to occur (100).

Arguably, the courts are not seeking 100% accuracy with regard to assessing the likelihood to future violence: "[O]bviously we do not require the therapist, in making that determination, [forecasting future dangerousness] [to] render a perfect performance . . . " (101). However, jurisdictions upholding the duty to warn and/or protect seem to consistently refer to and demand that the psychotherapist predict *foreseeable* violence, with little regard to any time parameter.

Concomitant with the prevailing need for the courts and state legislatures to provide some practical, realistic guidance regarding what constitutes "dangerousness" for purposes of *Tarasoff*-type rulings, guidance is sorely needed in defining "foreseeability." An important part of any definitional assistance from the court should include delineating the temporal limits of a psychotherapist's "predictive" responsibilities.

To date, no court has established or described a set time limit in which a violent act would be considered foreseeable and thus reasonably capable of prediction. In general, the courts vary widely concerning the length of time during which they consider an act of violence foreseeable and thus "actionable." For example, in *Tarasoff,* the length of time between the patient's last contact with his psychotherapist and the actual incident of harm was approximately 10 weeks (102). In the *Lipari* case the period was 6 weeks, and in a 1983 Michigan case, *Davis v. Lhim* (103), the period of time was 2 months.

A recent Delaware case aptly illustrates the unrealistic requirements that a court can sometimes place on a therapist and how it can seemingly dismiss significant clinical considerations, such as time parameters, as only minimally important. In a case that rendered a damages verdict of 1.4 million dollars, the Delaware Supreme Court found in *Naidu v. Laird* (104) that an inpatient psychiatrist was negligent for failing to foresee a former patient's potential to commit a dangerous act. On September 6, 1977, a man was (apparently) deliberately killed when his vehicle was struck by another vehicle driven by a Mr. Putney. Mr. Putney had a long history of mental illness, having already been treated a seventh time at Delaware State Hospital by the defendant $5\frac{1}{2}$ months prior to the accident. The victim's wife claimed that the defendant and two other psychiatrists were grossly negligent in their treatment and decision to discharge Mr. Putney (nearly 6 months earlier). A lower court found for the plaintiff against the defendant and awarded 1.4 million dollars. On appeal, the Delaware Supreme Court in affirming the verdict rejected defendant's two main arguments—that Mr. Putney was not committable and that the proximate-cause link between the psychiatrist's treatment and the fatal accident was too remote to be legally sufficient. The court, accepting the testimony of the plaintiff's experts, concluded that the patient did meet commitment requirements and that he was foreseeably dangerous. With regard to the proximate-cause argument, the court concluded that a 6-month lapse of time between discharge and the fatal accident was not, in and of itself, a bar from recovery but one factor to be weighed by the jury.

While not all cases have so casually dismissed the element of time as a critical issue in evaluating the foreseeability of a patient's violence (104\5), the need for careful and uniform consideration of this element continues to be noticeably lacking in recent decisions.

Confidentiality and Liability

The court in *Tarasoff* considered and rejected the argument that imposing on therapists a duty to act reasonably to prevent public harm would infringe on existing ethical and legal requirements that communications between therapist and patient be kept confidential (106). It is apparent, despite explicit judicial recognition of the significant role that confidentiality plays in psychotherapy (107), that confidentiality is not absolute and that deference must be given to certain exceptions that are "necessary in order to protect the patient or the community from imminent danger" (108). Prior to *Tarasoff,* a physician had a duty to breach confidentiality in order to safeguard society in very circumscribed situations such as reporting contagious or infectious diseases, child abuse, gunshot wounds, and mental illness requiring involuntary commitment. These disclosures could be made without fear of civil reprisal by a patient for an unauthorized violation of the doctor-patient privilege. The *Tarasoff* rationale recognized these circumstances and simply extended the exception to include patient expressions of potential violence to others.

One of the initial concerns that arose following the holding of *Tarasoff* was whether a psychotherapist could be held liable for breaching a state's statute regarding doctor-patient confidentiality and/or privilege laws in order to discharge a duty to warn. Because in 1978 the duty to protect was law only in California and is currently only addressed in approximately 60% of the states, how can a responsible psychotherapist in the other 40% of the country resolve the obvious conflict between maintaining confidentiality and warning a potential victim of possible patient violence?

Interestingly, this matter has rarely surfaced. In a Pennsylvania case, *Hopewell v. Adebimpe* (109), a psychiatrist reacted to a patient's apparent threats against her coworkers and wrote a letter warning her employer of this general threat without the patient/employee's consent. The patient sued the psychiatrist for breach of confidentiality. A Pennsylvania trial court ruled that the *Tarasoff* rationale did not apply and upheld the plaintiff's claim. This case has never been appealed, but two subsequent lower court opinions (110) have accepted *Tarasoff* and rejected the claim that a breach of confidentiality was actionable.

In the 1980 case of *Shaw v. Glickman* (111), the Maryland Court of Special Appeals addressed the issue of whether a psychiatrist had a duty to warn a woman's lover that her estranged husband was unstable, violent, and likely to represent a danger to him. The court ruled that the disclosure of the patient's (i.e., husband's) present condition and violent propensities would violate the Maryland statute regarding privileged communication (112). This case ruling, which held for nearly 9 years, was legislatively overruled in July 1989 by a new statute that not only recognizes the duty to protect, but immunizes from liability good-faith efforts by mental health professionals who discharge the duty according to the statute (113).

This new Maryland statute is consistent with the case holdings and statutes of other states that recognize the duty to warn (see Appendix 2). Even in these jurisdictions, however, some level of immunity will only be given to an applicable mental health professional who discharges the duty to protect in good faith and pursuant to any expressed guidelines promulgated by the state. For example, the Louisiana duty-to-warn statute (114) explicitly states that the psychotherapist must make a "reasonable effort to communicate the immediate threat to the potential victim and law enforcement authorities in the vicinity of the victim's residence." A Louisiana mental health professional, to avoid liability for breach of confidentiality, would have to make a reasonable effort both to warn the victim and to contact the law enforcement authorities in the vicinity of the victim. Failure to do one of these steps could conceivably result in a successful lawsuit against the mental health professional.

In states where there currently is no duty-to-warn law (e.g., South Dakota, Illinois, Hawaii), it is incumbent upon professionals to review their state privilege laws in terms of any public policy exceptions that require safeguarding society. Moreover, any effort to protect a potential victim should concentrate on the method or methods that are most effective but least invasive to the patient. This strategy will serve the public's interest and maintain the privacy rights of the patient. Of course, as with any treatment decision, careful, thorough documentation of the rationale and plan taken should be accomplished. Consultation with appropriate colleagues should also be considered.

Patient Self-Harm

It is not surprising that lawyers, as well as the courts, have often misunderstood, misinterpreted, or misapplied the doctrine of the duty to warn and/or protect in an attempt to assist their clients in either recovering damages or using it as a defense (115). Certain cases attempting to rely on *Tarasoff* reasoning do not factually involve a question of whether there is a duty to warn and/or protect a third-party victim. Nonetheless, the holdings in these decisions do provide some indication of just how far the courts might expand or restrict the duty articulated in *Tarasoff*.

This pattern is particularly important to mental health professionals, because a broad interpretation might impose an unfair burden on psychotherapists who provide treatment to patients who represent a variety of scenarios of "potential dangerousness." For example, does the duty to warn arise in cases of suspected suicide or self-harm? If so, to whom is the duty owed?

This issue was addressed in 1978 in the California case of *Bellah v. Greenson* (116). The First District Court of Appeals considered a malpractice action against a psychiatrist for alleged negligence in failing to warn the parents of a deceased child concerning their daughter's suicidal tendencies. The plaintiff parents claimed, among other things, that the earlier *Tarasoff* ruling created a duty on the part of the defendant psychiatrist to breach confidentiality and reveal to them disclosures their daughter had made in treatment about her suicidal tendencies. The court soundly rejected this interpretation of the *Tarasoff* holding by stating:

> [F]ar from imposing a duty to warn others of the likelihood of any and all harm which might be inflicted by a patient, *Tarasoff* requires that a therapist *not* disclose information *unless* the strong interest in confidentiality is counterbalanced by an even stronger public interest, namely safety from violent assault. (117)

In clearly differentiating the parameters of disclosing confidential information to safeguard against potential danger to the public, the court further held:

> We conclude that *Tarasoff* (II) . . . requires only that a therapist disclose the contents of a confidential communication where the risk to be prevented thereby is the danger of violent assault, and not where the risk of harm is self-inflicted harm or where property is damaged. We decline to further extend the holding of *Tarasoff*. (118)

Despite the fact that this decision is authority only in California, it is generally acknowledged as a reasonable summary of the law with regard to the application of *Tarasoff* and patient suicide. This ruling does not, of course, relieve a psychotherapist of the duty to exercise reasonable care in the treatment of a suicidal patient (i.e., keep the patient from killing himself or herself).

An interesting aberration in recent statutory law regarding the duty to protect throws a wrinkle in the general holding enunciated in *Bellah*. Florida's 1988 statute states that a duty to warn or protect is owed when there is "clear and immediate probability of physical harm to the *patient* or society" (119). It would seem that a duty would extend to a suicidal patient under this provision. No other state has such a law, and the Florida courts have not yet interpreted or applied this statute.

Fourth Party: Duty?

A corollary question regarding the parameters of the duty to protect is whether the duty extends to "fourth parties"? For example, what if during the course of treatment, a patient states that his current girlfriend plans to kill his ex-girlfriend. Assuming that the psychotherapist believes that the patient is reliable, does *Tarasoff* and its developing law apply?

Reviewing the variety of applications of the *Tarasoff*/duty-to-protect doctrine, it is highly doubtful that any court would extend it to a fourth party, as described above. In that example, the psychotherapist's relationship is with the patient (e.g., the boyfriend) and not his girlfriend. There is no "special relationship" with either the girlfriend or her potential victim. Moreover, a psychotherapist would be in no position to reliably evaluate the lethality or validity of the girlfriend's threats in "accord with professional standards." Even the most liberal application of the public policy exception of "safeguarding society" would not likely extend to this degree in light of the many tenuous and remote circumstances connecting the psychotherapist to his patient's girlfriend and to her potential victim. Although the legal requirements surrounding this case do not mandate an affirmative action on the part of the therapist, clinical indifference should be avoided. Attempts should be made to explore the implications of the girlfriend's behavior on the patient, as well as indirectly attempting to circumvent a possible fatal mishap by her through the patient.

The above analysis should generally apply to all psychotherapists except possibly those residing in Minnesota. A novel and unique aspect of that state's duty-to-warn statute is the trigger requirement that the duty arises "when a patient or *other person* communicates a specific, serious threat of physical violence against a specific, clearly identified or identifiable potential victim" (120). It would appear that the duty to warn and/or protect is owed in Minnesota when either a patient or someone other than the patient (e.g., "fourth party") expresses a threat. Without subsequent case law to clarify this interpretation, as well as the numerous clinical considerations that would attach to owing a duty of care to a nonpatient or stranger, it is not currently possible to determine precisely how Minnesota applies this provision.

Unreachable but Identifiable Victims

A situation may arise in which the intended victim of a patient's threat is known but the victim is not reachable (e.g., out of town, moved). What does the conscientious psychotherapist do then? Is any "good-faith effort" on the part of the psychotherapist to contact the intended victim sufficient, or is more required?

The general standard by which a psychotherapist's actions will be judged is whether his or her acts were reasonable under the circumstances (121). As a rule, the more imminent the threat of violence, the more aggressive and invasive the protective act. Therefore, if the threat of violence can be effectively contained by treating the patient (e.g., hospitalization or adjusting the current therapy approach), then the whereabouts of the identified victim becomes less critical. However, if it is reasonably clear that the patient will carry out his or her threats as soon as possible, and a direct approach involving contacting the victim is unsuccessful, it is doubtful that a court would deem a single contact effort sufficient. In the case of imminent danger, and when the victim is unreachable, alternative invasive strategies are likely to be required. These strategies might include hospitalization (voluntary, involuntary); notifying the police or some other similar agency; or contacting a close friend or family member. Every attempt should be made to contact the victim personally; however, when this is not possible or becomes increasingly inefficient, then alternative direct methods must be employed.

Preexisting Threatened Victims

What if a psychotherapist knew that calling the police and/or contacting the intended victim would make little difference in the ultimate occurrence of a patient's violent behavior?

This scenario is poignantly illustrated in the case of *Jablonski v. United States* (52). In this case, the victim, Melissa Kimball, was the common-law wife of the defendant's patient. She was fully aware of her husband's violent tendencies in light of his history of beatings of her and his rape of his former wife, his attempted rape of her mother, an extended involvement with the police, and a history of psychiatric treatment. His more recent acts of violence included threatening Ms. Kimball's mother. The patient, Mr. Jablonski, agreed to obtain psychiatric help at the V.A. hospital, where he was diagnosed as an "antisocial personality" and "potentially dangerous." His treating doctor recommended that Jablonski voluntarily hospitalize himself, but he refused. His prior psychiatric records, which were never obtained by the V.A., indicated that he had "homicidal ideations toward his wife."

The patient continued to act in a threatening manner, and Ms. Kimball drove him back to the V.A. for a second visit. The doctors believed that Mr. Jablonski was "dangerous" and an "emergency case" possessing an "antisocial personality with explosive features," but concluded that they had no basis for involuntary commitment. Two days later, Mr. Jablonski attacked and murdered his common-law wife.

The plaintiff, Melissa Kimball's daughter, alleged that the treating psychiatrists had acted negligently in their care of Mr. Jablonski and that those acts directly resulted in the death of her mother. The district court concluded that the defendants had committed several actionable acts of malfeasance or nonfeasance, including their failure to obtain Mr. Jablonski's prior psychiatric records, their failure to warn the victim of her husband's foreseeable dangerousness to her, and their failure to record warnings by the police regarding Mr. Jablonski's behavior and propensities.

The defendants' major counterargument was that they owed no duty of care to Ms. Kimball because Mr. Jablonski had made no specific threats against her. Moreover, even if they had, she was fully aware of the patient's dangerous tendencies. The court rejected this argument, stating:

> Although the case before us falls somewhere between the extremes of *Tarasoff* and *Thompson v. Alameda,* we find *Tarasoff* to be more clearly on point. Unlike the killer in *Tarasoff,* Jablonski made no specific threats concerning any specific individuals. Nevertheless, Jablonski's previous history indicated that he would likely direct his violence against Kimball. He had raped and committed other acts of violence against his previous wife. His psychological profile indicated that his violence was likely to be directed toward women very close to him. This, in turn, was borne out by his attack on Pahls [Kimball's mother]. Thus, Kimball was specifically identified or "targeted" to a much greater extent than were the neighborhood children in *Thompson.* . . . Moreover, the difficulties in giving a warning that were present in *Thompson* are not present here. . . . Warning Kimball would have posed no difficulty for the doctors, especially since she twice expressed her fear of Jablonski directly to them. Neither can it be said, as was the case in *Thompson,* that direct and precise warnings would have had little effect. (122)

The reasoning of the appellate court is difficult to understand and may be seen by some as an attempt to place blame and liability on the defendants. Granted, there were deficiencies in the defendants' care of Mr. Jablonski (e.g., failure to obtain his prior records), but it is unlikely that a more "direct" warning would have protected the victim. The record indicates that several individuals, including both doctors, a friend, and a priest, advised the victim to "stay away" from Mr. Jablonski. Moreover, the court acknowledges that the victim was afraid of the patient, and very well she should have been, given his extensive history of instability and physical violence, all well known to the victim. The court's statement that "neither can it be said . . . that direct and precise warnings would have had little effect" is speculative at best and ignores the stark reality of the victim's inability or unwillingness to extricate herself from an obviously abusive and dangerous relationship. It is hard to imagine that directly telling the victim the obvious—that Mr. Jablonski posed a risk of danger to her as the court states should have been done—would have made any difference.

In a more recent case, a jury awarded 4.5 million dollars to the decedent's estate for the brutal murder of a woman by a long-time patient of the defendant psychiatrist. In this case, *Rotman v. Mirin* (123), the plaintiff contended that the defendant's failure to adequately treat his patient's chronic disorder (paranoid schizophrenia) and failure to adequately warn the decedent of the patient's ongoing intention to kill her was a deviation from the standard of care. The decedent was the former girlfriend of the patient (Mr. Gould), and as such, she and her parents were fully aware of his mental condition and proclivity to destructive behavior and threats. For example, in 1975, presumably while delusional, the patient amputated his right arm by placing it on a MTA subway track. Before and after this incident, Mr. Gould was in and out of different hospitals for treatment, whereupon he would occasionally state that he had "to kill the decedent to save the Jewish people." Following a period of stabilization, the patient was discharged with the option of living at a halfway house or with his parents and receiving continued outpatient treatment with the defendant. Subsequent threatening behavior required rehospitalization as well as communication by telephone and letter to the plaintiff's home regarding Gould's threats to harm the decedent. Following a subsequent discharge, while the plaintiff was not at home, Mr. Gould told her parents that he had to kill her. The parents filed a criminal complaint, which resulted in probation and an order to continue treatment. Several months later, Mr. Gould stalked the decedent and stabbed her 37 times. At trial, two board-certified psychiatrists testified that the defendant's treatment of the patient was inadequate and the patient should have been committed. Further, they contended that the warning given to the decedent's parents was inadequate and did not sufficiently express the seriousness of Mr. Gould's condition. The defendant, in denying liability, stated that based on his observations, Mr. Gould was not committable and no longer represented a threat to the plaintiff.

Troublesome questions spring out of this case. If the plaintiff was indeed not commitable, it is unclear what the defendant could have done in treating Mr. Gould. The defendant relied, in part, on the parents to notify him if they observed any deterioration in the patient's condition. (There was no notification prior to the assault.) Plaintiff's experts claimed that this reliance on the parents' reporting, as well as that of his own patient, was negligent. The plaintiff and her parents *did know* that Mr. Gould was a threat to her. Their contention that the defendant understated Mr. Gould's condition to them in his letter is questionable because of the patient's visit to their home stating that he must kill their daughter.

There are many questions unanswered and issues left unexplained in this case. The case is currently on appeal, and many of these issues should be addressed in the appellate decision (124).

Like *Jablonski*, the *Rotman* decision leaves one straining to understand the rationale of the court, especially in light of the clear understanding of the risk that each victim personally had. The only consolation to either of these opinions is that California (125) and Massachusetts (126) now have duty-to-warn statutes that specifically prescribe what steps a psychotherapist is to take if the duty to protect should arise.

Duty to Protect Property?

Does the *Tarasoff* ruling extend to anything other than another person? Two states, one by case law and the other by statute, have stated that a duty to warn and/or protect is owed when there is threat of property damages. The initial opinion to establish this unique position was the case of *Peck v. Counseling Service of Addison County* (127). The patient, a 31-year-old epileptic with a long history of impulsive, dangerous, antisocial behavior, was treated at the defendant's counseling center for 3 years before he left the area and moved into a halfway house. Following a fight with another resident he was asked to leave, so he moved in with his parents, with whom he did not get along. He restarted counseling at the center with the therapist whom he had not seen for nearly 2 years.

His father suggested that his son lie to Social Security in order to obtain benefits to which he was not entitled. The son refused and became angry. The father told him that he was sick and that he belonged in a hospital. The patient left his parents' home and went to the counselor. She assisted him in finding a place to stay. The following day he told her about the argument that he had had with his father and that he was angry at him. Five days later he told her that he was angry enough that he would probably burn down his father's barn. In treatment, they explored this matter, and the patient assured the counselor that he was not going to burn down his father's barn. She believed him. The next day he burned the barn down.

The therapist, a master's level counselor with a degree in education, was supposed to seek consultation with the staff psychiatrist as needed. In this case, she wrote down a description of the threat but never apprised the psychiatrist. Also, she contacted the patient's former counselors but not his most recent physician. In the absence of conferring with the patient's most current doctor and the lack of opportunity to review past records (because they had been ordered but not yet received), the therapist was unaware that the patient was under heavy medication.

The patient's parents sued the counseling center for the damage to their barn. They claimed that the defendants should have known that their son posed a danger to them and their property, and that the defendants failed to notify them or others who could have taken steps to protect them. Moreover, they alleged that the counseling center's failure to properly assess the patient's potential for violence directly resulted in the destruction of their barn.

The court held that a reasonably prudent counseling center would have had a system for cross-referencing between physician and nonphysician for patients with severe medical problems; that the counselor should have consulted her supervisor or the past treating physician; and that the counselor should have obtained a more thorough history regarding the patient's threat.

On the issue of negligence the court ruled that not having the patient's recent medical history or the cross-referencing system was not actionable nonfeasance. It further concluded that the counselor had acted in good faith, even though her belief was based on inadequate information and insufficient consultation. However, the court did conclude that the counseling center should have recognized the substantial risk that the patient was capable of carrying out his threat. The court did note that the father was 50% negligent because of his conduct toward his son.

As a matter of law, the court held that if *Tarasoff* was in effect in Vermont, the counseling center would have had a duty to warn the Pecks. However, the court declined to recognize a *Tarasoff* duty in this case. The court dismissed the complaint and explicitly left to the state legislature or the Appeals Court the responsibility of determining whether Vermont law would incorporate a duty to warn. On appeal, the Vermont Supreme Court created that duty, stating:

> [W]e hold that a mental health professional who knows or, based upon the standards of the mental health profession, should know that his or her patient poses a serious risk of danger to an identifiable victim has a duty to exercise reasonable care to protect him or her from that danger. (128)

Unanswered questions abound from this decision. How does the threat of property damage equate to the aforementioned "serious risk of danger to an identifiable victim"? The only answer that the Vermont high court gives in response to this question is contained in a footnote that states, "[A]rson is a violent act and represents a lethal threat to human beings who may be in the vicinity of the conflagration (*sic*)" (129). This note is very tenuous and obviously places no limit on what constitutes "vicinity." Also, what are the professional standards for making predictions of violence by a master's level counselor? How are such predictions to be made and then judged? The court's opinion again offers no guidance. Equally vague is the court's reference to a generic "mental health practitioner" for whom the duty is to be discharged. In the absence of any elaboration, such a generic term can literally encompass anyone who provides professional counseling services.

Since this decision in 1985, no other court has followed Vermont's lead in extending *Tarasoff* to include danger to property. However, one state, New Hampshire (130), has by statute.

Scope of the Law and Trends

In 1987, the *Wall Street Journal* quoted an attorney from the American Psychiatric Association as saying, "[L]awyers for psychiatric and psychological groups advise members to consider *Tarasoff*-type lawsuits as an ever present possibility." It was estimated that over 100 such cases were pending, "two or three in every state" (87). While this prediction has fallen far short of the number of published and unpublished cases concerning malpractice cases involving the duty to warn, there is growing evidence that the warning that it is an "ever present possibility" is beginning to become apparent.

The majority of jurisdictions that have accepted the duty to warn have adopted some variation of the specificity rule first enunciated in *Thompson v. Alameda*. This rule and its general equivalents hold that a duty is owed if a specific or identifiable threat of danger is made toward a specific or identifiable victim. It would appear that this rule reflects both the majority and the general trend in recent opinions. Occasional court opinions and statutes, however, continue to reflect the more expansive "foreseeability" requirement as first described in *Lipari v. Sears, Roebuck and Co.*

AIDS: an emerging consideration.   A major trend in the law regarding duty to warn appears in the emerging cases involving acquired immune deficiency syndrome (AIDS). While relatively little case law currently exists in this area, multiple questions arise by practitioners regarding the treatment of AIDS patients. For example, a number of medical-ethical questions arise with respect to confidentiality and the general testing of psychiatric patients for the HIV virus (131). May patients be tested indiscriminately, or should testing only be reserved for patients who are high-risk candidates for AIDS, or for those who request testing? Once an AIDS patient is identified within the hospital, how should this information be communicated to other patients, if at all (132)? Especially on a sexually active coed ward in a psychiatric hospital, where a mentally incompetent AIDS patient may be present, what precautions must be taken by the staff to avoid others being infected (133)? What is a clinician's duty to warn and protect when a patient who is a health care provider develops signs and symptoms of AIDS dementia complex (134)?

Perhaps the most frequently asked question by clinicians is how to effectively manage within the rules of the law a patient who is HIV positive or who has AIDS symptoms who refuses to name his sexual contacts and refuses to stop having sexual intercourse with his partners (135). Must the psychiatrist, before releasing such a patient from the hospital, warn the intended sexual partner, if he or she can be identified? Must the psychiatrist keep the patient in the hospital to prevent infection to others?

Obviously, there are many confusing, complex, unanswered questions with respect to AIDS patients and the concept of dangerousness with duty to warn (136). As in all cases in which the psychiatrist is uncertain about future behavior of his or her patient who may be infecting others or who may be physically violent to others under certain clinical conditions, the psychiatrist is advised to seek legal consultation with respect to further action regarding discharge. In some cases, the psychiatrist is advised to seek judicial determination regarding discharge following a full court hearing on the issues. If the court then orders discharge of the patient, the psychiatrist must follow the court's order but must do so within proper and reasonable clinical precautions. Merely following a court's order does not necessarily protect the psychiatrist from further liability if his or her behavior is negligent and not in keeping with the standards of care within the profession.

Conclusions

The duty-to-warn/protect doctrine represents a classic dilemma for psychotherapists to balance the interests of society to be protected against threats to its welfare and a patient's interest in privacy and the maintenance of confidentiality. Whether one agrees or disagrees with the existence of this doctrine, the overriding reality is that it is an accepted theory of civil liability in at least two thirds of the states. As a result, when a patient threatens potential harm to a third party, psychotherapists must do something to guard against the potential risk of violence. While a therapist's first inclination in this situation might be to warn the potential victim or notify the police, this action should be resisted in favor of more clinically oriented alternatives. Also, because of the continued insistence of the courts to require therapists to render predictions of violence toward others when such ability is no better than 1 in 3, the need for careful, thorough, and probing assessments cannot be overstated.

References

1. 248 NY 334, 162 NE 99 (1928)
2. Palsgraf v Long Island Railroad Co, 248 NY 339, 162 NE 100
3. See, e.g., Dillon v Legg, 69 Cal Rptr 72, 441 P2d 912 (1968); Leong v Takasaki, 55 Hawaii 396, 520 P2d 758 (1974)

4. Tarasoff v Regents of the University of California, 13 Cal 3d 177, 529 P2d 553 (1974)
5. See, e.g., Comment—Where public peril begins: a survey of psychotherapists to determine the effects of Tarasoff. Stanford Law Review 31:165–190, 1978
6. See Harper FV, Kime PM: The duty to control the conduct of another. Yale Law Journal 43:886–905, 1934
7. Keeton WP, Dobbs DB, Keeton RE, et al: Prosser and Keeton on Torts, 5th Edition. St. Paul, MN, West Publishing, 1984, pp 383–385
8. Restatement (Second) of Torts § 319 (1965)
9. Ibid, comment (a), illustrations 1 and 2
10. Hoffman v Blackmon, 241 So 2d 752 (Fla App 1970)
11. Wocjik v Aluminum Co of American, 18 Misc 2d 740, 183 NYS2d 351 (1959); Davis v Rodman, 147 Ark 385, 227 SW 612 (1921)
12. Semler v Psychiatric Institute of Washington, DC, 538 F2d 121 (4th Cir 1976); Vistica v Presbyterian Hospital, 67 Cal 2d 465, 62 Cal Rptr 577, 432 P2d 193 (1967)
13. 272 F Supp 409 (D ND 1967)
14. McIntosh v Milano, 160 NJ Super 466, 403 A2d 500 (1979)
15. Merchants National Bank and Trust Co of Fargo v United States, 272 F Supp 417–419 (D ND 1967)
16. Givelber DJ, Bowers WJ, Blitch CL: Tarasoff—myth and reality: an empirical study of private law in action. Wisconsin Law Review, 1984, pp 443–497
17. Runck B: Survey shows therapists misunderstood Tarasoff rule. Hosp Community Psychiatry 35:429–430, 1984
18. See, e.g., Note—Tarasoff v Regents of University of California: the psychotherapist's peril. University of Pittsburgh Law Review 37:155–168, 1975; Rachlin S, Schwartz HI: Unforeseeable liability for patients' violent acts. Hosp Community Psychiatry 725–731, 1986; Stone AA: Vermont adopts Tarasoff: a real barn-burner. Am J Psychiatry 143:352–355, 1986; Greenberg LT: The evolution of Tarasoff: recent developments in the psychiatrist's duties to warn potential victims, protect the public, and predict dangerousness. Journal of Psychiatry and Law 12:315–348, 1984; Beck JC (ed): The Potentially Violent Patient and the Tarasoff Decision in Psychiatric Practice. Washington, DC, American Psychiatric Press, 1985
19. Cal Welfare & Inst Code §§ 5000–5401 (Lanterman Petris Short Act)
20. People v Poddar, 26 Cal 3d 438, 103 Cal Rptr 84 (1972), reversed, 10 Cal 3d 750, 518 P2d 342 (1974)
21. Tarasoff v Regents of University of California, 118 Cal Rptr 129, 529 P2d 553 (1974) [Tarasoff I]
22. Tarasoff v Regents of University of California, 118 Cal Rptr 130–131, 529 P2d 554–555
23. Tarasoff v Regents of University of California, 118 Cal Rptr 131, 529 P2d 556
24. Tarasoff v Regents of University of California, 118 Cal Rptr 135, 529 P2d 559
25. Tarasoff v Regents of University of California, 118 Cal Rptr 139–140, 529 P2d 563–564, citing Cal Welfare & Inst Code § 5201
26. Tarasoff v Regents of University of California, 118 Cal Rptr 140–141, 529 P2d 564–565

27. See, e.g., McDonald M: Court reaffirms "warning decision." Psychiatric News, Vol 11, August 6, 1976, pp 1, 18

28. Stone AA: Suing psychotherapists to safeguard society. Harvard Law Review 90:358–378, 1976

29. Comment—Where public peril begins: a survey of psychotherapists to determine the effects of Tarasoff. Stanford Law Review 31:165–190, 1978

30. Tarasoff v Regents of University of California, 17 Cal 3d 425, 131 Cal Rptr 14, 551 P2d 334 (1976) [Tarasoff II]

31. Tarasoff v Regents of University of California, 17 Cal 3d 438–439, 551 P2d 345–346

32. Tarasoff v Regents of University of California, 17 Cal 3d 438–439, 551 P2d 345–346

33. Tarasoff v Regents of University of California, 17 Cal 3d 440–441, 551 P2d 347

34. Appelbaum PS: Tarasoff and the clinician: problems in fulfilling the duty to protect. Am J Psychiatry 142:425–429, 1985

35. Tarasoff v Regents of University of California, 17 Cal 3d 425, 439, 551 P2d 334, 345 (1976)

36. Tarasoff v Regents of University of California, 17 Cal 3d 431, 551 P2d 345

37. Tarasoff v Regents of University of California, 17 Cal 3d 439, 551 P2d 345

38. Tarasoff v Regents of University of California, 17 Cal 3d 437–438, 551 P2d 344 n 10

39. Rubin BM: Prediction of dangerousness in mentally ill criminals. Arch Gen Psychiatry 126:397–398, 1972

40. Monahan J: Predicting Violent Behavior: An Assessment of Clinical Techniques. Beverly Hills, CA, Sage, 1981

41. Melton GB, Petrila J, Poythress NG, et al: Psychological Evaluations for the Courts. New York, Guilford, 1987, p 194

42. Appelbaum PS: The new preventive detention: psychiatry's problematic responsibility for the control of violence. Am J Psychiatry 145:779–785, 1988

43. Monahan J, Steadman H: Crime and mental disorder: an epidemiological approach, in Crime and Justice: An Annual Review of Research, Vol 3. Edited by Morris N, Tonry M. Chicago, IL, University of Chicago Press, 1983

44. Levinson RM, Ramsey G: Dangerousness, stress, and mental health examinations. J Health Soc Behav 20:178–187, 1979

45. Holland TR: Diagnostic labeling: individual differences in the behavior of clinicians conducting presentence evaluations. Criminal Justice and Behavior 6:187–199, 1979

46. Monahan J: The prediction of violent behavior: developments in psychology and law, in Psychology and Law. Edited by Schreier J, Hammonds BL. Washington, DC, American Psychological Association, 1983, pp 147–176

47. Melton GB, Petrila J, Poythress NG, et al: Psychological Evaluations for the Courts. New York, Guilford, 1987, p 205

48. Monahan J: The Clinical Prediction of Violent Behavior (Crime and Delinquency Monograph). Washington, DC, U.S. Department of Health and Human Services, 1981, pp 31–38

49. Simon RI: The duty to protect in private practice, in Confidentiality Versus the Duty to Protect: Foreseeable Harm in the Practice of Psychiatry. Edited by Beck JC. Washington, DC, American Psychiatric Press, 1990, pp 23–41

50. Ibid, pp 71–82
51. Tardiff K: A model for the short-term prediction of violence potential, in Current Approaches to the Prediction of Violence. Edited by Brizer DA, Crowner ML. Washington, DC, American Psychiatric Press, 1988, pp 1–12
52. Jablonski v United States, 712 F2d 391 (9th Cir 1983)
53. Tarasoff v Regents of University of California, 17 Cal 2d 439, 551 P2d 334, 131 Cal Rptr 25 (1976) [emphasis added]
54. 780 F2d 97 (DC Cir 1986)
55. 168 NJ Super 466, 403 A2d 500 (1979)
56. NJ Stat Ann 2A:170-25.7 et al (1987)
57. McIntosh v Milano, 403 A2d 511–512 [emphasis added]
58. 497 F Supp 185 (D Neb 1980)
59. Lipari v Sears, Roebuck & Co, 497 F Supp 188 [emphasis added]
60. Lipari v Sears, Roebuck & Co, 497 F Supp 194 [emphasis added]
61. 100 Wash 2d 421, 671 P2d 230 (1983)
62. Peterson v State, 671 P2d 230, 237 (1983)
63. Schuster v Altenberg, 144 Wis 2d 223, 424 NW2d 159 (1988)
64. Schuster v Altenberg, 144 Wis 2d 223, 424 NW2d 159 (1988), rev'd, Schuster v Altenberg, 86-CV-1327 (Cir Ct Racine Cty 1990)
65. 749 SW2d 696 (Ky Ct App 1988)
66. Ky Rev Stat § 202A.400 (Baldwin 1987)
67. 39 Ohio St 3d 86, 529 NE2d 449 (1988)
68. Littleton v Good Samaritan Hospital & Health Center 529 NE2d 449, 455 n 3 (Ohio 1988)
69. 775 P2d 1122 (Ariz 1989)
70. See Dillon v Legg, 69 Cal Rptr 72, 441 P2d 912 (1986); Rodrigues v State, 472 P2d 509 (Haw 1970)
71. 768 P2d 1198 (Colo 1989)
72. Lipari v Sears, Roebuck & Co, 497 F Supp 185 (D Neb 1980); Peterson v State, 100 Wash 2d 421, 671 P2d 230 (1983)
73. Ind Code Ann § 34-4-12.4-1 (Burns Supp 1987)
74. Minn Civ Code § 148.975 (Cumm Supp 1986)
75. Ky Rev Stat Ann § 202A.400 (Baldwin 1987)
76. Fla Stat Ann § 4900.0147 (Cumm Supp 1987)
77. 27 Cal 3d 741, 614 P2d 728, 167 Cal Rptr 70 (1980)
78. Thompson v County of Alameda, 614 P2d 735 [emphasis added]
79. Leedy v Hartnett, 510 F Supp 1125 (MD Pa 1981) (interpreting Pennsylvania law); Cairl v State, 323 NW2d 20 (Minn 1982); Doyle v United States, 530 F Supp 1278 (CD Cal 1982); Heltsley v Votteler, 327 NW2d 759 (Iowa 1982); Okerblom v Baskies, No 74-2570 Middlesex Cty Super Ct (Mass March 8, 1983); Cain v Danville State Hospital, No 1871-1982 Civil Monroe Cty Ct Comm Pleas (Pa January 12, 1984); Brady v Hopper, 751 F2d 329 (10th Cir 1984); Sharpe v South Carolina Department of Mental Health, 281 SC 242, 315 SE2d 112 (1984); White v United States, 780 F2d 97 (DC Cir 1986); Bardoni v Kim, 151 Mich App 169, 390 NW2d 218 (1986); Williams v Sun Valley Hospital, 723 SW2d 783 (Tex Ct App 1987); Jackson v New Center CMH Services, 404 NW2d 688 (Mich Ct App 1987)

80. Alaska, California, Colorado, Kansas, Louisiana, Maryland, Massachusetts, Minnesota, Montana, Nebraska, Utah, Washington

81. 377 SE2d 125 (SC Ct App 1989)

82. See also Sharpe v South Carolina Department of Mental Health, 292 SC 11, 354 SE2d 778 (Ct App 1987), cert dsmd, 294 SC 469, 366 SE2d 12 (1988)

83. Rogers v South Carolina Department of Mental Health, 377 SE2d 125, 126 (SC Ct App 1989)

84. 870 F2d 1098 (6th Cir 1989)

85. Davis v Lihm, 124 Mich App 291, 335 NW2d 481 (Mich App 1983), remanded on other grounds, 422 Mich 875, 366 NW2d 7 (1985), on rem, 147 MichApp 8, 382 NW2d 195 (1985), revised sub nom, Canon v Thumudo 430 Mich 326, 422 NW2d 688 (1987); Hinkelman v Borgess Medical Center, 403 NW2d 547 (Mich Ct App 1987); Jackson v New Center CMH Svcs, 404 NW2d 688 (Mich Ct App 1987)

86. Bisbing S: Duty to warn: current overview and trends. Unpublished manuscript, October 1989

87. Otten AL: More psychotherapists held liable for the actions of violent patients. Wall Street Journal, March 2, 1987, Section 2

88. Most lawsuits in psychiatry involve suicide. Clinical Psychiatry News 17(1):1, 13, 1989

89. Smith J, Bisbing S: Sexual Exploitation by Health Care and Other Professionals, 2nd Edition. Potomac, MD, Legal Medicine Press, 1987

90. Psychiatric News, Vol 22, April 3, 1987, p 11

91. American Psychological Association: Appendix to White Paper on Duty to Protect: Suits against mental health care professionals for the violent acts of patients. Unpublished manuscript, Washington, DC, American Psychological Association, September 1985

92. Simon RI: Concise Guide to Psychiatry and Law for Clinicians. Washington, DC, American Psychiatric Press, 1992

93. Roth LH, Meisel A: Dangerousness, confidentiality, and the duty to warn. Am J Psychiatry 134:508–511, 1977

94. Mills M: The so-called duty to warn: the psychotherapeutic duty to protect third parties from patients' violent acts. Behavioral Sciences and the Law 2:246, 1984

95. Flemming J, Maximov B: The patient or his victim: the therapist's dilemma. California Law Review 62:1025–1044, 1974

96. Wexler DB: Patients, therapists, and third parties: the victimological virtue of Tarasoff. International Journal of Law and Psychiatry 2:1–28, 1979

97. Leonard JB: A therapist's duty to potential victims: a non-threatening view of Tarasoff. Law and Human Behavior 1:309–317, 1977

98. Tupin JP: The violent patient: a strategy for management and diagnosis. Hosp Community Psychiatry 34:37, 1983

99. Beck JC: When a patient threatens violence: an empirical study of clinical practice after Tarasoff. Bull Am Acad Psychiatry Law 10:189–201, 1982

100. Simon RI: Clinical Psychiatry and the Law, 2nd Edition. Washington, DC, American Psychiatric Press, 1991, Chapter 13

101. Tarasoff v Regents of the University of California, 17 Cal 3d 425, 439, 551 P2d 334, 345, 131 Cal Rptr 14, 25 (1976)

102. Tarasoff v Regents of the University of California, 17 Cal 3d 430, 551 P2d 339, 131 Cal Rptr 19
103. 124 Mich App 291, 335 NW2d 481 (1983), remanded on other grounds, 422 Mich 875, 366 NW2d 7 (1985), on rem, 147 Mich App 8, 382 NW2d 195 (1985), revised sub nom, Canon v Thumudo 430 Mich 326, 422 NW2d 688 (1988)
104. 539 A2d 1064 (Del 1988)
105. Doyle v United States, 530 F Supp 1278 (CD Cal 1982) [one month after discharge considered too tenuous]; Januszko v State of New York, 47 NY2d 774, 391 NE2d 297, 417 NYS2d 462 (1979) [negligent discharge case where violence occurring 5 months after release was held to be too distant in time]
106. Tarasoff v Regents of the University of California, 17 Cal 3d 440–441, 551 P2d 346–347, 131 Cal Rptr 26–27
107. Tarasoff v Regents of the University of California, 17 Cal 3d 425, 457, 551 P2d 334, 358, 131 Cal Rptr 14, 38 (1976) (Clark J, dissenting)
108. American Psychiatric Association: The Principles of Medical Ethics With Annotations Especially Applicable to Psychiatry. Washington, DC, American Psychiatric Association, 1989, Section 4, Annotation 8
109. No GD 78-82756 Allegheny Cty, Ct Comm Pleas (Pa June 1, 1981)
110. Cain v Danville State Hosp, No 1871-1982 Civil Monroe Cty Ct Comm Pleas (Pa January 12, 1984); Kreiser v Kreiser, No 1775 Civil Lebanon Cty Ct Comm Pleas (Pa February 5, 1986)
111. 45 Md App 718, 415 A2d 625 (1980)
112. Shaw v Glickman, 45 Md App 718, 415 A2d 625 (1980)
113. MD Cts & Jud Proc Code Ann § 5-315 (1989)
114. La Rev Stat Ann § 9:2800.2 (Cumm Supp 1986)
115. Cole v Taylor, 301 NW2d 766 (Iowa 1981) [no civil duty owed to (criminal) defendant, based on duty to warn, to protect victims from his own violent acts]; Glazier v Lee, 171 Mich App 216, 429 NW2d 857 (1988) [no civil duty owed to (criminal) defendant, based on duty to warn, to protect victims from his own violent acts]; CAU v RL, 438 NW2d 441 (Minn Ct App 1989) [no duty of fiance to warn wife-to-be that he was infected with AIDS]; Division of Corrections v Neakok, 721 P2d 1121 (Alaska 1986) [state government liable for negligent failure to control dangerous parolee—foreseeable violence is sufficient without requirement of specifically identifiable victim]; Duffy v City of Oceanside, 179 Cal 3d 666, 224 Cal Rptr 874 (1986) [no duty of county to warn city workers of foreseeably dangerous parolee coworker]; Eckhardt v Kirts, 179 Ill App 3d 863, 534 NE2d 1339 (1989) [no duty of psychiatrist to warn husband of his wife's violent tendencies in light of no specific threats against husband or other foreseeable risks]; Hawkins v King County Dept of Rehab Services, 24 Wash App 338, 602 P2d 361 (1979) [no duty of attorney to warn victim of threat already known to her]
116. 81 Cal App 3d 614, 146 Cal Rptr 535 (1978)
117. Bellah v Greenson, 81 Cal App 3d 622, 146 Cal Rptr 535, 539 [emphasis in original]
118. Bellah v Greenson, 81 Cal App 3d 622, 146 Cal Rptr 535, 539–540
119. Fla Stat Ann § 490.0147 (Supp 1988)
120. Minn Stat Ann § 148.975 (West 1989)

121. Tarasoff v Regents of the University of California, 17 Cal 3d 425, 439, 551 P2d 334, 345, 131 Cal Rptr 14, 25 (1976)
122. Jablonski v U.S., 712 F2d 391, 398 (9th Cir 1983)
123. No 88-1562 (Middlesex Cty Super Ct, Mass 1988) [opinion not yet released]
124. Lindheimer SK, personal communication, April 1989
125. Cal Civ Code 43.92(West Supp 1989)
126. Mass Ann Law ch 112 § 129A(c)(2) (1988)
127. 499 A2d 422 (Vt 1985)
128. Peck v Counseling Service of Addison County, 499 A2d 422, 427 (Vt 1985)
129. Peck v Counseling Service of Addison County, 499 A2d 422, 424 n 3 (Vt 1985)
130. NH Rev Stat Ann § 329.31 (1986)
131. Zonana H, Norko M, Stier D: The AIDS patient on the psychiatric unit: ethical and legal issues. Psychiatric Annals 18:587, 587–593, 1988
132. Zonana H, Norko M, Stier D: The AIDS patient on the psychiatric unit: ethical and legal issues. Psychiatric Annals 18: 587–593, 1988 (see p 591), citing Mathews GW, Neslund VS: The initial impact of AIDS on public health law in the United States. JAMA 257:344–352, 1987
133. Zonana H, Norko M, Stier D: The AIDS patient on the psychiatric unit: ethical and legal issues. Psychiatric Annals 18:587–593, 1988; see p 591
134. Simon RI: AIDS dementia complex in healthcare providers: do treating physicians have an ethical and legal duty to protect endangered patients? Court, Health Science and the Law, Summer 1991
135. See, e.g., Bisbing SB: Psychiatric patients and AIDS: evolving law and liability. Psychiatric Annals 18:582–586, 1988; see pp 582, 585–586
136. See, e.g., Dyer AR: AIDS, ethics, and psychiatry. Psychiatric Annals 18:577, 578–580, 581, 1988

Chapter 9

Premature Release of Potentially Violent Patients

P sychiatrists face difficult clinical and legal responsibilities with regard to potentially dangerous patients when a decision to release or discharge is contemplated. The duty of clinicians to exercise reasonable care when deciding whether to allow a patient out on pass or to be discharged from a hospital is no less paramount than the duty owed to a patient when treatment is first initiated.

Clinical Decision Making When Releasing an Inpatient

In general, there are two distinct considerations when contemplating the release of a patient. The first, and probably most important, is the exercise of reasonable professional judgment in the decision whether to release in the first place. The second consideration, which is actually an extension of the original duty, is the implementation of a sound referral and follow-up plan.

The decision to consider discharging a patient may be due to any number of factors. For example, part of treatment may include permitting the patient to visit his or her family on a weekend pass; the patient is eligible for a full or conditional release; hospitalization is no longer beneficial; or an order for commitment has run. It is a well-established rule in the law that physicians (psychiatrists) are not warrantors of perfect results and therefore will not be held liable for mere mistakes in judgment (1). Instead, the standard by which a psychiatrist's decision to release a patient will be judged is that of an "ordinary and reasonable member" (2) of psychiatry.

In a large number of cases in which liability has been found for the negligent release or discharge of a dangerous patient, there has been a consistent finding of a failure to adhere to or to apply standard psychiatric procedures. For example, cases in which individual psychiatrists or hospitals have been found liable for the conduct of a released patient have included the following negligent acts:

❖ Failure to conduct a reasonable discharge interview (3)
❖ Failure of one psychiatrist to transfer to the discharging psychiatrist the records of a patient documented as being violent (4)
❖ Failure to comply with a judicial order requiring notification to the court before releasing the patient (5)
❖ Arbitrary and capricious release of a patient because of his or her "imperious manner" (6)
❖ Failure to carefully examine the patient and all available information about him or her (7)
❖ Failure of a hospital to maintain contact with a patient whom it had conditionally released (8)

The decision to release or discharge a patient must be weighed carefully, particularly if there is evidence of current assaultive behavior or a history of violence. It is well documented that except for an expressed intent to commit a violent act, there is no single conclusive factor or even constellation of factors that reliably predicts future dangerousness (9). This fact, however, does not relieve a psychiatrist from exercising reasonable professional judgment in determining whether it is appropriate for a patient to be released or discharged. Reasonable care generally dictates that a patient's records be carefully reviewed, the patient be interviewed, the input of other care providers be solicited whenever possible, and any other relevant and reliable data sources be consulted (e.g., family members).

Because every patient is different, there are often considerations that only apply to that individual. Simon, in the *Concise Guide to Clinical Psychiatry and the Law* (10), outlines numerous factors that, from a practical clinical perspective, should be considered in assessing a patient's violence potential. Among these factors are the following:

❖ Plan and motive
❖ Therapeutic alliance
❖ Other relationships
❖ Psychiatric diagnosis (Axis I and II)
❖ Actuarial data (age, gender, race, socioeconomic status, marital status, violence base rates)
❖ Availability of lethal means
❖ Expressed intended victims or threat

- ❖ Past violent acts
- ❖ History of alcohol abuse
- ❖ History of drug abuse
- ❖ Mental competency
- ❖ History of impulsive behavior
- ❖ Central nervous system disorder
- ❖ Low intelligence

Smith (11) highlights four major considerations of which hospitals and treating psychiatrists should also be aware:

1. Does the patient manifest an overt risk of violence, either to himself or herself, or to others? For example, is he or she involved in pending litigation (e.g., court-order detention or commitment)? Also, has the patient displayed a reduction in deviant behavior that is consistent with favorable community adjustment?
2. Has the patient received maximum hospital benefit as an inpatient? This can be gauged by reviewing admission records and progress notes to determine whether the patient has made significant improvement in the behaviors that precipitated hospitalization. Also, the question of whether the patient has developed insight into his or her problems and now assumes responsibility for his or her behavior should be evaluated.
3. Is the patient in good contact with reality and capable of rationally discussing his or her situation? In part, this can be assessed by several practical factors. Is the patient returning to a stable environment? Do his or her symptoms appear to be in stable remission? Is outpatient treatment available if needed? Is appropriate and meaningful psychosocial support available? Is the patient capable of adhering to a prescribed treatment plan alone (e.g., medication) or with the assistance of an accessible third party?
4. Does the patient possess sufficient social, emotional, and personal hygiene skills to sustain his or her living status outside of the hospital?

These are obviously not easy questions for psychiatrists to assess and answer. It is not likely that a patient will adequately meet all of these factors before being released, and probably it is not necessary. Some considerations, such as potential violence toward others, should always be assessed, whereas considerations like "maximum hospital benefit" are more flexible. In order to make decision making easier as well as to demonstrate the "reasonableness" of the ultimate decision of whether to release or not, psychiatrists should consider the six steps advanced by Klein and colleagues (12):

1. Records of previous treatments and hospitalizations should be obtained and carefully reviewed (13).

2. The clinical record should clearly and thoroughly document the decision-making process regarding the decision.
3. A consultation with relevant professionals, such as a senior staff psychiatrist, an attorney, or a hospital administrator, should be solicited whenever there is any question regarding clinical or legal aspects of the contemplated release. This consultation should also be carefully documented.
4. If a patient is to be discharged and it is determined that the patient presents a potential risk of danger, it is incumbent upon the discharging psychiatrist to make a reasonable effort to identify the potential victim and to communicate an appropriate warning (14).
5. After a careful assessment, if any doubt exists regarding the potential danger to self or others because of the contemplated release, the patient should be encouraged to remain in the hospital. If this recommendation is resisted, involuntary commitment should be considered.
6. If a patient has a history of violence, a postdischarge treatment and care plan should be developed. This plan should be formulated with the understanding that *appropriate follow-up* by the discharging psychiatrist or staff will be done.

Discharge and release planning should be a continuous process of assessment and revision. As noted earlier, it is not likely that a patient will satisfactorily meet all discharge considerations; yet this does not automatically preclude a patient from consideration for release. The prudent psychiatrist will conduct a risk-benefit analysis that systematically assesses all of the available clinical data that favor and oppose both releasing and retaining the patient (15). This weighing of relevant clinical factors should be done whether the decision involves a 1-day pass or final discharge. As noted by Simon: "If, after reasonable clinical examination and evaluation the clinician feels that the benefits for the *patient's recovery* outweigh the specific risks of any given psychiatric intervention, then these judgments should be recorded in a risk-benefit note in the patient's chart" (16).

Every psychiatrist has a "system or process" that he or she follows or employs when making difficult clinical decisions such as if and when to release a psychiatric patient. Regardless of the specific procedure, the essential consideration, ethically as well as legally, is whether "reasonable care and judgment was exercised in arriving at a decision" (17).

Negligent Release: Scope of the Case Law

Since the original *Tarasoff* decision in 1976, it appears that duty-to-warn/protect cases have garnered much of the professional liability and malpractice spotlight in both the lay and the psychiatric media. In one respect this concern is understandable in light of the apparent "added" responsibility placed on psychiatrists and other mental health professionals to predict violent behavior and responsibly safeguard the potential victim. However, what many mental health professionals and psychiatric hospitals are likely not to realize is that cases involving the injury or death of individuals because of the *negligent release or discharge* of a violent patient far outweigh in number and frequency those cases involving *Tarasoff*-type situations.

For example, one review of the case law before 1980 revealed 26 cases involving negligent discharge or release (18). What is notable about this compilation is that it was not intended to be comprehensive, it does not include settlements, and it only addresses cases that were heard on appeal. Therefore, it is easy to project that the actual number of adjudicated and settled cases is considerably higher. Moreover, a casual review of recent issues of many case reporter publications such as *Medical Malpractice: Verdicts, Settlements and Experts; Personal Injury Verdicts Review; Medical Liability Reporter; or The National Jury Verdict Review and Analysis* consistently reveals numerous cases involving negligent release or discharge. While no comprehensive review of the case law concerning this area of malfeasance has been published to our knowledge, at least 150 settled and adjudicated cases have been documented (19). Moreover, because of the increasing number of discharges influenced by insurance considerations and managed care decisions and the annual increase in lawsuits involving allegations of negligent release decisions, it would not at all be surprising if this type of case eventually supplanted suicide cases as the number one source of liability involving psychiatrists and psychiatric facilities.

Liability Considerations

In determining whether the release of a patient, either for a day pass or final discharge, is consistent with the standard of "ordinary and reasonable care," the courts have considered a number of facts. These include, but are not limited to, the following:

❖ The treatment of mental illness and mental health care in general are not an exact science (20).

❖ Release from the artificial confines of a hospital, even for a short period of time, can be both symptom reducing and therapeutic (21).

❖ Certain risks to the public are inherent in the release of many mental patients (22).

❖ The risks to the public (and to the patient being released) must be balanced against the need of the patient to reenter society (23).

Much of the problem associated with the decision whether to release a patient, especially when there has been past evidence of self-abuse or violence toward others, has been the conflict between the patient's right to autonomy and freedom and the potential risk of harm to others. This risk-benefit dilemma is aptly illustrated in cases in which the "open door" treatment approach is employed. It is no longer automatic that the standard of care for treating individuals with destructive or violent tendencies involves constant observation, ward restrictions, and strict confinement of movement (24). Psychiatrists have long recognized that effective treatment requires a considerable amount of trust, collaboration, and rapport between patient and doctor in order to be successful. Accordingly, a therapeutic approach that emphasizes patient responsibility, independence, and autonomy is likely to engender the kind of trust that most clinicians perceive as being essential to the stabilization of a patient's overt symptomatology and general well-being. Even severely disturbed patients tend to act and respond more appropriately to treatment demands when on an open ward. Open doors and relative freedom of movement, especially if they can lead to a temporary and permanent release from the unit, can bolster a patient's self-confidence, motivation to improve, and willingness to accept treatment. However, not all patients can be treated successfully in this modality. Proper selection of patients for various treatment settings involves the sound clinical judgment of the psychiatrist and the application of "reasonable" care and judgment.

In order to effect these desired patient qualities and results, some hospitals have adopted what is known as the "open door" policy (25). The difficulty for psychiatric decision-makers in attempting to weigh how much freedom to give a patient (e.g., freedom of movement on the hospital floor, a weekend pass, or final discharge) is often highlighted in legal cases in which an open-door policy is in effect. This difficulty, fortunately, has not been overlooked or minimized by some courts. For instance, a Florida federal district court in *Johnson v. United States* (26) noted:

> Modern psychiatry has recognized the importance of making every reasonable effort to return a patient to an active and productive life. Thus the patient is encouraged to develop his self-confidence by adjusting to the demands of everyday existence. . . . Furthermore, all the expert witnesses for both parties agreed that *accurate prediction of dangerous behavior, and particularly suicide and homicide, are almost never possible*. Especially in view of this fact, the Court is persuaded that modern psychiatric practice does not require a patient to be isolated from normal human activities until every possible danger has passed. Because of the virtual impossibility of predicting dangerousness, such an approach would necessarily lead to prolonged incarceration for many patients who would become useful members of society. It has also been made clear to the

Court that constant supervision and restriction will often tend to promote the very disorders which they are designed to control. . . . On the other hand, despite the therapeutic benefits of this "open door" approach, the practice admittedly entails a higher potential of danger for both the patient and for those with whom he comes in contact. . . . The Court is aware that some psychiatrists adhere to the older, more custodial approach. However, it has proved to the Court's satisfaction that *the "open door" policy and the judgmental balancing test are an accepted method of treatment.* Therefore, no liability can arise merely because a psychiatrist favors the newer over the older approach. [emphasis added]

The use of the open-door policy or some similar philosophy does not relieve the primary care professional from the responsibility to act reasonably and in accord with professional standards. For instance, in the 1988 malpractice case of *Littleton v. Good Samaritan Hospital and Health Center* (27), the Supreme Court of Ohio held that a psychiatrist will not be held liable for the violent acts of a voluntarily hospitalized mental patient subsequent to his or her discharge if the following applies:

1. The patient did not manifest violent propensities while being hospitalized, and there was no reason to suspect that the patient would become violent after discharge.
2. A thorough evaluation of the patient's propensity for violence was conducted, taking into account all relevant factors, and a good-faith decision was made by the psychiatrist that the patient had no violent propensities.
3. The patient was diagnosed as having violent propensities, and, after a thorough evaluation of the severity of the propensities and a balancing of the patient's interests and the interests of potential victims, a treatment plan was formulated in good faith that included discharge of the patient (27).

Professional Judgment

The threshold issue, regardless of whether the court applies a simple negligence theory or the more particularized "professional judgment" rule (as in *Littleton*) is determined by the reasonableness of the decision. Cases in which liability has been upheld because of an unreasonable failure to foresee a released patient's risk of danger to himself or herself, or others, include the Georgia decision of *Swofford v. Cooper* (28). In *Swofford,* a patient was involuntarily committed to the state hospital, in part because of his past threats to kill his family. Following 11 months of treatment, his treating psychiatrist permitted him to visit his family on a pass. While home the patient murdered his father. At trial, the court returned a verdict for the psychiatrist, concluding that the patient was contributorily negligent. The Georgia Court of Appeals reversed part of the lower court's ruling and reinstated the malpractice action against the psychiatrist. It concluded that while the psychiatrist was immune from liability with respect to the decision to permit the patient to leave the hospital, she was not immune on other grounds. According to the court, the issue was not whether the psychiatrist should have been able to anticipate the precise consequences that actually occurred, but whether "some kind of injury could have resulted from her act or omission." In reinstating the plaintiff's action for negligent treatment and failure to control (and therefore not release) the patient, the court took note that the patient was actively psychotic when he stabbed his father. This fact, coupled with the patient's known violent feelings against his family, created an unreasonable risk that the discharging doctor failed to guard against.

In another case, *Poss v. Regional Hospital of Augusta, Georgia* (29), a federal district court also rejected a claim of statutory immunity for a hospital whose treating physician discharged a suicidal patient 1 day after he had attempted to overdose on sleeping pills and who several hours later fatally shot himself in the head. Notwithstanding the statutory technicalities of government immunity in this case, it appears rather obvious that the unconditioned release of a patient less than 24 hours after a serious suicide threat had been made would create a rebuttable presumption of negligence and substandard care.

It is important to distinguish that it is *not* the proximate time element between the moment of release and the fatal act that determines the reasonableness of a doctor's decision, but the basis behind the decision and any follow-up care that is provided. For instance, in *McGrady v. United States* (30), the federal government was concluded to be not liable for a murder that a mentally ill patient committed 5 hours after being evaluated and released by a V.A. psychiatrist. It was determined that although the psychiatrist was aware of the patient's serious mental condition, he was not negligent in failing to diagnose the patient's dangerousness and take precautions to protect other persons. The court based this conclusion on the fact that the patient was being regularly treated at a county mental health facility, had not been violent or threatened harm to anyone, and had not manifested psychotic behavior during a 1-hour evaluation of his head pain complaints. Moreover, expert testimony established that he had not been psychotic on the morning of the examination, and the state murder conviction established that he was legally sane at the time of the murder.

Follow-up Treatment

Psychiatrists are advised that, in addition to conducting a thorough risk-benefit assessment before deciding to release a patient, they also should formulate plans for appropriate follow-up. This follow-up should theoretically begin the moment the patient prepares to leave the hospital. Depending upon the circumstances, a psychiatrist's failure to anticipate foreseeable risks to the patient or a third party anytime immediately following the physical departure of the patient could expose the doctor and/or hospital to liability. For instance, a wrongful death action was reinstated against the state of Indiana when a patient, just released from a state hospital, was killed by a motorist as he was walking to his home many miles away. A staff psychiatrist, as part of his release order, indicated to the staff, "discharge as soon as transportation can be arranged." Unbeknownst to the doctor, the patient was discharged without transportation. The appeals court noted that sufficient evidence was presented to allow a jury to decide whether the state negligently released the patient (31).

Other cases involving claims of wrongful or negligent release have been based on alleged negligent assessment of a threat of self-harm (32), failure to seek appropriate professional consultation (33), failure to notify authorities as agreed before releasing a violent patient (34), and release based on poorly or vaguely formulated and implemented discharge plans (35).

Defenses

As with any cause of action, various defenses may exist that partially or completely protect a defendant from liability. Claims of negligent release or discharge are no different from and are subject to the usual defenses raised by psychiatrists and hospitals who are sued. Of course, what dictates the defense or defenses employed are the particular circumstances surrounding the case and the defendant's acts or omissions in treating the patient.

Sometimes lost in the stress and anxiety that the mere mention of a lawsuit creates is the fundamental fact that just because someone is sued *does not* mean that the care rendered was negligent, substandard, unreasonable, or even a mistake (36). In fact, many times the "winning" defense argument is that there was no breach in the standard of care, that appropriate professional judgment was exercised, and that the psychiatrist's decision making was reasonable under the circumstances. For instance, in *Moran v. Westchester County Medical Center* (37), a New York court concluded that a hospital could not be held liable for malpractice when a psychiatric patient, following his release, killed his brother. The patient had been civilly committed after an incident of creating a public disturbance and manifesting unusual, psychotic-like behavior. After about a month of treatment, he was discharged from the hospital. Shortly thereafter, he murdered one of his brothers and injured another brother and two police officers. An appellate court held that the hospital was not responsible for the injuries resulting from the patient's conduct. The patient's release, they determined, was a matter of "professional judgment." Moreover, the patient's family was unaware of his whereabouts subsequent to his release, and the hospital was found to be not required to search for him.

In addition to defenses based on professional judgment and reasonable medical care, statutory immunity (especially for psychiatrists working in state hospitals and other government facilities) is fairly common. Depending upon state statute, governmental and public employees, as well as agencies and the state itself, may be partially or completely immune from any liability caused by the acts of released mental patients.

In the 1988 case of *Tobis v. Washington* (38), judicial immunity was found to preclude liability of the state and mental health professionals for their evaluation recommending that a state hospital patient be granted unconditional release. Pursuant to a request by the court, the patient, originally committed as a criminally insane individual, was evaluated for possible release. Following the evaluation by state psychiatric personnel, it was recommended to the court that the patient be given an unconditional release. The court accepted the recommendation and released the patient. Subsequently, he killed a woman. In affirming a lower court's ruling, a Washington appeals court found that the defendants were entitled to judicial immunity (39), ruling that they were acting as an arm of the court when they gave the court advice about the patient's mental condition.

A similar verdict was given in the case *Barnes v. Dale* (40), in which the Alabama Supreme Court indicated that a state psychiatrist's decision to release a patient, who later committed murder, illustrated the "depth of the defendant's discretionary public function." The court took particular notice of the psychiatrist's numerous data-gathering methods in arriving at his decision to release the patient. These methods included consultation with two staff psychiatrists who had direct observation of the patient, the patient's expressed willingness to continue in outpatient treatment, and the best judgment of all of the doctors involved that the patient had received the maximum benefits of hospitalization. It should be noted that in some situations, governmental immunity may pertain to one aspect of a defendant's conduct but not another. For example, in *Brown v. Northville Regional Psychiatric Hospital* (41), government immunity was extended to the decision to discharge a schizophrenic patient, but not to the defendant's failure to follow established discharge procedures.

Another defense that is sometimes successful in negligent release cases is that the harm committed by the discharged patient was too far ahead in time to be considered "reasonably foreseeable." This argument epitomizes the general contention nearly always raised or at least contemplated in negligent release cases that psychiatrists cannot predict dangerousness. The professional literature (42) and common sense tell us that "time attenuates predictive accuracy" and quite obviously precludes the clinician from foreseeing intervening factors that might create or exacerbate a patient's preexisting hostilities. Fortunately for psychiatrists, many courts recognize this limitation. In *Urbach v. United States* (43), the Fifth Circuit Court of Appeals affirmed the rejection of a malpractice action against a V.A. mental hospital by the family of a man who was beaten to death in a Mexican prison while out on an approved furlough. The court found that the patient's death was unforeseeable, stating that the beating by fellow prisoners was an "extraordinary" event that constituted an intervening force in the chain of causation. Other cases in which the time and circumstances surrounding the release of a patient and some subsequent damage were considered too tenuous or unforeseeable include the murder of a young boy by an escaped patient who never expressed any violent threats (44); an assault that occurred 5 weeks after a patient, who was not foreseeably dangerous, was discharged (45); and a shooting spree by a patient who had been released 19 months earlier (46).

Conclusions

Sometimes the need for a doctor to "act in a reasonable manner" and "practice ordinary care" must stretch to the limits of clinical practice in order to satisfy the courts. This is particularly true in cases in which violent acts are considered possible. No recent case probably better illustrates the sometimes unusually stringent application of civil law principles than the previously discussed case of *Naidu v. Laird* (47) (see Chapter 8). Although couched in language suggestive of the *Tarasoff* duty to warn and/or protect, this case is more like a negligent discharge case, because there was no threat or reasonable indication of violence potential.

What is noteworthy and worth repeating in discussing the issue of discharge decision making is the Delaware court's rejection of the defendants' argument that at the time of the patient's release the patient posed no threat of danger to anyone. Alternatively, the defendants argued that the patient was not eligible for involuntary commitment. This too was rejected. The court stated that based on plaintiff's expert opinion, at the time of discharge, the patient was a danger to himself and uncooperative, and refused to take his medication. Moreover, the plaintiff's expert opined that the patient was eligible for civil commitment. Further, the court concluded that the defendants had a responsibility to consider a patient's complete history and not just his most recent acts. Mr. Putney had been hospitalized 19 times between 1962 and 1977. He had been hospitalized 7 times at Delaware State Hospital. Specifically, the court cited the patient's many previous hospitalizations and Dr. Naidu's awareness that his patient had two previous car accidents while in a psychotic state, that the patient had a driver's license at the time of discharge, and that it was reasonable to assume that he would drive after being released and therefore could be involved in an auto accident.

Notwithstanding the simplicity of the court's argument and disparateness with other duty-to-protect and negligent discharge decisions (48), this decision provides a discomforting lesson that no predischarge decision making can be too thorough. In light of the *Naidu* decision, it is a reasonable option for psychiatrists to consult with an attorney if doubts exist regarding the legal parameters of appropriate release considerations. Counsel may be able to supply the psychiatrist or hospital with examples of discharge-related cases that provide some guidance on how the courts view this area of clinical practice. Of course, and it cannot be stressed enough, the ultimate consideration(s) must be clinical concerns, not legal.

Trends and Clinical Considerations

In general, the major concern with negligent release and duty-to-warn cases is the difficulty in assessing and the inability to predict future violent behavior. The clinician is advised to use acceptable clinical practices in making such assessments and to word the conclusions in clinical terms, rather than in ambiguous, poorly defined legal conclusions such as "dangerousness." The psychiatrist really does not know what dangerousness means, except as defined in the legislation in his or her jurisdiction. Therefore it is imperative that the psychiatrist make all assessments of the risk of violence within clinical guidelines (see Simon RI: *Clinical Psychiatry and the Law*, 2nd Edition. Washington, DC, American Psychiatric Press, 1992, Chapter 13). The issue of general foreseeability of violent behavior, as noted above, is a distinct problem for psychiatrists, who have no such skills at making these predictions.

If the courts mandate that the protection of society is the important issue, rather than confidentiality or the psychiatrist's ability to predict or foresee such violent behavior, then it behooves the psychiatrist to step aside from previously accepted responsibilities that are no longer within the therapist's expertise. For example, according to *Naidu v. Laird* (47), the psychiatrist is now forewarned that the decision to discharge a patient is no longer a psychiatric one alone. Psychiatrists cannot determine with any degree of reasonable medical or psychiatric certainty or probability that in several months a particular former patient would likely commit a particular violent crime or a violent reckless negligent act. If the psychiatrist is to be held liable for such precision in decision making, then he or she must have help from others in the community. Making decisions to discharge potentially violent patients is no longer exclusively a psychiatric function. Suppose Dr. Naidu had enlisted the aid of the committing court to determine whether Mr. Putney was committable and should remain in the hospital or be released by court order? If the court orders the release, Dr. Naidu and his colleagues will not be legally responsible for consequences of Mr. Putney's behavior, because they are obliged to follow the court's order. If the court determines that Mr. Putney is still a danger to "foreseeable but unidentifiable others in the undetermined future," then the court may recommit Mr. Putney until such time as the court sees fit to discharge him.

Suppose the court had determined that Mr. Putney was not committable, but the court was still concerned about his potential for violent behavior under certain circumstances? The court could then commit the patient to outpatient treatment and maintain jurisdiction over the patient (49). Should the patient become noncompliant with his treatment or make threats to others that may result in violent behavior, the court may then rehospitalize the patient after a thorough examination and evaluation by a competent psychiatrist.

The implication from this case appears to be to assess liability to psychiatrists who make decisions in areas that are extremely difficult and for which they have little or no expertise. Therefore, the responsive and responsible action by psychiatrists should be to consult the court in the determination of when confinement (which often has been imposed by the court) may be ended and freedom returned to the patient. The courts have determined that liberty is the overriding issue in commitment cases—that is, a patient has a right to a full due-process hearing before his or her liberty interests are restricted and he or she is involuntarily confined to a hospital. Similarly, it is logical to conclude that in cases involving the foreseeability of the violent behavior, the court has an interest in protecting the public and in determining when such deprivations of freedom are no longer necessary.

Another implication arising from this case involves the defense offered by psychiatrists that it was their clinical judgment at the time of release or discharge that the patient was not committable and was not a "foreseeable danger." Clinical judgment is not a sufficient defense in these cases (50). It is not the judgment per se, but rather the means by which that judgment was reached that determine whether or not liability exists. If the examination was incomplete, or the assessment lacked thoroughness, or significant individuals were not consulted for an appropriate history, the clinical judgment may be impaired and liability imposed.

Fortunately, the trend is toward the specific identifiable victim, and not a generic foreseeableness on the part of the psychiatrist. It is suggested that in those jurisdictions in which a generalized foreseeability of danger exists, the psychiatrist consult the attorney for the hospital before releasing a patient who has had a history of violence or who may have a "potential for foreseeable violence." It may also be appropriate to bring this case before the appropriate court for ultimate determination of committability or ability to be released to the community. In jurisdictions that require that a specific, identifiable victim must be threatened during psychotherapy (i.e., *Tarasoff II, Thompson*), the psychiatrist may make adequate clinical judgments based on information obtained in the course of therapy with the patient.

Psychiatrists and clinicians may learn what not to do when faced with a situation in which an identifiable third party is not threatened. For example, sending a letter to the employer is likely to be a breach of confidentiality, and the lack of a specific third-party victim is not a classic "duty to warn" case. The psychiatrist, in order to prevent violence, has many options before warning victims or breaching confidentiality with patients. Warning an endangered third party is rarely sufficient by itself. The psychiatrist may follow the guidelines presented in Chapter 8 (see section on foreseeable victims) as reasonable alternatives to warning potential victims who may be distressed or harmed by such news of potential violence toward them. Warning potential victims also may stimulate them to become the perpetrators of violence in order to defend themselves from the patient. Therefore, the clinician must continue to use common sense, good clinical judgment, and appropriate consultation when involved in cases of potential violence to others.

Finally, with the advent of managed care and the increased participation of insurance carriers in health care planning, discharge decisions are being influenced by economic considerations. Psychiatrists must make discharge decisions based on the clinical needs of the patient. Economic factors must not adversely affect the standard of care. The physician, not corporate administrators or insurance carriers, is responsible for making clinically sound discharge decisions (51).

References

1. Annot, § 38 ALR3d 3 (1971)
2. 79 Corpus Juris Secundum Physicians and Surgeons § 41 (1951)
3. Bell v New York City Health and Hospital Corporation, 90 AD2d 270, 456 NYS2d 787 (1982)
4. Underwood v United States, 356 F2d 92 (5th Cir 1966)
5. Hicks v United States, 511 F2d 407 (DC Cir 1975)
6. Dearcy v New York, No 66789 Binghamton Court of Claims (NY 1986)
7. Clark v New York, 99 AD2d 61, 472 NYS2d 170 (1984)
8. Whalen v Nevada, No 14457 (Nev Sup Ct, January 25, 1984)
9. Melton GB, Petrila J, Poythress NG et al: Psychological Evaluations for the Courts. New York, Guilford, 1987, pp 197–203
10. Simon RI: Concise Guide to Psychiatry and Law for Clinicians. Washington, DC, American Psychiatric Press, 1992
11. Smith JT: Medical Malpractice: Psychiatric Care. Colorado Springs, CO, Shepard's/McGraw-Hill, 1986, p 542

12. Klein JI, Macbeth JE, Onek JN: Legal Issues in the Private Practice of Psychiatry. Washington, DC, American Psychiatric Press, 1984, pp 23–24

13. See, e.g., Jablonski v United States, 712 F2d 391 (9th Cir 1983)

14. See, e.g., County of Hennepin v Levine, No CO-83-207 (Minn 1984); Hicks v United States, 511 F2d 407 (DC Cir 1975)

15. Simon RI: Clinical Psychiatry and the Law, 2nd Edition. Washington, DC, American Psychiatric Press, 1992

16. Simon RI: Concise Guide to Psychiatry and Law for Clinicians. Washington, DC, American Psychiatric Press, 1992 [emphasis added]

17. Smith JT: Medical Malpractice: Psychiatric Care. Colorado Springs, CO, Shepard's/McGraw-Hill, 1986, p 543

18. American Psychological Association: Appendix to White Paper on Duty to Protect: Suits against mental health care professionals for the violent acts of patients. Unpublished manuscript, Washington, DC, American Psychological Association, September 1985

19. S. B. Bisbing, personal communication, December 1990

20. See, e.g., Cameron v State, 37 AD2d 46, 49, 322 NYS2d 562, 565 (1971)

21. See Baker v United States, 343 F2d 222 (8th Cir 1965)

22. See Hayes v Perotti, 419 F2d 704, 707–708 (DC Cir 1969)

23. See Littleton v Good Samaritan Hospital and Health Center, 39 Ohio St 3d 86, 529 NE2d 449 (1988)

24. See, e.g., Perr I: Suicide responsibility of hospital and psychiatrist. Cleveland-Marshall Law Review 9:427, 1960

25. See Meir v Ross General Hospital, 67 Cal 2d 420, 425, 445 P2d 519, 523, 71 Cal Rptr 903, 907 (1968)

26. 409 F Supp 1283, 1293 (MD Fla 1976)

27. 39 Ohio St 3d 86, 529 NE2d 449 (1988)

28. 360 SE2d 624 (Ga Ct App 1987)

29. 676 F Supp 258 (SD Ga 1987)

30. 650 F Supp 379 (D SC 1986)

31. Overall v Indiana, 525 NE2d 1275 (Ind App Ct 1988)

32. Cornelius v Retreat Mental Hospital, Colbert County Cir Ct (AL 1985), cited in Medical Malpractice: Verdicts, Settlement and Experts 1:15, 1985 [$225,000 settlement for negligent discharge of patient who killed his wife]

33. Martin v Washington Hospital Center, 423 A2d 913 (DC App 1980) [$202,000 verdict based in part on emergency room physician's failure to obtain a psychiatric consultation]

34. Williams v United States, 450 F Supp 1040 (D SD 1978)

35. Kirkland v Florida Department of Health and Rehabilitative Services, 424 So 2d 925 (Fla Dist Ct App 1983)

36. Charles SC, Kennedy E: Defendant. New York, Free Press, 1985

37. 145 AD2d 474, 535 NYS2d 431 (1988)

38. 52 Wash App 150, 758 P2d 534 (1988)

39. See Bader v Washington, 43 Wash App 223, 716 P2d 925 (1986)

40. 530 So 2d 770 (Ala 1988)

41. 153 Mich App 300, 395 NW2d 18 (1986)

42. Simon RI: Concise Guide to Psychiatry and Law for Clinicians. Washington, DC, American Psychiatric Press, 1992

43. 869 F2d 829 (5th Cir 1989)

44. Furr v Spring Grove State Hospital, 53 Md App 474, 454 A2d 414 (1983)

45. Holmes v Wampler, 546 F Supp 500 (ED Va 1982)

46. Phillips v Roy, 494 So 2d 1342 (La App 1986)

47. 539 A2d 1064 (Del 1988)

48. Bisbing SB: Delaware Supreme Court affirms $1.4 million award against psychiatrist for failure to protect. American Academy of Psychiatry and Law Newsletter 14(April):8–9, 1989

49. Stefan S: Preventive commitment: the concept and its pitfalls. Mental and Physical Disability Law Reporter 11(July/August):288, 298–302, 1987

50. But see Littleton v Good Samaritan Hospital & Health Center, 39 Ohio St 3d 86, 529 NE2d 449 (1988) [reasonableness of professional's "professional judgment" considered threshold determinant of whether standard of care was breached]

51. Wickline v State of California, 183 Cal App 3d 1175, 228 Cal Rptr 661 (Cal Ct App 1986); Wilson v Blue Cross of Southern California, 222 Cal App 3d 660, 271 Cal Rptr 876 (Cal Ct App 1990)

Chapter 10

Coping With a
Malpractice Suit ─────────

Between 1984 and 1985, the average annual professional liability premiums of self-employed psychiatrists rose 18.2% (1). To what extent the proclivity to practice defensive psychiatry (2), or to act in a way to avoid malpractice liability, escalated during that time is unknown. In 1983, 1 in 25 psychiatrists could expect to be sued compared with just 1 in 50 in 1979 (3). It is apparent that psychiatrists have not been spared from the continued increase in malpractice litigation.

A psychiatric malpractice suit can be one of the most devastating experiences in the professional life of a psychiatrist. The anxiety generated by the accusation that the psychiatrist was negligent in his or her practice and that the patient suffered damage as a result may be extreme and debilitating. Most psychiatrists are unaware of the procedures involved in a lawsuit, and specifically a malpractice suit. Understanding the process by which the suit is developed and the mechanisms involved may help to lessen the tension and decrease the anxiety involved in coping with such lawsuits.

In this chapter, guidelines are presented for psychiatrists who have been sued or are afraid they may be sued, alerting them to the dangers inherent within the system. The purpose of this chapter is to educate the psychiatrist who needs to know what to do or what not to do in the event of a psychiatric malpractice lawsuit.

The Malpractice Lawsuit Process

Frivolous Suits

A frivolous suit, as the name implies, is a lawsuit that has no legal merit or is legally worthless. There are many reasons why such suits are filed (e.g., to harass, to "fish" for a quick monetary settlement, or to gain some advantage). Despite their inherent legal inadequacy, frivolous lawsuits may survive a motion to dismiss and must be taken seriously. For instance, while a lawsuit against a psychiatrist may blatantly lack medical or legal merit, it may, nevertheless, have courtroom appeal. A sympathetic plaintiff who has suffered severe injuries can incite a jury's emotions, leading to a large monetary award for the plaintiff even if the doctor is legally and medically innocent. It is not too far-fetched to assume that a relatively small but significant number of cases are decided against defendants (e.g., physicians) based primarily on the emotional appeal of the facts or the plaintiff's injuries. Moreover, most United States courts now impose liability for civil claims instigated with "malicious" intent that have no probable cause (4).

Any suit has the potential for creating a domino effect upon a psychiatrist's practice. A single malpractice suit (regardless of its merit) may trigger licensure investigations, create problems with the obtaining or renewal of hospital staff privileges, and/or cause malpractice insurance to be dropped or premiums greatly increased. It may also result in the levying of requirements for additional continuing medical education. Brooten (5) warns that the physician's response to a meritless suit should be no different from his or her response to any other malpractice claim.

Meritless suits aimed at obtaining a quick settlement or intended to injure a person's character or practice, even though the physician has not been negligent, typically are not successful. Possibly physicians today seem less intimidated and more willing to fight malpractice suits than in the past. Furthermore, attorneys representing plaintiffs scrutinize cases more carefully due, in part, to pretrial screening panels and tort reforms. As a result, a significant number of plaintiff complaints, at the outset, are considered meritless, inappropriate for litigation, or too shaky to invest the time and money to litigate the case. However, with the creation of the National Practitioner Data Bank, frivolous or nuisance suits will more likely be litigated to verdict by physicians. Settlement of a malpractice suit requires reporting to the National Practitioner Data Bank (6).

Initial Notice of Malpractice Allegations

When a patient, former patient, or family of a former patient wishes to sue the psychiatrist, an attorney is consulted who reviews the charges and allegations made by the patient or the patient's family. Before accepting the case, the responsible attorney will investigate the charges by reviewing the records of the psychiatrist and/or the hospital where the patient was treated. The attorney will investigate further by asking questions about the psychiatrist involved and about his and her reputation in the community. The lawyer will search out information about the psychiatrist through various publications listing the psychiatrist's background and education. Primarily, the attorney will want to review the medical records prepared by the psychiatrist so that he or she may note consistencies or inconsistencies in the psychiatric record and in his and her client's allegations.

In order for the attorney to properly assess the validity of the case, he or she should consult a colleague of the psychiatrist who is in no way related to the patient or to the psychiatrist (7). That expert psychiatrist can assess the records and the case in a neutral, dispassionate, and objective fashion. Only after such examination and evaluation of the records, and perhaps examination of the plaintiff, will the expert psychiatrist render an opinion to the plaintiff's attorney. In many cases, that opinion may be that the attorney does not have a valid case and should not pursue it any further. At that point, the attorney is free to turn to a second opinion to either confirm the first or perhaps to differ from it. If the lawyer receives a second opinion that is in opposition to the first, he or she may request a third psychiatrist as a tie breaker, to determine how strong a case may be made and to what extent the claim should be pursued.

It should be noted that attorneys are also in the business of turning a profit, as well as pursuing claims for their clients. Competent attorneys will not take a frivolous case that has no merit and little or no chance of winning. Attorneys work on a contingency fee in these cases and will take up to 40% of the settlement or of the award granted by the court. However, 40% of nothing is still nothing, and time for attorneys, as for psychiatrists, is money. It may take a great deal of money to mount a significant malpractice case, and attorneys need to know that they will not be losing a great deal of money on a case they cannot win. Therefore, competent and respectable attorneys will obtain objective and neutral psychiatric consultation before ever filing a lawsuit to be certain that they have a good case.

When the attorney is convinced that a valid case can be made, he or she will file the appropriate papers in the appropriate jurisdiction within the time allowed by the statute of limitations for malpractice cases. Statutes of limitations are usually construed strictly by courts, and deposition of such cases frequently turns on questions such as the appropriateness of the jurisdictional basis for suit.

In addition to filing the case with the appropriate jurisdiction within the statutory time limits, the attorney must give the defendant (psychiatrist) notice of such cause of action. Notice may be effectuated by 1) personal delivery of a summons containing the complaint which sets forth the general allegations that support the cause of action; or 2) delivery by mail of the summons and complaint. Personal service is regarded as the most efficient way of giving notice of the suit for purposes of due process. Thus, it is the preferred mode of letting the defendant know that he or she is being sued so that steps can be taken by the defendant to respond in a timely fashion. This notice that the psychiatrist is being sued by a particular person in a particular court also advises that the psychiatrist should obtain an attorney and contact his or her insurance carrier. It is at this point when the psychiatrist receives the notice of suit that his or her response to the malpractice suit begins.

Initial Response of the Defendant Psychiatrist

The immediate response by psychiatrists who receive a notice that they are being sued in malpractice is frequently one of shock, disbelief, and fear. The fear may later turn to anger and resentment, because the psychiatrist begins to justify that he or she was always good to the patient and had only the patient's best interest at heart. The psychiatrist begins to question his or her own competency and wonders whether or not other colleagues will find out about the complaint and refer no further patients.

It is an extremely traumatic experience for a psychiatrist to be sued for the first time. Psychiatrists are physicians who usually do not hurt their patients and are typically individuals who see themselves as kind, helpful, and interested in the sufferings of others. Psychiatrists often tend to be passive and nonaggressive, nonhostile individuals who obtain great pleasure from low tension environments and nonthreatening experiences. Much of their work is carried out in the privacy of their offices, in which they surround themselves with reflections of their personality and their interests. The exposure to the outside world of anything gone wrong is an even greater shock for those who are fairly isolated in their work.

There are those psychiatrists who have been sued several times and who work in high-tension, high-risk environments, for whom the lawsuit is not as threatening and therefore not as traumatic. Some psychiatrists will defend themselves emotionally by projecting whatever guilt or blame they may feel onto the patient, indicating that the patient is litigious. They may also believe the suit is frivolous and become angry at the attorney who takes such a case. Psychiatrists speak of the "deep pockets theory" of the law, in which the psychiatrist, with his or her expensive malpractice insurance, becomes an apt target of attorneys and their clients. Some may even believe they were "set up" for the lawsuit by their paranoid, psychopathic, or borderline patients.

Psychiatrists tend to handle trauma much as they handle their patients—by maintaining confidentiality and secrecy. Some may not even tell their spouses that they have been sued because of the feeling of shame and humiliation. On a practical level, psychiatrists should inform their insurance carriers immediately. They may also call their own personal attorney, or find the name of a competent defense lawyer who may advise them during the early stages of the suit.

It is most important for the psychiatrist who is sued not to panic and not to say or do inappropriate or confessional things, such as altering records or admitting guilt by calling the patient, apologizing, and offering to settle. Negotiations must be left to the attorneys, who are experts in the field and know the pitfalls and dangers of such expressions of remorse and conciliation. This is, after all, an adversarial procedure in which the sides line up in order to attack each other and defend themselves.

Scholars are now beginning to consider the countertherapeutic impact of some tort litigation (8). The psychiatrist may be hurt as well and may believe that further damage can be prevented, both to himself or herself and to the patient, by being "reasonable" and conciliatory. Defense attorneys may advise psychiatrists that such responses do not necessarily work in the hardened adversarial system that governs malpractice lawsuits. This is not to say that the psychiatrist should not be "humane" when confronted by the family of a patient who committed suicide. It is appropriate for the psychiatrist to express feelings of sadness to the family for their loss; however, it is not appropriate to accept the blame for the suicide and admit negligence in the treatment process. Working with families of patients who kill themselves or others, to console and comfort, is part of the healing process and is necessary when the psychiatrist is consulted. However, one should not cross the fine line of consolation to self-blame. The admissions made at the time of consolation may haunt the psychiatrist later, when the lawsuit is filed and processed.

Selecting the Proper Attorney

Physicians are often advised to consult their own attorneys when they are sued in malpractice. Most physicians are covered by adequate and competent insurance companies who retain their own firms of defense attorneys experienced and competent in handling these cases. It is essential that the psychiatrist contact his or her insurance carrier immediately upon learning that he or she has been sued. The insurance carrier will receive the records, study the problem, and refer it to one of the attorneys retained by the insurance company. These attorneys are usually well-picked, experienced attorneys who have worked on many similar cases in the past. It is probably safe to assume that the attorney selected by the insurance company will be competent and experienced and will provide the psychiatrist with reasonable and important information and consultation about how to go about defending the lawsuit.

Why, then, should a psychiatrist consult his or her own attorney in some cases? The advice to have one's own attorney is given because the attorney, then, is beholden to the psychiatrist as his or her client. In malpractice cases, the insurance company is regarded as the "client" (i.e., the defendant). The insurance company is said to stand in the psychiatrist's shoes for his or her benefit. The psychiatrist is the client of the insurance company, and the attorney is representing the best interests of the insurance company and, presumably, the psychiatrist as well. Should there arise a conflict between the insurance company and the psychiatrist regarding the optimal way of handling the defense, the attorney, as the representative of the insurance company, will have to take sides with the client rather than with the psychiatrist. For example, if the insurance company wishes to settle the claim, even though the psychiatrist is convinced that it is frivolous and can be won in court, the insurance company may choose to settle for economic reasons (7). Also, if the insurance company determines that the activity that brought on the complaint falls outside of the scope of the policy, it may decline to provide coverage and/or counsel (9). Thus, there may be a number of reasons for the psychiatrist who is sued to consult his or her own attorney in addition to utilizing the services of the attorney appointed by the insurance company to defend the malpractice lawsuit.

It is very expensive to mount an adequate and competent defense of any malpractice case. If the plaintiffs are willing to settle for an amount less than the expenses that will be incurred in order to properly defend the case, the insurance company, solely on business and economic grounds, may choose to settle rather than to defend. Other insurance companies may wish to defend in order to deter other attorneys from bringing frivolous lawsuits for low amounts of money. For this purpose, the insurance company may in the long run pay out more money for the defense of frivolous claims. However, as a deterrent it has the effect of alerting plaintiff attorneys that they may waste resources on a case that they may lose because of frivolity. In the long run, the insurance company may pay out more for the frivolous suits that add up than it would by defending a suit in order to alert the plaintiffs' attorney that he or she will need to spend money in order to pursue the case and, perhaps, lose it.

Psychiatrists should be aware of the inherent conflicts that may occur with their attorneys and the insurance company's representatives. If the insurance company wants to settle and the psychiatrist does not, the insurance company, under its contract, may opt out of the case, leaving the expenses to the psychiatrist who wishes to defend both honor and professional integrity. For some psychiatrists, the cost of defense is worth the price of their honor, because when the insurance company settles it has an impact beyond the insurance company–psychiatrist contractual relationship.

When an insurance company settles a frivolous plaintiff claim, yet meritorious to the defendant if defended, it labels the suit as a "loss." This is unfair to the psychiatrist who has not been adjudicated as negligent but who has lost the suit for purposes of his or her insurance coverage. The insurance company then structures the psychiatrist at a higher risk, or may even drop him or her from coverage because of the "lost suit." It is important for psychiatrists, when purchasing malpractice insurance, to check the fine print of the contract to be certain that they are not subject to such victimization in the event of a frivolous lawsuit. Furthermore, hospital privileges, licensure, or professional advancement may be adversely affected by a lawsuit that is settled or lost.

Providing Treatment Records of Patients

Following the filing of a suit and the initiating of pretrial discovery, the defendant-psychiatrist frequently will receive a subpoena for the patient's records by the attorney representing the plaintiff (10). A *subpoena* is a demand for records by an attorney who believes he or she has appropriate cause to receive these records (11). The psychiatrist may feel that the cause is not appropriate and to release the records would be a breach of confidentiality. The psychiatrist should obtain legal advice before releasing the records to be certain that the attorney who subpoenas them has a valid cause to obtain them. If the attorney advises the psychiatrist to release the records on the basis of the subpoena, the psychiatrist should do so after recording such advice and retaining a copy of the subpoena for his or her records.

If the attorney advises the psychiatrist not to release the records on the basis of the subpoena, the attorney will take the case to court and argue before a judge regarding the validity of releasing the records. If, after a court hearing in which arguments are presented by both sides, the judge orders the records to be released to the attorney who subpoenaed them, the psychiatrist must release the records upon court order. A *court order* is a command rather than a demand. The psychiatrist may be held in contempt if he or she does not obey the court order with whatever restrictions or limitations the court imposes upon the release. For the most part, court orders are not necessary, and records are usually released upon service of the subpoena by the plaintiff's attorney.

It is essential for the psychiatrist not to make any changes in the records before release. Once the subpoena is served or the court order is given, the records become evidence in a court case. Tampering with evidence is a felony that could result in a stiff fine or jail sentence.

Psychiatrists who anticipate that records will be subpoenaed are advised not to change them. It may be that upon review of his or her records, the psychiatrist finds information that may be harmful, prompting him or her to change them before they are subpoenaed. *This, however, should not be done.* The records stand as they are, and if they are changed, the change may negatively affect the psychiatrist in future matters. It should be expected that the plaintiff's attorney has a copy of the records even before they are released, especially if they are hospital records. There is very little chance the attorney will have a copy of private office records before the subpoena is served. However, it is not unknown that physicians have changed records before the subpoena but after notice that they will be sued in court. The plaintiff's attorney then can produce both sets of records before the court, indicating that the psychiatrist or physician has already begun to defend himself by "doctoring" the records. This is known as a "smoking gun" matter in the law, and it is very difficult, if not impossible, to defend.

If any changes need to be made in the records, the acceptable manner of changing records is to draw a single line through the erroneous record and write in, legibly, the new, corrected material. The psychiatrist should then initial and date the time of the change so that anyone reviewing the records later will know who made the change and when it was made. This protocol will indicate that there is a change but that there is nothing to hide, because the erroneous material below is still legible. The psychiatrist may then wish to put an addendum at the end of the record, indicating the reason for the change (12).

It should be noted that the actual physical records themselves belong to the doctor or the hospital, but the information contained in the record belongs to the patient, who has a right to see the records or to review them under certain conditions, according to the laws of each jurisdiction. The physician may feel that there are some parts of the records that are especially harmful to the patient and choose not to release them. The doctor cannot discriminate about what parts of the record to release and what parts not to release with impunity. The psychiatrist may file a petition to the court or argue before the judge that it would be unwise to release all the records as requested. An ethical basis exists for the psychiatrist to ask the court to show the records in chambers, to the court alone, for the judge to make a determination about the appropriateness of certain parts of the record that may be damaging to the plaintiff-patient, to his or her family, or to others, if the information is revealed (13). The court's decision is usually based on the existing state and federal laws governing release of mental health records in such cases (14). The judge will then decide whether to release records based on the laws of each jurisdiction.

Generally, the records are available when the plaintiff has filed the lawsuit. Anything contained in the records may be available for review by all sides and may be disclosed in open court. Plaintiffs should be so informed by their attorneys about the openness of records in order to give the plaintiff-patient the chance to exert competent decision making before proceeding with the lawsuit. The practice is comparable to informed consent in psychiatry or in medicine (15). Plaintiffs often complain during the course of litigation that they were never forewarned about the dangers and pitfalls of becoming involved in the lawsuit by their lawyers. They claim that if they had been so warned ahead of time, they may have chosen not to proceed with the lawsuit.

Similarly, patients should be alerted to the difficulties they will encounter once they file a malpractice lawsuit. They should be told of the proceedings that will affect their privacy and their family's privacy. They should also be told about the length of time it takes to pursue the lawsuit and the challenges that will be made upon them by the defense attorney in interrogatories and depositions, and at court testimony.

The emotional toll on the plaintiff may be considerable and may result in continued "emotional damage." It may be difficult to distinguish the original emotional damage from the alleged negligence and the continued emotional and mental suffering that results from the litigation process. Clearly, treatment of such plaintiffs is more difficult during the legal proceedings, and significant improvement is often delayed until the lawsuit is completed. Some psychiatrists are reluctant to begin treatment until all legal proceedings are completed.

Interrogatories

In addition to seeking the production of records pursuant to pretrial discovery procedure, the plaintiff's attorney has several other means by which to review the physician's recollection or testimony of the treatment of the plaintiff. After reviewing the records and obtaining expert witness evaluation of the case, the plaintiff's attorney may request (and usually does) a set of interrogatories from the defendant (16). Interrogatories are a set or series of written questions prepared to elicit information of interest in the case from the litigants. Attorneys are very careful about how they handle the information that goes into the responses to interrogatories. They are aware that these answers may be used against them later if, at deposition or a trial, their responses differ from those in the interrogatories. Similarly, the defendant's attorney may also request answers to a set of interrogatories posed to the plaintiff regarding the charges and allegations made.

Psychiatrists often find that responding to such forced questions, which may be intrusive, continues the traumatic experience of the lawsuit. They are forced to respond to accusatory questions that may be intimidating or humiliating. Most of the questions are based on information contained in the records, but some are used to inquire about the physician's background, economic, family matters, and professional associations.

Depositions

In addition to the medical records and the interrogatories, the plaintiff's attorney may request a deposition of the psychiatrist. A *deposition* is a set of questions asked directly of the psychiatrist by the plaintiff's attorney, which is taken under oath and recorded by a court stenographer. Under certain controlled circumstances, the deposition may also be videotaped, as well as recorded (17). In this atmosphere, the plaintiff's attorney has the opportunity of inquiring, in depth, about the treatment procedures and the reasons for the alleged negligence. Sometimes the plaintiff is present during the deposition, a circumstance that may add to the emotional trauma for the psychiatrist. Depositions may occur several months, or even several years, after the alleged malpractice. The psychiatrist must be prepared for the deposition by the attorney so that the presentation is not seen as arrogant or defensive, but rather, objective and professional. The deposition may last for several hours, or it may go on for days at a time, depending on the complexity of the issues and the manner in which the questions are asked.

Technically, there are two types of depositions: 1) the deposition for information or discovery purpose, taken by the opposing attorney, as noted above; and 2) the deposition in *bene esse,* taken to preserve testimony for trial when one of the witnesses is not able to be present. The deposition in *bene esse* applies primarily to an expert witness who may, for example, be on vacation, in which case the attorney wishes to preserve the testimony on videotape to replay to the court. Depositions may have the added utility in malpractice cases of obtaining additional information because they may be obtained from nonparty witnesses. Other forms of discovery, such as interrogatories, can only be obtained from party witnesses.

The discovery deposition may appear to be inquisitorial, and even intrusive into the psychiatrist's privacy. It is for this reason that the psychiatrist's attorney will be present during the deposition to protect the client. The attorney does not allow responses to irrelevant or incompetent questions and thereby protects the client, who is usually not aware of the fine points of the law with regard to evidence and testimony. However, most questions are answered despite attorney's objections that are related to complex evidentiary rules. The attorney also helps in the framing of the questions if they are unclear, and cautions the client not to respond if he or she does not know the answer and that he or she should not guess. If the physician does not remember, that is an appropriate response at deposition.

Attorneys can battle in depositions as to what is appropriate and what is not, what will be allowed, and what they may need to have the judge decide. Attorneys may object to questions based on their form or relevance. Generally, attorneys stipulate that during the deposition they will only object to the form of the question asked. Objections based on relevance are left to be objected to at trial; usually the judge will decide if a question is relevant or not. Sometimes, a deposition needs to be extended because there are unanswered questions that are in dispute.

The problem is the length of time it takes to develop and mount such a malpractice case. It is not uncommon for a trial to occur as long as 7 to 10 years after the alleged malpractice, or 5 or 6 years after the filing of the malpractice suit.

Working With the Attorney and the Insurance Company

It is important for the psychiatrist, who is usually a neophyte in litigation, to obtain very careful advice from his or her attorney and from the insurance company. The psychiatrist should not make statements without being asked and without being monitored by the attorney and/or the insurance company. The insurance company has a stake in the outcome of the case and thus has a right to counsel and advise the psychiatrist. If the psychiatrist does not work effectively with the insurance company, the psychiatrist may hurt his or her own case. The psychiatrist may also not cooperate to the point where the insurance company, by its contract, may abandon him or her. There are internal procedures that need to be followed; if they are not, the insurance company may feel that the psychiatrist is not working in good faith with them and may cost them an excessive amount of money. In order to protect against that situation, some insurance companies have clauses that may allow them to opt out if the psychiatrist does not cooperate effectively.

The psychiatrist must also work with the attorney, who recognizes and knows all the pitfalls and dangers involved along the path that is to be tread from the time of the summons to the appearance in court. A personal attorney can be consulted about conflicts that arise with the insurance company or its attorneys (18).

Preparation for Trial

Finally, it is *essential* that the psychiatrist work with the attorney in preparing for trial. The psychiatrist must be intimately familiar with the records and with what each witness has said on deposition and on interrogatories. The psychiatrist must be able to respond to the questions asked by the attorney, but more importantly he or she must be able to respond to the cross-examination questions presented by the plaintiff's attorney. The difference between the two types of questioning—direct and cross-examination—lies in the type of question and its form. During cross-examination, the attorney is permitted to ask leading questions. Leading questions are close-ended questions that usually suggest an answer. The difference in questioning is that the rules of evidence restrict the direct testimony to responses to open-ended questions that are not leading.

On cross-examination, the plaintiff's attorney may lead the psychiatrist by suggesting things and then by asking whether they are not true. However, the subject matter of cross-examination is limited to that covered during the direct questioning. Cross-examination may be done in a very demeaning and humiliating way, which may only tend to inflame or anger the psychiatrist. The psychiatrist, when a witness, must maintain a professional composure and demonstrate that no wrong was done. The psychiatrist is there to point out to the court what happened, and not to get involved in a shouting match or an argument with the plaintiff's attorney. Jurors expect attorneys to be argumentative and, sometimes, to be emotional. They do not expect psychiatrists or witnesses to be emotional, but rather expect them to respond directly, firmly, and professionally to the questions asked.

The psychiatrist must also be prepared emotionally and must prepare his or her family for the trial and its outcome. The outcome may mean loss of money by the insurance company and, perhaps, reassignment to a higher risk category if the plaintiffs prevail and the psychiatrist loses the case. However, some malpractice cases involve unethical behavior, which may then be reviewed by the licensing board or by the professional associations to which the psychiatrist belongs. The outcome of such a trial may lead to loss of license or to expulsion from professional groups and associations, or both, if the charges are proven (19).

While awaiting trial, it is often a good idea for the psychiatrist to obtain counseling from a respected colleague, preferably one who has gone through the experience, or one who works within the court system and is familiar with the problems inherent in the system. The psychiatrist will need to work on feelings of shame, humiliation, and concern about guilt, or even, perhaps, about the loss of a patient who may have committed suicide during the course of treatment. Psychiatrists have difficulty accepting these problems and may need counseling in preparation for such a trial and, perhaps, even beyond the trial.

The Malpractice Trial

The time between the filing of suit and the trial of an alleged malpractice action is often anxiety provoking and difficult for the psychiatrist, as well as for the plaintiff. Trial calendar delays vary radically from jurisdiction to jurisdiction; generally, federal delay is substantially less than the delay in state systems.

At the time of the trial, the psychiatrist has been well prepared for testimony. The physician should be aware of the details of testimony of others and know what is expected.

The plaintiff's attorney has, by the time of trial, the medical records, the notes of testimony of the deposition, and the answers to interrogatories. All of these are available for cross-examining the psychiatrist. The attorney may utilize the information contained in these documents, as well as information received from other fact and expert witnesses. The trials usually do not last more than several days, but they can last for several weeks, depending upon the complexity of the case and the number of witnesses that are called. In civil trials, there may be as few as six jurors, or as many as 12, as in criminal cases (20). In many jurisdictions, the jury does not have to be unanimous in its decision, as it does in criminal cases (21). The jury will find liability as well as damages. Without liability, there are no damages. If the psychiatrist is found liable for malpractice, damages may be assessed anywhere from one dollar to an unlimited amount, whatever is reasonable to the jury in light of the circumstances and facts presented. In some jurisdictions, the amount may be based up to the amount sought by the plaintiff in the complaint. In other jurisdictions the amount of damages may only be what the jury awards, because by statute, plaintiffs are not allowed to make a claim for a specific amount in the complaint (22). A number of states have enacted statutes that place caps on monetary damages for pain and suffering.

There is often relief following the verdict. The ordeal is over, and, depending on the outcome, the relief may be ecstatic or sad. Nevertheless, there is relief, because the pressure of waiting for trial and the pressure during the trial can be enormous.

Depending upon the outcome of the case, there may be an appeal, which will then usually lead to a settlement conference. For example, if a jury awards 10 million dollars in damages, the insurance company will certainly appeal. The plaintiff knows that there may be a wait of several years for a retrial or for the results of the appeal. The plaintiff may decide that 4 million dollars in hand is better than 10 million dollars that may be reduced or not be present after several years following all appeals.

Settlement Conference

The settlement conferences may occur before the trial, or, usually, the settlement may be agreed upon at the doorstep of the courthouse at the time of trial. Both parties will attempt to settle for the lowest and highest amount possible. Usually the judge will encourage the parties to settle. The prevailing public policy promotes settlement of claims in order to save court time and resources. The plaintiffs will hold out for as much as they can, and the defense will try to get by with paying as little as it can. When the case finally comes to court and backs are against the wall, with the encouragement of the judge, the settlement usually occurs. Very few cases actually go to trial (less than 3 percent of all tort claims), and most are settled before trial for an agreed upon amount, which is usually sealed and kept secret.

The Emotional Toll

Charles et al. (23) reported a study on the impact of malpractice litigation on physicians' personal and professional lives. Both sued and nonsued physicians reported changes in professional behavior and strong emotional reactions to both the threat and the actuality of litigation. However, sued physicians reported significantly more symptoms than nonsued physicians. In more than half of the cases studied, these symptoms included one of two clusters of symptoms descriptive of depressive and stress-induced illnesses. Significantly more sued physicians reported that they were likely to stop seeing certain types of patients, to think of retiring early, and to discourage their children from entering medicine. In a powerful book entitled *Defendant* (24), Drs. Sara Charles and Eugene Kennedy describe the ordeal of a 4-year-long malpractice litigation trial. Any psychiatrist contemplating a countersuit should first consider reading this book.

We have discussed the emotional toll on the psychiatrist from the lawsuit, especially if it is his or her first one and is unexpected. What needs to be emphasized is the emotional toll on the psychiatrist's family and especially on the plaintiff and his or her family. When conducting examinations on plaintiffs in any medical malpractice suit, one may note the enormous amount of tension, anxiety, and stress imposed upon the plaintiff as a result of the malpractice suit. Many have expressed that they feel worse for having sued because of the pressure on them than they felt as a result of the injury initially sustained at the time of the alleged negligence.

It is essential for attorneys to provide proper information to their clients in order to obtain true informed consent to enter the lawsuit. The attorney needs to explain to the plaintiff-patient the pressures that will be placed upon him or her and the stress that he or she will incur as a result of entering the lawsuit. The plaintiff will be questioned about personal and private matters, and family members will be drawn into the fray. Some plaintiffs may decide not to pursue lawsuits, or will request early settlement of a bona fide lawsuit to avoid the pressures anticipated in such cases.

Countersuits

Some legal commentators (25) state that one measure that will reduce frivolous malpractice suits is the filing of a countersuit whenever a physician perceives malpractice litigation to be meritless. Countersuits, for example, involving a question of malpractice are essentially a retaliation against the original suing patient, his or her attorney, or both, for having filed malpractice suits that are perceived to be baseless (26). Even though the countersuits may not be won, plaintiffs' attorneys who file meritless suits will be placed on notice that they, themselves, may become defendants and accountable for their actions (27).

From the outset, it should be understood that countersuits are very difficult to win because of the demanding "burden of proof placed on the plaintiff by applicable legal doctrines" (28) and that very few have succeeded. Four genuinely successful countersuits are known to have been won by doctors and subsequently upheld on appeal in Nevada (29), Kansas (30), Kentucky (31), and Tennessee (32). These successes are but a minute fraction, however, of the total number of meritless or suspect lawsuits filed each year. Also, all four malpractice cases were particularly egregious, malicious prosecution cases, which suggests that only countersuits to the most blatant or bad-faith suits have a reasonable probability of success. Notwithstanding this fact, it has been noted that the number of countersuits filed has increased considerably (33).

In order for a countersuit to be *brought,* the doctor must obtain a favorable termination of the malpractice suit against him or her (34). This occurs if 1) the doctor wins the case in court, 2) the plaintiff drops the suit, or 3) the case is dismissed by a pretrial motion (e.g., motion to dismiss).

If the suit is settled, the physician generally cannot bring a countersuit (35). A release of all claims is sought by each side in most settlements. This precludes the necessary requirement for the physician to have a favorable termination. Moreover, the release typically serves as an agreement that there will not be any further litigation flowing from the original dispute in question.

Some psychiatrists become so enraged when served with a meritless claim that they want to file a countersuit immediately. This can be a major tactical error, because it may only antagonize plaintiffs and strengthen their resolve, thereby losing the chance that the suit will later be dropped. Also, in court, a countersuit may backfire and invoke sympathy for the plaintiff. The impression conveyed is that the plaintiff-patient is being harshly treated by an uncaring (and well-off) physician.

In order for a countersuit to *prevail,* the suing physician must prove that 1) the suit was brought without probable cause (36), 2) the suit was brought with malice (36), and 3) damages were suffered by the physician (37).

Probable Cause

To establish the probable cause element in a countersuit, the psychiatrist must show that 1) no reasonable lawyer would have filed the claim, or 2) the plaintiff's lawyer's investigation of the case was grossly inadequate (38). It is usually very difficult to prove that no probable cause existed, because fault can be found with almost any treatment, especially in psychiatry. Moreover, it is noted that "advice of counsel to the effect that there is a reasonable chance that the claim will be found to be valid is enough to establish probable cause" (39).

Malice

Malice, in a civil countersuit context, may consist of a primary motive of ill will, or knowing lack of belief in any possible success of the (initial) action (40), but neither is necessarily essential. Some courts have found malice where the defendant's conduct (in the countersuit) is probably only reckless or negligent but where the conduct is a clear abuse of the defendant's position of power (e.g., hospital suing a physician employee) or an exploitation of the plaintiff's position of weakness (41). Malice is generally quite difficult to prove. Rarely is there documentation of its existence. Evidence must be presented that the malpractice suit was filed and pursued with reckless abandon. Simple spite is not enough. Reckless abandon, for example, may be proved in countersuits in which it can be shown that the suit was brought with the sole intent of forcing a quick settlement or in which the charges brought by the plaintiff's attorney were totally speculative (42).

Damages

The psychiatrist must prove, in most states, that he or she suffered some form of cognizable loss. Some examples of possible types of damages that might meet the "loss" requirement (43) include the following:

1. Monetary losses or a decrease in volume of patients
2. Loss of reputation
3. Emotional distress
4. Other health problems
5. Cost of a malpractice defense

Courts are beginning to recognize that when a physician is sued and there is no factual basis for the suit, the physician nevertheless may suffer real damage to his or her reputation and mental tranquility (44). This realization, coupled with the need for legal redress, has led some courts to loosely interpret, or dispense with the requirement of proving, special damages. The damage normally sustained when one is made a defendant in a lawsuit rather than the special damages of interference with the physician or his or her property is sufficient for some of these courts (45).

The courts attempt to balance the interest of patients to free and open access to the courts against the need of physicians to be able to practice without unnecessary legal entanglements. The patient has a fundamental right to his or her day in court as long as there is evidence that a claim might exist. Furthermore, the plaintiff's attorney, once the case has been accepted, is duty bound to pursue such claims so long as investigation does not clearly refute the patient's allegations (46). There are occasions, however, when because of time constraints (e.g., statute of limitation), an attorney may file a lawsuit with only minimal investigation into its merits. In these situations, plaintiff's counsel is obviously taking a risk, not necessarily of being countersued, but of having the claim summarily dismissed and raising the ire of the presiding judge.

One consideration that litigants involved in frivolous lawsuits and countersuits sometimes fail to acknowledge is the financial aspects associated with litigation. According to Belli (47), the top award for a countersuit in this country was $175,000. By contrast, the legal expenses in pursuing a countersuit can easily cost $30,000 or more. Legal costs for countersuits are not covered by malpractice carriers. Funds must come out of the doctor's pocket or from special funds established by medical organizations that help doctors finance countersuits.

Malpractice insurance carriers are reluctant to finance countersuits against plaintiffs' attorneys because they remain unconvinced that countersuits significantly decrease the number of malpractice suits filed against physicians (48). In addition, financing countersuits would raise professional liability insurance premiums even higher. Belli (47) feels that awards in successful countersuits tend to be low for four reasons:

1. Juries feel that doctors do not need the money.
2. Most plaintiffs do not have the resources to pay large awards.
3. The wrong committed by the plaintiff's attorney does not compare with medical malpractice cases in which patients are left brain damaged, crippled, or dead.
4. Most countersuits are not upheld at the appellate court level.

The desire to file a countersuit can be a very strong temptation for the psychiatrist who feels insulted and angered by a frivolous lawsuit. However, the psychological stamina required to pursue a countersuit is prodigious. The traumatic experience surrounding the original malpractice suit likely will be relived. Moreover, psychiatrist-litigants can likely expect to spend 2 to 5 years in litigating the *original* malpractice suit. The countersuit will take at least an additional 2 to 5 years to litigate. Thus, the psychiatrist can face anywhere from 4 to 10 years of bitter litigation that may culminate in two arduous trials. Furthermore, the possibility always exists that a counter-countersuit may be filed against the psychiatrist.

Psychiatrists should seriously consider any decision to retaliate against a frivolous lawsuit with a countersuit. The filing of a countersuit will inevitably disrupt the psychiatrist's personal equanimity, family life, and professional practice (49). Most psychiatrists require peace and quiet in their lives in order to properly perform their work. The legal arena is a boisterous and unfriendly place for anyone to enter, especially the psychiatrist who wants to maintain that professional calm so necessary in treating emotionally disturbed patients (50).

Nevertheless, if principle or vindication is an overriding need for the psychiatrist, an alternative approach may be available. In a few states, physicians who have been successful in the defense of a malpractice suit have requested and obtained letters of apology from plaintiffs and their attorneys (45). The letters have been published in medical journals and local newspapers, thereby helping to repair some of the damage to the physician's reputation.

A Clinical Philosophy for Litigious Times

Avoiding Destructive Defensive Practices

Given the current legal climate, only the most naive physician would not consider taking certain defensive measures when treating violent patients. For instance, it is foolhardy to ignore careful documentation of risk-benefit assessments made in the course of treating violent patients, particularly in those cases in which detailed record keeping is not inimical to good clinical care. The trick is to know when to turn defensive measures on and off and, at the very least, to be certain that patients are not harmed by such practices.

Some defensive practices are rooted in the best conservative traditions of medicine and are not necessarily reactions to litigation fears. The fundamental rule of *first do no harm* is quintessentially defensive, but originates from the physician's deep concern for the patient's welfare. The use of careful documentation and appropriate consultation represents good clinical practice on behalf of the patient while secondarily providing a shield from litigation. The *unduly* defensive psychiatrist, however, puts his or her own welfare (e.g., to avoid being sued) first in the course of attending the patient.

Defensive psychiatry comes in two fundamental forms, positive and negative, with some psychiatrists practicing both (51). Positive and negative do not refer to value judgments, but rather indicate acts of commission or omission. The *positive* defensive psychiatrist orders procedures and treatments to prevent or limit liability. These actions may or may not be in accord with good clinical practice. The *negative* defensive psychiatrist avoids procedures or treatments out of fear of a suit, even though the patient might benefit from these interventions. This latter course is particularly unconscionable and potentially medically and legally catastrophic. Defensive practices do not automatically shield the psychiatrist from malpractice claims. To the contrary, in an effort to avoid being sued, the defensive psychiatrists' commissions or omissions may be the very evidence that their care was substandard and the proximate cause of the patients' injuries.

The Dangers of Denial

Mental health professionals frequently point out to their patients the maladaptive aspects of denial that prevent a more harmonious accommodation to reality. However, mental health professionals themselves are not immune to this problem, particularly regarding the legal requirements governing the practice of their profession. The denial of these requirements inevitably leads to blind spots that can be legally disastrous. Although therapists do not need to be lawyers, it is a reality that they must practice within the law. A clear knowledge of legal issues relevant to clinical practice is essential in diminishing fears of legal entanglement with patients that often interfere with good clinical practice.

In fact, the personal and career problems arising from the fear of malpractice suits have become so widespread that support groups have mushroomed for physicians and their families. An increasing number of state medical societies are establishing programs to help physicians manage the emotional and physical stress produced by the liability crisis. For example, doctors in New York facing malpractice suits will be able to network with other practitioners to discuss their concerns. According to the American Medical Association, at least 19 states have medical societies that provide formal malpractice support programs (52).

Just a little knowledge can go a very long way. As an example, knowing that honest errors in patient care by themselves do not constitute malpractice can help immunize against destructive defensive practices as well as alleviate unnecessary anxiety and uncertainty. Even if the patient is unfortunately harmed, careful documentation that reasonable care was provided in the diagnosis and treatment of the patient will likely defeat any malpractice claim. The law does not require perfect treatment.

Primary Duty of the Therapist

There are three main factors that influence the practice of mental health professionals: 1) the therapist's professional, moral, and legal duty to provide competent care to patients; 2) the patient's rights to receive or reject such care; and 3) the decisions and directives of the courts, legislatures, and nongovernmental agencies that regulate professional practice. These three factors overlap to varying degrees depending on the specific clinical situation. The mental health professional must learn how to manage these sometimes conflicting spheres of influence so that proper care can be provided to the patient (53).

For example, the imposition of the *Tarasoff* duty upon therapists to protect endangered third parties in an ever-increasing number of jurisdictions has been viewed with much alarm (54). Because of the liability consequences of this duty, some therapists have resisted accepting it, viewing the duty as an external, adversarial intrusion by the law into their professional discretion and practice. Thus, the moral principles underlying the duty to protect victims from violence by mental patients are often overlooked. Few therapists would disagree with the need to protect an endangered third party if the therapist believes that his or her patient intends physical harm to another person. What initially appears to be an insurmountable conflict between the therapist's duty to maintain the confidentiality of patients and the law's requirement to safeguard the public is largely illusory. The duty to warn can be viewed with less rancor and often turned into a therapeutic account for the patient when the commonality of the underlying moral concern for the safety of fellow human beings by both the law and therapists is appreciated.

Furthermore, patients' rights movements, the ascendancy of the informed consent doctrine, the right to refuse treatment, and the "right to treatment" may appear to conflict with the mental health practitioner's duty to provide a reasonable standard of care. For example, the psychotic patient who needs treatment may refuse treatment. The refusal may be upheld by the court (55). However, many of these "externally derived duties" are not necessarily in conflict with good clinical practice. The requirement of informed consent can be utilized to enhance trust and the therapeutic alliance with the patient. Preoccupation with the law causes therapists to discharge their duties to patients in legally formalistic ways that may interfere with the all important therapeutic alliance with the patient. An iatrogenic liability neurosis can take hold of the therapist's professional judgment, interfering with patient care and management and paradoxically increasing malpractice liability.

For example, the patient with a serious refractory depression who is unresponsive to drugs and clearly requires electroconvulsive therapy may be deprived of this lifesaving treatment because of unfounded fears of malpractice. The patient experiencing suicidal ruminations who can be treated safely as an outpatient but is defensively hospitalized is poorly served.

In the area of drug therapy, does not the psychiatrist who prescribes nontherapeutic doses of medication in the vain hope of helping the patient without risking any harm abrogate his or her moral, professional, and legal duty to provide good clinical care to the patient? Is not the patient unnecessarily exposed to harm from the drug without the possibility of receiving proper benefit? Thus, the patient may continue to suffer and remain disabled. Shame and guilt can accompany such defensive practices, causing practitioners ultimately to disdain themselves and their work.

In another example, the therapist may be legally correct in following the dictates of a confidentiality statute that prohibits warning endangered third parties, but the therapist is eschewing good clinical practice in not warning an intended victim if it is clear that the patient represents a significant threat of harm and warning is the only option available. The therapist can be legally right but professionally and morally wrong.

It is the rare legal problem in psychiatric treatment that cannot be productively addressed through the utilization of good clinical practice and knowledge of pertinent legal issues. The key is to never lose sight of the primary duty of the therapist—to render good clinical care to the patient. The therapist has a professional and moral duty in providing care for patients that transcends standards imposed by the law or regulatory agencies. This is not to impute a moral superiority of the therapist's ethical and clinical responsibility over that of the law's requirements. Legal standards, however, are fixed at a minimum level by necessity. The professional and moral duty of the therapist regarding patients is set at a maximum level. The difference represents the gulf that exists between the human condition and the human spirit (56).

Legal Requirements

In regard to the law, the clinician should have a clear working knowledge of the relevant legal requirements governing professional practice. For instance, courts may consider that what is not documented was not done. Even this tiny bit of legal knowledge can go a long way in easing the anxieties of therapists who fear being second-guessed by plaintiffs' experts in a court of law. Yet, it is truly astounding how infrequently mental health professionals keep even minimally acceptable records.

Whenever a legal issue arises in clinical practice, every opportunity should be taken to turn it to therapeutic advantage for the patient. When the patient is to be informed about the risks of tardive dyskinesia before administering neuroleptic medication, the process of informing should be utilized to enhance the therapeutic alliance with the patient. Can warning an endangered third party be done in such a way as to include the patient's participation that preserves the therapeutic alliance? If not, can the damage be contained by a very discreet warning? Can a therapist make the difficult choice of potentially permanently disrupting the treatment relationship in order to warn a clearly endangered person of the patient's violent intention or to seek involuntary hospitalization of the patient? If the answer is "yes," this action will be initiated most often from a professional and moral concern for the patient and the intended victim, and not simply because of some legal mandate like the *Tarasoff* doctrine.

The traditional rule of tort law that a person has no duty to come to the aid of another in distress is probably an unacceptable position for most psychiatrists. The therapist does not act in these situations strictly from an obligation to meet the law's requirements. Long before *Tarasoff,* therapists protected others who were endangered by their patients or sought involuntary treatment for violent patients when all else failed. Moreover, long before confidentiality statutes were enacted, most clinicians maintained and still maintain a level of confidentiality that far exceeds current statutory requirements.

Positive Treatment Experience

At the most basic level, a knowledge of the duties of the therapist, the rights of the patient, and the legal and regulatory duties imposed upon psychiatrists and their clinical practices will allow for a more positive treatment experience for both patients and therapists. Hopefully, a comfortable familiarity with the law will diminish defensive practices that can inhibit good quality care. But at the highest level, the clinician must understand the overriding truth that professional concern for the patient is the fundamental principle. With this knowledge comes professional freedom.

The legal regulation of mental health practitioners and their interventions undoubtedly will increase in the years ahead. The necessity for the practitioner to possess a working knowledge of relevant legal requirements that govern professional practice is now an unblinkable reality. Legally knowledgeable therapists are in a much better position to provide quality care. Ignorance of the law makes the law appear like an unmanageable monster rather than a workable partner, thus diminishing professional gratification and effectiveness. As a lifelong dedication, the practice of medicine should be enjoyed. Knowledge rather than ignorance of the legal requirements governing psychiatric practice can be utilized to significantly diminish malpractice fears threatening personal and professional well-being. Once more, good clinical practice will be restored so that treatment decisions are unflinchingly made in the best interests of patients.

References

1. American Medical Association: Socioeconomic Characteristics of Medical Practice, 1986. Chicago, IL, American Medical Association, 1986
2. Simon RI: Clinical Psychiatry and the Law, 2nd Edition. Washington, DC, American Psychiatric Press, 1992
3. Slawson PF, Guggenheim FG: Psychiatric malpractice: a review of the national loss experience. Am J Psychiatry 141:979–981, 1984
4. Kaufman v A H Robins Co, 223 Tenn 515, 448 SW2d 400 (1969); Cisson v Pickens Savings & Loan, 186 SE2d 822 (SC 1972); Restatement (Second) of Torts § 674 (1965)
5. Brooten KE: How to handle a nuisance suit. Physician's Management, July 1986, pp 14–18

6. Johnson ID: Reports to the National Practitioner Data Bank. JAMA 265:407–411, 1991

7. Sadoff RL: Psychiatric malpractice, in Preparing and Winning Medical Negligence Cases. Edited by Preiser SE, Wecht C, Preiser ML. Charlottesville, VA, Michie, 1989, pp 475–512

8. Wexler D: Therapeutic Jurisprudence. Durham, NC, Carolina Academic Press, 1990

9. Leggett v Home Indemnity Co, 461 F2d 257 (10th Cir 1972)

10. See Chapter 1, this volume.

11. Fed R Civ P 34

12. Sadoff RL: Legal Issues in the Care of Psychiatric Patients. New York, Springer, 1982, p 62

13. American Psychiatric Association: The Principles of Medical Ethics With Annotations Especially Applicable to Psychiatry. Washington, DC, American Psychiatric Association, 1989, Section 4, Annotation 9

14. See, e.g., Hague v Williams, 37 NJ 328, 181 A2d 345 (1962)

15. Sadoff RL: Informed consent, confidentiality and privilege in psychiatry: practical applications. Bull Am Acad Psychiatry Law 2(June):101–106, 1974

16. Fed R Civ P 26 and 33

17. Fed R Civ P 30(b)(4)

18. Sadoff RL: Forensic Psychiatry, 2nd Edition. Springfield, IL, Charles C Thomas, 1988, p 195

19. Sadoff RL: New malpractice concerns for the psychiatrist. Legal Aspects of Medical Practice, March 1978, pp 31–35

20. Tillman v Ailles, 13 Miss 373 (5 S & M) (1845); Hibdon v United States, 204 F2d 834 (6th Cir 1953)

21. Fed R Civ P 48

22. NY Civ Prac L & R § 3017(c)

23. Charles SC, Wilbert JR, Franke KJ: Sued and nonsued physicians' self-reported reactions to malpractice litigation. Am J Psychiatry 142:437–440, 1985

24. Charles SC, Kennedy E: Defendant. New York, Free Press, 1985

25. Fish RM, Ehrhardt ME: Malpractice Depositions. Oradell, NJ, Medical Economics Books, 1987

26. Wong v Tabor, 422 NE2d 1979 (Ind App 1981)

27. Berlin L: Countersuing the attorney to stop frivolous lawsuits. Medicolegal News 5(Fall):3–4, 14–15, 1977

28. Birnbaum SL: Physician counterattack: liability of lawyers for instituting unjustified medical malpractice actions. Fordham Law Review 45:1003, 1029, 1977

29. Bull v McCuskey, 615 P2d 957 (Nev 1980)

30. Nelson v Miller, 607 P2d 438 (Kan 1980)

31. Raine v Drasin, Nos 80-SC-480-DG & 80-SC-501-DG (Ky S Ct filed June 16, 1981) (unpublished)

32. Peerman v Sidicane, 605 SW2d 242 (Tenn App 1980)

33. Smith WT: Medical malpractice: the countersuit fad. Trial 12:45, 1976

34. Keeton WP, Dobbs DB, Keeton RE, et al: Prosser and Keeton on Torts, 5th Edition. St. Paul, MN, West Publishing, 1984, pp 892–893

35. Natarors v Superior Court of Maricopa County, 113 Ariz 498, 557 P2d 1055 (1976)
36. Bertero v National General Corporation, 13 Cal 3d 43, 118 Cal Rptr 184, 529 P2d 608 (1974)
37. Keeton WP, Dobbs DB, Keeton RE, et al: Prosser and Keeton on Torts, 5th Edition. St. Paul, MN, West Publishing, 1984, pp 894–896
38. Belli MM: Belli for Your Malpractice Defense. Oradell, NJ, Medical Economics Books, 1987, p 195
39. Keeton WP, Dobbs DB, Keeton RE, et al: Prosser and Keeton on Torts, 5th Edition. St. Paul, MN, West Publishing, 1984, p 894, citing Harter v Lewis Stores, 240 SW2d 86 (Ky 1951)
40. Southwestern Railroad Co v Mitchell, 5 SE 490 (Ga 1880)
41. Robinson v Goudchaux's, 307 So 2d 637 (La 1975)
42. NY Civ Prac L & R 23
43. NY Civ Prac L & R 24
44. Sonnichsen v Streeter, 4 Conn Cir 659, 239 A2d 63 (1967)
45. Keeton WP, Dobbs DB, Keeton RE, et al: Prosser and Keeton on Torts, 5th Edition. St. Paul, MN, West Publishing, 1984, p 896
46. Hirsh HL: Physician countersuit: to sue or better not to sue? Medical Trial Technique Quarterly 34:59–76, 1987
47. Belli MM: Belli for Your Malpractice Defense. Oradell, NJ, Medical Economics Books, 1987, pp 193–200
48. Ky MD sues lawyers for 'malicious' malpractice action. AMA News, January 13, 1989, p 8
49. Levonian WP: I won my countersuit—but lost most of my practice. Medical Economics, March 16, 1987, pp 60–63
50. Simon RI: Clinical Psychiatry and the Law, 2nd Edition. Washington, DC, American Psychiatric Press, 1992
51. Simon RI: Coping strategies for the defensive psychiatrist. International Journal of Medicine and Law 4:551–561, 1985
52. Professional briefs. Medical Economics, June 6, 1988, p 13
53. Simon RI: Clinical Psychiatry and the Law, 2nd Edition. Washington, DC, American Psychiatric Press, 1992
54. Beck JC (ed): The Potentially Violent Patient and the Tarasoff Decision in Psychiatric Practice. Washington, DC, American Psychiatric Press, 1985
55. Bouvia v Superior Court, 179 Cal 3d 1127, 225 Cal Rptr 239 (1986)
56. Simon RI: Clinical Psychiatry and the Law, 2nd Edition. Washington, DC, American Psychiatric Press, 1992

Duty to Warn: Current Overview and Trends ———————

Jurisdiction	Source of law	Status
Alabama	Case law	Acknowledges[1]
Alaska	Statute	Accepts
Arizona	Statute	Accepts
California	Statute	Accepts
Colorado	Statute	Accepts
Delaware	Case law	Accepts
District of Columbia	Case law	Accepts
Florida	Statute	Accepts
Georgia	Case law	Acknowledges[1]
Illinois	Case law	Acknowledges[2]
Indiana	Statute	Accepts
Iowa	Case law	Accepts
Kansas	Statute	Accepts
Kentucky	Statute	Accepts
Louisiana	Statute	Accepts
Maryland	Statute	Accepts
Massachusetts	Statute	Accepts
Michigan	Statute	Accepts
Minnesota	Statute	Accepts
Montana	Statute	Accepts
Nebraska	Case law	Accepts

New Hampshire	Statute	Accepts
New Jersey	Case law	Accepts
New York	Case law	Accepts
North Carolina	Case law	Acknowledges[2]
Ohio	Case law	Accepts[3]
Pennsylvania	Case law	Accepts/rejects[4]
South Carolina	Case law	Undecided
Texas	Case law	Accepted
Utah	Statute	Accepted
Vermont	Case law	Accepted
Washington	Statute	Accepted
Wisconsin	Case law	Accepted

Tally (as of January 1991)

Total jurisdictions: 34

Statutes: 18

Total cases: no fewer than 54 (involving mental health professionals)

Source. **Researched and compiled by Steven B. Bisbing, Psy.D., J.D. (January 1991).**

[1]Acknowledged circumscribed duty, but none found in this case.

[2]No duty pursuant to case facts but a narrow one was acknowledged.

[3]Opinion is expressly limited to inpatient situations.

[4]Opposite trial opinions (3 accept/1 reject)

Duty to Warn and/or Protect: Scope of the Law ───────

Note: Researched and compiled by Steven B. Bisbing, Psy.D., J.D.

Jurisdiction	Source of law: case law/statute

Key: a = When the duty arises
b = Required action to be taken

Alabama[1]   *Morton v. Prescott*, **564 So 2d 913 (Ala 1990);
also see *King v. Smith*, 539 So 2d 262 (Ala 1989);
Donahoo v. State, 479 So 2d 1188 (Ala 1985)**

a) Specific threat of harm to a specific victim or "to any identifiable group of which the victim might have been a member."

b) Duty of care to the victim.

Alaska   **Alaska Stat Ann § 08.86.200 (1987)**

a) Immediate threat of serious physical harm to an identifiable victim, to a psychologist, or to a psychological associate.

───────

[1]While the court affirmed the lower court's finding that a psychiatrist owed no duty to warn or protect a person who was assaulted by a patient he allegedly prematurely discharged, the court specifically cited the language of *Thompson, Brady,* and other cases in rejecting the theory. By implication, the court appeared to endorse strongly the threshold requirement that a "specific threat to a specific victim" occur before a duty to warn could be accepted.

b) Disclosure to an appropriate authority.[2]

Arizona   **Ariz Rev Stat Ann § 36-517.02 (Supp 1990);**
but see *Tamsen v. Weber*, 802 P2d 1063 (Ariz Ct App 1990),
remanded for new trial

a) Explicit threat of imminent, serious physical harm or death to a clearly identified or identifiable victim or victims, *and* the patient has the apparent intent and ability to carry out such a threat.

b) "[R]easonable precautions [by mental health provider] to prevent harm threatened by a patient" are discharged by any of the following:

1) Communicating when possible the threat to all identifiable victims.

2) Notifying a law enforcement agency in the vicinity where the patient or any potential victims reside.

3) Taking reasonable steps to initiate proceedings for voluntary or involuntary hospitalization, if appropriate.

4) Taking any other precautions that a reasonable and prudent mental health provider would take under the circumstances.

California   **Cal Civ Code § 43.92 (West Supp 1991)**

a) Serious threat against reasonably identifiable victim.

b) Reasonable effort to communicate threat to victim or law enforcement authorities.

Colorado   **Colo Rev Stat § 13-21-117 (1987)**

a) Serious threat of imminent violence against specific victim.

b) Reasonable and timely effort to notify victim as well as appropriate law enforcement agent or other appropriate action including, but not limited to, hospitalization.

Delaware   ***Naidu v. Laird*, 539 A2d 1064 (Del 1988)**

a) Presentation of an unreasonable risk of harm to others.

b) Whatever precautions are reasonably necessary to protect potential victims (e.g., "may have a duty to warn potential victims or a class of victims and/or control, to some appropriate degree, the actions of the patient").

District of Columbia   ***White v. United States*, 780 F2d 97 (DC Cir 1986)**

a) Knowledge that patient presents a serious risk of violence to another.

b) Reasonable care to protect a foreseeable victim from danger.

---

[2]The referenced statute does *not* specifically address what is to be done if the trigger element is met. The above stated "disclosure to appropriate authorities" is *inferred* based on the recognized Alaska exception to confidentiality for reporting child, elderly, or disabled person abuse.

Florida   **Fla Stat Ann § 490.0147 (West 1991)**

a) Clear and immediate probability of physical harm to *patient* or *society.*

b) Communicates the information [threat] only to potential victim, appropriate family member, law enforcement officer, or other appropriate authority.

Georgia   *Allen v. Jenkins,* **No.—— Clark Cty Cir Ct, (Athens GA 1989),**
cited in Am Psychol 20:20 (March 1989)[3]

a) Immediate threat of physical violence to a readily identifiable victim.[4]

b) Inform the police or warn the victim.

Illinois   *Eckhardt v. Kirts,* **534 NE2d 1339 (Ill App 2d Dist 1989);**
also see *Kirk v. Michael Reese Hospital & Medical Center,*
117 Ill 2d 507, 111 Ill Dec 944, 513 NE2d 387 (1987)

a) Specific threats of violence are directed at a specific and identified victim.

b) "Duty to warn victim."

Indiana   **Ind Code Ann § 34-4-12.4-1 (Burns Supp 1988)**

a) Actual threat *or* conducts oneself or makes statements indicating imminent danger of using physical violence or other means to cause serious personal injury or death to others.

b) One or more of four measures: 1) attempt to notify victim; 2) attempt to notify police; 3) seek commitment; or 4) take steps "reasonably available…to prevent use of physical violence…until LEA…can take custody."

Iowa   *Heltsley v. Votteler,* **327 NW2d 759 (Iowa 1982)**

a) Knowledge of patient's violent nature and threats.

b) Take reasonable steps to ensure the safety of others.

Kansas   **Kan Stat Ann § 65-5603 (6) (Supp 1990)**

a) A person, specifically identified by the patient, who is threatened with substantial physical harm and [treatment personnel] believes there is a substantial likelihood that the patient will act on the threat in the reasonably foreseeable future.

b) Notification should be given (warning). The patient shall be notified that such information has been communicated.

---

[3]Additional information provided by Russell Newman, Esq., Director of Legal and Regulatory Affairs, American Psychological Association Practice Directorate, Washington, DC.

[4]The court in this case held for the defendant. It has been inferred from the scant information available that if the threat of violence had been more explicit and directed toward an identifiable victim, the court would have recognized the duty.

Kentucky   **Ky Rev Stat § 202A.400 (Supp 1990)**

a) 1) Actual threat of physical violence against clearly or reasonably identifiable victim, or 2) actual threat of some specific violent act.

b) 1) Communication of threat to victim, police, and victim's residence, or 2) communication of threat to law enforcement authorities.

Louisiana   **La Rev Stat Ann § 9:2800.2 (West Supp 1991)**

a) Immediate physical threat against clearly identifiable victim coupled with apparent intent and ability to carry out that threat.

b) Reasonable effort to communicate the immediate threat to the potential victim and law enforcement authorities in the vicinity of the victim's residence.

Maryland   **MD Cts & Jud Proc Code Ann § 5-315 (1989)**

a) Mental health care provider or administrator knew of the patient's propensity for violence, and the patient indicated to the mental health care provider or administrator that he or she intended to inflict imminent physical injury upon a specified victim or group of victims.

b) Mental health care provider or administrator makes reasonable and timely efforts to 1) seek civil commitment of the patient; 2) formulate a diagnostic impression and establish and undertake a documented treatment plan calculated to eliminate the possibility that the patient will carry out the threat; or 3) inform the appropriate law enforcement agency and, if feasible, the specified victim or victims of i) the nature of the threat, ii) the identity of the patient making the threat, and iii) the identity of the specified victim.

Massachusetts   **Mass Gen Ann Law ch 112 § 129A (West Supp 1991)**

Option One

a) "The client has communicated to the psychologist an actual threat of physical violence against a clearly identified or reasonably identifiable victim or victims."

Option Two

a) "Where the client has a history of physical violence which is known to the psychologist and where the psychologist has a reasonable basis to believe that there is a clear and present danger of physical violence against a clearly identifiable or reasonably identified victim or victims."

b) "In such circumstances [option one or two], the psychologist has a duty to warn or take reasonable precautions to provide protection from violent behavior. This duty shall be discharged...[through] one or more of the following: i) make reasonable efforts to communicate the threat to the victim or victims; ii) seek civil commitment of the patient pursuant to the chapter; iii) [make] reasonable efforts to notify appropriate police department or another law enforcement agency (LEA)."

Note: *Part 4:* "...nothing contained herein shall require a psychologist to take any action which, in the exercise of reasonable professional judgment, would endanger himself or increase the danger to a potential victim or victims."

Part 5: "the psychologist shall only disclose that information which is essential to protect the rights and safety of others."

Michigan   Mich Comp Laws Ann § 330.1750 (West Supp 1991)[5]

a) If a patient communicates to a mental health practitioner (psychiatrist, psychologist, or social worker) a threat of physical violence against a reasonably identifiable third person, *and* the patient has the apparent intent and ability to carry out that threat in the foreseeable future.

b) The duty is discharged if the mental health practitioner, subsequent to the threat, *does one or more* of the following in a "timely manner":

1) Hospitalizes the patient or initiates proceedings to hospitalize the patient.

2) Makes a reasonable attempt to communicate the threat to the third person and communicates the threat to the local police department or county sheriff for the area in which the third person resides or for area in which the patient resides, or the state police.

3) If there is a reason to believe that the third person who is threatened is a minor or incompetent, steps outlined in (2) should be taken *and* the threat communicated to the department of social services in the county in which the minor resided and to the third person's custodial parent, non-custodial parent, or legal guardian, whoever is appropriate in the best interests of the third person.

4) If the patient described in part (a) is being treated in a hospital and is being considered for discharge, the hospital shall designate an individual to communicate the threat to the necessary persons.

Minnesota   Minn Stat Ann § 148.975 (West 1989)

a) When patient or other person communicates a specific, serious threat of physical violence against a specific, clearly identified or identifiable potential victim.

b) Reasonable effort to communicate threat to victim, and if unreachable, then to the law enforcement agency closest to victim.

---

[5]This opinion is expressly limited to psychiatrists, thereby providing no guidance for psychologists, counselors, and other mental health professionals (see 390 NW2d at 222, n.4).

Montana   **Mont Code Ann §§ 27-1-1101, 2, 3 (1989)**

a) Actual threat of physical violence by specific means to clearly or reasonably identifiable victim.

b) Reasonable efforts to convey threat to victim and to notify appropriate law enforcement agency.

Nebraska   ***Lipari v. Sears, Roebuck & Co.*, 497 F Supp 185**
(D Neb 1980)

a) Foreseeable violence to unspecified class (public at large).

b) Reasonable precautions to protect potential victims.

New Hampshire   **NH Rev Stat Ann § 329.31 (1990)**

a) Serious threat of physical violence against a clearly identified or reasonably identified victim, or serious threat of substantial damage to real property.

b) Reasonable effort to communicate threat to victim, notifying police department nearest to victim or obtaining civil commitment.

New Jersey   ***McIntosh v. Milano*, 403 A2d 500 (NJ Super 1979)**

a) When patient presents a probability of danger to an intended or potential victim based upon the factual situation and applying the standards of the profession to make the assessment.

b) Reasonable steps to protect potential victim.

New York   ***Moskowitz v.* MIT, No. 14786/79 (NY Sup Ct**
December 1982), appeal denied 474 NYS2d 742
(AD 1984); also see *Oringer v. Rotkin*, 556 NYS2d 67 (App Div 1990);
***McDonald v. Clinger*, 446 NYS2d 801, 84 AD2d 482**

a) Foreseeable danger.

b) Reasonable effort to communicate threat to victim.

North Carolina   ***Currie v. United States*, 644 F Supp 874 (MD NC 1986),**
affirmed No. 86-2643 (4th Cir December 28, 1987);
also see *Cantrell v. United States*, 735 F Supp 670 (ED NC 1988);
***Moye v. United States*, 735 F Supp 179 (ED NC 1990)**

No duty (of outpatient therapists) to protect unidentifiable victims; no common law or statutory duty to control potentially violent patients by initiating commitment.

Note: Duty to control arises if a confined patient presents a foreseeable harm to anyone (identifiable or not).

Ohio   *Littleton v. Good Samaritan Hospital and Health*
Center, **529 NE2d 449 (Ohio 1988)**

a) Actor taking charge of person "knows or should know that person is likely to cause bodily harm to others if not controlled"

b) A psychiatrist will not be liable for the violent acts of a voluntarily hospitalized mental patient subsequent to the patient's discharge if:

   1) the patient did not manifest violent propensities while being hospitalized and there was no reason to suspect the patient would become violent after discharge; or

   2) a thorough evaluation of the patient's propensity for violence was conducted, taking into account all relevant factors, and a good faith decision was made by the psychiatrist that the patient had no violent propensity; or

   3) the patient was diagnosed as having violent propensities, and, after a thorough evaluation of the severity of the propensities and a balancing of the patient's interests and the interests of potential victims, a treatment plan was formulated in good faith that included discharge of the patient.

Note: Opinion *is expressly limited* with inpatient situations and appears to only relate to psychiatrists.[6]

Pennsylvania   *Hopewell v. Adibempe,* **No. GD-78-82756 CD**
(Allegheny Cty Ct Comm Pleas, Pa June 1, 1981)

Duty to warn preempted by state confidentiality statute.

Cain v. Danville State Hospital, **No. 1871-1982**
Civil (Monroe Cty Ct Comm Pleas, Pa January 12, 1984);
also see *Dunkle v. Food Service East Inc.,* **582 A2d 1342**
(Pa Super Ct 1990)[7]

a) Specific threat to readily identifiable victim.

b) Reasonable effort to warn a potential victim.

---

[6]**Also note:** State statute expressly immunizes professionals for "any harm that results to any other person as a result of failing to disclose confidential information about a mental health client, or failing to otherwise attempt to protect such other person from harm by such client. This applies [also] to expert witnesses who testify at hearings under this chapter" (Ohio Rev Stat § 5122.34 [1989]).

[7]The court noted that neither a psychologist nor a psychiatrist has a duty to warn or otherwise protect a third party absent a threat to inflict harm on a particular patient. To hold otherwise would "hinder the psychotherapist-patient relationship; frustrate treatment; and infringe upon the psychotherapist-patient privilege."

**South Carolina   *Sharp v. S.C. Department of Mental Health*, 315 SE2d 112
(SC 1984), writ dismissed 366 SE2d 12 (SC 1988)
[affirmed]; also see *Rogers v. S.C. Department of
Mental Health*, 377 SE2d 125 (SC Ct App 1989)**

The South Carolina Supreme Court did not explicitly recognize a duty to warn, because they found that on the facts of *Sharp* (i.e., no identifiable threat to a specific victim) that it would be untenable to "create" a general duty to the public at large based upon a patient's dangerous propensities. However, their holding could be interpreted to suggest that they might consider accepting a narrower view (majority trend) if the facts indicated an "identifiable threat to an identifiable victim."

Tennessee   Tenn Code Ann § 33-10-302 (Supp 1990)

a) A qualified mental health professional (psychologist or psychological examiner, certified or licensed social worker, and psychiatric mental health nurse) or mental health facility owes a duty of care when a patient "has communicated . . . an actual threat of bodily harm against a clearly identified victim and the qualified mental health professional, using the reasonable skill, knowledge, and care ordinarily possessed and exercised by his or her professional specialty under similar circumstances, determines that the patient has apparent capabilities to commit such an act."

b) "The duty to warn or take reasonable precautions . . . shall be discharged by any one (1) of the following:

1) Informing the clearly identified victim of the threat;

2) Having the patient admitted on a voluntary basis to a hospital;

3) Taking steps to seek admission of a patient in a hospital or treatment facility on an involuntary basis (pursuant to state law); or

4) Pursuing a course of action consistent with current professional standards that will discharge the duty."

**Texas   *Williams v. Sun Valley Hospital*, 723 SW2d 783
(Tx Ct App 1987)**

a) Threat or danger to a readily identifiable person.

b) Not addressed; no duty to warn found.

Utah   Utah Code Ann § 78-14a-102 (Supp 1988)

a) "...communication of an actual threat of physical violence against a clearly identifiable or reasonably identifiable victim."

b) "...[makes] reasonable efforts to communicate the threat to the victim, and notifies a law enforcement officer or agency of the threat."

Vermont *Peck v. Counseling Center of Addison County,* **499 A2d 422 (VT 1985)**

a) Based on knowledge, or upon standards of the mental health profession, that there is a foreseeable risk of harm to victim or property.

b) Reasonable effort to convey threat to identifiable victim.

Washington **1987 Wash Laws, ch 212, Part III(2); also see Wash Rev Code § 71.05.390 (10) (West 1989)**

a) Actual threat of physical violence against reasonably identifiable victim.

b) Reasonable efforts to communicate threat to the victim and law enforcement personnel.

Wisconsin *Schuster v. Altenberg,* **144 Wis 2d 223,** 424 NW2d 159 (1988)

a) Foreseeable harm to a third party (public at large).

b) Action to protect the patient from himself or herself, or a third party from the patient.

Note: Connecticut, as reflected in *Kaminski v. Fairfield,* 216 Conn 29, 578 A2d 1048 (1990), came close to recognizing the duty to warn when it rejected a police officer's counterclaim that the plaintiffs owed him a duty to warn of their schizophrenic son's violent tendencies. The court distinguished the instant case by noting that there were no "specific threats against a specific victim" and that the plaintiffs did not have a professional relationship with the police officer. While the court attempted to avoid the appearance of recognizing *Tarasoff*—"[W]hatever the merits of *Tarasoff,* the principles it establishes have no applicability in this case"—its use of the prevailing requirements in most duty-to-warn cases suggests that a mental health–type of duty-to-warn situation with a "specific threat to a specific victim" might be accepted.

Index of Cases

Index